GROWING RESTORATIVE REGULATION

GROWING RESTORATIVE REGULATION

MIRANDA FORSYTH,
FELICITY TEPPER,
DEBORAH HOLLINGWORTH
AND ALISTAIR NAIRN

Australian National University
ANU PRESS

Australian
National
University

ANU PRESS

Published by ANU Press
The Australian National University
Canberra ACT 2600, Australia
Email: anupress@anu.edu.au

Available to download for free at press.anu.edu.au

ISBN (hardcover): 9781760467319
ISBN (online): 9781760467326

WorldCat (hardcover): 1574882112
WorldCat (online): 1574883007

DOI: 10.22459/GRR.2026

Cover design and layout by ANU Press. Cover photograph by Daniel Fernandez.

This book is published under the aegis of the Public Policy editorial board of ANU Press.

Contents

List of illustrations

Figures

Tables

Preface

Growing Restorative Regulation explores the possibility of restorative approaches to regulation. The storyline in this book uniquely weaves together the emerging field of scholarship and practice in environmental restorative justice with the realities and challenges of environmental regulation.

This book emerged from a research collaboration funded through the Australian Research Council in 2018. The idea for the research project arose in the context of a period of significant change and reform. Following a review of the Environment Protection Authority Victoria (EPA Victoria/ the EPA) and the *Environment Protection Act 1970,* Victoria was on the brink of a radically new prevention-focused framework for environmental protection. It was in this context that the 'regulatory-academic' collaboration was conceived by the EPA's former Chair, Cheryl Batagol, and RegNet Emeritus Distinguished Professor John Braithwaite at The Australian National University (ANU). They each recognised an opportunity for an interdisciplinary approach that brings research into the dynamic space of regulatory practice—at a time of transformation.

The original questions that formed the basis of this research initiative were twofold. Firstly, how might the principles and practices of restorative justice enhance the practice of environmental regulation? And then: how might they help prevent harm from occurring, and heal and repair when it has occurred? The book is just one of the outcomes of this multiyear research initiative commencing in 2018.

The new regulatory framework in Victoria is a world-leading first. The *Environment Protection Act 2017* is formulated around a central premise— that there is a positive, legally enforceable duty on anyone undertaking an activity that poses a risk of harm to human health and the environment from pollution and waste. The EPA, together with the wider Victorian community, is embarking on a journey with this new approach to environmental regulation, one that will continue to evolve and mature with time. This legislative framework comes with a mandate but also new powers, tools and functions by which to protect, and prevent harm to, human health and the environment from pollution and waste. It is formulated and designed to switch the focus from pollution response to prevention. This is done by placing an obligation on those undertaking an activity to identify, assess and mitigate any likely risk of harm to human health and the environment. While this is explored and referenced in the book, it is important to note that as the new Act did not become operational until 1 July 2021, many of the case studies and interviews reference the pre-existing 1970 Environment Protection Act. That said, the book is very much conceived and written in anticipation of the preventative and restorative potential of the new legislative framework.

The circumstances in which EPA Victoria agreed to this collaboration build an important context for readers of this book. While public institutions like EPA Victoria will commonly participate in, and are consumers of, research, it is typically tightly defined and controlled. The ethnographic and explorative approach of researchers at ANU makes this unusual. Readers will hear the voices of EPA field practitioners and staff as they reflect openly on the challenges of their work and roles. They will read about the frustrations of community members, and the perspectives of duty holders and other regulators. Beyond this, readers will learn about the emerging global scholarship and interest in environmental restorative justice, and they will be challenged to consider whether the real-life scenarios depicted in the book can be improved with restorative innovations.

The narrative arc of the book takes the reader on a journey across the spectrum of environmental regulatory terrain. It moves from major environmental incidents and offending to licensing decisions about necessary controls of pollution and waste, revealing the way in which regulatory systems both enable and constrain the management of environmental concerns. *Growing Restorative Regulation* combines both 'insider' and 'outsider' perspectives on the nuance, facets, frustrations and imperfections of regulation. The research approach allows insights that might not otherwise emerge through a more conventional research methodology. To ensure that this research effort would be meaningful and authentic, the ANU researchers were provided with access to EPA people, systems and approaches. Of course, this was governed by a research agreement. However, given the nature of this research collaboration, it is important to clarify that the material in this book does not include information that is confidential or should not be in the public domain.

In this context, the role of the Industry Research Partners is another unique aspect of the collaboration. As the 'insiders', we have been the facilitators helping our 'outsider' research partners to follow their lines of research and inquiry. This has enabled access to EPA people and activities. Across the years (which spanned COVID-19 and significant organisational changes), we have been conscious of the EPA's role as a regulator, and the limits and boundaries on how information is used and how situations are presented. To this end, it is important for us to acknowledge that while the research was undertaken in a collaborative manner, the ANU researchers have also conducted their research independently. They have drawn research data from multiple sources, including community members, industry, Traditional Owners and other regulators. Together we have sought to navigate these multiple perspectives and situations while recognising their complexity and holding to the research objective to seek out restorative opportunities.

EPA Victoria, like all regulators, strives to provide public value and to achieve its statutory mandate. Readers of this book are invited into the ever-present challenge of regulation, one that is often accompanied by competing interests, some of them impossible to resolve, and the perennial reality that no solution will satisfy everyone. Regulators, like people generally, inhabit an imperfect world. As the premise of the book reveals, *being* or *growing* a restorative regulator speaks to a wider yearning for public institutions to understand that they operate and live within a network of relationships with all those within their regulatory remit.

The evolution of this book has been a journey in itself, commencing in 2018. Winding forward to the present day, we can see that the EPA and the ANU research team have been through numerous evolutions. Many of the original members of the research team and people involved in the interviews have moved on to other endeavours. The new EPA Act is not so new, and the 1970 Act is part of the EPA's history, yet the situations presented in the book remain ever present. Indeed, most of the case studies referenced in this book concern matters that the EPA continues to actively regulate. That said, the situations discussed here are dynamic, and some details may have changed between writing and publication.

Our thanks go to the many individuals who have contributed their time, reflections and ideas on how we might address the challenges that are constant companions in the quest of achieving responsive, responsible and restorative regulation.

Alistair Nairn and Deborah Hollingworth
Industry Research Partners of the Environment Protection Authority, Victoria

Acknowledgements

We, the authors, wish to acknowledge key individuals who made this journey so enriching, informative and insightful.

First, we would like to thank our wonderful research collaborators within the Environment Protection Authority Victoria (EPA Victoria): more than a hundred individuals who generously shared their wisdom and experience throughout this project. We particularly thank the former CEO of EPA Victoria, Cathy Wilkinson, and former EPA Chair Cheryl Batagol, each of whom gave so much of themselves in mentoring us in the ways of EPA Victoria. Their insight and dedication have left a lasting impression, and we came to admire them greatly. Many EPA staff gave generously of their time to further our research, including field officers, First Nations staff, and staff in regional offices, several of whom offered desk space, guided us on tours, and even walked with us to local lunch spots during our fieldwork visits – gestures of care and goodwill. Special thanks go to the restorative champions dotted throughout the EPA who helped us set up a pilot project (sadly scuttled by COVID-19). They gave us the inside stories of what it is like to think restoratively in the workplace, and they shared many ideas about dialling up the restorative nature of their work.

Second, we would like to thank the many individuals and groups outside EPA Victoria who also shared their thoughts, activities and hopes on the topic of environmental regulation, and their ideas about restorative approaches. The friends and critics of EPA Victoria—members of the community, the organised environmental movement and First Nations communities; those who experienced environmental and health harms firsthand; practitioners, and representatives of business and other areas of government—all brought fresh and enlightening perspectives on how restorative regulation might enrich future regulatory actions and relationships. Their ideas were wide-ranging, covering community participation, business interactions and, more broadly, systemic changes.

Third, we would like to thank some important people without whom this book would not have existed. We thank Emeritus Distinguished Professor John Braithwaite for trailblazing the ideas and creating all the best words that underpin the foundations of this book, and for demonstrating how beautiful and illuminating organisational ethnographic research can be when a breadth of disciplines, backgrounds and interests converge to nose out the truffles hidden in plain sight. This book began in the cauldron of his expansive vision of good, responsive and restorative regulation—one that trusts people to reveal what is possible, rather than confining them within structured research processes or filtering their words and actions through the lens of researcher comfort. After all, accompanying EPA inspectors to abattoirs and landfills really did stretch us beyond our comfort zone!

We also thank Emeritus Professor Valerie Braithwaite, whose gentle and patient guidance remained foremost in our minds: to always seek the moments of hope and to truly engage with the struggles and resilience of communities. Valerie's extensive experience with communities, the interplay between regulators and those regulated, welfare, health and safety, and much more besides, informed our approach, instilling in us the imperative to follow her lead in paying careful and respectful attention to impacted communities. Valerie shaped our thinking around hope, care and noticing the little things that matter greatly.

Our ANU colleagues also deserve our gratitude. They did the hard yards behind the scenes, from research and soundboarding to footnotes and photos. Dr Deborah Cleland, who has the wonderful ability to see the person and not the role, was a colleague researcher in the first years of the project. Her work with Indigenous issues spans many years, both overseas and in Australia, and helped guide our understanding of the cultural challenges facing First Nations communities in Victoria with respect to environmental harm. Her research on the frog ponds gave us moments of hope and joy. We further thank ANU colleagues Dr Yan Zhang and PhD candidate Mutiara Indriani, each of whom kindly gave so much help with things other people are not keen to do, such as formatting footnotes and chasing down obscure references.

We are also grateful to our volunteer photographer, Daniel Fernandez, whose compelling images grace the cover and several pages of this book, adding depth and visual resonance to its themes.

In addition, we thank our various reviewers, both known and anonymous—we truly appreciated your giving of your time and wisdom to guide us. Your help was instrumental in ensuring a robust, inclusive and accurate rendering of our research findings. We also thank Malcolm Sparrow, who read the first report, prepared by John Braithwaite, from which this book grew, giving incisive feedback that has wended its way into this iteration in all the right places.

We are grateful to have learned so much from the insights that all these people so generously shared with us.

We would also like to thank our editor, Glenine Hamlyn. Her thorough and insightful editing has helped to shape this work into a clearer, more cohesive and more accessible book. We are especially grateful for her care in engaging with both the substance and structure of the text.

Our gratitude extends further to our colleagues in the Environmental Restorative Justice Working Committee for the European Forum for Restorative Justice, with whom we have started to seed the new field of environmental restorative justice.

Finally, we thank our readers for taking the time to learn more about restorative regulation. We hope you find much to inspire you.

Funding

This project was funded by an Australian Research Council Linkage Grant with the EPA and the ANU. It spanned the years 2018 to 2025.

Notes on terminology and citations

First Nations terminology

In this book, we often refer to the First Nations people of Australia and their ways of being, doing and knowing. We wish to emphasise their perspectives on how we might move forward together to create a regenerative, restorative and shared approach to regulation.

When we use the term 'Indigenous peoples', we are referring to all Indigenous groups globally. When referring specifically to Aboriginal and Torres Strait Islander peoples in the country now known as Australia, we mainly use 'First Nations people', 'First Nations communities' (or groups), 'First Nations', or 'First Nations Australians'; sometimes we use 'Aboriginal and Torres Strait Islander peoples'. These terms are used with the understanding that:

> [m]any Aboriginal and Torres Strait Islander people do not like to be referred to as 'Indigenous' because it is considered too generic and can be applied to all indigenous peoples of the world. There is a growing preference for First Nations Australians as a more encompassing term, because while it also is generic, it acknowledges the diversity of Aboriginal and Torres Strait Islander peoples.[1]

Where relevant, we use specific names of communities or nations, respecting the terms by which First Nations groups self-identify.

In some instances, we use the term 'Indigenous' or 'Aboriginal' as an adjective (e.g. Indigenous regulation, Indigenous knowledge/practices, Aboriginal language/worldview or Indigenous perspectives/values). This is done with the understanding that while there are shared elements across First Nations cultures, each group has distinct practices, beliefs and worldviews.

1 Australian Institute of Aboriginal and Torres Strait Islander Studies (AIATSIS), 'First Peoples of Australia', accessed 14 March 2025, aiatsis.gov.au/explore/first-peoples-australia#toc-what-term-is-best-to-use.

We also refer to 'First Law' in recognition that the country now known as Australia has had laws in place for tens of millennia—an ancient, relational and reciprocal collective system of laws derived from the continent's lands and waters,[2] a 'body of laws which have governed relations between and within First Nations and between the human and non-human since the beginning of time'.[3]

Our use of these terms is guided by respect for the diversity of Aboriginal and Torres Strait Islander peoples and the richness of their cultures, connections to and custodianship of Country, and the unique sovereign status of their nations based on language groups.

Interview citations

For all interviews, anonymity was a condition of participation unless the interviewee explicitly agreed otherwise. This approach helped to facilitate candid, thoughtful reflections and a level of comfort that supported the depth and richness of information shared. To honour this, we identify most of our interviewees only by a general description of their role or affiliation (e.g. 'EPA officer' or 'community member') rather than by name, location or date. Where necessary for reasons of context, we add the year in which the interview took place.

2 Marcia Langton and Aaron Corn, *Law: The Way of the Ancestors*.

3 Martuwarra RiverOfLife, Anne Poelina, Donna Bagnall and Michelle Lim, 'Recognizing the Martuwarra's First Law Right to Life as a Living Ancestral Being', *Transnational Environmental Law* 9, no. 3 (2020): 541–68, 544, doi.org/10.1017/S2047102520000163.

Introduction: The need for restorative regulation

Source: Author.

This chapter introduces the concept of *restorative regulation* and explains the different ways the book can be read—as an account of one regulator's restorative journey, or as a guide to developing or growing restorative regulation more broadly. The chapter also outlines the benefits to be gained by integrating restorative values, practices and ethics into regulatory institutions and regulatory ecosystems.

In the sizzling summer of 2014, a large open-cut coalmine caught fire on the outskirts of Morwell, a rural township at the heart of the fossil fuel power-generation industry in the Australian state of Victoria.

Weather conditions on 9 February were the worst they had been for years: hot and windy, temperatures hovering around 40 degrees centigrade. By mid-afternoon, 70 fires were burning around the state. Smoke surrounded the township. Residents attempting to flee the bushfire threat struggled to find safe roads to escape. Multiple fire fronts threatened the mine, and, eventually, embers from one or two of the grassfires closest to the mine ignited the open-cut pit, leading to what was—at first—a small fire inside the coalmine itself.

Amid the general anxiety and reaction to the multiple fires, the gravity and extent of the one at the mine was not fully understood at first. But the mine fire could not be extinguished as easily as the bushfires. Within just a few days, the township that had already experienced so much anxiety and exhaustion was covered in a thick, choking blanket of smoke. The smoke was to linger for many weeks to come.

Unsurprisingly, the residents quickly became fearful for their health and safety as the smoke refused to lift, with fumes and ash—or 'black dust', as many would come to call it—building up, and the fire continuing its inexorable burn.[1] It wasn't long before people started to identify a variety of health impacts on themselves and their families, including respiratory and cardiovascular problems, dizziness and nosebleeds.[2] The Environment Protection Authority Victoria (EPA Victoria, the EPA) set up mobile air-monitoring around the town. As a safety and preventive measure, residents were asked to stay indoors where possible.

The fire kept burning. Three weeks after it started, vulnerable residents were advised to leave South Morwell, the suburb closest to the mine fire.

1 Jarni Blakkarly, 'Latrobe Valley a Litmus Test for Clean Energy Transition'.

2 Susan Yell and Michelle Duffy, 'Community Empowerment and Trust: Social Media Use During the Hazelwood Mine Fire'. Furthermore, the health department only decided to move people out 19 days into the incident: Blakkarly, 'Latrobe Valley a Litmus Test'; Sally A. Weller, 'Just Transition? Strategic Framing and the Challenges Facing Coal Dependent Communities'.

It would take 45 days before the fire was officially declared extinguished. It had been Latrobe Valley's 'largest and longest burning mine fire'.[3]

Nine days into the fire, the emergency response team, consisting of multiple government agencies, held a community meeting at Morwell's Town Hall. Describing the meeting many years later, the then- CEO of EPA Victoria reflected, '[It was] the absolute antithesis of what I think about community engagement.' The government agency representatives sat on the elevated stage, a single microphone positioned in the middle. The public, on the other hand, were all seated at ground level.

The first person who rose to ask a question wore a gas mask to emphasise his point. Removing it to ask his question, he enquired: 'I've looked this up on Google. And it says there's arsenic in the coal. Are we all now being poisoned by arsenic which must be in the smoke?' Next, a woman rose to explain that just two hours prior to the meeting, she had picked up her child from kindergarten, and that he had been covered in grey ash. She asked: 'Is he going to die?'

Recalling that day, the former Chair of EPA Victoria, Cheryl Batagol, shook her head sadly. Reflecting on it, she said that of course, with a setup like they had, only the loudest voices in the audience felt comfortable voicing their concerns to the experts seated high up on stage. It was just an impossible situation, she said, guaranteed to fail to generate the trust and calm needed.

The EPA later prosecuted the owners of the mine for a range of pollution offences. A lengthy and costly trial ensued. Victim impact statements taken from 50 members of the community were presented to the court. In 2020, six years after the fire and its wide-ranging impacts, the owners were convicted for these environmental offences. Their sentence? A mere A$380,000.[4]

The judge noted in sentencing that little had been done to rehabilitate the exposed areas ravaged by the fire. Even less had been done for the local community. Post-disaster engagement with community by the mine's

3 State Government of Victoria, *Hazelwood Mine Fire Inquiry Report 2014* (Victorian Government Printer, 2014), 12, www.latrobe.vic.gov.au/sites/default/files/2024-06/Hazelwood%20Mine%20Fire%20Inquiry%20Report%20%282009%29.pdf; Blakkarly, 'Latrobe Valley a Litmus Test'; Weller, 'Just Transition?'.

4 Weller, 'Just Transition?'. This reflected available penalties under the former *Environment Protection Act 1970* (Vic).

operators had largely involved the dispersal of $100 gift vouchers to the town's population, a meagre offering in the face of a great deal of suffering, loss and pain.

Although EPA Victoria was not the government agency responsible for managing the risks that led to the fire or for coordinating and managing the emergency,[5] its role in providing expert analysis on environmental impacts during the fire, coupled with its active participation in community engagement, made it a target of community anger and frustration. For the multiple agencies involved, including the EPA, the Hazelwood Mine fire cast a lasting shadow over subsequent regulatory discussions and decisions. More specifically for the EPA, the fallout from the mine fire led the government to establish an independent inquiry into the EPA's regulatory powers, duties and governance arrangements, ultimately sparking new legislation that has resulted in the transformation of the regulator. The community anger with the regulatory response serves as a stark reminder of the need for regulation that is attuned to community-specific risks and burdens, emphasises prevention as a core regulatory strategy, and prioritises authentic, timely communication and engagement to support communities in their time of need.

This book presents restorative regulation as a way forward for regulators seeking to respond to such needs and rebuild trust in regulatory institutions.

What is restorative regulation?

> *Because crime hurts, justice should heal.*[6]

This famous maxim of restorative justice scholar and Emeritus Distinguished Professor John Braithwaite emphasises that the aim at the heart of restorative justice is to repair harm that has occurred. Whether that harm has resulted from the domination of crime, war, pollution or school bullying, healing is central to recovery and the prevention of recurrence. In the same vein, we see restorative regulation as a way to orientate regulatory systems towards

---

5 State Government of Victoria, 'Hazelwood Mine Fire Inquiry Report 2014'.

6 John Braithwaite, 'Restorative Justice and De-Professionalization', *The Good Society* 13, no. 1 (2004): 28–31, muse.jhu.edu/article/175203.

repairing and preventing harm. We adopt a broad definition of regulation, seeing it as being broader than just law and including a wide range of informal factors that seek to influence the 'flow of events'.[7]

Restorative justice is often thought about as a form of sanctioning procedure that brings together those who have created harm with those who have been harmed. While this aspect is important, restorative justice can be interpreted more broadly. Howard Zehr, one of restorative justice's founders, conceives of restorative justice as a compass for living,[8] while others consider it an ethos.[9] Yet others see it as both, where a way of living through restorative practices serves as a visible manifestation of the restorative ethos, values and principles.

Our conceptualisation of restorative regulation involves a significant shift away from the conventional framing of a regulatory response. Restorative regulation is a way of doing regulation that emphasises healing over punishment, requires active accountability for harm caused, focuses on maintaining and building relationships, places ownership of conflict with those most impacted and seeks for opportunities to do better rather than bare-bones compliance. Instead of trying to enforce conformity primarily through coercive and punitive means, a restorative approach amplifies victims' voices to help offenders understand the impact of their action and to collaborate in working out what needs to be done to move forward.

At its core, restorative regulation is guided by the restorative values of equality, dignity, respect, trust, empowerment, and mutual care and concern.[10] Key practices involve ensuring active accountability of the person or entity that caused harm and facilitating dialogue that shares the perspectives of those impacted by harm or potential harm. Relational justice is a fundamental dimension of restorative regulation because healing, listening and empowerment cannot be enabled without a focus on relationships.

7 Christine Parker and John Braithwaite, 'Regulation', in *The Oxford Handbook of Legal Studies*, ed. Peter Cane and Mark Tushnet (Oxford University Press, 2003), 119–45.

8 Howard Zehr, *Changing Lenses: Restorative Justice for Our Times*.

9 Theo Gavrielides, 'Restorative Justice—the Perplexing Concept: Conceptual Fault-Lines and Power Battles Within the Restorative Justice Movement', *Criminology & Criminal Justice* 8, no. 2 (2008): 165–83, doi.org/10.1177/1748895808088993.

10 For a discussion of the reasons, see Miranda Forsyth et al., 'A Future Agenda for Environmental Restorative Justice?', *The International Journal of Restorative Justice* 4, no. 1 (2021): 17–40, doi.org/10.5553/tijrj.000063.

According to restorative scholar Chris Marshall, conceptualising restorative justice as a relational justice of care enables us to highlight its underlying commitment to vulnerability, reciprocity and relational personhood. [11]

Restorative regulation shares common ground with other disciplines and theoretical perspectives that reflect similar values and practices. Adaptive governance, responsive regulation, organisational psychology and various forms of justice (participatory, deliberative, environmental and procedural) propose techniques and practices that align with restorative regulation. Research by American psychologist Gary Klein and his colleagues provides a notable example. Their 'Good Strangers' project studied police officers and military personnel who excelled at managing civilian encounters without creating hostility. The study identified key characteristics that resonate with restorative approaches, including a conscious effort to build trust rather than rely on coercion. Effective individuals also demonstrated strong skills in building rapport and taking the perspectives of civilians.[12]

Many of the practices and values we discuss are, therefore, not unique to restorative justice or restorative practices. However, restorative regulation provides a coherent conceptual framework for bringing them together and explaining why and how they operate. It also provides the normative justification for considering their broader applicability across the regulatory spectrum.

We see in the convergence of similar approaches to justice and governance a sign that these are valuable ideas worth exploring. Basic as it may seem, the evidence shows that outcomes improve when people are given a space to express themselves, feel respectfully listened to and are met with curiosity rather than scepticism.[13] When others acknowledge and understand their pain, disappointment or frustration, things tend to work out better.

---

11 Christopher D Marshall, 'Justice as Care', *The International Journal of Restorative Justice* 2, no. 2 (2019): 175–85, 181, doi.org/10.5553/IJRJ/258908912019002002001.

12 Gary Klein et al., 'Police and Military as Good Strangers', *Journal of Occupational and Organizational Psychology* 88, no. 2 (2015): 231–50, doi.org/10.1111/joop.12110.

13 Sidney Dekker, Amanda Oates, and Joseph Rafferty, eds., *Restorative Just Culture in Practice: Implementation and Evaluation* (Productivity Press, 2022), 73–82, doi.org/10.4324/9781003162582. On curiosity, see Lynn Borton, 'Curiosity in Restorative Justice, with Kimiko Lighty', *Choose to Be Curious*, 5 January 2022, lynnborton.com/2022/01/05/curiosity-in-restorative-justice-with-kimiko-lighty/.

As journalist Amanda Ripley's story in Chapter 1 will demonstrate, many of the approaches proposed here are, in fact, the same basic tools we teach our children: express your feelings with words, ask for help in resolving problems, say sorry when you've caused harm and think of suggestions to make things right again.

This book brings a holistic understanding of restorative justice to the context of regulation, imagining what could happen if restorative approaches are applied across varied domains of an agency's regulatory work. We see this reimagining as opening possibilities beyond the typical focus on using restorative justice for sanctions, in areas such as compliance and enforcement, change management and, ultimately, the transformation of organisational culture. Moreover, while our research has focused on environmental regulation, the insights into restorative regulation have relevance and applicability to other regulatory domains as well.

At the heart of our approach is the idea of regulators embodying a restorative way of 'being humane' in all aspects of their daily practice. We aspire to open up the imagination to the diversity of spaces where restorative justice already thrives and where it could be a valuable and beneficial addition to a regulatory agency's practice. In conceptualising this through the organic metaphor of growing restorative regulation, we aim to cultivate a diverse and vibrant landscape of restorative practices and values that can flourish not only in environmental regulation but across all other regulatory contexts.

Growing restorative regulation: An overview

This book is the outcome of multi-year research collaboration between the Victorian environmental regulator, EPA Victoria and researchers at The Australian National University (ANU). This collaboration involved an exploration of the potential for restorative justice in environmental regulation, a new and evolving area for restorative justice that has gained significant attention in recent years.[14] This book shares what we have learned about the potential for restorative regulation, both within environmental regulation, and in regulation more broadly.

14 Brunilda Pali, Miranda Forsyth, and Felicity Tepper, eds., *The Palgrave Handbook of Environmental Restorative Justice* (Palgrave Macmillan, 2022).

In the rest of this chapter, we will outline the concept of restorative regulation and present the evidence supporting its merit for regulators. In Chapter 1, we clarify the restorative values and practices we reference throughout the book, establishing a foundational understanding for our use of specific terms and concepts. Chapter 2 offers a brief history of EPA Victoria, our principal regulatory research subject, and details how our research was conducted.

This leads us to Chapter 3, where we discuss the importance of community and citizen empowerment. We start here because, as senior regulator Kate Gavens recently emphasised in relation to the role of regulators, 'Really, at the end of the day, we're here to deliver outcomes for the community.'[15] As restorative justice researchers, we, too, view community as being at the heart of regulation, a thread we will keep weaving through all chapters.

In chapters 4 to 8, we explore ways in which restorative innovation can make a difference. These chapters cover restorative harm prevention, restorative monitoring of harm, restorative responses to harm, restorative repair of harm and restorative learning from harm. We chose these five areas to highlight different aspects of the regulatory spectrum, illustrating the broad applicability of restorative approaches.

Based on the insights learned through our research with EPA Victoria, we propose restorative innovations and practices that could benefit regulators in various domains, such as health care, finance, welfare, consumer affairs, aged care and criminal justice.

In Chapter 9, we critically examine the pressing need for regulators to engage effectively with First Nations Australians and offer suggestions for ways in which a restorative regulator might acknowledge and support Indigenous-led regenerative outcomes. Our final chapter wraps up with a set of recommendations for growing as a restorative regulator, including suggestions for supporting the restorative champions essential to this organisational transformation.

15 Kate Gavens, 'Incentivising Compliance: Using Behavioural Insights to Encourage and Persuade' (panel discussion with Liam Smith and John Merritt, Australia and New Zealand School of Government and the National Regulators Community of Practice, Melbourne Business School, 2 June 2023), anzsog.edu.au/learning-and-development/events-and-conferences/incentivising-compliance-using-behavioural-insights-to-encourage-and-persuade/.

The structure of the book is designed to provide flexibility, allowing you to delve into specific sections and explore them at your own pace. Threads connecting case studies, restorative values and practices, and recommendations for growing restorative innovations in daily regulatory activities weave a cohesive narrative throughout. We invite you to chart your own unique path of exploration, navigating the content as it aligns with your interests.

Navigating two perspectives on the book

This book can be read in two ways.

First, it is a detailed description of the spaces where restorative innovation has been tried, or where it could potentially be tried, within one particular regulatory organisation: EPA Victoria. This reading of the book draws upon the multi-year research journey with EPA Victoria mentioned above. Prior to our research, EPA Victoria had already been experimenting with restorative justice for several years, laying an important foundation for the further integration of restorative justice across its regulatory activities.

In this research journey, instead of starting with a narrow focus on tried-and-true restorative practices such as restorative conferences, we took an ethnographic approach in order to identify spaces where restorative practices and values already existed within the EPA—even if they were not explicitly labelled as 'restorative' by those using them.

Our approach was rewarded when we uncovered a multiplexity of restorative spaces in the EPA, some already 'in action' and some emerging as potential restorative spaces awaiting activation. The book details these discoveries, drawing out their diversity and emphasising the substantial challenges associated with increasing the spaces for restorative justice within a regulatory ecosystem.

Our research shows that some restorative innovations have worked well and others not so well. However, it is not our purpose here to evaluate them systematically. Rather, we seek to share possibilities for restorative innovation at all stages of the regulatory cycle and to reflect upon the many different places and forms in which it can take shape.

The second way of approaching this book, which we hope will resonate with regulatory practitioners and scholars, positions it as a *guide to a process* for nurturing restorative innovation within the regulatory framework. Read this way, the book presents EPA Victoria and its journey as an *exemplar* of how—and where—a regulator from any domain might initiate the search for spaces of restorative justice, both in current practice and in the potential for future use. This second approach encourages consideration of the transformative possibilities and the challenges of developing restorative practices in any given regulatory context. We show how a regulator intent on creating a restorative culture should first search for both existing and potential restorative practices before reflecting on how these can be nurtured and grown.

In seeking out restorative spaces, it is important to consider the potential application of restorative regulation across the entire spectrum of a regulator's activities, starting with the design of law reform principles, then encompassing the whole regulatory landscape, from licensing to the oversight of licensees' compliance. It could then be applied to operational responses to incidents and emergencies, and, further, to clean-up, law enforcement and prosecution.

As we consider each space in this book, we ask whether a more restorative approach could strengthen the preventive capacity of regulation. This focus on prevention, a core tenet of all restorative approaches, is increasingly central to environmental regulation and other regulatory domains such as health, finance, and consumer protection. Importantly, the preventive emphasis plays a pivotal role in rebuilding trust because it demonstrates a proactive commitment to safeguarding the wellbeing of individual citizens, communities and the environment.

We do not expect that a single restorative space will be a game-changer on its own. We have certainly found no evidence of any shift that radical. However, fostering a holistic imagination—one that aims to make many spaces more restorative—can be transformative. Wicked problems cannot be tamed in a restorative way without simultaneous efforts across multiple restorative spaces. This is why it has been important to map the many possible restorative spaces, opening our regulatory imaginations to a multispace, interconnected restorative vision.

The case for restorative regulation

Much of this book explores how to grow restorative regulation. First, however, we need to lay the groundwork for why it is worth planting in the first place. This is particularly important given the pervasive but incorrect rhetoric that restorative justice is a 'soft option'. In fact, a growing evidence base supports restorative justice as an effective regulatory approach across diverse regulatory domains,[16] including education,[17] health care,[18] human services[19] and criminal justice.[20] Restorative justice has already proven successful in diverse settings, from resolving conflicts in aged care and corporate governance[21] to addressing issues in the workplace (including workplace bullying).[22] It has been applied effectively in lawyer regulation[23] and measures to foster harmony on university campuses.[24] A substantial evidence base demonstrates that restorative approaches enable victims to play an active part in the justice process by empowering them to have a voice, ask questions and get answers, and to gain closure and move forward, thereby reducing their levels of stress and fear.[25] While most evidence comes from the criminal justice and educational sectors, these positive outcomes could benefit and strengthen regulatory processes more broadly.

16 John Braithwaite, *Restorative Justice and Responsive Regulation: The Question of Evidence*; John Braithwaite, 'Street-Level Meta-Strategies: Evidence on Restorative Justice and Responsive Regulation', 205–25.

17 Ernesto Lodi et al., 'Use of Restorative Justice and Restorative Practices at School: A Systematic Literature Review'; Rose Short et al., 'The Long-Term Impact of a Whole School Approach of Restorative Practice: The Views of Secondary School Teachers', 313–24.

18 Dhara Aminet et al., 'A Need to Embrace Restorative Justice at the Heart of the Patient Safety Movement', 183–84; Dekker et al., *Restorative Just Culture in Practice*.

19 Gale Burford et al., *Restorative and Responsive Human Services*.

20 Jonathan Hobson et al., 'Restorative Justice, Youth Violence, and Policing: A Review of the Evidence', 62; Carrie Menkel-Meadow, 'Restorative Justice: What Is It and Does it Work?', 161–87; Barton Poulson, 'A Third Voice: A Review of Empirical Research on the Psychological Outcomes of Restorative Justice', 167–204; Lindsay Fulham et al., 'The Effectiveness of Restorative Justice Programs: A Meta-Analysis of Recidivism and Other Relevant Outcomes'.

21 John Braithwaite, *Restorative Justice and Corporate Regulation* (Routledge, 2003).

22 Nathan Robert Neale et al., 'Managers' Restorative Versus Punitive Responses to Employee Wrongdoing: A Qualitative Investigation', 603–25. On workplace bullying, see Shirley Jülich and Noel S. B. Cox, 'Good Workplaces: Alternative Dispute Resolution and Restorative Justice'.

23 Linda Haller, 'Restorative Lawyer Discipline in Australia', 316–32.

24 David Karp and Megan Schachter, 'Restorative Justice in Universities: Case Studies of What Works with Restorative Responses to Student Misconduct', 247–63.

25 Caroline M. Angel, 'Crime Victims Meet Their Offenders: Testing the Impact of Restorative Justice Conferences on Victims' Post-Traumatic Stress Symptoms' (PhD diss., University of Pennsylvania, 2005); Rebecca Banwell-Moore, 'Just an "Optional Extra" in the "Victim Toolkit"?: The Culture, Mechanisms and Approaches of Criminal Justice Organisations Delivering Restorative Justice in England and Wales', *International Review of Victimology* 29, no. 2 (2023): 217–35, doi.org/10.1177/02697580221079993; Joanna Shapland, Gwen Robinson, and Angela Sorsby, *Restorative Justice in Practice: Evaluating What Works for Victims and Offenders* (Routledge, 2011), doi.org/10.4324/9780203806104.

When applied correctly, a restorative approach leads to greater stakeholder involvement, inclusivity, engagement and empowerment.[26] These attributes are especially relevant for addressing several pressing regulatory challenges, including the erosion of public trust and legitimacy, and for improving compliance, as discussed below.

While the explicit use of a restorative approach in regulatory institutions is still in its early stages, the evidence supporting its efficacy is steadily emerging. Encouragingly, EPA Victoria, whose innovative experience we explore in this book, is stepping up to the challenge. Similarly, New Zealand, under a previous government, envisioned a new framework for a restorative health system; if its recommendations are implemented, this framework could be transformative.[27] Existing restorative examples and innovations like these demonstrate the potential of restorative justice within regulatory frameworks. That said, we note that the uptake in practice is slower than is warranted by the evidence base. It strikes us as strange that approaches as basic as 'listen to people' and 'apologise when something goes wrong' are still seen by many as deeply challenging to regulatory orthodoxy. We hope this book helps them seem a little less so.

We now turn to several ways in which a restorative approach can help a regulator.

Increasing trust in the regulator

> Trust and cooperation are essential to a healthy, vibrant, well-functioning democracy.[28]

In today's world, citizens are increasingly losing trust in their institutions of governance.[29] Scholars talk about a crisis of legitimacy, reflecting concerns that states are finding it 'increasingly difficult to forge meaningful

---

26 Gerry Johnstone and Daniel W. Van Ness, 'The Idea of Restorative Justice', in *Handbook of Restorative Justice*, ed. Gerry Johnstone and Daniel Van Ness (Willan Publishing, 2007), 1–3.

27 The National Collaborative for Restorative Initiatives in Health, *He Maungarongo Ki Ngā Iwi: Envisioning a Restorative Health System in Aotearoa New Zealand* (The National Collaborative for Restorative Initiatives in Health, 2023), www.hqsc.govt.nz/assets/Our-work/System-safety/Restorative-practice/Publications-resources/Envisioning-a-Restorative-Health-System-May-2023.pdf.

28 Daniel Balliet et al., 'Political Ideology, Trust, and Cooperation: In-Group Favoritism Among Republicans *and* Democrats During a US National Election', *The Journal of Conflict Resolution* 62, no. 4 (2018): 797–818, 814, doi.org/10.1177/0022002716658694.

29 Samuel Wilson, et al., '5 Charts Show How Trust in Australia's Leaders and Institutions Has Collapsed'; Sarah Cameron et al., *The 2022 Australian Federal Election: Results from the Australian Election Study* (Australian Election Study, 2022), apo.org.au/node/321025.

connections with those governed'.[30] A common and popular narrative has emerged, casting regulators as 'technocratic', 'out-of-touch', entangled in 'red tape' and focused on 'bureaucratic nonsense'.[31]

The increasing lack of trust by the public in public institutions is sometimes called a democratic deficit—shorthand for the failure of governmental institutions to 'reflect the real values and ideas of citizens'.[32] This crisis or deficit is not necessarily a reduction in support for democratic values and principles, which still receive much support.[33] Rather, it is about low trust in, and suspicion towards, representative democracy—the politicians, the government, executive institutions, parliaments and elections.[34]

This distrust has arisen due to issues such as low transparency, limited engagement with citizens by officials,[35] regulatory capture,[36] anti-intellectualism,[37] risk-averseness and complexity in delivery of government services,[38] negative sentiment[39] and anti-science attitudes.[40] In turn, distrust has been fuelled by various converging challenges, including polarisation,[41]

30 Eline Severs and Alexander Mattelaer, 'A Crisis of Democratic Legitimacy? It's about Legitimation, Stupid!', European Policy Brief no. 21 (March 2014), Egmont Royal Institute for International Relations, aei.pitt.edu/63549/.

31 This type of rhetoric is sometimes referred to as 'bureaucrat bashing', through which the 'public sector workers have become a symbol of incompetence within society, and this symbol has been internalized by the public as a stereotype.' Gabriela Szydlowski, Noortje de Boer, and Lars Tummers, 'Compassion, Bureaucrat Bashing, and Public Administration', *Public Administration Review* 82, no. 4 (2022): 619–33, 621, doi.org/10.1111/puar.13485. It is further embedded in public discourse and media commentary by narratives spun using 'attack politics' by some politicians who place 'aggressive emphasis on failures over successes and the exploitation of organizational vulnerabilities,' 626.

32 Joan C. Tronto, *Caring Democracy: Markets, Equality, and Justice*, 1st ed. (NYU Press, 2013), 17.

33 Australian Government, *Strengthening Australian Democracy: A Practical Agenda for Democratic Resilience* (Department of Home Affairs, 2024), www.homeaffairs.gov.au/about-us-subsite/files/strengthening-australian-democracy.pdf; Severs and Mattelaer, *A Crisis of Democratic Legitimacy.*

34 Cameron et al., *The 2022 Australian Federal Election*; Simon Tormey, 'The Contemporary Crisis of Representative Democracy', *Democratic Theory* 1, no. 2 (2014), doi.org/10.3167/dt.2014.010211; Severs and Mattelaer, *A Crisis of Democratic Legitimacy?*; Charles Taylor, Patrizia Nanz, and Madeleine Beaubien Taylor, *Reconstructing Democracy: How Citizens Are Building from the Ground Up*, 1st ed. (Harvard University Press, 2020).

35 David Levi-Faur, 'Regulation and Regulatory Governance', 3–21.

36 Gary Becker and Richard Posner, '"Capture" of Regulators by Fannie Mae and Freddie Mac', *The Becker-Posner Blog.*

37 Yongjin Choi and Ashley M. Fox, 'Mistrust in Public Health Institutions is a Stronger Predictor of Vaccine Hesitancy and Uptake Than Trust in Trump', 1–10.

38 Peter Coaldrake, *Let the Sunshine In: Review of Culture and Accountability in the Queensland Public Sector: Final Report.*

39 Pew Research Center, *Americans' Views of Government: Decades of Distrust, Enduring Support for Its Role.*

40 Choi and Fox, 'Mistrust in Public Health Institutions'; Aviva Philipp-Muller et al., 'Why Are People Antiscience, and What Can We Do About It?', 1–10.

41 Anthony Painter, 'A Crisis of Legitimacy?', 10–15; Kevin Vallier, *Trust in a Polarized Age* (Oxford University Press, 2020).

the existential threat created by climate change,[42] rising populism and attack politics,[43] inequality,[44] botched automated administration of welfare and care,[45] and generally frustrating and dismissive citizen-government interactions.[46]

Instruments used to assess the state of the public's trust in its social and political institutions show a marked downturn in political trust.[47] In Australia, the Edelman Trust Barometer showed 'sharp declines in trust across all Australian institutions, eroding the record-high levels of public trust recorded in 2021',[48] whereas now 'just 30 percent of Australians believe people in government can be trusted.'[49] Worldwide, 'there is a low public perception of government integrity and governments could do better in responding to citizens' concerns.'[50]

When relations between regulator, regulated and citizen break down, information tends to be withheld rather than shared. When this happens, it hinders on-site accident investigation, preventive interventions, and remedial action, consequently inhibiting overall regulatory effectiveness.[51]

To understand how restorative practices help build trust, we can consider Valerie Braithwaite's concept of trust norms—shared community beliefs about what members must do to be considered trustworthy.[52] She argues that trust norms can be divided into two categories: (1) *exchange trust norms*, based on the other's reliability and informed by the person's or institution's competence, commitments, and track record; and (2) *communal trust norms*, based on whether or not 'the other is respectful, attentive and responsive

42 Coaldrake, *Review of Culture and Accountability*; Painter, 'A Crisis of Legitimacy?'.

43 Szydlowski et al., 'Compassion, Bureaucrat Bashing, and Public Administration'; Ethan Zuckerman, *Mistrust: Why Losing Faith in Institutions Provides the Tools to Transform Them.*

44 Tronto, *Caring Democracy: Markets, Equality, and Justice.*

45 Valerie Braithwaite, 'Beyond the Bubble that is Robodebt: How Governments That Lose Integrity Threaten Democracy', 242–59; Ryan Calo and Danielle Keats Citron, 'The Automated Administrative State: A Crisis of Legitimacy', 797–845.

46 Coaldrake, *Review of Culture and Accountability.*

47 Severs and Mattelaer, *A Crisis of Democratic Legitimacy?*; Tormey, 'The Contemporary Crisis of Representative Democracy'; Edelman, *Trust Barometer 2022 Australia.*

48 Edelman, *Trust Barometer 2022 Australia.*

49 Cameron et al., *The 2022 Australian Federal Election*, 5.

50 OECDgov, 'Building Trust to Reinforce Democracy' (YouTube video), 5 August 2022, www.youtube.com/watch?v=xNc45gpZJao.

51 Neil Gunningham and Darren Sinclair, 'Regulation and the Role of Trust: Reflections from the Mining Industry', *Journal of Law and Society* 36, no. 2 (2009): 167–94, doi.org/10.1111/j.1467-6478.2009.00462.x.

52 Valerie Braithwaite, 'Understanding and Managing Trust Norms', *International Journal for Court Administration* 12, no. 3 (2021): 1–13, doi.org/10.36745/ijca.425.

to needs, consultative, accountable, and understanding of their position'. Critically, she argues that even for institutions like government and courts, people need both exchange trust norms (competence and consistency) and communal trust norms (compassion and fairness) to ensure trustworthiness.

Restorative regulation is particularly valuable in building communal trust. Unlike top-down methods, restorative approaches are inclusive and based on dialogue. By emphasising relationship-building, restorative regulation creates opportunities for citizens to engage directly with regulators, making them accessible rather than hidden behind seemingly unaccountable layers of bureaucracy that often foster suspicion and mistrust. Attentiveness, care and open-mindedness, key aspects of a restorative approach, contribute to growing positive relationships between citizen and regulator through supporting communal trust norms.[53]

Alongside their strengths, each type of trust norm contains a weakness. As Braithwaite observes, 'Exchange trust norms lack an imperative for compassion, while communal trust norms lack an imperative for consistency: [a]ttending to both types of norms means that one can off-set the weaknesses of the other.'[54]

Of course, in practice, both forms of trust norm cannot always be given equal weighting. This book does not suggest that restorative approaches are *always* the right approach. Regulators must navigate a careful path between listening and responding on the one hand and following established protocols on the other. One way to manage potential tensions between these two sets of norms is through careful management of expectations: outlining when each approach will be used, noting any legislative requirements for a particular approach, defining the boundaries of processes like consultation in context, and providing clear justifications for these boundaries.[55]

Our final point on the issue of trust is to highlight findings from recent research by Mark Duckworth, Christine Horn and Michele Grossman on what they term 'trust flows' between community and government.[56] They argue that for a trust relationship to be successfully created and sustained,

53 Alec Clott, 'Restorative Justice as a Form of Collaborative Governance: A Theoretical Analysis of Mediation and Collaboration', *SPECTRA* 5, no. 1 (2016), spectrajournal.org/articles/73.

54 Braithwaite, 'Understanding and Managing Trust Norms', 7.

55 Braithwaite, 'Understanding and Managing Trust Norms', 11, drawing on the work of Pearce Laanela.

56 Mark Duckworth, Christine Horn, and Michele Grossman, *Do Governments Trust Communities? The Trust Flows Project Research Report* (Centre for Resilient and Inclusive Societies, 2024), doi.org/10.56311/FZLZ2190.

trust must flow in both directions: communities must trust government actors, and governments must actively demonstrate trust in communities. A central finding of their work is the importance of interpersonal relationships between government officials and citizens as the foundation of trust, alongside the need to invest time and resources in relationship-building activities.

Duckworth, Horn and Grossman also emphasise the following as key to building trust:

- recognising communities as assets and not 'problems to be managed'.
- establishing functional relationships before a crisis arises, ensuring communication channels and systems for interventions are in place when needed.
- sharing power and facilitating collaborative processes, noting that '[c]ommunity organisations want to be involved in decision-making processes and want to have their voices heard.'[57]

While these suggestions reaffirm longstanding principles of community engagement and participatory governance, they also emphasise the enduring relevance of relational approaches to addressing contemporary challenges. As we will show in the following pages, these objectives align strongly with those of restorative approaches, which are particularly well suited to encouraging trust through shared power, relational attentiveness and meaningful collaboration.

This book aims to highlight the opportunities and possibilities for restorative approaches, advocating for their conscious inclusion alongside more business-as-usual regulatory practices. Restorative approaches can tend to slip into the background, overlooked as legitimate alternatives. This tendency arises partly because individuals' inclinations to be restorative in outlook and practice vary, leading to restorative approaches being seen as a matter of individual discretion rather than deliberate policy. To address this, it is necessary for leaders to recognise, and publicly celebrate, the successes of restorative approaches. Doing so provides tangible examples of these alternative approaches and legitimises them. This is the ultimate insight of projects like The Good Strangers described above.[58] In other words,

57 Duckworth et al., *Do Governments Trust Communities?*

58 Klein et al., 'Police and Military as Good Strangers'. Klein and colleagues found that police officers and military personnel who excelled at managing civilian encounters without creating hostility made a conscious effort to build trust.

organisations can and should consciously develop the skills and reflexes needed to recognise and apply restorative approaches where appropriate, rather than relying on good luck or the presence of innately restorative team members.

Providing opportunities for learning and change instead of punishment

Despite the pervasive belief that punishment offers a satisfactory answer to crime and wrongdoing,[59] the evidence clearly shows this is not the case.[60] The assumption of regulatees as rational actors has been found to be deficient, and regulatory responses based on simplistic threat frameworks often fail.[61] Large fines on corporations are often not as effective as legislators expect. They may not be high enough to rationally deter the worst corporate crimes, as the mine fire example showed. Alternatively, if the fines are high enough to be deterrent, the company may go into bankruptcy and never pay the fine. Moreover, as John Braithwaite argues, punitive approaches also increase defiance, meaning that, in some cases, the threat of punishment provokes defiant reactions that can make crime more likely, not less.[62]

Restorative regulation offers an alternative to the usual punitive approach. It seeks to achieve accountability through active engagement by those responsible for causing harm or who have the potential to cause harm. A core insight of the International Institute of Restorative Practice is that 'human beings are happier, more cooperative and productive, and more likely to make positive changes in their behavior when those in positions of authority do things with them, rather than to them or for them.'[63] Examples we discuss throughout this book will demonstrate how industries and businesses that sustainably improve their environmental stewardship over time are more likely to have had supportive regulators who worked *with* them rather than punishing them.

59 United Nations Office on Drugs and Crime, 'Topic Two—Justifying Punishment in the Community', (March 2019), www.unodc.org/e4j/en/crime-prevention-criminal-justice/module-7/key-issues/2--justifying-punishment-in-the-community.html.

60 John Braithwaite, 'Minimally Sufficient Deterrence', *Crime and Justice* 47 (2018): 69–118, doi.org/10.1086/696043.

61 Dudley, Susan E. and Zhoudan Xie, 'Designing a Choice Architecture for Regulators', *Public Administration Review* 80, no. 1 (2020): 151–56, doi.org/10.1111/puar.13112.

62 Braithwaite, 'Minimally Sufficient Deterrence'.

63 Ted Wachtel, 'Defining Restorative', *International Institute for Restorative Practices* (2016): 1–12, www.iirp.edu/images/pdf/Defining-Restorative_Nov-2016.pdf.

Restorative justice improves regulatory compliance by promoting mechanisms that encourage relationship-building, as well as supportive, collaborative and even empathic engagement with those who have caused, or may cause, environmental harm. When offenders understand and gain insight into the consequences of their actions, they are more likely to take responsibility for repairing harm and develop more considerate behaviour towards others in the future.[64] While this may seem more challenging with corporate entities or businesses rather than individuals, a substantial body of literature supports the positive effects of using restorative approaches for addressing white-collar crime as well.[65] We discuss this further in Chapter 1 under the concept of 'active accountability'.

In terms of accountability for harm caused, restorative approaches can reinforce a commitment to implementing agreements to rehabilitate, repair harm and reform. In domains such as criminal justice and occupational health and safety, restorative justice has proven more effective in implementing successful remedies than court orders.[66] Preliminary research suggests a combination of restorative justice and court orders may be more effective than either approach used separately.[67]

Restorative justice enables offenders to apologise directly to those they have harmed. This can help lessen resentment, build relationships, and open the way to restoring the offender's social licence to operate in the future. This provides a significant incentive for regulatees to engage with a restorative

64 John Braithwaite, *Crime, Shame and Reintegration* (Cambridge University Press, 1989), doi.org/10.1017/CBO9780511804618.

65 Ivo Aertsen, 'Restorative Justice for Victims of Corporate Violence. Victims and Corporations', in *Victims and Corporations: Legal Challenges and Empirical Findings*, ed. Gabrio Forti (Wolters Kluwer, 2018): 235–58; Zvi D. Gabbay, 'Exploring the Limits of the Restorative Justice Paradigm: Restorative Justice and White Collar Crime', *Cardozo Journal of Conflict Resolution* 8, no. 421 (2006–2007): 421–86; Siti Nur Intihani, *Regulation of Deviations Local Government Grant Funds to the Private Sector Through Restorative Justice,* Proceedings of the 2nd International Conference on Law, Economy, Social and Sharia, vol 2 (2024): 545–67, proceeding.icless.net/index.php/icless22/article/view/105; N. Leeper Piquero, S. K. Rice, and A. R. Piquero, 'Power, Profit and Pluralism: New Avenues for Research on Restorative Justice and White-Collar Crime', in *Restorative Justice: From Theory to Practice,* ed. H. Ventura Miller (Emerald Group Publishing Limited, 2008), 209–229, doi.org/10.1016/S1521-6136(08)00409-0; Brent Fisse, 'Reconstructing Corporate Criminal Law: Deterrence, Retribution, Fault and Sanctions', *Southern California Law Review* 56 (1982): 1141–246; Brent Fisse and John Braithwaite, *Corporations, Crime and Accountability* (Cambridge University Press, 1994), doi.org/10.1017/CBO9780511659133.

66 John Braithwaite, *Restorative Justice and Responsive Regulation* (Oxford University Press, 2002), doi.org/10.1093/oso/9780195136395.001.0001.

67 Heather Strang et al., 'Restorative Justice Conferencing (RJC) Using Face-to-Face Meetings of Offenders and Victims: Effects on Offender Recidivism and Victim Satisfaction. A Systematic Review', *Campbell Systematic Reviews* 9, no. 1 (2013): 1–51, doi.org/10.4073/csr.2013.12; John Braithwaite, 'Restorative Justice and Responsive Regulation'.

process. While there are, of course, concerns that offenders might engage in restorative processes purely for prosaic and non-restorative motives, empirical research indicates that engagement in these restorative processes increases offenders' insights into the impact of their offending. This, in turn, often results in a significant change in attitude, even for offenders who start from a cynical standpoint, stimulating their intrinsic motivation to heal the harm caused.[68]

Creating better pathways forward following regulatory failures

What do better pathways forward look like when it comes to restorative regulation? Throughout this book, we explore how restorative approaches can be used to repair harm and build or rebuild relationships with the impacted people and communities. This ranges from practices involving community engagement and empowerment, such as co-production and reporting feedback, to encouraging and supporting regulatees to do the right thing, using practices such as praise and motivational interviewing. To be truly restorative, this pathway must be laid down not only after harm has occurred, but also proactively to prevent future harm.

Restorative justice enables offenders and those affected to collaborate in determining what is required to repair the damage inflicted on the environment, the community, and the relationships impacted. By widening the circle of participants, better decisions can be made collectively, drawing on new forms of knowledge and perspectives.[69] Working together, the solution is more likely to reflect what those impacted by the harm want to see happen. This can lead to long-term involvement not only in remediating the harm, but also in maintaining the improvements made and the relationships formed. Ultimately, this can foster a sense of communal ownership and a deeper commitment to the restorative process.

But what does this look like in practice?

68 Hadeel Al-Alosi and Mark Hamilton, 'The Ingredients of Success for Effective Restorative Justice Conferencing in an Environmental Offending Context', *UNSW Law Journal* 42, no. 4 (2019): 1460–88, doi.org/10.53637/ZEAN8618.

69 Jennifer J. Llewellyn, 'Responding Restoratively to Student Misconduct and Professional Regulation: The Case of Dalhousie Dentistry', in *Restorative and Responsive Human Services*, ed. Valerie Braithwaite, Gale Burford, and John Braithwaite (Routledge, 2019), 127–42, doi.org/10.4324/9780429398704-9.

A pertinent example comes from an incident of environmental harm in New Zealand in 2019. Following an accidental discharge of geothermal liquid into a river, the electricity company responsible for the harm, Contact, entered into a restorative justice process. One of the outcomes was that Contact made an apology to the impacted community, while another was the initiation of direct collaboration between the company and the affected community. On its website, the company states:

> We accept responsibility for the accidental, unauthorised, unlawful discharge into the Waikato River, and are very sorry that this happened. We have a longstanding connection with the Taupō community and *tangata whenua* that we value and want to strengthen. We also have a deep connection to the Waikato River and we were devastated to have caused this damage.
>
> We have put a lot of effort into remediating the damage we caused to the environment, the plant and our community. This has included working with *Ngāti Tūwharetoa* on a restorative justice process which resulted in a cultural impact assessment being undertaken, and a commitment from Contact to address the issues raised as part of their assessment.
>
> We acknowledge the mauri of the Waipuwerawera and Waikato River, and the deep connection that *Ngāti Tūwharetoa* have to these waterways. We committed to addressing the impact we've had environmentally, culturally, and on our relationship.[70]

Reaching out to those who have direct experience of the harm and who know what would improve the challenges they face because of the harm highlights the importance of firsthand experience. Lived experience cannot be replaced by standardised, business-as-usual statistical analyses, expert reports or mea culpas that lack the crucial follow-up actions. In a health care context in which the lived experience of those receiving the services is championed, the following has similarly been noted:

> One of the problems with addressing safety issues within well-established services is that there is little challenge to group thinking. New thinking and outside challenge are important if some of the more intractable safety issues are to be successfully managed. Patients can and should provide this challenge.[71]

70 Contact, 'Restoration of Environmental and Cultural Impacts of the 2019 Karapiti Incident', 3 December 2023, contact.co.nz/aboutus/media-centre/2021/05/13/karapiti-incident-report.

71 Dekker et al., eds., *Restorative Just Culture in Practice*, 81.

Thus, the knowledge required to move forward is often held by those outside the regulatory relationship. As discussed in Chapter 9, in certain contexts, the circle of healing must be further widened to include First Nations cultural values alongside other forms of expertise. Doing so ensures a well-rounded and inclusive outcome that genuinely repairs harm and promotes regeneration.

Increasing compliance and deterrence

It is clear that, despite the dominance of the 'command-and-control' model that underpins many standard regulatory approaches, behaviour is influenced by a wide range of factors, including the social environment of the regulatee. Often, the most impactful tools and mechanisms for achieving improved compliance outcomes involve direct interactions between the regulator and regulatee.[72] Generating a shared sense of responsibility enables the regulator to explain the rules, provide broad advice, offer guidance and share ideas of tools and techniques, all before any compliance issues become a problem. Even where compliance issues do arise, these relational approaches are often preferable to immediately ratcheting up the enforcement pyramid, as many regulatees are more likely to respond positively when given the opportunity to put things right.

Research has shown that even in areas such as tax compliance, where one may assume that economic motivations are central, what can, in fact, affect compliance behaviour are legitimacy and the approval of the regulatory authority and its goals.[73]

Direct interactions do not need to be costly or involve large time commitments. Behavioural scientist Liam Smith recalls a story in which the regulator included a laminated infographic explanatory sheet with a notice of a possible upcoming inspection. The regulator framed this as wanting the regulatees to 'be in a better position when the regulator comes'. He then relates the unexpected yet highly positive compliance outcomes from this small, simple gesture:

---

72 Joel Edwards et al., 'Implementing General Environmental Duties: Challenges and Opportunities', *Australian Journal of Public Administration* 80, no. 3 (2021): 474–92, doi.org/10.1111/1467-8500.12456.

73 Valerie Braithwaite, Kristina Murphy, and Monika Reinhart, 'Taxation Threat, Motivational Postures, and Responsive Regulation', *Law and Policy* 29, no. 1 (2007): 137–58, doi.org/10.1111/j.1467-9930.2007.00250.x.

> One, when the inspectors did come, we actually found they reported back to us that they had less animosity—usually when the inspector comes knocking, it's 'Get the hell out of here, I don't want to know you.' But they were like, 'Noo, come in and I'll show you where I did this, look, there it is, ta-da!' So that was one thing that was a little bit surprising.
>
> The other thing was, the sheet that we'd sent them was stuck up on the wall. Well, why did you stick it up on the wall? They said, 'Well, it's laminated.' It's such a simple thing, right, but that's exactly what happened. And so, it sat there in lunchrooms and recreation areas, where it was really prevalent.[74]

Of course, this is not to say that punitive approaches are never warranted. We see restorative justice as existing within the responsive regulation pyramid, a concept developed by regulatory scholar John Braithwaite. He argues that having restorative justice near the base of a regulatory pyramid, which begins with less intrusive options and escalates to increasingly deterrence-oriented options, has the effect of providing greater deterrent power and cost-effectiveness. It achieves this by maximising the compliance effect of the threat of enforcement.[75] In an environmental context, where there is the potential for exponential harm to occur quickly, as in the factory fires discussed throughout this book, it may be to respond immediately through a highly intrusive sanction. The key is having a range of options, with restorative approaches complementing more punitive measures.

Widening the circle of responsibility for avoiding and repairing harm

One of restorative justice's earlier theorists, Nils Christie, argued that the state had 'stolen' conflicts from community by framing them solely as crimes that needed to be punished, rather than also seeing them as violations of people and fractures in interpersonal relationships.[76] Rather than allowing the law to take full ownership of conflicts, Christie argued for the importance of putting degrees of control back in the hands of those affected. Restorative regulation seeks to involve not only those harmed and

---

74 Kate Gavens, 'Incentivising Compliance: Using Behavioural Insights to Encourage and Persuade'.

75 Lawrence W. Sherman, Peter Neyroud and Ken Pease, *Offender-Desistance Policing and the Sword of Damocles* (Civitas, 2012).

76 Nils Christie, 'Conflicts as Property', *The British Journal of Criminology* 17, no. 1 (1977): 1–15.

those who caused harm in preventing and responding to the harm, but also the wider community. This way of diffusing responsibility back through society ensures that change becomes more transformative.

A restorative approach broadens the range of entities and individuals who have a stake in taking responsibility for preventing and responding to harm. It shifts us away from relying solely on state employees or self-regulation to fix everything in the regulatory space. Given the limited regulatory capacity and geographically dispersed nature of many forms of harm—ranging from environmental harm to health care malpractice, financial misconduct, cybersecurity breaches and exploitative labour—extending responsibility for harm prevention makes good sense. It acknowledges that a range of perspectives and diverse possible solutions can improve the overall decision, while drawing upon the many willing eyes and ears in the community who are invested in seeing the right things happen.[77]

In this way, restorative justice promotes the growth of grassroots democracy among the citizenry. In the environmental regulatory space, the restorative approach shows a pathway forward for business, community members, citizen scientists, First Nations peoples, ecosystem stewards and environmentalists, among others, to form a shared 'regulatory community'.[78] Genuine participation is 'the politically most feasible and socially most just form of conservation possible'.[79]

Finally, widening the circle of actors connects to the larger project restorative justice lays claim to—that of transformation of cultures and institutions into more restoratively minded entities. In time, this transformation has the potential to exert influence beyond the institutions, infusing communities, businesses, cities and towns with a restorative 'just culture' approach that builds trust, repairs relationships and emphasises collaborative decision-making to mend and prevent harm, positioning everyone as part of the solution.

77 Forsyth et al., 'A Future Agenda for Environmental Restorative Justice?'. On the 'potentially remedying role of public participation' in the context of citizen environmental monitoring, see Per M. Stromberg and Ranjula Bali Swain, 'Citizen Monitoring in Environmental Disclosure: An Economics Perspective', *Journal of Environmental Management* 356 (2024), doi.org/10.1016/j.jenvman.2024.120567.

78 Errol Meidinger, 'Regulatory Culture: A Theoretical Outline', *Law & Policy* 9, no. 4 (1987): 355–86, doi.org/10.1111/j.1467-9930.1987.tb00416.x.

79 Anja Nygren, 'Contested Lands and Incompatible Images: The Political Ecology of Struggles Over Resources in Nicaragua's Indio-Maíz Reserve', *Society & Natural Resources* 17, no. 3 (2004): 189–205, doi.org/10.1080/08941920490270221.

How might regulators grow restorative regulation?

As explained above, our research project aimed to discover the spaces where restorative approaches have already taken root in the regulatory structure and cycle, as well as to identify openings for planting and nurturing new restorative ideas and processes. We have developed this into a three-stage process that can be used by all regulators:

1. **Plant and nurture seeds of restorative practice**. Identify spaces within the regulatory landscape where it is possible to plant restorative regulatory approaches alongside existing approaches, or where restorative approaches are already taking root.
2. **Embed, nurture and expand restorative practices**. Support the transition from pilot efforts to sustained and operationalised practices, recognising that restorative and conventional approaches can coexist and enrich one another.
3. **Find ways to connect restorative approaches across the entire regulatory ecosystem**, such as developing a shared language, fostering restorative organisational culture, empowering staff to use restorative approaches, building in incentives, supporting innovation and sharing stories.

This book shares our journey through this three-stage process with EPA Victoria in the hope that it will inform or inspire other regulatory journeys. Many of the chapters are concerned with stages one and two—identifying potential and incipient restorative practices and nurturing them. We share insights from our qualitative research into the spaces where restorative approaches have already been realised, no matter how undeveloped they may be, as well as the untapped potential waiting to be explored. Along the way, we coin new terms to describe the innovative approaches, when relevant. The last chapter explores the third stage, drawing on the EPA to illustrate the concept of the need to embed values and practices across the regulatory system.

Our approach views the regulator as working within, and being part of, a broader regulatory ecosystem that includes regulatees, communities, related businesses and relevant government institutions. This framing lessens the focus on institutions and tools, reorientating us instead towards relationships and interconnections between entities in the system. It offers a more holistic view of how regulatory processes impact—and are impacted by—various interconnected elements within a larger system. For instance, it reveals how economic, social, regulatory and cultural behaviours are shaped by powerful forces and interrelationships within a system. It also illuminates how entrenched behaviours, shaped by these systemic forces, can be hard to break out of because they become habitual or are rewarded, or because the costs of not conforming are too high.[80]

Viewing regulation as part of a larger ecosystem shapes our theory of change. Systems theory suggests that to create sustainable change, we must engage the deeper dynamics of the whole system. Small interventions in just one part of the system often bring about change that is short-lived, as the system will eventually resettle into conformity with its own powerful, deep currents.[81] Our research seeks to engage with these deeper dynamics as a whole by identifying, creating and supporting *spaces for restorative regulation* across many parts of the regulatory system. In this way, the restorative approach can have a lasting impact by transforming ingrained habits embedded in the system's underlying dynamics.

Our overall contention is that restorative justice, as a discrete and clearly defined *technique* such as restorative conferencing, probably proffers something worthy, though relatively modest, to improved regulatory outcomes. In contrast, a restorative justice *sensibility* weaving across all stages of regulatory decision-making is likely to make a much greater impact and be more enduring. This idea finds expression in schools that successfully imbue a restorative ethos across their entire school,[82] as well as in cities that become 'restorative cities'.[83]

In the next chapter, we explore the restorative values and practices we focus on throughout the book, ones that inform and support a regulator's transformation to becoming truly restorative.

80 Danny Burns, 'Systemic Action Research: Changing System Dynamics to Support Sustainable Change', *Action Research* 12, no. 1 (2014): 3–18, 6, doi.org/10.1177/1476750313513910.

81 Donella Meadows, *Leverage Points: Places to Intervene in a System* (The Sustainability Institute, 1999); David Peter Stroh, *Systems Thinking for Social Change* (Chelsea Green Publishing, 2015).

82 Lodi et al., 'Use of Restorative Justice and Restorative Practices at School'; Annmary S. Abdou et al., 'Restorative Schools: A Consultation Case Study for Moving from Theory to Practice', *Journal of Educational and Psychological Consultation* 33, no. 4 (2023): 421–48, doi.org/10.1080/10474412.2023.2192205.

83 Grazia Mannozzi, 'The Emergence of the Idea of a "Restorative City" and Its Link to Restorative Justice', *International Journal of Restorative Justice* 2 (2019): 288–92, doi.org/10.5553/IJRJ/25890891 2019002002006; Martin Howard, 'Restorative Cities: 8 Examples Changing the World', Restorative Justice 101, accessed 5 March 2026, restorativejustice101.com/restorative-justice/the-restorative-city-10-examples-changing-the-world.

1

Foundations of restorative regulation: Values and practices

Source: Author.

We actually spent time together, and we talked about things.
—Amanda Ripley[1]

1 Amanda Ripley, 'These Radically Simple Changes Helped Lawmakers Actually Get Things Done'.

This chapter offers an overview of the key values, theories and practices foundational to restorative justice, as developed by practitioners and scholars over recent decades. It defines and explains many of the central concepts used throughout the book, arguing that restorative regulation involves aligning restorative values with restorative practices.

Intractable conflict and political polarisation are increasing around the world, particularly in the United States.[2] One political analyst after another points to the increasing trend of Democrats and Republicans being unable to cooperate on almost everything.[3] Even at the individual level of social interaction, research has found that 'most Democratic and Republican voters live in partisan bubbles', having 'almost zero interactions' with one another.[4] This divisiveness is amplified in Congress. One Democrat member of Congress apparently described working with a Republican as not only like being in a relationship with someone who had cheated on him, but being in a relationship with someone who cheated on him *with the person who was trying to kill him*![5]

Hence, it is not hard to imagine that by 2021, things were looking pretty dire for the Select Committee on the Modernization of Congress, a Committee made up of six Democrats and six Republicans, all of whom initially refused to even sit in the same room together.[6] However, following some radical new approaches, the Select Committee on the Modernization of Congress became one of the most high-functioning bipartisan workplaces on Capitol Hill.

2 News from Brown, 'U.S. Is Polarizing Faster than Other Democracies, Study Finds'.

3 For example, Christina Pazzanese, 'Democrats and Republicans Do Live in Different Worlds'; Pew Research Center, *Americans' Views of Government: Decades of Distrust, Enduring Support for Its Role*; Daniel Balliet et al., 'Political Ideology, Trust, and Cooperation: In-Group Favoritism among Republicans *and* Democrats during a US National Election'.

4 Pazzanese, 'Democrats and Republicans Do Live in Different Worlds'; see also, Jon Yates, *Fractured: Why Our Societies Are Coming Apart and How We Put Them Back Together Again* (HarperCollins, 2021), 22, who refers to 'social bubbles filled with people "just like me"' as an underlying cause of our fractured societies.

5 Ripley, 'These Radically Simple Changes'.

6 The Select Committee on the Modernization of Congress, a bipartisan committee established every 20 to 30 years, seeks to 'study how the institution is working and to propose reforms that will improve operations so that members can work more effectively for the American people'. See Derek Kilmer, *Final Report: Select Committee on the Modernization of Congress*, 1.

Journalist and author Amanda Ripley investigated the factors behind this turnaround. She found that prior to the reforms, 'basic practices you would use to prevent anarchy in any kindergarten classroom were not being followed in Congress'.[7] In particular, there were no opportunities for people to sit down together, work on shared goals or talk things through when they disagreed.

Basic changes were put in place to bring people together, and things slowly started to change. Then the 'January 6 United States Capitol riot' occurred and ruptured the emerging new way of working. Rather than bowing to the seemingly inevitable and abandoning the Committee, two of its leaders decided to bring all the Committee members together for a confidential conversation about their experiences on January 6 and how it was affecting their ability to work together.

No red jerseys or blue jerseys ... just fix Congress jerseys

Chair Kilmer and then-Vice Chair Graves decided to change the usual House's tradition of dividing the Committee budgets and staff along party lines. The slogan 'one staff, one budget' provided an approach that modelled 'strong bipartisan collaboration'. This helped to make the Committee a 'uniquely nonpartisan entity', sharing everything from social media accounts to office space, keeping everyone 'on the same page'.

(Select Committee on the Modernization of Congress, December 2022, 28–29)

One by one, the members opened up about what had happened to them during that period and how they had felt. Other members were then asked to acknowledge what they had heard and identify what resonated with them. Ripley asserts that '[w]hen people in intractable conflict sit down and listen to each other under the right conditions, they make surprising discoveries'. She quotes one observer who noted that '[b]oth sides believed the other side had been acting politically. And something happened where they realized they were all people—people who had been through something traumatic.'

7 Ripley, 'These Radically Simple Changes'.

Ripley continues:

> [A]s Congress returned to in-person hearings, committee members did something truly startling: they stopped sitting up on high, on a dais, like every other committee and started sitting in a round table format, at the same level of the people who came to testify. Turns out that fixing politics starts by rearranging the furniture. 'You can foster more productive conversation when you can look each other in the eye,' Kilmer says when I ask him to explain the obvious.[8]

Kilmer is a reference to Chair Derek Kilmer. Chair Kilmer himself further noted that the dialogue was fruitful:

> Our Committee had spirited debate and disagreements on a number of issues, but I was heartened by the fact that every member of our Committee had the same North Star— to make Congress work better for the American people.[9]

Neither Ripley, Chair Kilmer, nor the members of the Select Committee on the Modernization of Congress conceptualised what was being done in terms of restorative justice. However, as this book unfolds, we will see that many of the actions they took reflect the values and practices of restorative justice that underpin what we call restorative regulation:

- People's interpersonal relationships with each other were acknowledged and nurtured (focusing on relationships).
- Opportunities were created for telling stories and being emotionally vulnerable (engaging emotions).
- Deep listening and engagement with other people's perspectives were emphasised (adopting a dialogue-based approach).
- Difficult issues were addressed directly through dialogue, rather than being left to ferment in the background (creating safe spaces for meaningful conversations).
- Participants sat in circles, a geometrical arrangement symbolising equality and interconnection (building restorative circles and structures).

We explore many of these concepts in this chapter in an overview of key restorative values and practices, as developed by restorative justice practitioners and scholars over the past several decades. While we draw on

8 Ripley, 'These Radically Simple Changes'.

9 Kilmer, *Final Report*, 3.

these values and practices throughout the book, we also build upon, expand, and in some cases, innovate on them to help deepen the understanding of what is possible to achieve through restorative approaches in the context of contemporary regulatory challenges.

Core values and guiding principles of restorative regulation

This section details some of the core values and principles that help to guide restorative regulation, depicted as an overview in Figure 1.1.

Figure 1.1. Core values and guiding principles of a restorative regulation framework

Source: Generated by authors using Bing Image Creator, 27 November 2024. Prompt: 'Healing circle within Australian bush scene'

A fundamental orientation towards healing

Healing is both a central restorative value and an intended outcome. In conceptualising harm caused, restorative justice treats crime or wrongdoing as a source of suffering for individuals and communities that disrupts relations in social life. In response, the healing process must focus on mending these social ruptures while also repairing any direct physical impacts of the offence.

The healing potential of restorative justice is well supported by research. Psychologically, it can reduce negative emotions, alleviate post-traumatic stress, and help victims regain their sense of agency and self-efficacy.[10] A restorative approach to healing extends beyond individuals, addressing multiple forms of harm, including relational and physical harm to both humans and other-than-humans, including nature, and repairing multiple sets of relationships.[11]

Healing is motivated through respectful relationships and care for the safety of others. It is inherently a relational journey because restorative justice recognises that harm disrupts not only an individual's experience but also the interconnected web of relationships within a community or society. The impact of harm extends beyond the victim and offender, affecting their families, friends, and the wider community. Healing, therefore, must include restoring damaged relationships and addressing the emotional, psychological and social wounds.

Restorative approaches also emphasise the importance of understanding harm within a temporal context. This means it is often necessary to consider the historical and material circumstances underpinning a particular event to make sense of it and to understand the possible pathways forward. By facilitating a broader enquiry, restorative approaches can uncover broader and systemic issues behind individual events, creating opportunities for more macro-level regulatory interventions.

Indigenous-led restoration of Country is another approach to healing, one that complements healing in restorative justice. Sometimes referred to as 'caring for Country', the Indigenous-led approach to healing Country draws upon millennia of Indigenous environmental stewardship of all Australia, including Victoria. We will explore this more deeply, both when we address

10 Ana M. Nascimento et al., 'The Psychological Impact of Restorative Justice Practices on Victims of Crimes—a Systematic Review'.

11 Miranda Forsyth et al., 'A Future Agenda for Environmental Restorative Justice?', 20; Brittany Hill, 'Restoring Justice for Animal Victims'; Felicity Tepper, 'Restorative Justice for Animal Harm'.

the Djaara Peoples' restoration of what they call 'upside-down Country' as a case study in Chapter 7, and in Chapter 9, when we highlight the broader Indigenous-led approaches to healing Country.

The relational orientation to healing is often contrasted with the more classical regulatory approach of seeking to identify what rules have been broken and determine what sanction is applicable. However, as we discuss in this book, these two approaches are not always in opposition and can, in fact, complement one another.

Striving for active accountability

For a restorative approach to be viable, the actor responsible for causing harm must take active responsibility. This means not only acknowledging the harm but also accepting ongoing responsibility for remedying it.[12] In contrast, our dominant conventional justice systems usually enable passive responsibility, where offenders are represented by third parties, such as lawyers or advocates, and may not be called upon to engage with the process, merely to comply with imposed orders. Active responsibility involves inviting the offender to participate, often through a facilitated dialogue, where they hear firsthand about the impacts of the harm they have caused.[13] The offender then becomes a part of the process of determining what needs to be done to repair the harm and how to move forward. Restorative approaches emphasise that true accountability requires action.[14]

People often ask why an offender would be motivated to take responsibility like this. In fact, many people who cause harm do so accidentally or inadvertently, or bitterly regret their actions afterwards, even sometimes if those actions were initially deliberate. Restorative approaches are often welcomed as they provide the opportunity to 'make amends'. Even in cases

12 John Braithwaite and Declan Roche argue that the 'shift in the balance toward active responsibility occurs because the priority of restorative justice proponents is to be just in the way that [wrongdoers] heal'. John Braithwaite and Declan Roche, 'Responsibility and Restorative Justice', 63–84. Building on this, Braithwaite emphasises that moving beyond passive responsibility requires stakeholders to actively take responsibility 'for justice as a better future'. John Braithwaite, 'Restorative Justice'.

13 Lode Walgrave, 'Restorative Justice, Punishment, and the Law'.

14 The process of accountability in restorative justice occurs in three phases: the giving of account (offenders explain their actions), the taking of accountability (they acknowledge the harm caused), and the making of obligations (specific actions to remedy the harm are agreed upon). Thus, accountability is not merely a verbal acknowledgement of wrongdoing but a requirement for offenders to take active steps to repair harm and meet the victim's needs. True accountability is inherently linked to efforts to rectify the situation and address the needs of the victims meaningfully. William R. Wood and Masahiro Suzuki, 'Getting to Accountability in Restorative Justice'.

where companies cause environmental harm, John Pabon, a sustainability expert and author of an exposé on high-level unsustainable industries worldwide, noted 'there are far more companies trying to do better than those who would put profit before the planet'.[15]

In addition, as David Moore and Alikki Vernon argue from decades of experience running restorative processes, the process itself often results in emotional and cognitive shifts in the person who caused harm. Such changes can motivate offenders to engage in efforts to repair the harm. The authors state further:

> The *active participation* of people who are actually affected by the incident or situation most effects behavioural change on the part of the person-responsible [*sic*]. The greater the number of relationships present in the conference, the greater is the opportunity to set relations right.[16]

While this approach may work well when offenders are human actors, what happens when they are companies or businesses? The principle of offenders such as corporations proactively taking responsibility for wrongdoing was theorised by scholar Brent Fisse in his work on *reactive fault* in the 1980s. Addressing this topic in a 2023 speech on restorative justice in Brazil, John Braithwaite shared the following:

> [W]hen Brent Fisse first shared with me a draft of his original ideas on reactive fault in 1981, I was unconvinced that it would sit comfortably with the justice intuitions of ordinary people, and indeed perhaps my own intuitions about justice for corporate crime. Would justice as a better future which a defendant had proactively, apologetically, remorsefully, and effectively brought about satisfy citizens? After observing more than a hundred restorative justice conferences, including many for corporate defendants in my capacity as a regulator, and considering the evidence on victim satisfaction reviewed in Braithwaite (2002), I concluded that the answer was yes. My initial misplaced caution about Fisse's reactive fault was mistaken.[17]

---

15 John Pabon, *The Great Greenwashing: How Brands, Governments and Influencers Are Lying to You*, 70.

16 David B. Moore and Alikki Vernon, *Setting Relations Right in Restorative Practice: Broadening Mindsets and Skill Sets*, 59.

17 John Braithwaite, 'Transforming Corporate Criminal Law for the Challenges of Mining Disasters' (lecture), Brazil, 2023, on file with the authors; See also, Italian scholar Orsina's piece on working through the implications of reactive fault in civil law: Amalia Orsina, *La Responsabilità da Reato Dell'ente Tra Colpa di Organizzazione e Colpa de Reazione*.

As we explore in this book, restorative processes can be effective in a corporate context if the corporate veil is pierced. They require company representatives—those with genuine 'skin in the game'—to engage in relational ways that connect them directly with those impacted by the harms for which they are responsible.

Avoiding stigmatisation of those doing harm

Blaming, excluding and stigmatising wrongdoers appears to be on the rise across the globe. This mindset can be problematic, especially in situations where parties have no alternative but to continue engaging with one other. This is the case in many contexts, including workplaces, universities, and many of the cases described in this book, where communities and industry are co-situated in uncomfortably close proximity.

Stigmatisation can entrench defensiveness, making it less likely that wrongdoers will take responsibility or engage meaningfully in repairing harm. When people or companies feel permanently branded as 'bad actors', they may become more resistant to change rather than being helped to acknowledge harm and take positive steps forward.[18] Instead of encouraging accountability, stigma can create a sense of exclusion that reinforces denial, avoidance or adversarial responses.[19]

Restorative justice adopts a different approach. Rather than putting the person at the centre of the problem and denouncing them, or pointing to their weaknesses and failings, it focuses on the problem that led to the harm. This approach is supported by the theory of reintegrative shaming.[20] According to this theory, framing an offender (whether a person or company) as fundamentally good but having done a bad thing, rather than labelling them as inherently bad, creates space for accountability. It becomes possible for them to acknowledge the shame they may feel by, for example apologising, without fear of permanent rejection.

18 Erving Goffman, *Stigma: Notes on the Management of Spoiled Identity* (Prentice Hall, 1963).

19 Tom R. Tyler (ed.), *Why People Obey the Law*.

20 Braithwaite, *Crime, Shame and Reintegration*.

By shifting the focus from condemning individuals to addressing harm and its consequences, restorative approaches create conditions in which accountability is more likely to be embraced rather than resisted. They enable the offender to start building a new pathway forward, which may include co-creating this future with those harmed or with the wider community.

Focusing on relationships, not just individual actors

> Rooted in relational theory, restorative justice practices systematically address social, cultural, political, and economic dimensions of how individuals interact.[21]

Alongside reintegrative shaming theory, relational theory also provides the bedrock for many restorative approaches.[22] Relational theory is grounded in the empirical observation that people are not isolated individuals making purely rational life choices. Rather, we are all the products and progenitors of relationships, living in and through our relationships with others. These relationships shape, increase, limit and condition the choices available to us, structuring how we navigate the world.

Relational approaches have a human-centred focus, prioritising the wellbeing and dignity of individuals and communities. From a regulatory perspective, when organisations and individuals are able to see their relationships with others, they are more inclined to consider how their actions will impact those around them. For instance, when there is increased understanding of how compliance contributes to a positive and cooperative environment, it can increase the motivation to adhere to regulations. This dynamic is explored further in our case study of the Brooklyn Industrial Precinct in Chapter 3.

Relational approaches can also be helpful for addressing complexity in regulatory domains. As government scholars Janine O'Flynn and Gary L. Sturgess note:

> Relational approaches have been seen as a way to address more complex problems; [*sic*] the argument being that complexity demands higher levels of integration and connection at the local level, and deeper relationships with community.[23]

---

21 Christina Parker and Kathy Bickmore, 'Complexity in Restorative Justice Education Circles: Power and Privilege in Voicing Perspectives About Sexual Health, Identities, and Relationships'.

22 Jennifer J. Llewellyn, 'Transforming Restorative Justice'.

23 Janine O'Flynn and Gary L. Sturgess, *2030 and Beyond: Getting the Work of Government Done*, 23.

Relational approaches shift the regulator away from impersonal, goal-oriented and structured interactions towards more meaningful, long-term connections with individuals. These approaches are characterised by deeper engagement, mutual understanding and trust-building.

The relational lens of restorative regulation recognises that harm, conflict and regulatory breaches are not isolated events but are deeply entwined with the quality of relationships between individuals, regulators, businesses and communities. Harms and breaches are liable to reoccur more frequently, and often more blatantly, where the relational dimensions of regulatory encounters are neglected. For restorative regulation to be effective, therefore, regulators need to prioritise relational approaches in everyday regulatory encounters, laying the groundwork for increased compliance, preventive attitudes and stronger, more resilient relationships.

Prioritising safety

Safety is prioritised in restorative processes. Safety has multiple dimensions, such as the place where dialogue or meetings occur, attentiveness to power dynamics and emotional wellbeing.

First, the actual location or setting must be chosen with care. The physical environment should be neutral for all participants, and maximise comfort and safety. The setting should encourage a sense of equality and promote trust among participants. Settings that create divides between participants, such as upper and lower seating levels, should be avoided because they risk creating power imbalances or intimidating situations.

It is important that participants feel psychologically safe, comfortable about speaking up and sharing what they want to say, and able to express their emotions without being judged, dismissed or interrupted.[24] Restorative justice recognises that healing will only be possible where participants feel secure enough to engage in honest, and often vulnerable, conversations.[25]

Attentiveness to power dynamics is crucial in restorative interactions to ensure fairness and inclusivity. Addressing these dynamics at the outset and throughout the process helps avoid marginalising participants.

24 Paul Axtell, 'Meeting Management: Make Your Meetings a Safe Space for Honest Conversation'.

25 Lesley Parkinson, *Restorative Practices at Work* (Crown House Publishing, 2023).

No participant should feel coerced or silenced. Skilled facilitators play a key role in mitigating power imbalances, ensuring that each participant has an equal voice, thereby keeping the process fair and just.[26]

Another important mechanism for ensuring safety is the principle of voluntariness. Participation in a restorative process—whether by those who caused harm or those impacted by it—must always be voluntary.[27] This provides psychological safety by ensuring that all participants retain the freedom to choose whether or not to participate, and are at liberty to withdraw at any stage, without pressure.

Safety can also be created through less formal measures, such as clearly outlining the conditions for conversation at the outset and inviting participants to contribute to and agree on those conditions. In a regulatory context, this may involve regulators explicitly stating whether a conversation will be recorded for formal purposes and reassuring regulatees that they will always have an opportunity to explain their perspective.

Centring the needs of those most impacted by the harm

Centring the needs of those most affected means prioritising the wellbeing of individual victim(s) in the regulatory process. Where the victim is a community, this means addressing the needs and wellbeing of the community immediately affected. While challenges arise when large numbers of people are involved, techniques exist to navigate this, as discussed in our Hampton Park Landfill case study in Chapter 7 and illustrated through restorative forums, such as truth and reconciliation commissions.[28] Emerging technology such as community reporting applications and participatory tools enhanced by AI may also facilitate broader and more inclusive participation in the future.[29]

26 Ashanti Jones, 'The Heart of Facilitation in Restorative Justice'.

27 Steve Kirkwood, 'A Practice Framework for Restorative Justice'.

28 For a detailed discussion on how restorative justice processes can account for large numbers of participants, refer to Chapter 7.

29 One example of a reporting application (app) we learned about during the research was the 'Snap Send Solve' app. Many residents were familiar with its use. This Australian and Aotearoa New Zealand app enables residents to capture images of issues in need of fixing within their neighbourhood and send them directly to their local council and/or utilities for resolution: www.snapsendsolve.com/about (accessed 24 February 2025).

This approach contrasts sharply with standard regulatory and criminal justice methods, which often sideline victims after an initial complaint is made. In restorative processes, however, deliberate opportunities are created for those most impacted by harm to share how they have been affected, express what they need to heal, and suggest what they want to be done for the harm to be repaired.

An example of the power of this approach can be seen in the changes made to nursing-home management in the United States during the 1990s. In response to the *Untie the Elderly* campaign, which highlighted the use of physical and chemical restraints on elderly residents, operators of these facilities were forced to change their abusive practices. One significant change was the creation of Residents and Relatives Councils, which empowered the very residents who had previously been passive subjects of regulation to actively participate in the conversation. These councils enabled residents to voice their frustrations, revealing that their boredom and anger stemmed from the confinement that the nursing home had imposed on them.[30]

Engaging with emotions

Emotional engagement is a key element that makes restorative approaches effective on so many levels. The free expression of emotions among parties builds new relationships and social capital.[31] Building upon restorative scholar Chris Marshall's concept of an 'ethic of care',[32] restorative practices value emotions as an important motivator for participation in the restorative process. Emotions not only help build social bonds but also enable participants to fully express themselves and engage meaningfully.

In discussing the importance of the victim's narrative of harm and the offender's narrative of accountability, restorative justice scholar Meredith Rossner emphasises how important it is to engage with emotions:

30 John Braithwaite, Valerie Braithwaite, and Gale Burford, 'Broadening the Applications of Responsive Regulation'.
31 Wachtel, 'Defining Restorative'.
32 Marshall, *All Things Reconciled*, 175.

> In these narratives, a range of emotions can be expressed, including anger, fear, anxiety, shame, guilt, remorse, and hope. This expressive dimension, expressed through these narratives, is a particularly compelling part of restorative justice. Indeed, the emotional element of restorative justice may be its defining characteristic.[33]

We will examine narratives or storytelling below. In terms of emotional engagement, participants in restorative processes must feel safe expressing the full range of their emotions and know that their emotional engagement is respected, encouraged and seen as a normal part of the process.

While it is not common for emotions to be front and centre of regulatory strategy, it has struck us during our research journey how often regulators have referred to the need to engage 'hearts and minds'. For example, Kate Gavens, the inaugural Chief Conservation Regulator in Victoria, said:

> It's a hearts-and-minds piece, isn't it? … How do you shift an issue? Because there's a couple of different parts of it: one is getting the community to care, the other is getting your actors to care, getting your regulated entities to care. … [W]e need to win the hearts and minds.[34]

Gavens considers that 'hearts and minds' is 'the entry point into incentivising behaviour change', which requires openness to experimentation, looking for opportunities to connect directly with people and being open to 'thinking all sorts'.[35] For Gavens, this extends beyond individuals; it also requires regulators to be purposeful in appealing to the values and motivations of business entities.

For regulatory staff reaching out to communities, the hearts-and-minds approach reflects the importance of building the skills that aid emotional intelligence. This requires sensitivity to the motivations and attitudes of offenders, stakeholders and colleagues so that understanding, cooperation and positive change can be fostered effectively within the regulatory framework.

33 Meredith Rossner, 'Restorative Justice in the 21st Century: Making Emotions Mainstream'.

34 Gavens, 'Incentivising Compliance'.

35 Gavens, 'Incentivising Compliance'.

In discussing how regulators acknowledge and foster cultural connections to communities, Torres Strait Islander political scientist Dr Josephine Bourne emphasises the importance of engaging 'with a good heart … an open heart'.[36] She emphasises that engagement with Indigenous Australians must include respect for their culture and 'connection to Country'.[37]

However, it is important to recognise that this is not easy work. While many cultures (from societal to organisational) tend to shy away from conflict, restorative practices require confronting difficult emotions and situations. Engaging hearts and minds, therefore, involves not only the work of the participants but also care and support for staff, helping them develop the necessary skills to navigate sensitive situations effectively.[38]

Practices for restorative regulation

In this section, we discuss various practices that can facilitate restorative regulation. Many of these practices can be used in conjunction with other restorative practices, as well as with standard regulatory practices. Many valuable insights have been offered regarding the specifics of restorative regulation, including the nuts and bolts of practices; most of these are beyond the scope of this book. We highlight some of particular interest, visualising these in Figure 1.2. Moore and Vernon, for example, have recently explored additional restorative practices that may well resonate with those applying restorative approaches in regulatory contexts.[39]

---

36 ANZSOG, 'What is Culturally Responsive Regulation? And How Do We Get There with Our Aboriginal and Torres Strait Islander Partners?'.

37 ANZSOG, 'What is Culturally Responsive Regulation?'.

38 Zehavit Levitats and Eran Vigoda-Gadot, 'Yours Emotionally: How Emotional Intelligence Infuses Public Service Motivation and Affects the Job Outcomes of Public Personnel', 770; Jake Phillips et al., *Emotional Labour in Criminal Justice and Criminology*, 25.

39 Moore and Vernon, *Setting Relations Right*.

Figure 1.2. Core practices for restorative regulation

Source: Generated by authors using Bing Image Creator, 22 January 2025.
Prompt: 'Diverse group of people seated in a restorative circle in Australian bush'

Respectful restorative dialogue

The oldest and most widely used approach within restorative justice—dialogue—lies at the heart of restorative practices.[40] Respectful restorative dialogue is the primary means through which individuals, communities and other stakeholders share their perspectives on harm, conflict, and solutions. It promotes understanding, accountability, healing, and reconciliation among all participants. One of the earliest proponents of restorative justice, Howard Zehr, describes it as follows:

40 Mark S. Umbreit et al., 'Restorative Justice Dialogue: Evidence-Based Practice'.

> Restorative justice is a process where all stakeholders in an injustice have an opportunity to meet in a circle to discuss who has been harmed and the needs of stakeholders in order to reach agreement on what to do to heal the harms and meet those needs.[41]

Restorative dialogue involves a number of components:

- conditions of safety (including psychological safety)[42]
- acknowledgement of harm by those who have caused harm
- open and respectful communication
- deep listening by all participants
- empathy (cognitive, emotional, compassionate and critical):[43]
  - cognitive empathy: understanding another person's perspective or mental state
  - affective (or emotional) empathy: sharing or feeling another person's emotions
  - compassionate empathy: choosing to take action to help someone based on both understanding *and* feeling their emotions
  - critical empathy: recognising and reflecting on how broader socio-economic, historical and systemic factors shape another person's emotions, behaviours and perspectives
- empowerment of those impacted to tell their story in the manner they choose
- collaborative exploration of solutions.

41 Zehr, *Changing Lenses: Restorative Justice for Our Times*.

42 In restorative dialogue, kindness is an important aspect of psychological safety. It promotes a sense of connectedness within the team, between regulators, and with those being regulated, while enhancing communications with the communities served by regulators. By making people feel valued, kindness builds trust, facilitating openness and emotionally intelligent conversations during dialogue. Lesley Parkinson, *Restorative Practices at Work*, 53–54.

43 Francis Stevens and Katherine Taber, 'The Neuroscience of Empathy and Compassion in Pro-Social Behaviour'; Todd DeStigter, 'Public Displays of Affection: Political Community Through Critical Empathy'; Luke J. Rapa, Candice W. Bolding, and Cari Allyn Brooks, 'Integrating Critical Consciousness and Social Empathy: A New Framework to Enhance Conscientization'.

Acknowledgement of harm is an important precondition for restorative dialogue and frames how the dialogue unfolds. In most formal restorative processes, such as restorative conferences, the offender will have accepted responsibility for the harm caused, even if they may not have admitted to criminal or civil liability for an offence. This is a very different starting point from mediation, which assumes neutrality regarding fault between the parties.[44]

The empowerment of those impacted to tell their story is another important aspect of respectful dialogue. In a restorative process, everyone who is present has a voice and an opportunity to talk without being interrupted. This is often achieved by seating everyone in a circle and having protocols around taking turns to speak.

Restorative justice provides a space in which those impacted by the offender's action can explain, directly, how the harmful action has affected them. For example, in the Hampton Park Landfill case study involving a restorative justice conference (Chapter 7), affected residents were given the opportunity to tell both the landfill operator and EPA Victoria how they were impacted by the odour from the landfill and the regulator's perceived failure to act, and they were able to collaborate in considering solutions to address the harm.

In summary, respectful restorative dialogue requires attentiveness in setting up the process. This means, for example, ensuring that everyone is safe and having a guiding structure to frame the dialogue constructively. It is also crucial to make sure that all participants have the chance to tell their stories. Skilful facilitation is essential.

The following format is often used to help the dialogue proceed restoratively:

- **Start with situating everyone:**
  - What are your relationships?
  - Why are you participating in the dialogue?

44 Rachel Field, 'The Theory and Practice of Neutrality in Mediation'. We note that while this principle is widely accepted, it is also contested, as some scholars argue that complete neutrality may not always be feasible or desirable in mediation practices—see, for example, Susan Douglas, 'Neutrality in Mediation: A Study of Mediator Perceptions'.

- **Focus on key restorative questions:**
  - What happened?
  - Who has been impacted?
  - What needs to be done to make it better?
  - Whose responsibility is it to address these needs?
  - Who else might help to address the situation?
- **Encourage people's stories by asking further restorative questions:**
  - What were you thinking about at the time the incident occurred?
  - What have you thought about since?
  - What have been the hardest things for you?
  - Who else has been affected?
  - What do you think needs to be done to make things better?

In general, restorative dialogue is attained when all the components we have outlined are addressed. However, it also requires deep listening, to which we turn next.

Deep listening

Deep listening is an important aspect of restorative dialogue. It fosters trust, empathy and effective communication, and is 'foundational to understanding stakeholder and community needs'.[45] Deep listening is respectful, empathetic, self-aware and actively attentive.[46] The listener is fully present, prepared to understand the speaker's perspective beyond surface-level words. This means not only hearing what is said but also paying attention to the emotions, intentions and deeper meaning behind the speaker's words, as well as observing their body language. There is no judgement, and silence is valued as much as speaking.[47]

Effort is made to encourage the speaker to explore their thoughts and feelings more deeply. The listener can achieve this by asking open-ended questions and giving reflective responses to ensure they have understood correctly. Solutions and advice are not imposed; rather, the speaker is supported in realising their own insights and suggestions for repair and change.

45 Emily Kasriel, 'Deep Listening'.
46 Kasriel, 'Deep Listening'.
47 Kasriel, 'Deep Listening'.

Restorative justice involves listening that is not only deep but also patient. This has particular resonance for Indigenous communities, where their knowledge, sense of place and experiences require that all non-Indigenous outsiders check their pace and learn to follow the flow set by the Indigenous community.[48] In Australia, this concept and way of being is sometimes called *Dadirri*, which broadly translates as listening to Country and to one another.[49] *Dadirri* is a quiet, contemplative listening approach of 'watching, listening, waiting and then acting'.[50] It requires awareness, and comfort with silence. As Nauiyu elder, Dr Miriam-Rose Ungunmerr, puts it: 'We don't like to hurry. There is nothing more important than what we are attending to. There is nothing more urgent that we must hurry away for.'[51]

Yet, non-Indigenous staff, often bound by strict timetables and metrics over which they rarely have personal control, may view time as something to rush through. In a world shaped by mere centuries of managerialism, this pressure contrasts sharply with the millennia-long, deeply rooted temporal perspectives of Indigenous ways of being.[52] As one Indigenous interviewee who was very knowledgeable about EPA Victoria at a particular time told us:

> EPA has not had patience to wait. They want to rush in to mitigate the damage, without understanding what is actually significant about the site. There may be bones, there may be tools, all of which could be disturbed by the EPA. There needs to be a better relationship with cultural heritage officers. We need to set up meetings to explain how we can work together.[53]

48 Monty Nixon, 'Here's What "Deep Listening" Can Tell Us About the Natural World and Our Place in It'.

49 *Dadirri* is a 'word, concept and spiritual practice … from the Ngan'gikurunggurr and Ngen'giwumirri languages of the Aboriginal peoples of the Daly River region (Northern Territory, Australia)'. 'Dadirri: The Quiet Stillness Inside Us' (Miriam Rose Foundation), www.miriamrosefoundation.org.au/dadirri/. In English, it has the sense of 'listening to Country' but it is also a 'deep contemplative process of "listening to one another" in reciprocal relationships': Miriam-Rose Ungunmerr-Baumann et al., 'Dadirri: An Indigenous Place-Based Research Methodology', *AlterNative: An International Journal of Indigenous Peoples* 18, no. 1 (2022): 94, doi.org/10.1177/11771801221085353.

50 Ungunmerr et al., 'Dadirri'; Alasdair Vance et al., 'Culture, Health and Well-Being: Yarning with the Victorian First Nations Community', International *Journal of Indigenous Health* 19, no. 1 (2024): 1–17.

51 Ungunmerr et al., 'Dadirri'.

52 Seth Godin, *The Song of Significance: A New Manifesto for Teams* (Penguin Random House, 2023), 26–27. Godin notes that the industrial work of 'managers, assembly lines, tests, inspections, raises, bonuses, pink slips, avoiding the boss, quiet quitting, and layoffs […] is a recent invention, perhaps two hundred years old'.

53 Interview with Indigenous leader as part of a project involving The Australian National University and School of Regulation and Global Governance (RegNet) and EPA Victoria, 2018–24.

Patient listening is also emphasised by regulatory scholar Malcolm Sparrow. He advises regulators to carefully examine the character of the harm from all angles before trying to untie its knots.[54] Scholars Rawsthorne et al. call this aspect of deep listening '"loitering" in communities, spending time in the everyday life of the community, not merely engaging with the community instrumentally around an agenda'. They further add that 'deep listening is also about taking time to seek out people and experiences that are not usually included', viewing it as a vital way to shift power.[55]

Deep listening, with its emphasis on presence, empathy, patience and respect, deepens understanding between the participants in the restorative process. It forges connections between them and honours the diversity of voices and experiences of those sharing the journey towards healing. In particular, it shifts the human tendency from reacting to responding, encouraging a more reflective and open mode of engagement. Lawyer and person-centred counsellor Samu Czabán suggests that empathy 'creates a unique perceptual field that can dissolve boundaries between people, promoting shared meditative experiences and deactivating heuristic, fast-thinking pathways'.[56]

Of course, regulators may find that they are subject to pressures (including pressures from communities) that make it challenging to spend time listening deeply. The argument we make here is not that deep listening is always needed or appropriate, but rather that there is relational value for regulators in listening to different voices and hearing about the different relationships to, and perspectives on, harm. Listening is a skill that requires care, thought, skill development and practice; it is also a practice that encompasses self-care for those adopting it, including regulatory staff. In cultivating deep listening, regulators not only build stronger relationships

54 Malcolm K. Sparrow, *The Character of Harms: Operational Challenges in Control* (Cambridge University Press, 2008), doi.org/10.1017/CBO9780511753862.

55 Margot Rawsthorne et al., 'Understanding Community-Led Disaster Preparedness', *Australian Journal of Emergency Management* 28, no. 2 (2023): 49–54, 50, doi.org/10.47389/38.2.49.

56 Samu Czabán, 'A Lawyer's View of Irrelevant Influences in the Courtroom', *Psyche*, 23 January 2025, psyche.co/ideas/a-lawyers-view-of-irrelevant-influences-in-the-courtroom.

with regulatees and communities but also enhance their own self-awareness and wellbeing, contributing to more effective and compassionate regulatory practices.[57]

Yet, very rarely do regulatory organisations provide the space to engage in deep listening. By listening to different voices, regulators can build stronger relationships and be more attuned to the varied ways harm is experienced and perceived over time. Here are some suggestions as to ways of possibly addressing relationship-building without pressure:

- **Avoid waiting for crisis times**. Engage with business and community stakeholders during quiet periods. Host informal gatherings to foster open communication. Provide staff training on active and deep listening to develop listening and perspective-taking skills.
- **Task junior staff with fact-finding**. It can be beneficial for new and junior staff to develop their understanding of regulatory issues by being given tasks that require them to research and think about the concerns, goals and policies of business and community organisations. They can then suggest how regulatory goals and policies could be better understood in the light of what they have learned.
- **Do not make assumptions**. Rather than thinking about what would make you change your behaviour, be prepared to work with the influences, drivers and realities that communities and those regulated are dealing with.[58]
- **Create regular feedback loops**. Establish ongoing channels for feedback from stakeholders to continuously improve understanding and relationships. Encourage stakeholders to identify regulatory challenges and possible solutions in the spirit of mutual problem-solving.

57 In the context of health care, when patients are similarly positioned to regulatees and community members who wish to be fully heard, Ronald M. Epstein and Mary Catherine Beach note that 'training that promotes deep listening to oneself and others through contemplative practices, shared narratives, and appreciative interviews consistently shows improvements in compassionate patient-centred care and clinician well-being.' This emphasises the relational value of deep listening, not just for those being listened to, but also for the listeners, increasing self-awareness and improving the quality of their interactions with others. Ronald M. Epstein and Mary Catherine Beach, '"*I Don't Need Your Pills, I Need Your Attention*:" Steps Toward Deep Listening in Medical Encounters', *Current Opinion on Psychology* 53 (2023): 1–6, doi.org/10.1016/j.copsyc.2023.101685.

58 Liam Smith et al., *Inspiring Change: How to Influence Behaviour for a Better World* (Monash University Publishing, 2024).

Restorative circles and structures

The use of a circle for restorative processes is intended to facilitate equality and interconnectivity between participants. Every participant has an equal voice and is at the same level in the circle, reinforcing the idea that each person's perspective is valued and important, and that no single person, including the facilitator, can dominate.[59] The circle is a democratic practice, enabling participation, listening, learning and facilitating simultaneously.[60]

A circle supports openness and transparency. Every participant can see the other participants face-to-face. Emotions and intentions are evident to all, supporting honesty and sharing. This further encourages dialogue between participants and helps with turn-taking, as each person can see when a participant has finished speaking. Some circles include a talking piece, which helps to prevent interruptions and reduces the prominence of the facilitator.[61]

Circles bring structure to the restorative process. Structure heightens the respect shown towards the people participating, demonstrating that the situation is being treated seriously and with attentiveness. In bringing people together, the circle fosters positivity, defines shared goals and promotes positive feelings.[62]

In this book, we discuss a range of other structures that regulators can use for dialogue, such as Open House forums, that incorporate some of the key principles underlying circles, including inclusivity, transparency and open communication.[63]

---

59 Gerry Johnstone and Daniel W. Van Ness, *Handbook of Restorative Justice* (Willan, 2007), 215; Sue Roffey and Florence McCarthy, 'Circle Solutions, a Philosophy and Pedagogy for Learning Positive Relationships: What Promotes and Inhibits Sustainable Outcomes?', *The International Journal of Emotional Education* 5, no. 1 (2013): 36–55, files.eric.ed.gov/fulltext/EJ1085741.pdf; Yvon Dandurand and Annette Vogt, *Handbook on Restorative Justice Programmes*, 2nd ed., (United Nations Office on Drugs and Crime, 2020), www.unodc.org/documents/justice-and-prison-reform/20-01146_Handbook_on_Restorative_Justice_Programmes.pdf.

60 Parker and Bickmore, 'Complexity in Restorative Justice Education Circles'; Roffey and McCarthy, 'Circle Solutions'.

61 Johnstone and Van Ness, *Handbook of Restorative Justice*, 53; Parker and Bickmore, 'Complexity in Restorative Justice Education Circles'; Umbreit et al., 'Restorative Justice Dialogue'.

62 Roffey and McCarthy, 'Circle Solutions'.

63 For detailed discussion on Open Houses, see Chapter 3.

Fair process

> If Fair Process is observed, individuals are more likely to trust and cooperate with systems even if they themselves don't benefit from the system.[64]

> When authorities do things with people, whether reactively—to deal with crisis—or proactively, the results are better.[65]

Drawing from procedural justice theory, restorative practices acknowledge that when people feel they have been treated in a procedurally just and fair way from the beginning of the process, they are more likely to perceive the process as fair and legitimate, and to feel respected. As a result, people are more likely to participate, be engaged and comply with the outcomes, even if the resulting decision does not favour or convenience their own interests.[66]

In every restorative practice, key values must apply to ensure the process is fair for all parties involved. Fair process and a sense of fairness are achieved in restorative justice by making sure that the process is voluntary, safe, impartial, neutral, accessible and respectful. John McDonald, a highly experienced restorative justice facilitator, refers to this as ensuring fair rules, fair play and fair outcomes.[67]

Participation must be voluntary and based on informed choice.[68] People must be given the opportunity to give their side of the story and be listened to respectfully, genuinely and without interruption. This respect and genuine heeding of stories must be continuous throughout the practice.[69] The motives of authority figures or leaders who are participating (for example, facilitator, corporate manager, regulatory staff) must be evidenced as trustworthy through their careful listening, openness to doing the right thing and attentiveness to those harmed. It is important that explanations

64 Jake Garner, 'Restorative Practices in ResLife: The Role of Fair Process in Curriculum Development', *Roompact* (blog), August 2022, blog.roompact.com/2022/08/restorative-practices-in-reslife-the-role-of-fair-process-in-curricular-development/.

65 Wachtel, 'Defining Restorative', 6.

66 Gregory D. Paul and Ian M. Borton, *Creating Restorative Justice: A Communication Perspective of Justice, Restoration, and Community* (Lexington Books, 2021), 25; Susan L. Miller, 'The Importance of Storytelling for Restorative Justice', in *After the Crime: The Power of Restorative Justice Dialogues between Victims and Violent Offenders* (New York University Press, 2011), 172, doi.org/10.18574/nyu/9780814770382.001.0001; Donald Lee Mills, 'The Crashing Tide: Blending Restorative Practices and Trauma-Informed Care' (IIRP Graduate School, 2013).

67 Garner, 'Restorative Practices in ResLife'; Wachtel, 'Defining Restorative'; Mills, 'The Crashing Tide'.

68 Dandurand and Vogt, Handbook on Restorative Justice Programmes.

69 Garner, 'Restorative Practices in ResLife'.

for decisions, actions and choices are given, including an indication of how feedback or information provided by participants concerning the matter was treated.[70] Outcomes arising from the restorative practice must be clear so that all parties can move forward knowing what to expect.[71]

In summary, engaging the affected community through a fair and inclusive process reassures both direct victims and the broader public that their concerns have been genuinely considered. When done effectively, such engagement fosters stronger relationships between the regulator, the community and industry. It can also enrich citizen involvement, resulting in more robust citizen science initiatives, clearer pathways for public incident reporting, and more transparent updates from regulators and industry stakeholders.

Apology

From time to time, we will mention apology as part of the restorative process. While apology is not the primary goal of the restorative justice process, it does play a significant and valuable role. Among other things, it contributes to the perception that the process was fair, helps foster reconciliation, and increases victim satisfaction.[72] Apologies that are part of the restorative process can help repair relationships and restore community trust, especially where the wrongdoer takes full responsibility for their actions and demonstrates genuine remorse.

When given voluntarily, rather than as part of a court-ordered process, apologies are viewed as having a greater positive impact.[73] Within the context of restorative justice, a sincere acknowledgement of responsibility and remorse from the offender can provide the victim and affected community with a sense of validation and recognition of the harm they have experienced. This can be a crucial step towards healing. For an offender, an apology can be seen as a signal to move forward and grow, rather than to stagnate and potentially regress.

---

70 Garner, 'Restorative Practices in ResLife'.

71 Garner, 'Restorative Practices in ResLife'.

72 Masahiro Suzuki and Tamera Jenkins, 'Apology–Forgiveness Cycle in Restorative Justice, But How?', *International Review of Victimology* 29, no. 2 (2023): 259–76, doi.org/10.1177/02697580221079994; Masahiro Suzuki, 'Possibility of Sincere Apology in Restorative Justice: When and How?', *International Journal of Offender Therapy and Comparative Criminology*, 68, no. 13–14 (2022): 1342–56, doi.org/10.1177/0306624x221132238.

73 Alfred Allan et al., 'The Impact of Voluntariness of Apologies on Victims' Responses in Restorative Justice: Findings of a Quantitative Study', *Psychiatry, Psychology and Law* 29, no. 4 (2022): 593–609, doi.org/10.1080/13218719.2021.1956383.

Use of storytelling and narrative

The use of storytelling and, more broadly, narrative, is an important part of restorative processes. Storytelling gives victims a voice, helps to establish a shared account, gives meaning to what has happened, includes multiple perspectives, reconnects participants with their own knowledge and skills, and provides the opportunity to be truly heard.[74]

Storytelling is not driven by any defined parameters or directions; it is nonlinear, consists of what each participant wishes to tell and share, and is unhurried. In the restorative context, storytelling gives each participant the chance to contribute to creating 'new meanings and expanded storylines':

> These new understandings, developed through expanded storylines, may provide a preferred position in which to stand in relation to the harm that has been done. This repositioning in relation to the harm can happen when each participant is given the opportunity to tell stories in personally resonant ways, while the facilitator elevates points of resonance between participants' own stories and the storylines of the other.[75]

Storytelling involves the emotional engagement of both the teller and the listener in recounting what has occurred, moving beyond facts to surface the emotional and relational dimensions of what is being discussed. It enables the sharing of perspectives that might otherwise go unheard, such as those from the community, and emphasises the co-production of an account of harm that aims for justice and is capable of improving the future. While storytelling focuses on personal experiences, as a form of narrative, it also has the ability to reveal broader structural patterns and systemic factors contributing to harm, expanding responsibility and accountability to include businesses, government and regulatory organisations.[76]

Stories are powerful forms of communication that can provoke action and change. Danny Burns, a complexity and development scholar, suggests that the stories people choose to tell, and how they are received by an audience,

---

74 Janine Natalya Clark, 'Storytelling, Resilience and Transitional Justice: Reversing Narrative Social Bulimia', *Theoretical Criminology* 26, no. 3 (2022): 456–474, doi.org/10.1177/1362480620933230; Forsyth et al., 'A Future Agenda?'; Renee Handsaker, 'Narrative Approaches to Restorative Justice Settings: Considerations of Power, Struggle and Social Transformation', in *Intersecting Stories: Narrative Therapy Reflections on Gender, Culture and Justice*, ed. Dulwich Centre (Dulwich Centre Publications, 2020).

75 Handsaker, 'Narrative Approaches', 82.

76 Forsyth et al., 'A Future Agenda?'.

reveal what is really important in a given situation. He deliberately takes stories from one arena to another to do what he calls 'resonance testing'. He explains that when stories resonate with others, '[t]here is an acceleration of pace and an increase in emotional expression. One story leads to another, and a clear picture of what is important emerges.' Reflecting on what this means for action, Burns argues that '[t]his is a much more powerful process of legitimation than traditional methods. It leads to engagement and ownership.'[77]

In the community context, a community member who is able to tell their story directly to the regulator may feel a sense of empowerment and experience validation, knowing that their voice has been heard and that their concerns have mattered in the regulatory process. In discussing the value of storytelling as a restorative practice for regulators working with community, one EPA interviewee told us:

> There can be a general sense of disbelief or scepticism [from community] until you meet with someone who is sharing their story. There is enormous power in that, to bring that back into the organisation. Which is about being heard, which is what is truly hoped for, someone to really feel their pain and take it back in and do something with it.

At a broader level, community storytelling can make it possible for new stories to become an integral part of larger collaborative repair and restoration efforts, expanding the conversation beyond individual experiences to collective meaning-making and systemic change.[78]

Multiple perspective-taking

One of the key objectives of restorative processes is to enable participants to see issues from the perspectives of others and thus come to a more balanced understanding of what has occurred.[79] As Moore and Vernon write:

77 Danny Burns, 'Systemic Action Research: Changing System Dynamics to Support Sustainable Change', *Action Research* 12, no. 1 (2014), doi.org/10.1177/1476750313513910.

78 Anooj Bhandari, 'Restorative Practice: Developing a Community of Storytellers', *Teaching Artist Journal* 16, no. 3–4 (2018): 100–105, doi.org/10.1080/15411796.2018.1535645.

79 'Why Perspective Matters: Understanding the Importance of Different Viewpoints', *Resilience Dynamic*, updated 27 April 2023, resiliencedynamic.com/resilient-thinking/why-perspective-matters/.

> As participants in a restorative process work together to develop a shared understanding of a *bigger picture* that none has seen until now, the complex conflict within and between them transforms into cooperation.[80]

This is increasingly important for regulators, especially in the context of issues that are potentially highly divisive. For instance, in discussing the difficulties of managing student conflict at Berkeley University in the USA in response to the 2023 Israel/Gaza war, the Chancellor stated that she felt both pro-Palestinian and pro-Israeli groups were saying: 'See my pain. See where I am.' She observed that both groups felt to a certain extent unseen, and she noted: 'I think the task for us all is to figure out how we can bring together people of sharply differing views, and have them talk to each other with civility and respect.'[81] This approach stands in stark contrast to the position-embedding effects of the most prevalent forms of communication that now dominate the Anglosphere, which often reinforce existing biases and divisions rather than fostering understanding and dialogue.[82]

The Chancellor is effectively asking for forums that enable perspective-taking: spaces where participants are prepared to understand a situation from another person's perspective and to 'consciously listen to the perspective of others'.[83] When an individual considers the different perspectives of others, it can help them to identify biases and flaws in reasoning, make more informed judgements, and be more humble and more willing to adjust viewpoints when new information is brought to bear on the situation.[84]

80 Moore and Vernon, *Setting Relations Right*, 14.

81 Carol Christ, 'The Chancellor of Berkeley Weighs In', Interview by Molly Fischer, *The New Yorker*, 17 December 2023, www.newyorker.com/news/the-new-yorker-interview/the-chancellor-of-berkeley-weighs-in.

82 As politics scholar Matt Beech explains, there is a widening cultural polarisation within Anglosphere nations, attributed to their greater ideological divergence, decreased toleration in the public sphere and the effects of social media—see Paula Rossignoli, 'Matt Beech | Polarized Peoples—Examining the Culture Wars and How They Can be Transcended', *Institute of European Studies*, 20 June 2024, ies.berkeley.edu/news/matt-beech-polarized-peoples-examining-culture-wars-and-how-they-can-be-transcended. Similarly, a 'populist model of the Anglosphere', particularly evident in the United States and Australia, is characterised by 'polarised and volatile politics, media and public culture'. Andrew Mycock, 'The Anglosphere or Anglospheres? The English-Speaking World in Flux', *Centre for International Policy Studies*, 14 October 2020, www.cips-cepi.ca/2020/10/14/the-anglosphere-or-anglospheres-the-english-speaking-world-in-flux-2/.

83 Steffan Surdek, 'Why Understanding Other Perspectives Is a Key Leadership Skill', *Forbes*, 17 November 2016, www.forbes.com/sites/forbescoachescouncil/2016/11/17/why-understanding-other-perspectives-is-a-key-leadership-skill/.

84 Daniel Grabowski, 'Considering Multiple Perspectives In Critical Thinking', *Oxford Open Learning*, 23 March 2023, www.ool.co.uk/blog/considering-multiple-perspectives-in-critical-thinking/.

Perspective-seeking is an important skill that often involves being 'truly and authentically curious' about hearing and learning more about how others see the world.[85]

The ability to engage in respectful dialogue is an important theme throughout the book, particularly around the demands and challenges of engagement, which are fundamental regulatory concerns. In many ways, it relies on a process that emphasises the ongoing development of relational interactions (what is often referred to in social sciences as 'relationality'), which rarely happens in large-format forms of engagement such as town halls, public meetings or even some Open Houses that are more commonly used by regulators. Rather, the social impulse on display in public engagement often pushes in the opposite direction—contest rather than transformation: to public condemnation, shaming and grandstanding. These may not be inappropriate responses in themselves, but outside the context of a more relational process they tend to exclude the possibility of positive restorative values. In Chapters 3 and 8, we discuss various alternative practices that can be used to promote understanding, empathy, deliberation and the taking of responsibility, even in larger-scale public settings.

Scholar Val Braithwaite notes that where people are not given an opportunity to share their own perspectives, they are less likely to relate to other people's perspectives, or get on board with problem-solving or responding to regulatory action:

> Different narratives are constructed depending on values, expectations, social groups, political identities, and trust in authority. If these different narratives are not given voice and problems resolved, defiance and social fragmentation are likely to result.[86]

Restorative processes facilitate an environment in which multiple perspectives emerge organically and can be synthesised collaboratively. This occurs when accounts of what occurred are co-constructed, and when empathetic questions are used to explore who was impacted, such as, 'How did you feel?' and 'What have you thought about it since?'

---

85 Surdek, 'Understanding Other Perspectives'.

86 Valerie Braithwaite, 'Tax Evasion', in *The Oxford Handbook of Crime and Public Policy*, ed. Michael Tonry (Oxford University Press, 2012), 381–406, doi.org/10.1093/oxfordhb/9780199844654.013.0016; Valerie Braithwaite, *Defiance in Taxation and Governance: Resisting and Dismissing Authority in a Democracy* (Edward Elgar, 2009), doi.org/10.4337/9781848449077.

Why are multiple perspectives so important for restorative regulation? Here are a few reasons:

- **completing the picture**: Multiple perspectives join the dots, so to speak, and give a fuller, more nuanced understanding of the harm or breach and the complexities involved.
- **ensuring procedural and ethical fairness**: Each person has a chance to speak, express their experiences and needs, and to be properly heard.
- **promoting empathy**: Standing in another's shoes helps encourage participants to see what happened from different angles and understand motivations, and this facilitates healing.
- **providing accountability**: Having multiple perspectives on what has happened helps to hold those responsible to account for their actions by ensuring all affected participants have a voice in what happens next.
- **preventing harm**: Multiple perspectives can help prevent harm, such as where citizen scientists and Indigenous peoples share their local knowledge alongside conventional and technical regulatory perspectives, potentially bringing to light unknown hazards or opportunities to stop harm.
- **learning and improving**: Learning from different perspectives and making improvements and adaptations builds resilience for both people and regulatory systems.[87]

Being able to embrace multiple perspectives is not just a virtue but a necessity for all regulators. However, it is especially important for the restorative regulator, which must be able to see beyond singular viewpoints to understand the dynamics driving harm and conflict. Regulatory matters are multifaceted, and the complexity of regulating is on the increase. By actively seeking out, listening to and valuing diverse perspectives, the restorative organisation will be better informed, and in a position to prevent harm and build trust. This holistic approach reinforces restorative principles such as accountability and healing while laying the foundation for a more resilient and just regulatory system.

---

87 Jenny Campbell, 'Why Perspective Matters: Understanding the Importance of Different Viewpoints', *Resilience Dynamic*, accessed 23 January 2025, resiliencedynamic.com/resilient-thinking/why-perspective-matters/.

The extension of restorative practice

While restorative justice was originally seen as a specific technique for responding to harm, today it is conceptualised more broadly to also encompass approaches to preventing harm. It has become almost a reflexive process, moving from addressing the harm to identifying its cause, then focusing on future prevention. The preventive aspect of restorative justice can manifest in various ways, such as in the strengthening of relationships, in opportunities for constructive dialogue about how to mitigate potential future harm, or in learnings from previous incidents of harm.

Some practitioners and academics prefer the term 'restorative practice' to describe this broader approach to restorative justice. Restorative practices practitioners David Vernon and Alikki Moore explain that restorative practice not only helps repair ruptured relationships but also establishes, maintains and deepens positive relationships, and neutralise conflicts associated with damaged relationships.[88] In clarifying the relationship between restorative practice and restorative justice, Chris Marshall calls them both 'different facets of the same diamond'.[89] He observes they are all 'aimed at the creation of interpersonal relationships and societal institutions that foster human dignity, equality, freedom, mutual respect, democratic engagement, and collaborative governance'. In this book, we include both restorative justice and restorative practice under the umbrella of what we term 'restorative regulation'.

There are many different forms of restorative practice. One way to understand the range of alternatives is through restorative justice practitioner Ted Watchel's concept of a 'restorative practices continuum', which spans from informal to formal restorative processes. At one end, there are quicker processes involving fewer people, while at the other end, larger, more involved processes take place.[90] In Figure 1.3, we illustrate how we have reconceptualised the restorative continuum in an environmental context.

88 Moore and Vernon, *Setting Relations Right*, 1.
89 Christopher D. Marshall, *All Things Reconciled.*
90 Wachtel, 'Defining Restorative'.

Figure 1.3. Conceptualising the environmental restorative justice continuum as a river

Note: The different restorative approaches flow in as rivulets, gradually increasing the restorative values and practices. Towards the left of the continuum, restorative interventions are more informal, while towards the right, they become more formal and structured.

Source: Designed by upklyak/Freepik, www.freepik.com/free-vector/river-top-view-cartoon-curve-riverbed-with-blue-water-coastline-with-rocks-trees-green-grass_9396078.htm. Modified into river format from International Institute of Restorative Practices [IIRP, Josh Wachtel], Restorative Practices Continuum, en.wikipedia.org/wiki/File:Continuum-of-restorative-practices.gif, CC BY-SA 3.0).

Working with both restorative practice and restorative values

Both restorative justice and restorative practice are rooted in a set of values and ethics that inform their practice in real-life situations. While it is possible to discuss a precise type of practice, such as a restorative conference, or a specific value, such as active accountability, optimally, both are interconnected within a cohesive approach that aligns restorative values with practical implementation. In this way, restorative methods genuinely reflect the core values of restorative justice, while adapting to different cultural (community and organisational) contexts and unique circumstances:

> [T]he distinctiveness of restorative justice lies in its *peculiar* combination of processes, values and intended outcomes, so that any descriptive definition of restorative justice ideally should include all three elements.[91]

If we focus solely on restorative processes or practices without the associated values, there is a risk that it becomes performative, reduced to a tick-box exercise or simply routinised.[92] Unfortunately, this outcome is not uncommon in restorative justice initiatives across the globe, and it is a danger we must vigilantly guard against.

Since focusing on either values or practices alone is problematic, we tend to shy away from thinking of restorative regulation as a toolbox we can open to select the 'right' tool. Instead, we conceptualise restorative regulation as being more akin to the sensibility, knowledge and skills of a gardener—best approached holistically, with care, and keenly adaptive to the prevailing circumstances. Later in the book, we will further explore the metaphor of gardening as a way of understanding how to be restorative within a regulatory context—how to not only cultivate but also grow restorative approaches in practice.

Detailed descriptions of different forms of restorative regulation across the entire regulatory spectrum are presented throughout this book. This chapter lays out the theoretical foundation for the components that have informed

91 Marshall, *All Things Reconciled*.

92 Robert Weisberg, 'Restorative Justice and the Dangers of Community', Research Paper no. 50, Stanford Law School, February 2003, papers.ssrn.com/sol3/papers.cfm?abstract_id=373483.

our examples of restorative regulation. By understanding restorative justice's theory and guiding principles, readers can see how existing and new restorative spaces can be nurtured across diverse regulatory contexts.

Community voice and empowerment

In this book, we place emphasis on amplifying the community's voice in restorative regulation. Throughout the chapters, we provide numerous examples of how this occurs. In this section, we address a set of foundational restorative values and practices that support this participatory, empowering process. When we talk about empowerment, we mean that citizens should feel empowered to speak out, be heard and, at times, participate in collaborative policymaking. This goes beyond merely being consulted in decision-making; it encompasses a broader sense of having a meaningful impact at various stages, including when issues are identified, input and data are gathered, solutions are co-developed and outcomes evaluated.

Public participation and engagement

Restorative approaches involve direct participation from those who are responsible for harm, those impacted, their support communities and, at times, the broader public.

Involvement of the wider public in decision-making is not unique to restorative justice. It is highlighted by many other theories of public participation and deliberative democracy. Even in peacemaking processes, Séverine Autesserre argues: 'The people who have to live with the consequences of a decision should be the ones making it.'[93] This ensures greater ownership and accountability.

And yet, it remains hard to do in practice. O'Flynn and Sturgess, in their recent review of the Australian Public Service (APS), state:

> Whilst there has been plenty of talk over many years about more relational approaches in the APS—partnerships, community engagement, collaboration, partnership, client co-design, for example —this has not necessarily translated into widespread practice.[94]

93 Séverine Autesserre, *The Frontlines of Peace: An Insider's Guide to Changing the World* (Oxford University Press, 2021), doi.org/10.1093/oso/9780197530351.001.0001.

94 O'Flynn and Sturgess, *2030 and Beyond*, 23.

Many reasons underpin this reticence or inertia. According to O'Flynn and Sturgess, one major cause could be that 'relational approaches … fundamentally challenge the frameworks that are currently used to audit and assess practice'.[95] Other reasons can include concerns around conflict of interest, resource constraints, a short-term focus, risk aversion, resistance to change, legal and regulatory framework limitations, increasing complexities and the pressures of technocratic measurability.[96]

Yet, each of these concerns can be, and should be, addressed. Public participation and engagement in regulation achieves numerous goals. It:

- enables decisions that reflect the needs, aspirations and values of the public
- increases the transparency and legitimacy of decisions by clarifying the basis upon which decisions are made
- creates opportunities for public ownership of decisions, which can improve both implementation and monitoring.

Moreover, growing interest in community participation and engagement practices is evident across Australia, from local governments to the federal level, giving these practices growing legitimacy.[97]

There is no doubt that community engagement must be deep and authentic. But what does this mean in practice?

There are different levels of citizen participation and engagement, which can be formalised in various ways. Two well-known frameworks are Arnstein's 'ladder of public participation' (1969) and the International Association for Public Participation's *Public Participation Spectrum,* better known as 'IAP2' (2007).[98] These frameworks emphasise the following levels of participation

95 O'Flynn and Sturgess, *2030 and Beyond*, 23.

96 Katherine Margaret Pascoe, 'Subverting, Challenging and Working Within Bureaucratic and Managerialist Systems: Strategies for Upholding Relationship-Based Social Work Practice'; Rob Wilson et al., 'New Development: Relational Public Services—Reform and Research Agenda'.

97 Helen Christensen, 'Legislating Community Engagement at the Australian Local Government Level', *Commonwealth Journal of Local Governance*, no. 21 (2018): 1–30, doi.org/10.5130/cjlg.v0i21.6515; Kim A. Johnston, 'Community Engagement: Exploring a Relational Approach to Consultation and Collaborative Practice in Australia', *Journal of Promotion Management* 16, no. 1–2 (2010): 217–34, doi.org/10.1080/10496490903578550; Department of Climate Change, Energy, the Environment and Water, 'Community Engagement for Renewable Energy Infrastructure', last modified 2 October 2025, www.dcceew.gov.au/energy/renewable/improving-community-engagement-support-energy-infrastructure.

98 Sherry R. Arnstein, 'A Ladder of Citizen Participation'; International Association for Public Participation, 'IAP2 Spectrum of Public Participation'.

and engagement: inform, consult, involve, collaborate and empower. They range from providing the public with essential information about the decision-making process to empowering them to actively contribute to decision-making, including decision-making for themselves and their communities. Additionally, other models and strategies exist that emphasise different aspects of community engagement, with the similar goal of always ensuring a broad and inclusive approach.[99]

Not every officer working in a regulator will have the necessary skills, competencies, or even the inclination to engage with the community. However, for those who choose to work in roles that involve or would benefit from community engagement, support can be provided by embedding the practices and values of restorative regulation within the organisation. This can be achieved by making these a core part of the regulatory body's culture and ethos.

Regulators will always have restrictions on the degree to which the public can be involved in making final determinations. However, a restorative approach requires consistently asking whether, and how early in the process, opportunities for effective public participation through restorative means can be made. This approach differs from the more common pattern of regulators seeking individual feedback and then making sense of it internally; rather, it involves the regulator bringing people together to hear from each other and reach a collective position on what is needed to move forward. Ideally, regulators will be proactive in creating opportunities for such practices throughout the whole decision-making process, even beyond approval. We will explore these opportunities, and the importance of community participation and engagement, throughout the book, and with a particular focus on empowering the community in Chapter 3.

Collective efficacy

Collective efficacy is a natural extension of any discussion on community participation and engagement. It plays a crucial role in empowering communities to influence change, solve problems collaboratively and take shared responsibility for their community's wellbeing.[100]

---

99 For example, see Australian Government, *The Australian Public Service Framework for Engagement and Participation*; World Bank Group, 'Citizen Engagement and the CIVIC Facility', 2. United States Government, 'Framework for Public Participation and Community Engagement'.

100 John Braithwaite, 'Regulatory Mix, Collective Efficacy, and Crimes of the Powerful'.

At the individual level, personal efficacy is the sense of control an individual feels over their own life. At the community level, collective efficacy involves 'an increased sense of community and belonging' and helps instil in communities or groups a sense of agency and control in their governance, allowing them to shape their own destinies and influence the decisions impacting them.[101] Each type of efficacy increases resilience.[102]

Communities with high collective efficacy are more likely to have members who stay engaged in the long term, join community groups, attend meetings, and undertake grassroots initiatives like citizen science and civic ecology initiatives. In Chapter 3, we discuss our case study of a long-lived community group in the Brooklyn Industrial Precinct that appears to us to have high collective efficacy – it has lasted for over a decade and is still going strong.

Collective efficacy is a restorative value achieved and empowered through both restorative values and restorative practices. Practices such as circles encourage the expression of emotions and support shared decision-making.[103] Collective efficacy further helps build social capital, an important factor for ensuring collaboration, resilience and mutual support during times of hardship.

Importantly, collective efficacy among staff in the regulator can help empower the restorative champions, unifying them with a shared purpose so that they address complex challenges using restorative approaches and strive to create a common understanding of what a restorative workplace looks like. Ultimately, collective efficacy can provide staff with the confidence and agency to help the organisational culture evolve into a more restorative culture. We will detail the potential of collective efficacy in Chapter 10.

---

101 Ruby Long et al., 'Community Engagement Via Restorative Justice to Build Equity-Oriented Crisis Standards of Care'; Gina Baral Abrams, et al., 'Proactive Restorative Practices: Creating the Conditions for Individuals and Communities to Flourish'.

102 Baral Abrams, Hebling, and Smull, 'Proactive Restorative Practices'; Long et al., 'Community Engagement'.

103 Long et al., 'Community Engagement'; John Braithwaite, 'Motivational Interviewing and Restorative Justice Praxis', 33–40.

Recognition of cultural diversity

One of the important lessons that arose early in our research and was sustained throughout was the need to ensure that culturally and linguistically diverse (CALD) communities were fully included in regulatory responses to harm, recovery, and prevention. For example, in Chapter 6, we describe the case of a CALD community left out of the information stream during COVID-19, leaving its members feeling scared, ill-informed and alienated. Many of our interviewees stressed the high importance of making sure that information was accessible in a range of languages, and that it was appropriately conveyed and attentive to cultural sensitivities.

A restorative regulator recognises and values the importance of cultural diversity in several key ways:

- **creating cultural competency**: Invest in training and education to help staff understand the cultural diversity of the communities they serve. In Australia, this also means helping staff gain cultural competency in First Nations Australians cultures (see Chapter 9).
- **fostering cultural liaisons**: Create and maintain cultural liaison networks that staff can reach out to, both during times of crises for quick dissemination of safety information, and during all times when regulatory decisions impact CALD and Indigenous communities. This should include active engagement to co-create and adapt regulatory practices where relevant.
- **ensuring language accessibility**: Provide materials, websites, and other sources of information in all the languages spoken within the communities the regulator impacts.
- **enabling culturally sensitive decision-making**: Ensure that the cultural context and perspectives of CALD and Indigenous communities affected by decisions form part of the regulatory decision-making processes, to ensure culturally appropriate and respectful outcomes.

Cultural diversity is an inherent part of most of the communities a regulator serves. A restorative regulator must, therefore, make the effort to ensure that its regulatory approaches are inclusive and respectful of this reality.

What makes restorative regulation different?

Our overview of the values and practices underpinning restorative regulation is not intended to be exhaustive but rather directed towards the components we have identified as 'core'. These also reflect the values and practices that we will keep referring to, expanding upon, and developing in the chapters ahead.

We see the threads of restorative values and practices as interweaving and supporting each other. In a response to harm, these threads entwine iteratively to foreground relationality, collaboration, respectful dialogue, inclusiveness, attentiveness to emotions and illumination of the bigger picture. A regulator that is able to weave the threads of restorative values and practices into its mission and methodologies makes a significant step towards growing as a truly restorative regulator.

To understand some of the key contributions of restorative regulation that emerge from this combination of values and practices, it is helpful to contrast it with standard regulatory approaches as shown in **Table 1.1**. We stress that this table is just a tool to help explain concepts—the categories are often less clear-cut in real life.

Table 1.1. Comparing standard and restorative regulatory approaches

Regulatory dimension	Standard regulatory approach	Restorative regulation approach
Focus of effort	Breaches of rules and regulations	Emphasis on repairing harm and (re)building relationships
Parties involved	Regulatee	Regulatee, those impacted by harm and others with a stake in the issue
Whose voice is heard?	Regulator and regulatee	Regulator, regulatee, those impacted by harm and others with a stake in the issue
Form of accountability	Passive	Active, linked to actions to repair harm and (re)build relationships
Form of authority	Doing things ***TO*** the regulatee	Working ***WITH*** the regulatee
Motivation to change	Extrinsic (pressure from regulator)	Intrinsic (developing within regulatee)

Regulatory dimension	Standard regulatory approach	Restorative regulation approach
Procedures involved	Notices and other sanctions	Deliberation among main stakeholders
Sanctions	Fines	Repair, prevention and (re)building of relationships

In our next chapter, we begin by taking a historical tour of EPA Victoria, tracing its evolution and the forces that have shaped it. From there, we take a behind-the-scenes look at our research journey—who we worked with, what went into our research, and why storytelling proves to be a powerful tool for uncovering insights.

2

The Environment Protection Authority Victoria as an incipient restorative regulator

Source: Shan S, Unsplash.

The best research you can do is talk to people.

—Terry Pratchett, 2001[1]

1 David Freeman, 'In Conversation: Terry Pratchett and Gerald Seymour', *The Guardian*, 9 November 2001, www.theguardian.com/books/2001/nov/08/fiction.terrypratchett.

This chapter introduces EPA Victoria, the regulatory agency at the heart of our research. It describes our research methodology and outlines the four main case studies explored throughout the book. The chapter concludes with key caveats and limitations to our research, which are essential for understanding the context and scope of our findings.

From its headquarters in the heart of Melbourne, behind the bustling Southern Cross Railway Station, to its offices dotted around Melbourne's suburbs and Victoria's regional areas, EPA Victoria stands as Australia's oldest, and one of the world's earliest, environmental protection agencies.[2] This chapter explores EPA Victoria's more than 50-year journey—its history, its people and its evolving role since its founding in 1971—providing important context for the book's restorative insights. A brief history of EPA Victoria opens the chapter, after which we outline the five-year research journey that has shaped this work.

We recount this story as outsiders who, through long-term organisational ethnographic research with the EPA, have had the privilege of gleaning invaluable insider perspectives, just as long-term EPA insiders have benefited from engaging with the perspectives of academic outsiders.

'Between a Rock and a Hard Place': A potted history of EPA Victoria

> *The challenge is to lift our focus to embrace our total interaction with this part of the planet. EPA's role is to inform, to guide—still, sometimes, to chide—and to be a partner as we turn the rocks and hard places into pathways for the future.*
>
> —Dr Brian Robinson[3]

2 Environment Protection Authority Victoria, 'EPA Victoria Upgrades Its Compliance and Enforcement Action', *Australian Environment Review* 26, no. 7 (2011): 201–04, 201; Penny Armytage, Jane Brockington, and Janice van Reyk, *Independent Inquiry into the Environment Protection Authority* (Environment Protection Authority Inquiry Ministerial Advisory Committee, 2016), iv, apo.org.au/sites/default/files/resource-files/2016-03/apo-nid72340.pdf (hereinafter referred to in the text as the MAC Review).

3 Ari Unglik, *Between a Rock and a Hard Place: The Story of the Development of the EPA* (Environment Protection Authority, 1996), 120, citing Dr. Brian Robinson, a former chair of EPA Victoria.

We borrowed this section's title from the book *Between a Rock and a Hard Place: The Story of the Development of the EPA,* a historical account of EPA Victoria from an earlier era. This work traces EPA Victoria's coming-of-age journey from its establishment in 1971 to 1996, covering its first quarter-century. According to the author, EPA Victoria was created in response to people 'starting to realise that the beauty of their physical environment was fading—fast—and the quality of their own lives was diminishing in return'.[4] Growing concerns around waste volumes and 'the highly complex problems' this had caused created sufficient impetus in the early 1970s for the passage of environmental protection legislation and the establishment of EPA Victoria.[5]

EPA Victoria's legal foundation was the *Environment Protection Act 1970* (Vic) (EP Act 1970), a piece of legislation considered radical and progressive at the time.[6] One of the first in the world to adopt a fully integrated approach to protecting diverse components of the environment,[7] this legislation established a framework that included environmental crime offences, a licensing regime requiring public scrutiny of certain activities, and the creation of state environmental protection policies.[8] These policies set environmental objectives and standards that formed the foundation for environmental licensing, compliance and enforcement for over four decades.

EPA Victoria's early history revealed a range of challenges, many of which persist today. These included:

- managing relationships with both industry and community
- balancing support for polluters in complying with regulations, and coercive use of enforcement powers
- addressing public expectations that 'everything would be fixed at once'.

4 Unglik, *Between a Rock and a Hard Place,* 7.

5 Armytage et al., *Independent Inquiry* (MAC Review), iv.

6 Unglik, *Between a Rock and a Hard Place,* 7; Jane Hall, 'Review of the Victorian EPA—What May Change?', 138–44.

7 Unglik, *Between a Rock and a Hard Place,* 20.

8 These were known as 'SEPPs' for short. They have been discontinued under the *Environment Protection Act 2017* (Vic), except in some limited circumstances, and have been replaced by the general environmental duty (GED) and new subordinate instruments. EPA Victoria, 'Using SEPPs and WMPs in the New Environment Protection Framework Guide'.

EPA Victoria also faced confusion over agency responsibilities for environmental matters, rapid population growth (including residential encroachment on both environment and industry) and ongoing issues of contaminated land and waters. Additionally, it had to find innovative ways to regulate complex environmental harm, such as air and water pollution resulting from multiple, diffuse inputs. Over time, the EP Act 1970 would undergo multiple amendments in an attempt to keep up with emergent, changing environmental challenges. Yet, it must be acknowledged that at its inception, it was considered state-of-the-art environmental legislation worldwide.

In the mid-1980s, the introduction of a community liaison officer changed the way the regulator interacted with the community. This came about because '[t]he Authority had come to recognise in practice that the community was not an impediment but, in fact, the reason for its existence. Many EPA officers had been frustrated because the public's persistence would slow their progress … Until then, EPA's clients had to deal with a group of technocrats and scientists who were competent in the idiom, but poor at communicating with the greater public'.[9] A big restructure to create teams of EPA Victoria staff in different regional centres also brought the EPA closer to the people who lived and worked in the regions they served.

For some staff, these new expectations of personal interactions with the public were so confronting that they left the organisation. However, many others, especially staff below management level, were keen to adopt a more communicative and interactive approach. This change opened up new possibilities, with EPA Victoria Chairman at the time, Dr Brian Robinson, recalling the following:

> They could actually go outside the office and do things. They did not have to sit behind a desk, hand a licence down to some inspector who would go out, knowing nothing about the background of the licence, and inspect and bring back the reports which would never go back to the guy who'd issued the licence.[10]

In this revealing recollection, it is possible to glean the first small steps being taken towards a more restorative approach to regulation, with interpersonal relationships between regulator, industry and the community starting to be seen in a more positive light.

9 Unglik, *Between a Rock and a Hard Place*, 77.
10 Unglik, *Between a Rock and a Hard Place*, 78.

By the twenty-first century, environmental challenges and community expectations had shifted considerably, impacting on the EPA's level of responsiveness. The 1970 EP Act that had once attested to so much foresight began stumbling over its patchwork of amendments, resulting in inconsistencies and inadequacies in meeting the task of holistic environmental protection. Growing environmental complexities and broken legislation impacted how the public and industry perceived the EPA's effectiveness. Several external reviews criticised EPA Victoria's regulatory approach, citing concerns about its effectiveness and influence in environmental protection, and its outdated enforcement policy.[11] Among other things, external reviews made recommendations that the EPA 'streamline its enforcement approaches to make them more responsive'.[12] Concerns about the EPA's effectiveness in protecting the environment and need for better engagement with affected communities provide an important background to the EPA's more recent restorative journey.

As with most environmental regulators worldwide, restorative justice was not formally part of the EPA's strategy or vision for the first three decades of its operation. A small change came about in 2000, when a provision was inserted into the EP Act 1970 as section 67AC, to enable EPA Victoria to seek a 'restorative project' as part of a prosecution outcome:[13]

> In addition to, or instead of, any other penalty the court may [order] the person … carry out a specified project for the restoration or enhancement of the environment in a public place or for the public benefit (even if the project is unrelated to the offence).

An even bigger change came in 2011 following a major Compliance and Enforcement Review, known as the *Krpan Review*.[14] The Krpan Review recommended that EPA Victoria 'pilot a program for community conferencing based on the restorative justice principles … as part of

11 See, for example, Stan Krpan, *Compliance and Enforcement Review: A Review of EPA Victoria's Approach* (hereinafter referred to in the text as the Krpan Review); Mark Beaufoy and Rebecca Tompkins, 'EPA Victoria Releases Contaminated Environments Review Discussion Paper and Annual Compliance Plan 2012–13'; Environment Protection Authority Victoria, 'EPA Victoria Upgrades Its Compliance'.

12 Phillipa McCormack, 'Assessing an Assertive EPA Victoria', 16–17. McCormack further noted that one regulatory response to the reviews might be to include restorative justice regulation as part of a more tailored regulatory mix (17).

13 Nicola Pain et al., 'Restorative Justice for Environmental Crime: An Antipodean Experience', 290, citing section 67AC(2)(c). This section was inserted by means of the *Environment Protection (Enforcement and Penalties) Act 2000*, Victoria.

14 Krpan, *Compliance and Enforcement Review*.

its use of enforceable undertakings for environmental offences'.[15] This recommendation was based upon growing recognition of the importance of community engagement and an increasing push to ensure its advancement across government during the preceding decade. The Krpan Review noted how an earlier review undertaken by Professor Richard Macrory in the United Kingdom had 'consulted regulated communities in a range of regulatory settings and found overwhelming support for restorative justice initiatives'.[16] The time for EPA Victoria to invest in restorative approaches in the regulatory context had truly arrived.

The push for restorative approaches led to several important outcomes. Organisational and regulatory policies were established to maximise the use of restorative project orders as an outcome of prosecutions (section 67AC). The *Compliance and Enforcement Policy* was amended, and guidelines were developed to support opportunities for community-driven initiatives to restore environments impacted by environmental offending.[17] Between 2012 and 2013, courts awarded six restorative projects under section 67AC, totalling $802,000. In 2013–14, three projects were awarded, totalling $225,000, and in 2014–15, 10 projects were awarded, amounting to approximately $679,800.[18] In Chapter 7, we discuss the Hampton Park Landfill case study—the only instance in which EPA Victoria has used a restorative conference, as recommended in the Krpan Review.

Further, in the EPA's 2013 *Environmental Citizenship Strategy*, restorative justice formed a central part of the 'interdependent relationship between EPA and the Victorian Community and our joint responsibility to protect and improve the environment', which involved 'actively encouraging, supporting and empowering the community, business and organisations to create lasting pro-environmental behaviour change driven by: accessibility, participation and responsibility, environmental equity and restorative

15 Krpan, *Compliance and Enforcement Review*, 302.

16 Krpan, *Compliance and Enforcement Review*, 301, citing findings from Richard Macrory, *Regulatory Justice: Making Sanctions Effective: Final report*, (Better Regulation Executive, 2006), www.regulation.org.uk/library/2006_macrory_report.pdf.

17 For the former Compliance and Enforcement Policy under the EP Act 1970, see Environment Protection Authority Victoria, *EPA Victoria Compliance and Enforcement Policy* (EPA Victoria and State Government of Victoria, 2011), hazelwoodinquiry.archive.vic.gov.au/wp-content/uploads/2014/08/EPA.0001.004.0049.pdf. For the current policy under the EP Act 2017, see Environment Protection Authority Victoria, *EPA Victoria Compliance and Enforcement Policy*, (State Government of Victoria, 2025), www.epa.vic.gov.au/about-epa/publications/1798-2.

18 Pain et al., 'Restorative Justice for Environmental Crime', 290.

action'.[19] The restorative action included '[r]estorative processes to empower stakeholders by involving them in sanctions, enforcement and remedies' and 'restorative conferencing'.[20]

Following the Hazelwood Mine fire, a further major review into EPA Victoria was announced in 2015, in the form of a Ministerial Advisory Committee (MAC), with its final report released in 2016 (the MAC Review).[21] The MAC considered this to be 'a "once-in-a-generation opportunity to not just tinker at the edges, but to reflect on what we think the fundamental purpose and functions of the EPA should be"'.[22]

The MAC Review acknowledged how much the world had changed since the EPA's inception, noting that while waste and pollution remained key concerns for the EPA, both community expectations of EPA Victoria and environmental challenges had changed.[23] In response to the MAC Review, the Victorian Government announced a major overhaul of the EP Act 1970, including governance reforms (such as establishing a board) and the introduction of a statutory purpose that explicitly recognised the connection between human health and the environment. Ensuing reforms centred on the passage of new legislation, the *Environment Protection Act 2017* (Vic) (EP Act 2017). Although its commencement was delayed by unforeseeable factors, including the global COVID-19 pandemic, it finally became operational on 1 July 2021.

The EP Act 2017 introduced a new paradigm for protecting human health and the environment from the harmful effects of pollution and waste, shifting the focus towards prevention through a 'duties' framework. To support the objectives of this legislative purpose, the Act significantly expanded the powers and tools available to the EPA, specifically targeting the prevention of risks to both the environment and human health. In particular, the Act introduced a legally enforceable general environmental duty (GED) as central to the law, in recognition that protecting our

19 Environment Protection Authority Victoria, *EPA Environmental Citizenship Strategy* (EPA Victoria, February 2013), 1, available at the Wayback Machine, web.archive.org/web/20250420193958/https://www.epa.vic.gov.au/about-epa/publications/1519; see also Pain et al., 'Restorative Justice for Environmental Crime'.

20 Environment Protection Authority Victoria, *EPA Environmental Citizenship Strategy*, 5.

21 Armytage et al., *Independent Inquiry* (MAC Review); see also Hall, 'Review of the Victorian EPA'.

22 Hall, 'Review of the Victorian EPA', 138, citing Environment Protection Authority Inquiry Ministerial Advisory Committee, *Independent Inquiry into the Environment Protection Authority/ Environment*, (State Government of Victoria, August 2015), 3.

23 Armytage et al., *Independent Inquiry* (MAC Review).

environment is a shared responsibility, owed by everyone. This was another groundbreaking initiative in the development of environmental law, marking the first application of a risk-based approach as the foundation for environmental regulation.

More pertinently for our purposes, some of the legislative and internal reforms addressed specific demands for the inclusion of a restorative response. Further chapters in this book will explore these responses in detail.

The value of storytelling

Throughout the book, we will draw on stories to illustrate our arguments and provide depth to our insights and suggestions. Storytelling forms an important aspect of restorative justice, as sharing stories enables the surfacing of unique experiences, emotions and motivations of participants.

We use four key case studies to flesh out EPA Victoria's story of restorative regulation. While each of these is an actual case study, they can also be understood as 'ideal type' stories.[24] This is because they raise common regulatory conundrums experienced by environmental regulators the world over. By exploring them, we aim to capture various elements of restorative approaches across different points of the regulatory spectrum.

Here, we summarise the four case studies that illustrate restorative elements in practice:

- **the Hazelwood Mine fire**: This case study was introduced at the start of the book and is explored in greater detail in Chapter 6.
- **the Hampton Park Landfill**: This case study is set in the south-eastern suburbs of Melbourne on a major urban arterial road. The area contains many industrial sites, including waste disposal and recycling facilities. The study centres on a landfill releasing foul odours that affected the surrounding community. Following many complaints, EPA Victoria decided to use an instrument known as an 'enforceable undertaking', which obtains a promise from the alleged offender to fix the problem

24 Sociologist Max Weber used the term 'ideal type' as a sociological concept to refer to a conceptual model able to capture essential features or characteristics of a particular social phenomenon, or, as in our case, institution. It is a theoretical construct that does not purport to require exact reproduction in other regulatory instances but rather serves as a way of understanding and analysing the regulatory institutional phenomena in a way that can be informative for existing or future regulatory experiences. An 'ideal type' story, therefore, aims to embody an archetype or ideal for restorative regulation that can inform the shaping of restorative regulation policy and operational choices applied beyond the original examples.

and make improvements. In this case, the enforceable undertaking was developed through a restorative conference. This conference directly involved the community in determining the terms of the enforceable undertaking. This story is discussed in Chapter 7.

- **Brooklyn Industrial Precinct**: Located in Melbourne's west, this case involves a complex node of pollution sources, including meat processing factories, waste and recycling operations, and manufacturing plants. This story illustrates a 'perfect storm' of industry and residential areas encroaching upon each other at different points in time. Lax planning laws, insufficient foresight about buffer zones and other evolving historical factors have converged to make this area of Melbourne's west a hotbed of tensions between industry, residents and regulators. Problems include dust, fumes, noise, heavy truck traffic and foul odours. Of especial interest from a restorative perspective is the creation of a long-lived Brooklyn Community Reference Group (BCRG), which continues to hold regular meetings over a decade after its establishment, providing a space for industry, community and EPA Victoria to regularly discuss ongoing community concerns. This story is detailed in Chapter 3.
- **working with the Dja Dja Wurrung People**: Situated in central Victoria, a rural part of the state of Victoria, our fourth story is an important recognition that for the Traditional Owners and Indigenous peoples of this area, inclusion in environmental protection has not been a priority until recent times. This story reveals the moral imperative of building relationships, trust and ongoing collaboration with First Nations peoples. It focuses on the Traditional Owners of the Dja Dja Wurrung Country (the Djaara people) and their role in restoring a harmed environment. It explores how restorative processes can lead to greater involvement and ownership of environmental protection by Traditional Owners. More on this story is provided in Chapter 7.

While these four case studies, along with other illustrative stories we explore throughout the book, provide encouraging examples of how different forms of justice can emerge, we also document the very real limitations that exist. These include long delays in court cases, the fact that only a minority of cases have a restorative outcome, competing ideas about what constitutes a 'community' and who (or what) comprises it, and a lack of guaranteed flow-on effects for either environmental or ongoing partnerships. All these factors mean that outcomes can be hard won and ephemeral. And, like many restorative approaches, the success stories concern a relatively confined group of people. As such, the mechanisms that enabled them to occur can all too easily become forgotten before their learnings are widely imparted. We return to the need to share success stories in Chapter 10.

Thus, these four stories each demonstrate both the possibilities and the limitations of environmental restorative justice at different points across the regulatory spectrum. We have woven their common themes throughout the book, in particular:

1. **the impacts of harm**. The impacts of environmental harm are often experienced more profoundly, and in directly embodied ways, by disadvantaged communities, including lower socio-economic groups and First Nations peoples.
2. **the value of support**. Adopting restorative approaches to regulatory work can cascade to better environmental and health outcomes and encourage further restorative initiatives. However, these initiatives are neither certain nor predictable; they appear to be contingent on a confluence of four key factors: support structures, supportive actors, supportive relationships and supportive practices.
3. **relational values**. Restorative processes can humanise regulatory practice while observing the necessary objectivity and impartiality. This can transform a regulatory institution and its practices, enhancing the regulator's ability to recognise within its institutional process the importance of relational values. By embedding relational values within institutional approaches, regulation moves beyond a narrow focus on policies and processes. This shift enables a deeper understanding of what is occurring in practice, how relationships are being cultivated, and how they can be supported meaningfully.
4. **alleviation of tensions**. Restorative approaches have the potential to disrupt unproductive polarisation that may have developed, such as tensions between communities and regulators or between communities and industry.

The stories we recount in the book reveal how restorative approaches enable individuals to engage with each other by focusing on harm and collaboratively working out how to redress and heal it. This can lead to unexpected, organically shaped pathways forward. The restorative process holds promise for linking individuals' and communities' firsthand experiences of regulatory processes in ways that ensure all the impacts and needs are heard, accounted for, and meaningfully incorporated into the regulatory response. This, in turn, delivers more meaningful ownership of inputs into, and the ongoing delivery of, regulatory outcomes.

As we noted in the Introduction, Nils Christie once famously rebuked the Western criminal justice system for 'stealing' people's conflicts—excluding them from the opportunity to participate in, learn from, and grow through collaborative problem-solving.[25] Restorative justice, whether in environmental or other regulatory domains, offers a way to avoid such criticism by welcoming everyone into the arena and expanding the web of relationships involved in creating justice.

Next, we turn to a brief overview of our research journey. Conducting this research required us to cultivate a web of relationships with interviewees and supporters both within and beyond the EPA. We deeply appreciate the invaluable contributions of each individual, acknowledging that their reflections and experiences grounded us in a wide range of perspectives and made this research possible.

Contextualising our research

Our research journey started with an Australian Research Council Linkage grant awarded to the ANU and the EPA.[26] The key researchers from the ANU were Emeritus Distinguished Professor John Braithwaite, Emeritus Professor Valerie Braithwaite and Miranda Forsyth, along with Dr Deborah Cleland and Felicity Tepper. They were joined by two EPA staff, Deborah Hollingworth and Alistair Nairn. While all contributed to the research, only four are authors of this book. The book also draws, in part, on a substantial paper authored by John Braithwaite in 2021.

We gathered the information informing this book's findings from multiple stakeholders and sites of action. This multifaceted approach has enabled us not only to learn from a broad range of perspectives but also to see and understand the structural limitations of environmental regulation within a world that often places economic interests before human and ecological

25 Nils Christie, 'Conflicts as Property', *The British Journal of Criminology* 17, no. 1 (1977): 1–15, doi.org/10.1093/oxfordjournals.bjc.a046783.

26 Australian Research Council 17/18 Linkage Grant (LP170100906), Miranda Forsyth *Preventing and Addressing Environmental Harm Through Restorative Justice*, (School of Regulation and Global Governance, ANU, n.d.) regnet.anu.edu.au/Centre-Restorative-Justice/Preventing-and-addressing-environmental-harm-through-restorative-justice.

health. Fortunately, these multiple lenses have amplified for us the 'glimmers of possibility that exist in the here and now' for environmental restorative justice and restorative regulation.[27] The multifaceted lenses have given our research an orientation towards critical hope, an essential part of transformative change.[28]

To uncover these 'glimmers' across as diverse a set of environmental regulatory practices as possible, we adopted the broad methodology of organisational ethnography.[29] From late 2018 to 2024, we conducted ethnographic research within EPA Victoria and with many organisations that have strong relationships with the EPA, such as cognate regulators, corporations, environmental and community groups and Traditional Owner organisations. This included shadowing, interviewing, observing and meeting with over 200 stakeholders.

Interviews, observations, and conversations

The primary source of data is the 86 interviews we undertook with 190 EPA Victoria officers, mostly individually and sometimes as small groups or teams. To this we add multiple observations of EPA officers in meetings where training occurred, policies were debated with a range of actors (including cognate environmental agencies), enforcement decisions were made, business actors were consulted (sometimes pursuant to formal EPA decision-making, such as issuing licences), and community and Traditional

27 Katharine McKinnon, Katherine Gibson, and Linda Malam, 'Introduction: Critical and Hopeful Area Studies – Emerging Work in Asia and the Pacific', *Asia Pacific Viewpoint* 49, no. 3 (2008), doi.org/10.1111/j.1467-8373.2008.00376.x.

28 Valerie Braithwaite, 'The Hope Process and Social Inclusion', *The Annals of the American Academy of Political and Social Science* 592, no. 1 (2004), doi.org/10.1177/0002716203262096; Valerie Braithwaite, 'Collective Hope', *The Annals of the American Academy of Political and Social Science* 592, no. 1 (2004), doi.org/10.1177/0002716203262049; Jenny Cameron and Katherine Gibson, 'Alternative Pathways to Community and Economic Development: The Latrobe Valley Community Partnering Project', *Geographical Research* 43, no. 3 (2005), doi.org/10.1111/j.1745-5871.2005.00327.x; Donna Haraway, 'Situated Knowledges: The Science Question in Feminism and the Privilege of Partial Perspective', *Feminist Studies* 14, no. 3 (1988), doi.org/10.2307/3178066; McKinnon et al., 'Introduction: Critical and Hopeful Area Studies'; Iris Marion Young, *Inclusion and Democracy*.

29 Organisational ethnography is often understood as both an *approach* to exploring a group's daily practices and the *artefact* produced through engagement. A core 'method' within ethnography is participant observation, which involves 'being there' in an organisation, observing, asking questions and documenting what is seen and heard. The long-term relationships between researchers and organisational stakeholders facilitate iterative exploration of varied experiences and practices, free from judgment. This approach allows researchers to capture a richer, more detailed picture than other methods might provide in the organisational context. See further Jenna Pandeli, Neil Sutherland, and Hugo Gaggiotti, 'Outlining a Practical, Emotional and Reflexive Approach to Organizational Ethnography', in *Organizational Ethnography: An Experiential and Practical Guide*, eds. Jenna Pandeli, Neil Sutherland, and Hugo Gaggiotti (Routledge, 2022), 1–12, doi.org/10.4324/9781003021582-1.

Owner groups were consulted. Further to these, we sat in on EPA court cases, accompanied field inspections and attended meetings of an EPA community of restorative practice.

In addition, we conducted 54 interviews of non-EPA actors across business, academia, Traditional Owners' organisations, and community members, leaders and groups. As with EPA Victoria, wherever possible, we observed various meetings and activities held by these actors. From 2019 to 2022, we observed regular meetings held by two community groups concerned with issues in an industrial area of Melbourne. We also observed relevant court cases and spoke to legal professionals.

An additional line of inquiry in our interviewing was suggested by Dr Cathy Wilkinson, the CEO of EPA Victoria from 2018 to 2021. She requested that we explore the 'spaces' in which restorative practices can flourish and thrive. As part of this, she was curious about the qualities of a model EPA field officer.[30] She expressed her desire to 'bottle' these qualities, hoping to make it easier to transfer their intangible qualities to more junior and new officers. Inspired by her spontaneous idea, we referred to these interviews as our 'bottling interviews'.

This unexpected interview trajectory yielded rich data. While most of this data did not accord with the subject of this book,[31] it revealed striking insights. It became clear that the field officers regarded internally as outstanding environmental regulators within EPA Victoria were overwhelmingly those able to see the 'big picture' and 'have difficult conversations' with regulatees, often in challenging and complex circumstances. Their skill lay in successfully being able to convey the message in a way that even the most resistant regulatee could ultimately accept, however reluctantly. In other words, the intangible quality that set these regulators apart was their highly developed relational skills and an instinctive (or learned) understanding of the importance of relationship-building. Another key intangible quality was their willingness to seek to understand and work with different perspectives.

30 Known as Environment Protection Officers (EPOs), these officers are authorised to exercise certain powers under the EP Act 2017. Their responsibilities include conducting inspections, offering compliance advice and issuing remedial notices, such as those for pollution abatement, clean-up and remediation actions.

31 We are hopeful, however, that this process will form the basis of a future research, as it proved to be a fruitful inquiry with valuable insights for all regulators with field officers.

Our bottling interviews became a valuable means of identifying further glimmers of the potential places and actual spaces where restorative justice operates.

Our method has been to search widely for incipient or emergent restorative justice rather than to estimate its prevalence. We spent a lot of time hanging around EPA Victoria offices—central, suburban and regional—attending internal team meetings of disparate kinds. We joined in on countless casual and more serious conversations, whether in lunchrooms, on walks around the EPA, or on long car trips to regional offices and inspection sites. In the field, we participated in or observed inspections, 'Open House' sessions, approval and licensing decision-making conferences, community reference group meetings and other community consultations. We even visited a trade show where EPA Victoria had its own stand.

With the Dja Dja Wurrung People, a major Indigenous stakeholder, we went to Bendigo several times to visit the Dja Dja Wurrung Clans Aboriginal Corporation. During each visit, we attended two EPA consultation meetings with the Dja Dja Wurrung, observed Djaara's board and staff meetings, attended cultural and arts events, and spoke with seven people who held varied roles at The Bendigo & District Aboriginal Co-operative. We interviewed Indigenous staff members of EPA Victoria during the project, as well as Indigenous staff at various levels of seniority within what was then known as the Department of Environment, Land, Water and Planning (DELWP),[32] and former Aboriginal Victoria. Additionally, we interviewed Indigenous Elders and Aboriginal academics from nations beyond the Dja Dja Wurrung People who were civil society leaders in environmental regulatory policymaking.

Other stakeholders interviewed included:

- executives of many regulated corporate entities
- environmental non-government organisations (NGOs/ENGOs), both statewide and local, and four 'Friends of the River/Creek' organisations. This included spending time with group members on location where they were undertaking restoration work, attending community-led meetings regularly over four years and observing EPA-led community meetings.

32 Since 1 January 2023, the Department has been known as the Department of Energy, Environment and Climate Action, or 'DEECA' for short; see Department of Energy, Environment and Climate Action at www.deeca.vic.gov.au/.

- two water authorities
- environmental regulators from six local governments in Victoria
- other state and federal governmental agencies holding environmental responsibilities that partner with EPA Victoria. These included the former Department of Environment, Land, Water and Planning, Parks Victoria, former Aboriginal Victoria, Sustainability Victoria, Department of Health, Department of Justice and Community Safety, the Commonwealth Department of Climate Change, Energy, Environment and Water, prosecutors and private legal counsel
- Officers for the Protection of the Local Environment (known by all as 'OPLEs'), who (at the time of the research) had joint appointments between municipal councils and EPA Victoria. Our interviews also covered trips with these officers on inspections.

Finally, we engaged restorative justice NGOs (regional, statewide, national and international) and activists of diverse stripes in iterated yarning on the themes of this book.[33]

Other data we have relied upon in reaching our findings include a range of unpublished and public EPA Victoria and other governmental documents; information from duty holders (also known as licence or permit holders), community members and groups; case law, media and advocacy materials.

Some important caveats

Our framing of this journey through the experiences of the environmental regulator in the state of Victoria, explored by way of case studies, is intended to reveal how one particular regulator has experienced restorative regulation. Through concrete examples, we have sought to bring to life both what has occurred in practice and what might be possible in the future. However, the specific 'regulatory responsibility and reach' set by the Victorian Government, which grants the regulator its particular powers, will not align exactly with other regulatory contexts. Each regulator's capacities are shaped by the powers, duties and functions bestowed upon it by law, the resources it receives and the broader regulatory framework in which it operates. Yet, while the regulatory spaces in other contexts may differ, we hope these examples offer insights that resonate for regulatory situations elsewhere.

33 'Iterated yarning' is a term arising from the concept of yarning, a culturally significant practice common to Indigenous Australians. This storytelling approach, which we detail in Chapter 9, refers to reflective, ongoing and reciprocal conversations.

Another important limitation should be noted. Many of the spaces fundamental to contemporary regulatory transformation—such as those addressing climate change—involve significant and complex challenges that require policy development, shaping and responsiveness at the macro level of government.[34] Regulatory transformation can require detailed, lengthy and broad consultative policy work in the case of complex policy with far-reaching implications. This usually exceeds the remit of an operational regulatory agency focused on compliance and enforcement. For example, EPA Victoria does not currently have sole responsibility for the regulation of climate change actions. This reflects the reality that its mandate is to regulate pollution and waste, while the Department of Energy, Environment and Climate Action has primary responsibility for the comprehensive and coordinated response needed for approaching climate change.[35] This division of responsibilities is by no means an unusual situation in many jurisdictions, the U.S. Environmental Protection Agency included. However, in addition to considering regulatory spaces, readers seeking a broader perspective of environmental issues must also think about the restorative potential of civil society activism, the work of treaty secretariats, and the role of judges, prosecutors and diplomats in helping to bring forth the restorative potential for complex environmental challenges. While these other spaces are undeniably important, they fall outside the scope of this book.

We acknowledge that, while we have worked hard at interviewing and observing many people and situations, there is no way that 'saturation' has been achieved across the range of all perspectives on our case studies and sites. Time and again, we believed we had approached saturation—particularly among the most sampled respondents, EPA staff—only to be proven wrong. Notably, no interviews were conducted at institutions in which captive communities have so little control over their built environment, such as prisons or aged care facilities, nor with those who lack the power or resources to move somewhere else. This limitation in our methodology reflects a broader weakness of consultation—whether by EPA Victoria or

34 The EPA has sought to articulate it role in climate change regulation through a statement of regulatory intent: EPA, *EPA's Statement of Regulatory Intent on Climate Change*, (Engage Victoria and EPA Victoria, 2025), engage.vic.gov.au/epas-statement-of-regulatory-intent-on-the-causes-and-consequences-of-climate-change.

35 In Victoria, climate change targets and mitigation measures are determined under the *Climate Change Act 2017*. The EPA plays an important role in supporting these targets under the EP Act 2017, particularly through the GED [general environmental duty] obligations, which require duty holders to address and mitigate the causes and consequence of climate change in their activities.

any regulator tasked with taking responsibility for environmental harm—which pays little attention to voices whose firsthand experience and outrage will always be silenced by the institutions that confine them to a smelly, polluted or inescapable space.

Throughout this book, we have included quotes representative of the variety of views expressed to us, views that convey the tone, feel and vibe of the relevant context as accurately as possible. As we explained earlier, stories are central in restorative justice theory, and respecting those who tell us their stories openly is equally important. To protect our interviewees, all quotes have been made anonymous unless otherwise agreed or already public. In the few cases where identification might still be possible, we have adjusted key descriptors—such as position, location and gender—while ensuring fidelity to the meaning and context of the original statements.

The research and interviews for this book took place during a period of significant change for the EPA. While plans for operationalisation of the EP Act 2017 were under way during our research, the regulatory framework in force for the first half of the project remained the 1970 Act. As a result, the case studies and examples throughout this book are primarily grounded in the 1970 Act, reflecting an approach to environmental protection that has since evolved. However, research carried out after the implementation of the Act of 2017 is also included. While the EP Act 2017 introduces a new regulatory approach and its implementation is still in its early stages, this book acknowledges its different emphases and opportunities.

Now that we have explored the EPA's background and how we went about our research, the next chapter turns to discussing the first of our spaces for restorative regulation—citizen empowerment.

3

Restorative regulation through citizen empowerment

Source: John Englart, Flickr, CC BY-SA 2.0 (www.flickr.com/photos/takver/15013080821/).

> *[C]ommunity sits front and centre in any successful democratic nation. And when community cares, when it is engaged with democracy, real progress can be made.*
>
> —Stephanie Bull, 2023[1]

1 Stephanie Bull is the Director of the Museum of Australian Democracy (MOAD). This quote is taken from her speech at the Museum of Australian Democracy (MOAD), delivered 30 August 2023. Quote used with permission.

In this chapter, we discuss what it means to take relational justice seriously in terms of community engagement and empowerment, and we highlight the importance of genuine dialogue and relationship building. We identify the variety of roles that community can play in the regulatory process and the various entrance points that can be created to enable them to fulfil those roles.

When regulatory breaches occur, their effects ripple far beyond the immediate violation to touch the lives of entire communities.

Take, for instance, the familiar scenario of environmental breaches. Whether the breach be pollution in a local waterway or the acrid odour from a nearby abattoir, the resulting harm impacts the community's health and wellbeing. It makes sense, therefore, to directly engage community members in the regulatory process that is designed to both fix the problem and prevent future recurrences.

This chapter explores a narrative that casts citizens not as mere bystanders but as active agents in the regulatory process. While our focus is primarily on state regulators, we acknowledge that citizens themselves are often active regulators in their own right—a scope that is beyond this book yet fundamentally important.[2]

2 The clearest example is the regulatory work undertaken by First Nations communities worldwide, where Indigenous governance systems and traditional ecological knowledge play a crucial role in environmental stewardship. Additionally, community-based monitoring groups, citizen science initiatives and local advocacy organisations frequently contribute to oversight in the regulatory context, holding both industry and government to account. Examples include volunteer water-quality monitoring programs, neighbourhood air-pollution tracking initiatives and grassroots campaigns that push for better enforcement of environmental laws.

On what community means

The term 'community' is broad and dependent on its socially constituted context. We recognise that each community is unique and is not an object to be acted upon but a collective with its own agency and power.

When we refer to 'community', we look first to the neighbourhood community impacted directly by environmental harm in its locale. This means the individuals, families and groups located in close geographical proximity to one another. This community is directly impacted by regulatory processes responding to regulated harms.

Beyond this, we also consider community in a broader sense—people who share common experiences, conditions or values, such as 'factory workers', 'school-aged children' or 'environmentalists'. Although the members of these communities may not live near one another, they can still connect, engaging in community meetings, discussions and advocacy as affected or interested groups.

Existing practice and theories supporting citizen empowerment in regulation

> *In the real world, answers may not be clear-cut. There will be messy choices, and you're not going to be able to construct a policy response in a neat and tidy way. Being able to listen to other people, even as you stay true to your principles, that's how you actually succeed.*
>
> —Jake Sullivan[3]

As discussed in Chapter 1, citizen empowerment and engagement are central to restorative regulation. However, these ideas are not new. In this section, we discuss regulatory practice and theory that align with restorative understandings of citizen empowerment, while in the following section, we explore what makes a restorative approach distinctive.

Regulators everywhere are increasingly realising the valuable, diverse perspectives, roles and experiences that citizens and community organisations bring to regulation. There is growing awareness of the need to involve these perspectives, roles and experiences across many regulatory areas.

3 Jake Sullivan is an attorney and former US National Security Advisor from 2021 to 2025. Citation from BrainyQuote, www.brainyquote.com/quotes/jake_sullivan_763474.

In July 2021, Demos, a United Kingdom think tank, published a paper as part of its work on reimagining the public service in a post-COVID world.[4] It advocated for a shift from transactional to relational public services, stating:

> Relational public services can improve outcomes by giving citizens more control and confidence to resolve their problems. And relational public services can build communities that are able to mobilise and resolve problems by themselves, without relying heavily on the state.[5]

Making space for community participation and engagement[6] is increasingly recognised as good regulatory practice, grounded in the principles of informing, consulting and accountability: 'Broadening public participation and community engagement in the regulatory process can help agencies produce more responsive, effective, durable, and equitable regulations.'[7]

In their recent study, scholars Duckworth, Horn and Grossman identified a key recommendation for rebuilding trust in government:

> Co-production of policies and programs is one key method for building trust relationships. This means that communities have agency and are not just 'consulted' on program development and delivery. True co-production takes time and sustained effort to work with communities as partners. There needs to be a more widespread understanding of how these techniques could be used and the willingness to take the time to use them.[8]

---

4 Polly Mackenzie, *The Social State: From Transactional to Relational Public Services* (Demos, 8 July 2021), demos.co.uk/research/the-social-state-from-transactional-to-relational-public-services/.

5 Mackenzie, 'The Social State', 4.

6 'Public participation' refers to the involvement of the public in government decision-making, often emphasising 'stakeholders' with specific interests or 'stakes' in the regulatory matter. This includes individuals, government bodies from varied jurisdictions, industry and businesses, civil society organisations. 'Community participation and engagement' is a subset of public participation, focused specifically on community or communities likely to be affected by a regulatory process. While the term 'community' is context-dependent, it generally includes individuals, local/civil society organisations and Traditional Owner groups. Community engagement focuses on 'build[ing] trust-based, long-term, and two-way relationships with communities, including underserved communities that have been historically left out of government decision making': Executive Office of the President, Office of Management and Budget, 'Broadening Public Participation and Community Engagement in the Regulatory Process', Memorandum for the Heads of Executive Departments and Agencies (Executive Office of the President, 19 July 2023), 4, www.reginfo.gov/public/jsp/EO/fedRegReview/Broadening-Public-Participation-and-Community-Engagement-in-the-Regulatory-Process.pdf.

7 Executive Office of the President, 'Broadening Public Participation', 4.

8 Mark Duckworth, Christine Horn, and Michele Grossman, *Do Governments Trust Communities? The Trust Flows Project Research Report* (Centre for Resilient and Inclusive Societies, 2024), 39, www.crisconsortium.org/trust-flows-research-project.

Many jurisdictions require public participation as part of their regulatory framework.[9] Genuine public participation, however, demands more than the involvement of well-resourced and knowledgeable 'sophisticated stakeholders'; it requires the genuine inclusion of regulatory beneficiaries and members of the broader public.[10] Some commentators argue that community involvement is necessary not only for achieving better regulatory outcomes but also for regulators and other government actors to maintain their own 'social licence' to regulate, just as corporations must maintain their social licence to operate.[11]

In thinking through many of the issues that arise from citizen empowerment, particularly in relation to power sharing, we have found the theoretical concept of 'agonism'—developed by Belgian political theorist Chantal Mouffe—especially useful. Agonism is a political theory that emphasises the productive potential of ongoing conflict, not as a means of ushering in a new, perfect system, but as a mechanism for creating pathways that diminish the domination caused by power imbalances and hierarchies. Ideally this is achieved by creating a shared plane where all voices are heard and contribute.[12] As Rawsthorne et al. observe: 'It is through dialogue with community members that shared understanding emerges, challenging the assumptions about community and power.'[13] This perspective reflects our

9 For example, in the United States, the *Administrative Procedure Act* stipulates that regulatory agencies undertaking notice-and-comment rulemaking must 'give interested persons an opportunity to participate in the rule making through submission of written data, views, or arguments' (5 U.S.C. Section 553[c]). Further, section 6(a) of the Executive Order 2866, *Regulatory Planning and Review* (Sept. 30, 1993) directs regulatory agencies to 'provide the public with meaningful participation in the regulatory process' (Executive Office of the President, ' Broadening Public Participation'), 1. Other ways of giving the public an opportunity to participate include: informal consultation, public notice-and-comment, public hearings, advisory bodies and citizens' advisory panels. See also OECD, *Eight Ways to Institutionalise Deliberative Democracy*, OECD Public Governance Policy Paper, (OECD, 2021), www.oecd.org/content/dam/oecd/en/publications/reports/2021/12/eight-ways-to-institutionalise-deliberative-democracy_e1f898a0/4fcf1da5-en.pdf.

10 Michael Sant'Ambrogio and Glen Staszewski, 'Public Engagement with Agency Rulemaking: Final Report', (presented at the Administrative Conference of the United States, 19 November 2018), 2.

11 Julia Black and Andrew Murray, 'Regulating AI and Machine Learning: Setting the Regulatory Agenda', *European Journal of Law and Technology* 10, no. 3 (2019): 13.

12 According to Chantal Mouffe, agonistic pluralism is a possibility from this kind of balance. Here, agonistic pluralism means democratic interaction between a community of people who hold diverse beliefs and opinions. It becomes possible where the power is balanced, no one single group dominates, and room is made for different voices to have a say in shaping society. In such a space, no one person or group has an overwhelming advantage, thus making it easier to engage in respectful debates that can lead to innovative and fair solutions for political, social and environmental problems: Chantal Mouffe, *On the Political* (Routledge, 2005); Chantal Mouffe, *Agonistics: Thinking the World Politically* (Verso, 2013); Chantal Mouffe, *For a Left Populism* (Verso, 2018).

13 Margot Rawsthorne et al., 'Understanding Community-led Disaster Preparedness', *Australian Journal of Emergency Management* 38, no. 2 (2023): 50, doi.org/10.47389/38.2.49

position, discussed in the introduction, that embracing and managing political conflicts as constructive debates is a healthy and necessary part of democratic discourse. It is not necessary that there be agreement; rather, what matters is the possibility of genuine conversation, where diverse perspectives can contribute to innovative and fair solutions to complex issues.

We see a parallel to this theory in scholarship from a very different domain—that of marriage counselling. You may be familiar with Dr John Gottman's work, which for several decades has examined the dynamics of couples' relationships. In his book, *The Seven Principles for Making Marriage Work*, Gottman argues it is important to draw a distinction between 'solvable problems' and 'perpetual problems'.[14] He found that 69 percent of relationship conflicts are insoluble: conflicts that stem from perpetual problems all couples experience, the content of which may differ for each couple (for example, house cleaning, in-laws, sex, disciplining children), but not the fact of conflict itself.[15] Rather than solving perpetual problems, what matters most is whether a couple can establish an ongoing, constructive dialogue about them. If they cannot do so, conflict becomes gridlocked, and that is where the real troubles lie. However, if both partners learn to discuss their differences constructively, they create an opportunity for understanding and growth, enabling them to navigate towards a liveable acceptance of the realities involved in sharing a life together. Similarly, problems in the relationship between community and industry are not always fully solvable, but the relationship can be manageable when the necessary conditions for productive dialogue are in place.

Taken together, Mouffe, Braithwaite, and Gottman show that while a regulatory problem may never be resolved to the full satisfaction of all sides involved, empowering all actors to have a voice and be heard in relation to the issue makes a difference to how people feel about the outcomes and whether they accept them. Regulatory dialogue often takes place at a broad structural and political level, yet the real-world impacts fall on specific communities and individuals. This makes it particularly important to centre the voices of those most directly affected by regulatory decisions, voices and experiences that are too often overlooked in current regulatory processes.

---

14 John Gottman and Nan Silver, *The Seven Principles for Making Marriage Work: A Practical Guide from the Country's Foremost Relationship Expert*, Second ed. (Harmony Books, 2015).

15 Gottman and Silver, *The Seven Principles*.

Restorative regulation and citizen empowerment

With growing awareness of the need to meaningfully, respectfully and reciprocally engage citizens and those impacted by regulatory decisions in regulatory processes, we need to ask: What extra dimension comes from considering community engagement from a restorative perspective?

In this section, we consider citizen empowerment across a broad range of regulatory activities, from setting the standards and rules by which decisions are made—for example, in policies and regulations—through to making actual decisions, such as licence approvals. Through the restorative lens we are using, citizen empowerment means fostering relationships that enable the following:

- **knowledge empowerment**: providing citizens and organisations with the *tools, knowledge and opportunities* to understand regulations so they can voluntarily comply
- **accountability empowerment**: creating opportunities for citizens to play *a role in holding others accountable* for harm caused, particularly ensuring that those most impacted have a voice in determining how harm is repaired
- **deliberative empowerment**: establishing forums where citizens can *contribute to shaping* regulatory frameworks that affect them, as a form of deliberative democracy, rather than just responding to them
- **trust-building**: *strengthening trust* between citizens and the regulator through commitments to transparency and fairness
- **collaborative empowerment**: *providing avenues for citizens to report issues*, voice concerns and contribute to regulatory decision-making in a genuine and collaborative way.

As we discuss below, not all these forms of citizen empowerment will always be fully accommodated. However, breaking them into these different facets helps clarify the different contexts in which each can be most effectively enabled.

Understanding citizen empowerment in this way can be seen as a form of relational justice. However, relational justice goes beyond simply restoring balance or fairness; it aims to also transform relationships in ways that ensure they are healthier, more equitable and conducive to mutual flourishing.

According to Jennifer Llewellyn, a proponent of relational theory, the pursuit of relational justice must occur both at the interpersonal level and within the systemic or institutional contexts.[16]

From a regulatory perspective, relational justice means paying attention to the conditions that enhance and sustain relationships between regulators, regulatees and citizens, not just on interpersonal levels but also structurally. This means prioritising human dignity and inclusiveness, and creating participatory opportunities for dialogue to enable a genuine responsiveness to emerging issues. It up-ends the more hierarchical, one-way models of interaction that often underpin managerial regulatory approaches, which emphasise efficiency, standardisation and top-down control. Llewellyn argues:

> Through broad inclusion, such processes are able to ensure the appropriate balance between macro- and micro-justice issues and to avoid sacrificing the needs and interests of individual parties. Such processes also have the potential to be democratic in the sense that they strive to ensure that those affected can participate in the processes of decision-making about how to do justice in a particular situation. It is, thus, not sufficient for parties to simply be included, they must be given the opportunity to participate in a meaningful way, which includes, but is not limited to, taking part in a process of dialogue about the requirements of justice.[17]

So, how can this be achieved in practice? Many restorative practices and values combine to support community empowerment and relational justice.

Genuine inclusion of community voice requires a process that provides inclusive spaces where all relevant actors can be empowered to engage in meaningful discussion. A restorative facilitator plays a key role in actively enabling deep listening between participants, channelling their deliberation towards broadly acceptable solutions that both resolve the concerns and support healing. The facilitator may rely upon restorative mechanisms such as listening circles or restorative conferences to create spaces for constructive and deliberate dialogue. However, as we explore further below, there is plenty of room for creativity in finding innovative ways to include community voices.

---

16 Llewellyn, 'Transforming Restorative Justice'.

17 Jennifer Llewellyn, 'Restorative Justice: Thinking Relationally About Justice', in *Being Relational: Reflections on Relational Theory and Health Law*, eds. Jocelyn Downie and Jennifer L. Llewellyn (UBC Press, 2011), 89–108, 99, doi.org/10.59962/9780774821902-007.

Before we turn to the different spaces for community empowerment, we first outline the preconditions necessary for a regulator to engage in this space. As a structural issue, this requires the state to prioritise relational justice and to provide the authorisation and resources for the regulator to be an effective restorative regulator.

In addition, being open to direct communication with the public in restorative ways requires both institutional and individual courage, as well as an openness to emotional engagement. In particular, this requires openness to being placed in emotionally testing situations. Sometimes, pent-up frustration, passion, or feeling dismissed can lead to some individuals expressing outrage. In many societies, particularly within institutional or bureaucratic contexts, there is a growing tendency towards conflict avoidance, with regulatory strategies seeking to limit the expression of emotions. However, this is not always the case with the broader public, where strong emotional responses are often readily visible. In reflecting on an occasion when EPA Victoria was first working with community forums, Chief Conservation Regulator Kate Gavens recalls:

> I remember those community forums, and they were fierce events to start with, but over time calmed down. I remember when I started at the Conservation Regulator and I think we *were* quite scared to go and talk to the community because we got bashed and bruised quite a bit in doing so. And finding our confidence to get back out there again and what you see is the trust that you build then with your stakeholders as you go out and you talk to them and you agree to disagree. I think that's a really important piece for us as regulators, in terms of we're here to serve the community, we're part of the government, we are public servants. Getting out there and talking to people, and not just regulated entities, but talking to the community that we serve about the issues they care about, and that it's okay for them to disagree with us I think is a really critical part of the role.[18]

John Merritt, a former CEO of EPA Victoria, agrees:

> But it's that thing, the fear of it—it's us, we've got to guts it out to get into this game! And it's hard, it's bloody hard. But you can't fall into this myth that it's us and them and it's all a bloody war out there

18 Gavens, 'Incentivising Compliance'.

> and you can't try things and … Actually, it's the opposite. People are decent and they just want to see us having a crack at *their* problem. Not *our* problem, *their* problem.[19]

As the points made by these seasoned regulators illustrate, community outrage is not a reason to refrain from engagement, nor is it something for regulators to fear. When harnessed constructively, it becomes a compass for community concerns, a form of feedback highlighting what really matters to the community and giving impetus for efforts towards swifter resolution.

Relationship expert Esther Perel counsels us to distinguish between conflict that is productive, useful and restorative, and conflict that is destructive, useless and harmful.[20] Just as in our interpersonal relationships, leaning into constructive conflict can strengthen communities and support better regulation. However, it does require empathy, hard work and, at times, the development of new skills.

One way to do this is to support the restorative inclinations of regulatory officers, especially those at the frontline.[21] In our research, we found many regulatory officers who were interested in leaning into community engagement, with some telling us, 'We actually want to hear.' One officer recounted a conversation where community engagement was discussed, with another officer pushing back, cautioning: 'They may say something we don't like.' The first officer told us with a grin that she had replied cheerfully: 'Bound to!'

Here, the insights and experience of senior officers in the field—those who understand the importance of relationships and approach conflict in a humane, persuasive and participative way—can be invaluable. Placing less experienced officers alongside senior officers can help pass on valuable lessons in handling conflict and difficult conversations restoratively, helping them

19 John Merritt, 'Incentivising Compliance: Using Behavioural Insights to Encourage and Persuade' (ANZSOG, 2 June 2023), anzsog.edu.au/learning-and-development/events-and-conferences/incentivising-compliance-using-behavioural-insights-to-encourage-and-persuade/.

20 Esther Perel and Mary Alice Miller, 'Letters from Esther #50: Could it Really Be That Easy to Resolve Conflict?', *Esther Perel* (blog), 2023, www.estherperel.com/blog/letters-from-esther-50-could-it-really-be-that-easy-to-resolve-conflict.

21 Rachel Suff, *Managing Conflict in the Modern Workplace* (Chartered Institute of Personnel and Development, 2020), www.cipd.org/globalassets/media/knowledge/knowledge-hub/reports/managing-conflict-in-the-workplace-2_tcm18-70655.pdf.

to overcome their reticence to engage with complaints and grievances they might otherwise avoid. As former CEO John Merritt explained, 'The first behaviour we have to change is ours.' He goes on to say:

> Here's the thing, we are powerful beyond our wildest dreams as regulators. Like it is scary how powerful we are. But with that comes a very painful acceptance that whatever it is that's going on out there that we don't like, is modelled on us … Until I changed *my* behaviour, nothing happened. And once I changed, everything started to change. Nothing changes until we change.[22]

Restorative spaces for community empowerment

We now turn to the restorative and incipiently restorative spaces relevant to community participation and engagement we observed during our research with EPA Victoria. These include community consultation meetings (town hall meetings and Open Houses) and community reference groups (CRGs). We also address neighbourhood environmental improvement plans (NEIPs). Although NEIPs are no longer used by the EPA, we include them here because their past use offers valuable insights. We selected these examples for their ability to tell the restorative story, both immanent and incipient. The insights they provide can guide regulators who wish to implement similar participatory formats in the future.

To start, we first visit the Brooklyn Industrial Precinct. Here, we relate a story about a typical regulatory dilemma where a regulator finds itself entangled in the conflicting, often somewhat irreconcilable demands of both community and industry.

The Brooklyn Industrial Precinct

In *Between a Rock and a Hard Place*, the author relates how the deposit of industrial waste into Melbourne's rivers had generated so much putrid waste by the late 1800s that the city had become known as 'Smelbourne'. Melbourne's gentry, who had grown rich from the era's Victorian gold rush, were not amused by this term. At the time, Melbourne had 'more balls and parties, a larger measure of intellectual life … a larger leisured

22 Merritt, in panel discussion 'Incentivising Compliance'.

class than Sydney'.[23] And this leisured class was desirous of maintaining areas along the Yarra River in central Melbourne in a state fit for its leisure activities, such as boating and swimming.[24] Not content with just using the river for leisure, the gentry also wanted to build fashionable homes along the Yarra's banks. This led to the relocation of all the tanneries, knackeries and other befouling industries dotted along the Yarra to a different river in Melbourne's west—the Maribyrnong River.[25]

Back in the 1800s, and for the first half of the twentieth century, offensive industries continued to be placed away from people—or, at least, away from people who had a voice. Joyfully free from planning laws, a proliferation of abattoirs and rendering plants were built, often involving family businesses handed down from generation to generation. Gradually, over time, these noisy and odorous industries started to be ringed by houses. This occurred partly because it was an affordable area for families to build in and partly because this area was reasonably close to central Melbourne.

Over time, the families who had benefited from the lax planning laws that had facilitated building homes in what was essentially an industrial area, and their successors, naturally started to resent the intrusive smells and noises that invaded the fabric of their lives. Residents turned to EPA Victoria to demand enforcement of environmental standards guaranteeing them better-quality air and environment.

Unsurprisingly, this situation gave rise to a perfect storm of competing interests—a storm that continues swirling to this day, exemplified by the tensions in the Brooklyn Industrial Precinct in Melbourne's west. The Precinct includes many noxious industries such as landfills, recycling sites, construction material sites, abattoirs, knackeries, and tallow works—all in an area often serviced by unsealed roads, giving rise to problems of dust, fumes, noise and bad odours. In some cases, residential areas are located as close as 50 metres from the Precinct. The story about who came first is a

23 Richard Ernest Nowell Twopeny, *Town Life in Australia* (Elliot Stock, 1883), cited in Helen Doyle, *Thematic History—A History of the City of* Melbourne's *Urban Environment: Planning for Future Growth* (Context Pty Ltd, 2011), 92, mvga-prod-files.s3.ap-southeast-4.amazonaws.com/public/2024-05/history-city-of-melbourne-urban-environment.pdf.

24 Doyle, *Thematic History*, 92.

25 Ari Unglik, *Between a Rock and a Hard Place*, 8. Author Jeri Freedman, discussing similar experiences in the United States during the same era, notes that '[p]rior to the twentieth century, many factories were built near rivers and streams' and that '[i]t was common to discharge the industrial waste from the manufacturing process into those same waterways'. Jeri Freedman, *The Establishment of the Environmental Protection Agency* (Cavendish Square, 2018), 16.

contested one. Some residents say that when they arrived decades ago, there were just sheep paddocks surrounding them. Some businesses, on the other hand, have pedigrees going back over a century.

Whatever the historical truth about the encroachment of industry upon housing and vice versa, in the 21st century, many residents here live cheek by jowl with industry. This includes companies such as Australian Tallow Producers (ATP), which makes meal and tallow from mixed abattoir meats, an inherently smelly process giving rise to residents complaining of a 'rotting carcass smell'. One resident related a time when 'my little girl had a party, and we had to pack up and move away [because of the odour].' They then intoned, 'How embarrassing is that?' Many industries in the Precinct operate trucks that deliver and take away heavy materials. This constant activity causes clouds of dust that deliver gusts of grit to the eyes and hazy plumes into the lives of residents, described by one resident as being 'really, really unsettling'. Another said she felt the dust was 'basically the equivalent of smoking'. Yet another resident, describing a smell from a chicken processing industry, complained, 'It will knock you out of your car sometimes'.

Many thousands of complaints are lodged each year with the EPA—some on a daily basis—principally about the effects of odour and dust.[26] Eventually, EPA Victoria decided to take a systemic approach to the area and develop a multifaceted compliance strategy. The then Chair, Cheryl Batagol, and former CEO, John Merritt, committed to taking action and to demonstrating leadership in addressing the challenges facing Brooklyn.[27] Partly, this involved taking a tougher approach to compliance and enforcement. But it also involved several restorative dimensions, which are our primary focus.

The key restorative example involved the establishment in 2008 of a Brooklyn Community Representative Group Community Forum (BCRG). With representatives drawn from the community, industry, local city councils and the regulator, this 'enabled government and industry to see the level of anger and frustration across the community first-hand, and

26 The Annual Report for 2023-24 notes that the EPA received 25,000 reports across the whole of Victoria. EPA Victoria, *Annual Report 2023–24*, www.epa.vic.gov.au/annual-report.

27 Jen Lilburn, 'Background and Achievements' (Brooklyn Community Representative Group: Background and Achievements, January 2014), 7, www.brooklynip.com.au/wp-content/uploads/2014/02/BCRG-BackgroundAndAchievements-Report-A4-170114-web.pdf.

this has driven the need for change'.[28] Nearly two decades later, it is still going strong.[29] The aim of the Forum was to jointly manage the ongoing problems facing the Precinct. It meets quarterly, and for 10 years, it had the same facilitator, allowing her to build up knowledge and trust with BCRG until she was finally replaced by another long-term facilitator.

Two key factors are behind the BCRG's successes. The first is the commitment by all involved to 'stay the course'. This long-term dedication reflects a key ethic of restorative practice, demonstrated by people showing up, meeting after meeting. The second factor is the commitment to place-based engagement—all meetings take place in the Brooklyn Community Hall, which is hired for the sessions and treated as the BCRG's 'permanent home'.[30]

The regular meetings often attract 40 to 50 people, with over 90 attending in 2010.[31] EPA Victoria, along with Brimbank City Council, made a formal commitment in 2012 'to ensure the community's aspirations are reflected in the actions they take, and to provide feedback about how BCRG informs their decisions'.[32] EPA Victoria initially covered the cost of the independent convenor (since our research, the responsibility has shifted to the industry participants covering this cost). The personal presence of senior members of the EPA appearing regularly at each meeting has increased the existing good rapport and respect with the community members who turn up. As well as EPA Victoria, local councils, local area industry representatives and invited experts attend meetings. Asked about the purpose of the BCRG, members have variously said it is about 'industry and community working together to support change', 'maintain[ing] the momentum', 'deliver[ing] a message in a constructive and considered manner', and 'a chance to network and talk'. Together, these opinions reflect the agonistic approach.[33] In particular, the BCRG was said to have 'given the community a stronger voice'.[34]

We classify these community reference forums or groups as restorative. This interpretation stems from their role in facilitating conversations that centre the problem of harm, as well as from their structure, which facilitates respectful listening to different voices in a non-hierarchical way. Everyone

28 Lilburn, *BCRG*, 2, 5.
29 See Brooklyn Industrial Precinct, *BCRG Community Forum Meeting Notes*, accessed 13 February 2025, www.brooklynip.com.au/bcrg-meeting-notes/?mc_cid=44fc3f0d1a&mc_eid=8b61f57a4c.
30 Lilburn, *BCRG*, 2.
31 Lilburn, *BCRG*, 2.
32 Lilburn, *BCRG*, 2, 8.
33 Lilburn, *BCRG*, 3–4.
34 Lilburn, *BCRG*, 5.

has an equal opportunity to speak, the differing community reflections are respected, and the most recent scientific data is presented and discussed alongside firsthand experiences. The repeated nature of these sessions enables ongoing development and the maintenance of relationships, thereby advancing communication between all groups and actors between meetings, and keeping doors open for greater engagement. Over time, the necessity of having to live together leads to acceptance, however begrudging, and mutual tolerance. In such a context, dialogue really is the only satisfactory way forward.

Our research team attended a number of meetings of CRGs interacting with EPA Victoria over four years. We were struck by the feeling of camaraderie in the room,[35] which coexisted alongside often heated discussions. Of course, we also heard bitter complaints from some community members about never receiving feedback after repeated calls to the EPA, while others professed a lack of trust in local companies' promises to improve, a standard refrain being: 'They're just lying.' Others complained that businesses only complied when EPA officers were conducting their inspections: 'My problem is with the operators emitting dust and blaming others. They don't give a shit when you are not there.'

At the end of these meetings, it was not unusual for us to step out into the dark street and be met by a distinct and unpleasant odour in the air, experiencing for ourselves briefly the same brutal sensory impact that impinged on the residents much of the time. On one such occasion, to our surprise, some of the residents and EPA Victoria odour experts immediately started an animated discussion, trying to identify the direction of the odour and its particular 'notes'. Was it more metallic or organic in nature?

We asked ourselves how such relationality develops in some contexts, while in others, similar processes result in formulaic check-a-box exercises with no emotional engagement or impact.[36]

35 We had this same impression when meeting over Zoom (virtual meeting application), as some of the meetings were held online during the pandemic lockdown periods.

36 The term 'relationality' refers to the quality or state of being relational—how individuals and groups connect, interact and understand each other within a given context. It involves the creation and nurturing of meaningful relationships that enable mutual understanding and collective action. See further Downie and Llewellyn, eds., *Being Relational*.

The answer, at least in part, seems to lie in sustained, place-based engagement and the willingness of all parties to remain in dialogue over time. Over the decade and a half of its operation, the BCRG has led to increased sharing of information with the community as well as greater involvement of the community in air-quality monitoring, which began in 2009. The regulatory response has been significantly shaped by attentiveness to and engagement with the community, helping to increase trust in the regulator, despite the underlying problems not being fully resolved to anyone's satisfaction.

Most recently, the Brooklyn Precinct became the inaugural site of a Better Environment Plan (BEP). The BEP is a new initiative under the EP Act 2017, aimed at supporting businesses to propose innovative solutions to issues likely to impact human health and the environment. The BEP commits four of the Brooklyn industries to identifying and implementing strategies to reduce dust pollution and improve air quality while maintaining communication with the local community.[37]

The BCRG has been complemented by other strategies to address pollution concerns, including the enforcement of licence conditions through sanctions. In this regard, innovative experiments in sanctioning have incorporated a restorative dimension, blending traditional enforcement with more community-centred approaches.

An example of this approach is the sanctioning of ATP in December 2015 for atmospheric pollution offences, resulting in a $200,000 fine. Rather than the fine being paid to consolidated revenue, however, EPA Victoria applied for a court order to direct the funds towards restoring relationships with the impacted community, using the mechanism we referred to in Chapter 2: a section 67AC order under the old EP Act 1970.[38]

This process enabled the EPA to work with the community to develop project proposals by local groups to use the funds. Eventually, a project run by the Hobsons Bay City Council was chosen to develop a recreation area to benefit the affected community. Through the social capital the EPA had built up in the Precinct, and its understanding of the existing needs and concerns, it was also able to identify a number of restorative project options that were ready to activate in the case of future infringements. This fostered an ongoing relationship between ATP and the community—ATP

37 EPA Victoria, 'Inner West Dust and Air Quality Has a Better Plan', *Delta Group* (n.d.), www.deltagroup.com.au/inner-west-dust-and-air-quality-has-a-better-plan/.

38 We will discuss section 67AC order in more detail in Chapter 7.

representatives continue to attend BCRG meetings, while their engagement with community has involved ongoing commitments. As recently as September 2023, ATP committed to a new community engagement plan, which included an online Community Notice Board, an Odour Monitoring Program, and an online reporting form.[39] In an email to BCRG, an ATP employee conveyed the following:

> We aim to operate in our community without any offsite impacts such as odour. If our systems are challenged, we want to know immediately if you are impacted so we can promptly address the cause. To avoid any delays in this information getting to us quickly, we have set up a Community Noticeboard on our website … This is the best way to ensure that the problem is addressed quickly. The Noticeboard will also keep you up to date on our progress and any necessary operational changes or maintenance programs that could have an unintended impact.[40]

The story of Brooklyn Industrial Precinct illustrates how different points of interaction between a regulator, community/victim and offender can be used to achieve a range of restorative processes and beneficial outcomes. Referring to the different types of citizen empowerment introduced above, we can see that the BCRG enabled knowledge and collective empowerment; the s67AC order enabled accountability empowerment; trust was built between the community and the regulator and many industries in the Precinct, and the BEP enabled deliberative empowerment.

The case study also illustrates several limitations of existing restorative approaches. For community members who feel obliged to bear the responsibility of remaining engaged over many years—shouldering unremunerated and often emotionally taxing work—there is a limit to how much can be expected without adequate support. Another challenge involves the relative inaccessibility of these processes for community members from linguistically diverse backgrounds. Further, constraints within regulatory frameworks mean that unmotivated offenders may have little to no incentive to alter their practices, leaving the community feeling frustrated and unheard. In turn, this can put pressure on regulators to be seen to be

39 The BCRG's public email newsletter, 21 September 2023 (on file); for the Community Notice Board and reporting form, see Australian Tallow Producers, 'Community Notice Board' (5 September 2023), austal.com.au/community-notice-board/.

40 BCRG public email newsletter, 21 September 2023.

responding—'arriving with flashing lights'—in ways that are performative but fail to enable the kinds of constructive dialogue and planning necessary to make sustainable changes in a complex environment.

A well-thought through and attentive restorative approach must take heed of these limitations and address them *with* community, not *for* community.

This is an appropriate point at which to explore other spaces and practices for restorative community engagement that EPA Victoria has experimented with over the past decade.

Town hall meetings

Historically, community pressure over the siting of a new industrial development near homes or the approval of a new disposal site for 'toxic' waste has led EPA Victoria to hold town hall-style meetings with concerned citizens. Town hall meetings are among the most common forms of community engagement used by regulators, often intended to provide information and offer the community an opportunity to 'have a say' through asking questions. However, while they do facilitate face-to-face discussion, they frequently fall short of meaningful democratic participation. Instead, they tend to be reactive, invite grandstanding and suffer from reduced inclusivity, despite their stated participatory aim.[41]

Many of our EPA interviewees raised serious concerns about town halls, particularly their failure to provide a suitable platform for independent and credible expert advice, and their inaccessibility to CALD communities. Between vociferous politicians, probing media, government officials keen to set the record straight, corporate lobbyists angling for good optics, and committed environmental NGOs, the voices of ordinary local citizens who lack the confidence or courage to speak up and navigate past noisier voices are often crowded out. Unless town halls intentionally create the conditions for the necessary relationships to exist, the potential for genuine citizen empowerment is limited.

41 See, for example, Samantha Villegas, 'For Better Engagement, Torch the Town Hall (Meeting)', Raftelis, accessed 13 February 2025, www.raftelis.com/insight/for-better-engagement-torch-the-town-hall-meeting/; Michael Zuckerman, 'Mirage of Democracy: The Town Meeting in America', *Journal of Deliberative Democracy* 15, no. 2 (2019); Natalie Ricklefs, 'Why Your In-Person Town Halls Aren't Reaching People', *Citizen Lab* (19 July 2022), archived at the Wayback Machine, web.archive.org/web/20231026135212/https://www.citizenlab.co/blog/civic-engagement/why-your-in-person-town-halls-arent-reaching-people/.

Recognising these shortcomings, EPA Victoria has experimented with more tailored approaches to community consultation. In the following section, we explore two such approaches—'Open Houses' and community reference groups. Some examples already demonstrate clear restorative values and outcomes, while others provide glimpses of restorative potential. In the latter cases, we highlight opportunities to further enhance the restorative nature of these new engagement structures.

Open Houses

The Open House format features a setup of booths or tables, typically peopled by experts from EPA Victoria and relevant industry members. The aim is to provide a more intimate level of engagement with the community through face-to-face chats. The format frequently includes information-sharing and distribution of free explanatory materials. The Open House often starts in the late afternoon and continues into the evening, meaning that residents can wander into a community hall with children or grandparents in tow, after school pickup or work, before or after dinner, attending at a time that suits them. Depending on the setup, community members can ask questions about what is being done to reduce environmental impacts and comply with environmental protection laws, view maps and diagrams, and explore information displays. In some cases, residents can even interact with portable monitoring or pollution management equipment, gaining a hands-on experience of how monitoring works.

EPA surveys of participant satisfaction with the quality of participation have confirmed higher levels of satisfaction from participants attending Open Houses (and also for information sessions for the EPA's former 'works approvals') compared to town hall meetings. This was confirmed to us across various EPA interviews.

Observation of an Open House

During our research, we observed an Open House set up specifically for the Brooklyn Industrial Precinct and hosted by the BCRG.

The Brooklyn Open House featured multiple tables. Behind one table sat an EPA water quality monitoring expert. At the next table, an air quality monitoring expert discussed pollution levels. Behind each table, graphs displayed the latest pollution monitoring trends. Further along, an EPA officer was seated with a drone, dynamically demonstrating how this new, detective-based technology could scan for pollution hotspots. Addressing the residents gathered around, the officer explained how drones provide value above and beyond traditional stationary sampling and trend-based monitoring.

Moving along, we observed the industry tables. One such table was operated by Cedar Meats, a large —and sometimes smelly—abattoir. Its outreach staff were actively responding to the citizens who came with questions.

The next table was set up for the very large infrastructure company Transurban and its contractors, CPB Contractors and John Holland, along with the Western Distributor Authority. Together, these entities were managing the West Gate Tunnel Project, which involved digging a tunnel for the nearby West Gate expressway to provide a second means for crossing the river alongside the West Gate Bridge. They displayed project plans for discussion, highlighting proposed rehabilitation efforts that included tree planting and 14 kilometres of bike and walking paths, promising a continuous bike transit from Werribee to the city. Their pitch for the West Gate Tunnel included the claim that their smart management technologies to steer traffic flow would reduce pollution from cars and 'remove thousands of trucks from residential streets'.[42] Many attendees visiting this table were openly cynical, with many reiterating existing community concerns related to the potential for the release of toxic chemicals from old industrial sites disturbed by the excavation.[43]

Further tables featured representatives from additional companies, each answering questions about their particular pollution and waste impacts. Some corporate tables were almost totally focused on positive messages. For example, the message conveyed at the table for Sims Metal centred around their strategy of collaborating with building and construction waste recyclers to purchase the metal retrieved from concrete for recycling purposes.[44]

42 West Gate Tunnel Project, 'What We're Building: About', 18 February 2022, bigbuild.vic.gov.au/projects/west-gate-tunnel-project/about.

43 Meg Hill, 'Health Fears for Tunnel Project', *Dockland News*, 4 September 2019, www.docklandsnews.com.au/health-fears-for-tunnel-project_15623.

44 Sims Metal self describes itself as 'A Leading Metal Recycling Company' that buys, processes and sells ferrous and non-ferrous recycled metals: 'About Us: A Leading Metal Recycling Company', Sims Metal, accessed 13 February 2025, www.simsmm.com/about-us/.

Recovered Energy Australia explained how they conduct waste gasification conversion to energy from the contents of household waste bins.[45] Their literature claimed they will generate enough energy recovery to provide electricity for 16,000 homes from this gasification plant, with minimal local pollution. Some community members remained cynical, saying that the rich who create most waste should have this 'minimal pollution' in *their* backyards.

Hence, the challenges, risks and opportunities associated with 'progress' in a developed economy can be seen to play out in a local-scale precinct that stands at the crux of its history and transformation.

Finally, but importantly, two local councils (Brimbank City Council and Hobsons Bay City Council) had their own tables. These two councils often provide venues for the Open House forums and for some environmental organisations. They, too, had informative materials available and brought their local expertise to respond to questions. In each case, their presence gave local residents an opportunity to talk directly with council officers and community-based organisations about actions that could be taken to address local pollution issues.

Addressing the challenges of recording an Open House

Compared to the town hall meeting, the community hall is noisy in an Open House. Twenty conversations may be going on simultaneously at many tables, some with a little cluster of people standing together, others with citizens seated together around a table. Another couple stands sharing stories over cups of coffee just outside the hall. The cacophony of conversations, although a vibrant sign of democracy in action, does mean that recording the wisdom distilled from conversations can be difficult, for both regulator and business alike.[46] So, while the Open House may be superior to a town hall meeting in terms of participative empowerment, enabling community members to interact with the specialist experts and duty holders to discuss specific concerns, it is a challenging forum for listening deeply to, and taking on board, community feedback and concerns.

---

45 Recovered Energy Australia is a company that self-describes as being 'committed to converting household waste into a source of clean power', through 'gasification technology', 'What We Do', Recovered Energy Laverton, accessed 13 February 2025, www.recoveredenergy.com.au/what-we-do.

46 By 'recording,' we mean documenting or making note (in writing) of key points and issues raised by community members for record-keeping or prompts for future action; we do not mean using an audio device.

Several factors compensated for the limitations of the Open House format in recording community feedback. One approach involved experts and duty holders at each table sometimes taking notes of what was said to them. However, more often they did not do so, most likely due to the pressures of interacting with multiple individuals simultaneously. Another approach was the gathering of the dozen or so EPA table-masters at a 'stand-up' debriefing session after everyone else had left, where they discussed the biggest and most recurring concerns raised by attendees. This session ended with a reminder that a more formal meeting would soon follow to consolidate the learnings from the Open House, which we were later able to observe. It is important to note that only messages that came to EPA tables were compiled at this stand-up circle. Yet, some decisive responses resulted from this discussion, notably because many citizens expressed concerns about a specific problem with a particular duty holder. As a result, it was agreed that a site inspection would be scheduled to address this matter 'pronto'.

We detail the recording efforts because we think that the degree to which community members perceive their messages as being heard and accounted for is crucial. When an effort is made to note down community concerns and suggestions, it provides an important visual cue for residents, reassuring them that their input has been recorded and will be actioned in some way. Some restorative thinkers argue that a group recounting of what has occurred is essential to the emotional transformation that is a hallmark of collaborative problem-solving, as well as for fostering a shared sense of ownership of the solutions, which is typical of restorative approaches.[47]

An alternative method to record such events could be borrowed from the practice around *SpeakOuts*, another form of Open Houses. The developers of *SpeakOuts*, Wendy Sarkissian and Andrea Cook, explain:

> A trained Listener pays close attention to what people are saying and asks pertinent questions, while all their comments are clearly recorded (on butcher's paper or pre-printed panels/exercise sheets) by a trained Recorder. A range of interpretive material is used to encourage people to comment on issues of local concern. This is really a 'listening session' focussing on the community's views.

47 For example, Meredith Rossner, a criminologist and restorative justice scholar at The Australian National University, holds to this theory.

> As the *SpeakOut* progresses, the walls of the venue become covered with community views. Reading their neighbours' comments often encourages shy and hesitant people to speak out.[48]

The *SpeakOuts* creators note that, over time, they have developed the practice of engaging community members to take on the role of 'Listener' (facilitator), providing training and support for them to do this effectively themselves. They actively seek to include community members who speak other languages as community facilitators, noting that while having translators can sometimes be impractical, bilingual community facilitators help to increase participation.

Interactive activities at Open Houses and other community forums

A fun interactive element at one table of the Brooklyn Open House that really grabbed our attention was the display of gas canisters containing actual odours from the Brooklyn Industrial Precinct. The odours spanned a spectrum of offensive smells, from the pungency of a 'rending' smell of animal flesh from ATP to the acrid tang of paint thinner and the foul stench of decomposing organics. Through an interactive game, citizens were invited to 'guess the odour'. The rationale was not only to provide a hands-on display to encourage participation, but also to teach the community to identify the possible sources of the odours they were likely to report. A wheel of odour with character descriptors complemented this 'training of the nose' of citizens so that they could become better at distinguishing sulphurous odours from odours emanating from solvents, petrol, rotting, putrid waste, and different kinds of animal and vegetable waste. This ability to guess the odour can offer real benefits: whenever citizens can correctly identify the odours they are perceiving, this can, in turn, help EPA officers who do inspections to better ascertain the source of the odours, potentially allowing for quicker resolution.

48 Wendy Sarkissian and Andrea Cook, *Speaking Out in Community Engagement: A Review of Fifteen Years of Refinement of the* SpeakOut *Model* (Social Planning and Research Council of BC, 2000), www.sparc.bc.ca/wp-content/uploads/2020/11/speaking-out-in-community-engagement.pdf, 3. A *SpeakOut* is an 'interactive staffed exhibition that aims to provide an informal and interactive "public meeting" environment where a wide range of people have a chance to participate … [through] … structured "drop-in" participation': Andrea Cook, 'What Exactly is a SpeakOut?', *Wendy Sarkissian, PhD* (blog), accessed 13 February 2025, sarkissian.com.au/publications/inspired-books/speakout-the-ultimate-workshop-guide/what-exactly-is-a-speakout/.

This interactive display is a creative example of relational activity. It aligns the community's knowledge and perceptions with the regulatory lens of the EPA, strengthening citizen empowerment through knowledge. It also builds mutual understanding and, in the best case, rapport between all parties, contributing to the building of trust.

In addition, psychology research demonstrates that getting people moving and engaged in collaborative activities can have a dramatic impact in overcoming fixed viewpoints and entrenched disputes. As psychologist Peter T. Coleman explains:

> Recent advances in neuroscience and social science research have documented the benefits of movement—cognitive, motivational, emotional, and physical—for increasing our neuroplasticity (brain flexibility) and openness to new experiences. To find a way out of entrenched patterns, both simple locomotion and synchronization with others can free us and rewire our experiences and relations in a manner that can lead to more creative and constructive patterns in our life.[49]

In contrast, events reliant on seating participants in rows to keep them orderly, as happens in town hall meetings, are less likely to promote movement and may therefore miss the opportunity to inspire this type of shared learning opportunity.

Interactive activities can also capture the attention of children through being more engaging and fun. Through encouraging 'playfulness', children's voices can be brought forth with little or no prompting, as long as facilitators are paying attention. The perspectives of children on environmental issues are critical for enabling a more comprehensive understanding of the impacts. Interactive activities can also engage youth in proactive problem-solving rather than their feeling hopeless and disenfranchised.[50]

---

49 Peter T. Coleman, *The Way Out: How to Overcome Toxic Polarization* (Columbia University Press, 2021), 166, doi.org/10.7312/cole19740.

50 Anna Orrnert, *Youth Initiatives: Supporting Citizen Engagement with Government and Civic Life*, GSDRC Helpdesk Research Report 1418 (GSDRC, University of Birmingham, 2018), gsdrc.org/wp-content/uploads/2018/03/Youth_initiatives_citizen_engagement.pdf.

To illustrate this, we relate a story about the healing experience of children attending Gowrie Clare Court Early Learning Centre, located near a local water source known as Stony Creek, in Melbourne's western suburbs.[51] At the end of August 2018, an industrial fire broke out in a chemical storage warehouse in Tottenham, a suburb in western Melbourne. It became known as the 'Tottenham industrial fire'. Contaminants from the fire flowed into Stony Creek, including pollutants such as hydrocarbons, acetone, herbicides and heavy metals. This incident caused the deaths of many animals, including some 2,500 fish, and of trees and other plants.[52]

Having earlier participated in an Indigenous knowledge program for 3- to 5-year-olds, which had sought to help the children to think about Stony Creek through the perspective of its Traditional Owners, they spoke of 'Creek' as being one of them. When the catastrophe came, the children were deeply hurt.[53] This became clear from their submissions to a parliamentary inquiry held into the incident. In one parliamentary submission, the children explained that 'Creek is very sad'. In another, a three-year-old girl from the local kindergarten remarked: 'We've got to listen to the trees, they're drinking the poison.' Similarly, Annabelle from Clare Court echoed this sentiment in her submission, saying: 'We need to listen to the trees. Their roots are drinking the poison. They will show us.' Both of these young girls got it.

Other children's submissions made to the parliamentary inquiry were mainly in the form of paintings. Through their artwork, the children sent messages about their friend, Creek, who should be seen as having rights as a creek, just like they have rights as children. The youngest children of West Footscray were the ones who added the inspiring restorative vision that we all need to engage when healing from environmental trauma, to better understand that we suffer as one with our Creek, our trees, our sky.

---

51 Stony Creek flows through the western suburbs of Melbourne, namely, St Albans, Albion, Sunshine, Braybrook, Tottenham, Brooklyn, Kingsville and Yarraville. It eventually joins the Yarra River under the Westgate Bridge. Its overall condition is poor; it is mainly contained within concrete drain structures and, in some places, purposefully redirected underground. In the more natural sections of the creek, members of the Friends of Stony Creek, a local volunteer community group, have been actively restoring it by replanting native vegetation and removing invasive weeds, along with other conservation efforts.

52 EPA Victoria, 'The Tottenham Industrial Fire', updated 12 May 2025, www.epa.vic.gov.au/tottenham-industrial-fire. This fire is known by EPA Victoria as the 'Tottenham industrial fire' and by others as the 'West Footscray industrial fire'.

53 Parliament of Victoria Legislative Council Environment and Planning Committee, *Inquiry into Recycling and Waste Management: Interim Report* (Victorian Government Printer, August 2019), new.parliament.vic.gov.au/4a4bf9/contentassets/631c8359ad7f4dc487aef9d986fae1e7/interim-report-inquiry-into-recycling-and-waste.pdf.

To their credit, the parliamentarians listened and gave prominence to the paintings of the children in their report.

No 'wrong door'

Our community interviews underscored just how problematic 'wrong doors' are, especially in times of crisis. 'Wrong doors' means individuals seeking help are turned away from a range of access points and have to search to find the right 'door'. In the case of the Tottenham industrial fire, the issue of wrong doors took centre stage when no agency or authority could offer good answers on how serious the problem would ultimately prove to be. In West Footscray, for example, residents grew increasingly exasperated at what they perceived as the Maribyrnong Council, Melbourne Water, EPA Victoria, and the Metropolitan Fire Brigade each shifting responsibility to one other over something that appeared to warrant accountability from at least one of them. One EPA officer explained to us that:

> [Communities] don't understand the difference between what a Council can do, what a planning authority can do, what a regulator can do and what different regulators can do within their regulatory framework, and nor should they. For me, some of the really important features where we're in an approvals system is jointly running a process with Council, for example. So typically, in Victoria, to approve something that is 'scheduled', it needs a works approval[54] from EPA and … a planning permit from local government.
>
> So, there are two must-haves that sort of run a local government process separate to an EPA process, which just confuses people. They don't know who looks after trucks going in and out, who looks after open and closing hours at this facility, and they shouldn't have to know that. So, running those processes together is very important, and … now, with an EES [Environmental Effects Statement] process as well, [it] tends to centralise approvals, which I think is a very useful thing.
>
> But those Open House sessions—if you've got Council, EPA, proponents, interest groups and so forth, it's just really important that people can circulate between those different points of information to understand and to talk directly to people about what their role is and where they can help with their concerns. Because it's hopeless for us to say we can't talk about trucks entering the premises because

54 A 'works approval' is now known as a 'development licence' under the EP Act 2017.

> that's outside of our regulatory agreement—that's very unhelpful … Actually, those conditions are part of the planning permit; let's walk over here and talk to the planning guy.

By having tables representing many different parts of the regulatory problem, an Open House offers the community some level of transparency and accountability. In effect, it provides a 'no-wrong-door' resolution to questions arising from anyone in the community who wishes to ask. The diversity of perspectives offered in this way, and the responsiveness of the government and industry officers, when they share information openly, is inherently restorative. However, as we discuss next, achieving true restorative effectiveness in the Open House requires careful design.

Enhancing the restorative nature of an Open House

It is important to consider how the Open House format can best support the different facets of citizen empowerment as we have defined them above.

EPA Victoria has noted and applied the potential of using breakout areas to facilitate more focused or private opportunities for discussion. However, if Open Houses are not tied to particular events and actions, it has to be accepted that their purpose leans more towards knowledge and collaboration empowerment, such as through information-sharing, opening up pathways of two-way communications and checking in on broader common objectives.

The physical presence of regulatory officers is critical to the effectiveness of Open Houses. In some ways, their presence responds to the request the public often has for bureaucrats to 'front up and be real'. In this way, having regulatory officers available for direct interactions helps build the interpersonal relationship dimension of relational justice and through this, the relational underpinnings necessary for citizen empowerment. Answering questions about people's concerns and fears face-to-face is very different from putting information on a website that requires an individual to do the work of answering their own query. Open Houses can serve an important function for the community to feel they have been heard, and their questions honestly engaged with, even if they do not hear the result they are hoping for.

However, this is not just about the regulators being present. Those who have caused the problems must also be present. While we have related that some industry representatives were present in the Precinct story, a critical comment asserted by attendees at this Open House was that the polluters often do *not* turn up. One Open House attendee stated that alleged polluters won't come 'if they know they are going to be beaten up. They come when they have a good story to tell about improvement they have made.'[55]

When they do come, it must be for more than handing out glossy pamphlets of good deeds—they also need to engage with the community face-to-face, respectfully and with integrity. This is critical for ensuring active accountability, a key restorative principle. Ideally, they can explain what motivated their harmful actions and detail their repair intentions candidly, using straightforward, clear and simple language that the community can easily understand, as well as being willing to respond to the questions—and, yes, even the anger and frustration—of affected residents. This places an onus on business and industry to ensure they send the people who have the authority, experience and capability to engage openly with community. It is preferable that the CEO or head of the organisation attend as well, the one person who has the real authority and credibility to say, 'Yes, we hear you and we are sorry. We are fixing that. We will make sure it does not happen again.'

Even though some of the polluters they wanted to engage with were absent, participants at our observation felt the Open House format was information-rich and crucial in reducing anger and adversarial attitudes. This framing persisted, despite some of the community members and staff from EPA Victoria whom we interviewed perceiving it as a form of pacification rather than an unmitigated good. As discussed earlier, outrage is the essence of constructive politics that should motivate fixing the problem that drives the outrage. In John Braithwaite's view, regulators that seek to placate outrage rather than harness it to projects of transformation are not being serious about their mission. By contrast, regulators guided by a duty of care to their staff and community participants must seek to address problems and resolve issues in the most constructive ways possible.

We suggest that a hybrid design of Open Houses might strengthen their restorative nature. In other words, this would place the emphasis on having many one-on-ones and many small group encounters. These could be combined and sequenced with town hall-style meeting features that cater for a large group recounting their grievances. Such an approach would enable a full palette of restorative possibilities. In this mix, the town

55 Recorded during our research observation of a participation at an Open House observation.

hall-style meeting acts as a 'plenary', 'so everyone gets to hear at least some key themes',[56] while the Open House-style layout allows for developing the understandings and initial connections. Inclusion of a more restorative process can then emerge to ensure deep listening, long-term connectedness and ongoing repair.

Making Open Houses more restorative through an integrated feedback loop

> When it comes to in-person meetings, without a strong feedback loop to create continuous information and engagement they can have a high time and effort cost with seemingly low benefit, significantly limiting their reach.[57]

From our observations, Open Houses represent strong but vulnerable shoots of restorative regulation. The practice around them was rich and creative at EPA Victoria. However, they are costly in terms of human facilitation and financial resources, making them inherently susceptible to cost-cutting measures. To keep the advantages implicit in Open Houses going and make them more open to restorative innovations, an explicit authorising environment is needed that offers clear support and rules that allow them to self-sustain in the long term.

To make Open Houses more restorative and justify their use, they could be integrated more explicitly and robustly into the regulator's monitoring and compliance systems. At present, Open Houses are good opportunities for the regulator to gain valuable community information about what is happening in a particular locale. Yet, as our concerns about recording highlighted, there are no mechanisms to collate the information gathered and feed it back to the relevant sections within the regulator.

One way to improve this integration would be to explicitly require the use of Open Houses to support ongoing compliance and monitoring, especially when incidents occur. In cases where persistent concerns exist, such as the Brooklyn Industrial Precinct, it is important to keep the community informed. This can be achieved through developing consistent practices. The costs involved should not be borne solely by regulators—companies responsible for pollution or accidents should contribute. This could be a condition of a permit, licence, or even a condition of a penalty or

56 Interview with an EPA officer.
57 Ricklefs, 'Why Your In-Person Town Halls Aren't Reaching People'.

judgment outcome. Regulatory guidelines could use directives to set the expectations for regular information sessions to keep the community updated on mitigating, repair and preventive actions. Businesses should also be responsive to community feedback, including a requirement to report back to the regulator on progress in their community engagement efforts.

This integrated, restorative approach would create a cohesive feedback loop that encompasses regulator, regulatees and community, guaranteeing that information flows bi-directionally. Having in place a 'clear feedback loop … [ensures] people feel their opinions are being heard and see a direct impact for contributing to real policy action'.[58] The loop further ensures that community feedback is reaching those responsible for repair, mitigation and prevention of harm, fully embodying the restorative values of citizen empowerment through participation and engagement.

Community reference groups

We first introduced community reference groups (CRGs) when discussing the emergence and operation of the Brooklyn Community Reference Group (BCRG). Now we turn to a broader exploration of their role and impact.

A community reference group (CRG) is a forum that regularly brings together representatives of the local community and the offending company or companies, other local industry, the regulator, local council(s), and any additional regulators or key actors of relevance. In addition, the CRG may request to have visiting specialists, subject-matter experts, parliamentarians and other individuals the community wants to hear from. A CRG will meet regularly to give feedback, ask questions, discuss issues and raise the impacts its members are experiencing. For the main part, CRGs are geared towards empowering participants through increased knowledge and collaboration. They do this by creating and sustaining relationships between government, regulators, duty holders and community, offering regular opportunities to engage in facilitated dialogue. Ideally, this breeds greater collective understanding and awareness of the problem(s), possible solutions and who is responsible for fixing them.

Community reference groups are formed in response to a wide range of situations in Victoria, but most commonly in response to an application for an operating licence or permit. A CRG provides an appropriate forum for a company or local council to explain to the community how it will

58 Ricklefs, 'Why Your In-Person Town Halls Aren't Reaching People'.

comply with licence or permit conditions. It also offers a chance to outline ongoing monitoring efforts to prevent future harm. Just as importantly, these entities must explain what guarantees they will give as to making these results available to the CRG, including timeframes and accessibility for community enquiries.

The convention is that site owners bear the responsibility for managing CRGs. This is an appropriate expectation with respect to the responsiveness to operational issues that the CRG can facilitate, and expedient in terms of the resourcing required to sustain it over the long term. While cynicism about the industrial site's owner having responsibility for CRGs is understandable, the argument in support is that the business is responsible for managing the site, placing them in the best position to address issues as they arise and quickly implement improvements.

The site owner's responsiveness to concerns the community raises increases when direct lines of communication are kept open for engagement between an operator and its neighbours, provided there is sufficient trust to support this. For instance, we have observed CRGs in which companies have provided a direct phone number for residents to call at any time of day or night to report noises or odours, with a commitment that the company will respond swiftly where possible. Similarly, ATP's noticeboard and reporting form, discussed earlier in this chapter, is another way to enhance responsiveness to community.

What we learned from observing community reference groups

We have learned about CRGs not only through our interviews with stakeholders (EPA Victoria, community members, local government and industry) but also directly through our participation as observers in several such groups. In particular, we observed two CRGs over the course of several years. The first is the BCRG discussed earlier, while the second involved a CRG set up by the company AkzoNobel to address community health concerns about odour and noise emitted from its processes.

AkzoNobel is a Dutch multinational paint and coatings manufacturer that has run a facility in the western Melbourne suburb of Sunshine North for over 65 years.[59] In this instance, the community had expressed numerous

59 AkzoNobel Pty Ltd, *Communications and Engagement Strategy*, March 2021, www.akzonobel.com/content/dam/akzonobel-corporate/global/en/regional-assets/australia/akzonobel-communications-and-engagement-strategy-2021.pdf; 'About Us', AkzoNobel, accessed 13 February 2025, www.akzonobel.com/en/about-us.

concerns about the Sunshine North facility emitting smells and noises that were disrupting the lives of locals and causing them health concerns. AkzoNobel formed the CRG with the aim of being 'a good neighbour' and generating 'community confidence that its operations will not cause negative offsite impacts'.[60] Initially, there were several meetings held in the space of the first month, reflecting the intensity of local concerns and the need to be fully attentive. During our observations, we noted that senior management, including the CEO, would turn up to the regular community meetings to acknowledge the concerns, face questions and answer them. Of particular note was the determination of the CEO to be open, to follow up the community concerns and to give constant updates on the promised solutions to reduce odour and noise. This promise included creating and staffing a direct reporting line to the company and making regular website updates. EPA Victoria was also in attendance at the meetings.

The concerns were not materially addressed as quickly as the community would have liked, due principally to global supply chain problems caused by the COVID-19 pandemic. However, the CEO and other members from management continued to front up and explain what was being done to fix the problems and were willing to respond openly to questions from all members of the community present. In seeking to maintain its relationship with community, AzkoNobel has since continued to hold community meetings. It also has a 'report a complaint' button on the front page of its website, makes Community Report Tables public, and provides updated information for community 'to keep the community of Sunshine North informed about the facility and act as a means for members of the community to provide feedback and post questions to AkzoNobel'.[61]

By bringing together responsible duty holders several times a year for direct engagement with concerned citizens and community organisations, site-based CRGs exemplify restorative practice. In providing a forum where the duty holder explains how they are exercising their duties and answers community questions, we observed that site-based CRGs support core restorative practices such as healing, accountability, safety, deep listening and citizen empowerment.

60 AkzoNobel, *Communications and Engagement Strategy*, 3.
61 'AkzoNobel Sunshine North Community Hub', AkzoNobel, 2025, www.akzonobel.com/en/countries/australia.

Yet, as with many a well-intentioned commitment to regular group participation, long-term momentum relies heavily on enthusiastic leadership and dedicated community members. Interest can easily wane, whether through natural attrition, busy lives or dwindling enthusiasm. Continued participation is often rooted in participants' sense of scope for effecting change. If the scope for change is not demonstrated through identifiable results achieved promptly, the impetus for participation often diminishes. As one EPA officer described when relating a CRG's evolution over time, the group's longevity brings its own issues and is not necessarily reflective of its success. The same officer went on to explain their concern that people either 'aren't actually from the area' or that 'a lot of them don't show up'.

These are real challenges. However, awareness of the challenges and limitations is the first step towards learning how to respond effectively and reignite the momentum. This might mean strengthening the resources available to CRGs, making long-term ongoing engagement a licence condition or showcasing industry champions who have modelled excellent practice in working with these groups.

The value of community reference groups for restorative regulation

Successful CRGs need committed leadership, resource support and realisation of actual change. When done right, they are worth the effort, serving as a powerful example of the restorative value of citizen empowerment. By giving communities control of the conversation, CRGs help legitimise the social licence to operate, encouraging permit and duty holders to come to the table and engage meaningfully.

Other restorative values are met through CRGs. These include:

- **accountability**. By facilitating direct engagement with the licence holders and local industry representatives, CRGs can publicly encourage responsible actions and decision-making.
- **safety**. In creating a safe space where constructive dialogue can occur, CRGs promote an environment where participants feel comfortable sharing their viewpoints and experiences.
- **deep listening**. The way in which CRGs are conducted encourages attentiveness to diverse perspectives expressed by multiple stakeholders. This enables greater understanding and fosters empathy.
- **healing**. The accountability, safety and deep listening aspects of the CRGs lead to healing, as the open dialogue between stakeholders allows everyone to work through and address underlying conflict or concerns.

- **prevention**. By requiring ongoing meetings to provide action updates, the CRG process encourages proactive and collaborative efforts to prevent future harm and keeps the focus on the community's wellbeing.
- **learning and growth**. In providing a forum for experts to attend and where all participants can express their lived experiences and impacts, everyone present has the opportunity to learn and grow. Whether it is learning from mistakes or from expertise, more effective practices can be developed together to move forward constructively.
- **long-term engagement**. The value inherent in CRGs as an ongoing forum promotes sustained dialogue, the building and maintenance of relationships between stakeholders, and consistency of engagement. This element is essential for all forms of restorative empowerment.

By actively supporting CRGs through resource allocation, guidance, attendance at meetings, and placing expectations on permit holders and duty holders to be involved in CRGs, regulators can help nurture an environment where restorative values thrive.

Neighbourhood Environment Improvement Plans

During our research, we looked at one other engagement practice—Neighbourhood Environment Improvement Plans, usually known as 'NEIPs'. Neighbourhood Environment Improvement Plans formed part of the EP Act 1970, having been introduced in 2001. While they were not reintroduced in the EP Act 2017, EPA's experience with them yielded a valuable lesson worth sharing.

Neighbourhood Environment Improvement Plans were voluntary statutory agreements pioneered by EPA Victoria.[62] As part of 'second generation' environmental law at the time, they 'abandon[ed] command and control in favour of collaboration and community-based decision-making' and 'specifically engage[d] with diffuse and complex environmental problems at a neighbourhood geographic scale'.[63] These plans sought to develop community-based partnerships that accounted for the triad of economic, social and environmental considerations at the heart of sustainable development. Cary et al. described them thus:

62 Neil Gunningham, Cameron Holley, and Clifford Shearing, 'Neighbourhood Environment Improvement Plans: Community Empowerment, Voluntary Collaboration and Legislative Design', *Environmental and Planning Law Journal* 24, no. 2 (2007): 126.

63 Gunningham et al. 'Neighbourhood Environment Improvement Plans', 126.

> They typically involve a wide range of individuals, municipalities, water authorities, businesses and community-based organisations, which all have an important role to play in resolving broad-scale or diffuse source pollution. NEIPs are founded in community agreement and participation and can provide a direct response to community priorities for environmental improvements. The result of the extensive consultation between the various parties to a NEIP is a binding agreement between the various parties that is given statutory status by the Act.[64]

Earlier EPA pilot experiments with NEIPs faced significant challenges, particularly in sustaining participation.[65] While communities collaborated well to reach consensus, fundamental problems associated with resourcing likely exacerbated the other challenges NEIPs faced, including their complicated and drawn-out processes, the overly heavy reliance on volunteerism, and the difficulty of maintaining diverse community engagement. Additionally, their effectiveness was further eroded by regulator perceptions of costs outweighing benefits, and community perceptions that government controlled the decision-making and which actions went ahead. Despite their initial promise and innovative nature, NEIPs failed to gain traction due to these unresolved flaws. So, when the EP Act 2017 was drafted, it was no surprise that NEIPs were left behind.

The key lesson from the NEIPs' underwhelming legacy is that a collective approach only works if it has sustained funding and sufficient flexibility to build on existing pockets of collective efficacy.[66] Neighbourhood Environment Improvement Plans revealed a flaw in the imposition of overly specific initiatives on certain communities. The effort to establish a framework of community meetings may have been too ambitious, straining resources in pursuit of success. A better approach might be to let community participation to emerge organically—much like an architect waits for 'desire

64 Joanna Cary, Henry Jackson, and Wayne Gumley, 'Statutory Tools for Environmental Protection in Victoria—The Next Generation', *National Environmental Law Review*, no. 2 (2004): 38, www5.austlii.edu.au/au/journals/NatEnvLawRw/2004/34.pdf.

65 Gunningham et al., 'Neighbourhood Environment Improvement Plans'; Cameron Holley and Darren Sinclair, 'Deliberative Participation, Environmental Law and Collaborative Governance: Insights from Surface and Groundwater Studies', *Environmental and Planning Law Journal* 30, no. 1 (2013): 32–55.

66 Collective efficacy refers to a community's shared belief in its ability to work together effectively to achieve common goals, maintain social order and overcome challenges through mutual trust and coordinated action. See further the seminal article on collective efficacy by Robert J. Sampson, Stephen W. Raudenbush, and Felton Earls, 'Neighborhoods and Violent Crime: A Multilevel Study of Collective Efficacy', *Science* 277, no. 5328 (1997): 918–24, doi.org//10.1126/science.277.5328.918.

paths' to form before paving them in place, responding directly to what the public determines will work for its needs.[67] This way, the process evolves in step with the community's capacity, interests and motivations.

Our fieldwork suggests that expecting regulators to be flexible, adaptable and open to emerging community-led practices is not overly idealistic. Practically every creek near a city in Victoria has a 'Friends of the Creek' group, making it easy to identify local community groups and alliances that can be galvanised. Involving these groups and organisations is also a respectful way to include First Nations peoples in the conversation.

One Friends of the Creek group we interviewed fondly recalled the joy of welcoming students, civil engineers, bankers and other corporate workers to their river care activities. They highlighted how a spontaneous 'boot banquet, food out the boot of our cars!' became a simple but powerful way to draw people in. The shared experience of food and conversation, a human ritual as old as time, helped foster connections. One interviewee described how a casual morning tea chat led to a corporate participant taking on the role of group treasurer, adding that 'with food like this, it was nothing subtle!'.[68] This bonding between outside participants and the community group has come to matter to the workers who attend, to the point where one interviewee noted how some of the corporate participants were genuinely disappointed when told the group could only find space for them in working bees once a year.

A garden of varietals: Diverse approaches to restorative citizen empowerment

An integral restorative insight from our interviews is that combining different engagement methods creatively and responsively can be highly effective. Each stage of the participatory spectrum, from outrage to genuine collaboration, contains the seeds for more restorative approaches to take root and grow.

67 Desire paths or lines are the pathways people (and other animals) make, usually reflective of the most direct route, arising organically from what people prefer in their daily navigations. Robert McFarlane has described them as 'free-will ways', indicative of their emergent, unplanned appearance. Once they emerge, they can be harnessed as part of final design outcomes. Sian Johnson, 'What Desire Paths Can Tell Us About Safer, Better Public Spaces', *ABC News*, 23 April 2023, www.abc.net.au/news/2023-04-23/desire-paths-offer-insight-into-use-of-public-spaces/102191044.

68 Interview with the Friends of the Creek group.

A strong example of this interwoven restorative approach can be seen in the case of the Stevenson Brothers Industries (SBI) landfill. Located in Ballarto Road, Cranbourne—a suburb of Melbourne—SBI's landfill is a site licensed by EPA Victoria to process solid, inert wastes such as construction and demolition materials. Typically, this type of landfill is considered to pose a lower odour risk due to the minimal organic content. However, during a period of cold weather, following various site management issues, the SBI landfill started emitting strong 'rotten egg' odours (hydrogen sulphide). Local residents quickly filed numerous complaints with the EPA, but regulatory action failed to prevent the environmental issue from escalating. Frustration mounted, resulting in many frayed tempers.

Once the scale of the issue became apparent, EPA Victoria wanted to intervene using a restorative approach centred on direct personal contact. They began with online community information sessions, enrolling around 200 people to the first meeting.[69] While attendees had their questions answered, it was clear the format limited opportunities for expressing the understandable raw emotions. Recognising this, the EPA shifted its approach to a series of in-person 'pop-up' dialogues, allowing for more open and immediate interactions. Times and locations for the pop-ups were widely shared on social media to ensure broad community participation.

As a locally owned company, SBI was able to be more responsive to the community and actively engaged at every stage. Since July 2022, its website has featured regular updates to the community, including apologies for the 'inconvenience' caused and ongoing thanks to the community for reporting issues to the EPA, providing crucial data to help the company identify and address the problem.[70] The pop-ups led to the establishment of a community consultative committee, aimed at:

> providing a forum for discussion between the local community, stakeholders and SBI. The committee addresses issues relating to the landfill's operations, acts as a conduit to keep the community informed, and allows for SBI to receive collective feedback.[71]

69 This took place during the COVID-19 lockdown periods. Virtual meetings were necessary as the pandemic measures prevented in-person gatherings.

70 For an example, see SBI Group, 'Update from SBI Group—Friday 24th January 2025', www.sbiinertlandfill.com/news/. The earliest of these bulletins is dated 5 July 2022.

71 SBI Group, 'Community Consultative Committee', accessed 26 March 2026, www.sbiinertlandfill.com/community-investment/.

One regulator observed that it is now possible for all the parties to communicate about the issues with a degree of familiarity and trust that did not previously exist.

However, SBI's response was insufficient, leading EPA Victoria to suspend its licence and prosecute the company in the Supreme Court. SBI Landfill Pty Ltd was ordered to pay $200,000 'for the carrying out of a project for the restoration or enhancement of the environment in a public place or for the public benefit'.[72] The EPA interpreted SBI's agreement to this order as an acknowledgement to the community that it had failed to comply with its operating licence by not containing the odours to its site.[73]

This case study highlights the importance of both the regulator and the regulatee being willing to adapt and shift between different approaches to support community empowerment. When initial engagement efforts fail to capture the necessary breadth and depth of community input, a flexible approach allows for more responsive and inclusive engagement strategies. At times, it also requires the use of punitive sanctions, such as licence suspension and prosecution. A truly restorative and responsive approach involves remaining attentive to what works, being creative in exploring alternatives, and allowing space for the community to organically define the participatory framework that best meets its needs.

Other possible spaces for preventing harm through community engagement

Across the regulatory spectrum, numerous opportunities exist to empower citizens to proactively build relationships, learn from multiple perspectives and co-produce harm-prevention strategies.

One possibility lies in developing relational approaches for prioritising major community concerns. For example, the engagement process could draw inspiration from citizens' juries, a deliberative and participative democratic mechanism where a representative group from the community deliberates on a specific issue. Participants hear from experts and stakeholders, then

72 'EPA, SBI Settle Legal Action to Benefit Community', *The Mirage*, 2 August 2024, www.miragenews.com/epa-sbi-settle-legal-action-to-benefit-community-1288772/.

73 The historical data relating to the EPA's ongoing interactions with SBI concerning odour breaches can be searched at Environment Protection Authority Victoria, 'Search: SBI' accessed 13 February 2025, www.epa.vic.gov.au/search?q=sbi.

engage in constructive, informed discussions, and work towards collective recommendations. The aim is to reflect the collective wisdom of citizens through public engagement and help bridge the gap between the public and government decision-makers.

In Australia, several citizens' juries are currently being experimented with, for deliberation on matters as diverse as nighttime safety in cities to infrastructure spending.[74] Some city councils in Victoria have adopted citizen juries to inform budget planning, arguing that they improve both participation and the credibility of resourcing decisions. Similar participatory mechanisms, such as future councils and citizens' assemblies, have been successfully employed in other jurisdictions and offer valuable insights for further shaping this broader restorative approach.[75]

A less intensive yet equally valuable alternative is convening a restorative circle or symposium of citizens to engage in dialogue about specific regulatory issues.[76] This type of restorative gathering could bring together a diverse cross-section of the community to discuss localised environmental harms, or as a way of co-designing restorative projects to fulfil a restorative project order under the EP Act 2017.[77] A restorative circle or symposium offers a flexible and inclusive space for open, structured discussions that can lead to more responsive and effective regulatory solutions.

74 'Citizen Juries—An Overview', Victorian Local Governance Association, accessed 13 February 2025, www.vlga.org.au/citizen-juries-overview.

75 Citizens' assemblies are deliberative democratic processes that bring together a representative group of citizens to discuss and make recommendations about complex issues. The goal is to include a diverse range of citizens in shaping solutions and to enhance the legitimacy of government decisions. The citizens' assembly is not a once-off event—it includes the expectation that the participants can respond to the government's response, keeping the dialogue going. For instance, in the case of Scotland's Climate Assembly 2020–2022, members reconvened to consider the government's response and did not feel the government had sufficiently taken their recommendations into account. They made further recommendations based on their impression that the government had failed to address the significant changes the citizens had sought. 'Scotland's Climate Assembly: Recommendations for Action', *Participedia*, last modified 10 June 2023, participedia.net/case/12537. See further Charles Taylor, Patrizia Nanz, and Madeleine Beaubien Taylor, *Reconstructing Democracy: How Citizens Are Building from the Ground Up*, 1st ed. (Harvard University Press, 2020); Jon Alexander and Ariane Conrad, *Citizens: Why the Key to Fixing Everything Is All of Us* (Canbury Press, 2022); and OECD, 'Eight Ways to Institutionalise Deliberative Democracy'.

76 Lawrence Kershen, 'Can Environmental Mediation Save the Planet?', *Passlenet*, 28 January 2023, passle-net.s3.amazonaws.com/Passle/5b3f2cb9780ebf0410d034b3/MediaLibrary/Document/2023-01-26-17-20-50-655-CanEnvironmentalMediationsavethePlanet.pdf.

77 Section 332 of the EP Act 2017, 'Restorative project orders'.

Cultivating pluralism: The key to citizen empowerment

This chapter has shared the long journey of learning about community empowerment experienced by EPA Victoria, including the challenge of balancing the virtues of agonism and collaboration. Through the various stories shared here, we have illustrated how regulators can encourage and support the restorative value of citizen empowerment in multiple forms and at different levels of community, often for sustained periods of time. Some formats are more suited to the sharing of information and knowledge, with the aim of transparency, clarity and integrity of information. Other formats are better attuned to engaging with the wisdom of crowds, to gain a consensus on how to move forward. All, however, rely on strong relationships, as it is through our relational connections that empowerment truly takes root.

A key takeaway emerges: the best way to empower citizens is to ensure that diverse, pluralist restorative approaches are cultivated.

With this foundation in mind, we now shift our focus to the ways in which environmental and social harm can be addressed, always with an openness to citizen and community inclusion. We start in the next chapter by looking at the prevention of harm.

Image 1: EPA staff monitoring water quality

Source: EPA Victoria, used with permission.

Image 2: Smoke plumes from power generation in the Latrobe Valley, Victoria

Source: Andrew Wright, CSIRO, 20 March 2025, RS23078_AS0092 (Version 1).

Image 3: Morwell open cut coal mine, Victoria
Source: Andrew Wright, CSIRO, 21 March 2025, RS29697_EM0732 (Version 1).

Image 4: Temporary West Gate Tunnel air quality monitoring site, Yarraville, 14 June 2020

Source: Philip Marris, Flickr, CC BY-SA 2.0 (www.flickr.com/photos/122687277@N03/50004044296).

Fire Rescue Victoria
9 August 2020 ·

FRV firefighters have been working to extinguish a factory fire in Campbellfield today, with support from our colleagues at CFA (Country Fire Authority), Victoria Police, Ambulance Victoria, Victoria State Emergency Service and Environment Protection Authority Victoria. 🔥

At the height of the incident, more than 20 firefighting appliances were at the scene, along with a number of other specialist units. 🚒👨‍🚒

#WeWorkAsOne

Image 5: #WeWorkAsOne—an example of Victorian agencies working together to extinguish the factory fire in Campbellfield

Source: FRV, used with permission.

Image 6: The ANU research team meets with the Friends of Maribyrnong River during one of their restoration efforts, October 2019

Source: Authors' photo.

Image 7: The ANU research team and the EPA half-day presentation, 'EPA staff restorative justice symposium: restorative justice through enforcement action—enforceable undertakings, civil & criminal proceedings', 24 October 2019

Notes: This was one of the first presentations from the project for EPA staff, local scholars and members of industry. The panel (L to R: Dimity Kingsford-Smith, John McDonald, John Braithwaite, Alan Fels, Christine Parker and Rhianna Kerr. Cheryl Batagol was also a member of this panel (not pictured).

Source: Authors.

Image 8: Fellow researchers in our project, John and Valerie Braithwaite, attending a climate protest in Melbourne, Victoria, 15 March 2019

Source: John and Val Braithwaite, used with permission.

Image 9: Scar tree, Broulee NSW

Source: John Braithwaite, used with permission.

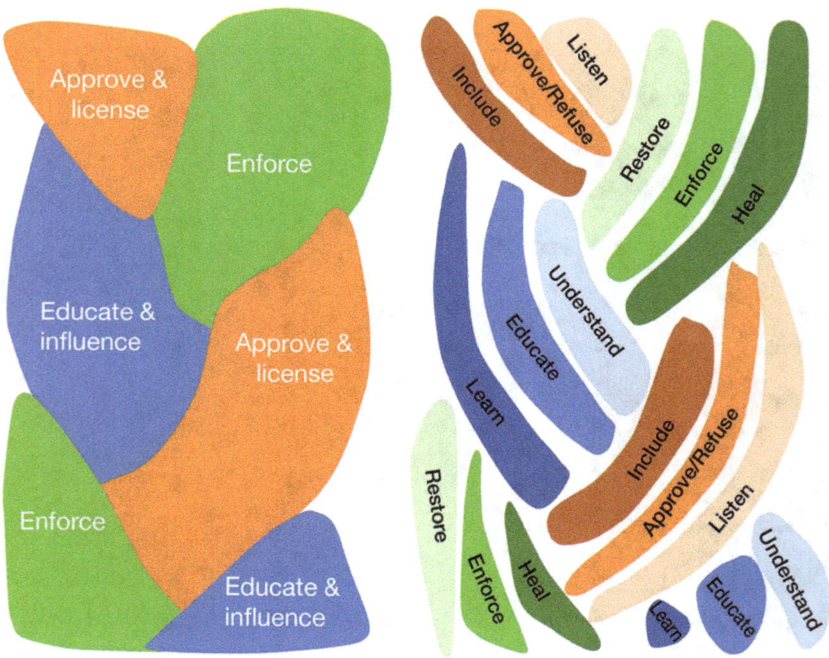

Image 10: The environmental restorative justice braids developed by Dr Deborah Cleland, a member of the ANU research team

Note: The braid images were used in several of our publications that were shared with project participants and members of the public to help explain the aims and applications of the research.

Source: Pixabay and Deborah Cleland.

Image 11: The environmental restorative justice wheel developed by Dr Deborah Cleland, a member of the ANU research team

Notes: The wheel image was used in several of our publications that were shared with project participants and members of the public to help explain the environmental restorative justice practices as an ongoing cycle of healing for communities and the environment.

Source: Wiki Commons, created with NASA World Wind from PD source data, and authors.

4

Preventing harm through restorative approvals processes

Source: Author.

We're not just trying to stop bad things, we're trying to lift everybody up, constantly up, up, up, whether it's environment protection and everything, safety, road safety—up, up, up.

—John Merritt[1]

1 John Merritt, 'Incentivising Compliance'.

This chapter explores how restorative approaches can be embedded in regulatory decision-making about permissions (approvals) and standards to improve future decision-making. Bringing in local expertise leads to better decisions by exposing regulators to different sources of knowledge, helping to generate creative approaches to mitigating harm. Restorative approaches also help build trust and strengthen relationships between communities, industry and regulators, improving communication pathways.

As we explained in chapter one, this book identifies a three-stage process to growing restorative regulation. The first process involves identifying spaces within the regulatory landscape where it is possible to plant restorative regulatory approaches alongside existing approaches, or where restorative approaches are already taking root. The second process involves looking for ways to nurture and expand these newly planted restorative approaches, helping them flourish. This chapter is the first in a series of chapters (4 to 8) that focus on identifying such spaces as opportunities to plant and to nourish restorative approaches along different parts of the regulatory spectrum.

In this chapter, we concentrate on the processes that take place before harm occurs. First, we look broadly at licensing—the regulator's approval or non-approval of activities that may pose a risk of harm to the environment or human health or have broader social impacts. Licensing processes can often be opaque to communities. When handled without inclusivity, they can lead to community resentment and even anger, especially when decisions affect daily life, such as the approval of a waste-to-energy facility or the expansion of an abattoir. However, if done well, licensing processes can help prevent future harm and build stronger relationships between industry, community and the regulator.

In a second step, we investigate community input into standards-setting, another key regulatory process for mitigating against future risks of harm by identifying the appropriate criteria against which to assess future applications.

Before discussing these two regulatory areas and our empirical findings on the incipient restorative potential within EPA Victoria, we first consider the role that restorative approaches can play in the prevention of harm. While restorative justice is commonly associated with responding to harm, it is equally geared towards proactively preventing harm, particularly through restorative practices.

Restorative approaches contribute to harm prevention in two main ways. First, they facilitate the genuine inclusion of local expertise and knowledge, helping to inform decision-making on licensing on granting licences for future activities by bringing in potentially highly relevant, often undocumented sources of knowledge about risks. This inclusion can also generate creative solutions for mitigating future harm. Restorative practices ensure that those contributing their expertise feel genuinely heard by those who have the power to respond to what they hear. Additionally, they help surface the depth and nature of community concerns about the proposed activity, which can prompt the regulator to respond by asking for more details or conducting independent assessments.

Second, many restorative practices centre around building strong relationships, thereby building trust and enabling effective communication between industry, regulator and the community. Establishing these relationships at the outset of an activity—such as the opening of a new tannery or composting facility—can reduce the risk of future harm by creating an environment where 'near misses' and other issues can be reported and discussed constructively rather than through blame-seeking.

Restorative practices can also create 'relational slack'—a form of flexibility or extra capacity within relationships that can function as a buffer if things do go wrong.[2] For instance, the Chancellor of Berkeley University, whom we discussed in Chapter 1 in relation to the challenges of dealing with polarised student bodies, observed: 'When you have relationships, it becomes in some ways easier to have the [difficult] conversation, because you have some credibility with people.'[3] This idea aligns with the perspective of restorative justice practitioners Terry O'Connell and Mark Vennen, for whom restorative practices encompass these relational dimensions: 'Restorative practice is a way of thinking and being, focused on creating safe spaces for real conversations that deepen relationships and build stronger, more connected communities.'[4]

2 The National Collaborative for Restorative Initiatives in Health, *He Maungarongo Ki Ngā Iwi*.

3 Carol Christ, 'The Chancellor of Berkeley Weighs In', *The New Yorker*, interview by Molly Fischer, 17 December 2023, www.newyorker.com/news/the-new-yorker-interview/the-chancellor-of-berkeley-weighs-in.

4 Terry O'Connell and Mark Vander Vennen, cited in John Braithwaite, *Restorative Justice and Reintegrative Shaming* (Routledge, 2020), 283.

We now examine the restorative potential we uncovered in what is now referred to under the EP Act 2017 as the 'permissioning' process.[5]

Restorative approaches to approvals and permissions

Regulatory approvals provide many spaces with restorative potential. In an environmental context, these include permissions for new or existing activities that may impact the environment and local communities, the permissioning of potentially high-risk activities, waste, discharge or emissions. Applying restorative approaches at the permitting stage of the regulatory cycle is an opportunity for the identification and mitigation—or even prevention—of future environmental harm, rather than a mere response to harm that has already occurred. As one of our EPA Victoria interviewees working in the approvals area stated, 'In many cases, we are at the front end of trying to reduce harm to the environment.'

EPA Victoria developed some incipient restorative practices for its former 'works approvals' processes under the EP Act 1970, and these practices have continued under the new EP Act 2017, as we discuss below.[6]

While integrating restorative approaches strengthens opportunities to mitigate or avoid future harm, it also presents challenges. The regulator is often constrained by legislative frameworks that define what is and is not permissible, as well as challenging timeframes for determining applications. Applications for approvals for developments and activities frequently involve long-term commitments and substantial commercial stakes, including outlay of resources, hiring of personnel and building infrastructure. These commitments serve as a weighty consideration in the minds of the regulatory decision-makers. Moreover, the perceived and actual limitations on the scope for communities to influence the ultimate decision about whether

5 EPA Victoria refers to their overall system of applying for and assessing licences, permits and similar permissions as a 'permissioning system'. This is administered under the *Environment Protection Act 2017* (EP Act 2017) and the Environment Protection Regulations 2021. See also, 'Managing the Permissioning System', EPA Victoria, 2023, and 'Permissions Scheme Policy', EPA Victoria, 29 January 2025, www.epa.vic.gov.au/17993-permissions-scheme-policy.

6 See EP Act 2017, Chapter 4—Permissions. This legislative chapter covers development licences, operating licences, pilot project licences, permits, registration and cases in which permission is not required.

a development or activity should go ahead, or the conditions on which they can proceed, make the approval stage of the regulatory process a highly fraught one.

As a result of prescriptive legislative frameworks, it is rarely the case that potentially impacted communities have actual decision-making power over whether activities proceed. Rather, the restorative dimension is relevant to ensuring there is a fair process for enabling the greatest scope of genuine community input that is allowed under the legislation. As we noted in Chapter 1, fair process depends upon:

- the provision of genuine opportunities for individuals to voice concerns about decisions affecting them
- clarity of expectations regarding the process so that all parties understand it
- adherence to procedures in a way that is not perceived as merely 'tick-box' or performative but instead facilitates meaningful engagement.

These three elements are central to effecting a respectful and collaborative regulatory approach.

So, what can this look like in practice?

In Victoria, approvals or permissions are granted through a 'permissions scheme'.[7] A regulatory approval must be issued when an applicant seeks to carry out an action, project or activity that requires authorisation. For example, an approval would be needed if something is proposed with a potentially high environmental impact, or for a major alteration to a licensed premises or to undertake activities that impact the environment.

When EPA Victoria receives an application for permission from an applicant under the EP Act 2017, it must decide whether to approve or reject it. While the EPA is guided by statutory criteria, the decision-making process allows for an opportunity for public submissions and, in some instances,

---

7 The EP Act 2017 introduced a new 'permissions' regime (e.g. see 'Permissions Scheme Policy'). It covers three tiers of permissions that match the level of seriousness of the potential risk to the environment: *licences* are required for the highest-risk activities, *permits* for medium-risk activities and *registrations* for lowest-risk activities, with the new EP regulations determining which activities fall under each tier (*Permission Schemes Policy*). Under the EP Act 2017, the term 'development licences' has replaced the former term 'works approvals', which was used under the EP Act 1970. Our case study discussion focused on the processes for works approvals because the EP Act 1970 was in force at the time of the fieldwork.

a public participatory process. The EP Act 2017 provides for a Charter of Consultation, a public document in which EPA Victoria explains its commitment to consultation with Victorians (pursuant to section 53 of the EP Act 2017). It gives guidance on the consultation process. In the Charter, the principles of legislative environmental protection that underpin the EPA's consultation approach are explained, the value of consultation discussed and the scope and content of consultation in relation to permissions and standards outlined. The Charter came about as a result of both legislative requirements and an organisational choice to consult to ensure the EPA was being accountable and inclusive.[8]

Currently, the key restorative opportunity in the decision-making process is referred to as the 'Conference of Interested Persons'. This conference is convened midway through the assessment period for the express purpose of gathering multiple perspectives on the application. The goal is to facilitate dialogue about the potential for harm and explore ways to prevent or mitigate it. The insights from this conference help inform the final decision.

Examples of what needs to be considered before permission is granted include:

- the applicant's fitness (an important consideration in an era where organised environmental crime such as illegal waste storage has risen)
- suitability of the proposed design
- what plans are in place to ensure that potential pollutants such as dust, odour and noise remain within acceptable limits
- existing issues of concern in the surrounding locale and how their impacts might interact with the new proposal
- level of consultation that has already taken place.[9]

Once an application is accepted for assessment, it is advertised, and there follows a comments period of at least 15 business days to actively encourage community and other stakeholder participation.

8 See also *Charter of Consultation*, EPA Victoria, 15 June 2021, www.epa.vic.gov.au/about-epa/publications/1928.

9 The Conference of Interested Persons replaced what was formerly known as the 'section 20B Conference' under the EP Act 1970. Although there are differences between the two processes, they share a common purpose in allowing the EPA to convene a process to bring parties together in a facilitated forum and in requiring that recommendations made by the forum are forwarded to the EPA for consideration in the decision-making process. For more details on the Conference of Interested Persons, see Environment Protection Authority Victoria, *Charter of Consultation*, 11 ff.

For significant applications, EPA Victoria may hold a drop-in information-sharing and listening session (not for less complex or lower-risk permissions).[10] In some cases, an online question-and-answer forum is offered instead. During the information session, the applicant gives an interactive presentation, and community members can pose questions to both the applicant and EPA Victoria and receive responses.[11] Citizens are given clear instructions on how to make a submission to the assessment process and where they can find information to stay updated. This approach has similarities to the Open House methodology discussed in the previous chapter. Concerned citizens are encouraged to address their questions directly to the proponent of the development. EPA staff who run these sessions receive training in what they describe as 'soft skills' and what we would call restorative skills, such as convening, active listening and explaining complex scientific information in an accessible way.

During our research, EPA Victoria typically handled around 60 works approvals in a normal year.[12] Of these, four or five resulted in what we refer to as a 'community conference' (formerly colloquially referred to by EPA staff as '20B conferences', named after their legislative provision of section 20B in the old Act).[13]

A community conference would be convened when:

- initial community submissions identified concerns that EPA Victoria judged needed further exploration with the community
- there was a large number of objections
- EPA Victoria wanted to better understand community concerns and explore solutions acceptable to the community.

Both conference types, the 20B conference and its successor, the Conference of Interested Persons, prioritise dialogue as the primary means for understanding community concerns. Further, they are a form of collective problem-solving, providing a constructive way to work through the sorts of conditions that ought to be put in place to mitigate community concerns.

10 This session is held only for major applications. It is not convened for less complex or lower-risk permissions.

11 Where this happens online, it occurs in the same manner as a face-to-face drop-in information session.

12 This number reflects the average amount for works approvals under the EP Act 1970.

13 The community conference refers to either section 20B conferences of the former EP Act 1970 or equivalent provisions under section 236 of the EP Act 2017. See Chapter 3 for more on 20B conferences.

In our interviews, EPA staff involved in former works approvals highlighted restorative values, such as deep listening, relational justice and citizen empowerment through direct participation, as important components of these conferences. Staff described asking questions such as, 'Why are you concerned about it?' and 'Have we understood it correctly?' These questions reflect an effort to engage meaningfully with the community rather than simply to fulfil regulatory obligations. The Charter of Consultation appears to reinforce the commitment to the restorative values of listening to community, learning from community, and seeking 'opportunities for greater collaboration and empowerment in environmental decision-making'.[14]

Like all regulators, EPA Victoria operates within defined limits when assessing applications—when an application meets specified and delimited policy criteria, the EPA's ambit of discretion is limited. After all, it is the EPA's compliance with the environmental protection legislation that will come under scrutiny when the lawyers pull on their robes and head to court. Adherence to these objective standards reinforces the exchange trust norms—built through competency and consistency—as we discussed in the introduction.

Despite these limitations, community involvement may catalyse EPA Victoria to double check. Public input may encourage the regulator to reassess what could be done within the bounds of existing standards and regulations to prevent and mitigate harm.[15] This exploration may lead to previously unconsidered, but legislatively available, licence requirements that could be imposed to increase the likelihood of harm prevention. As one EPA officer stated, 'It is a better process when we are encouraging community participation and encouraging companies to seek a social licence and to engage with co-design.'[16]

---

14 Environment Protection Authority Victoria, *Charter of Consultation*, 8.

15 Moreover, as part of EPA Victoria's risk-based approach, EPA Victoria has stated that to help it determine preventive strategies, the EPA 'seek[s] out and use[s] the insights from community and stakeholders'. Environment Protection Authority Victoria, *EPA Victoria Compliance and Enforcement Policy*, Publication 1798.3, 6.

16 Interview with an EPA officer.

How community conferences work

While there was considerable diversity in the format of the community conferences that we observed, all were convened under provisions of the EP Act 1970.[17] These provisions required the conference to be facilitated by an appointed chairperson (the Chair). The EPA typically appointed an independent Chair. Importantly, the Chair was responsible for reporting back to EPA Victoria with recommendations for consideration in the subsequent decision-making process.

At the start of a community conference, the independent Chair for the community consultation process would be appointed from a list of experienced facilitators. The Chair worked with the development proponent and key stakeholders to develop an agenda for the consultation. In some instances, the facilitators would meet local community members ahead of time to obtain their inputs into the agenda. One facilitator noted that this proactive engagement really helped to defuse the community's concerns and feelings of not being heard. The Chair was also tasked with communicating expectations for constructive dialogue, emphasising the importance of listening to one another and explaining what is expected when emotions run high, at the point when 'soft skills' become critical.

While independent facilitation was the gold standard, EPA staff themselves would chair the conference in rare cases—particularly when community submissions were few. In these instances, experienced EPA staff who were trained in facilitation, and who were independent of the works approval unit and delegated decision-makers for the application, took on the facilitation role. Although not ideal, this 'lean' approach ensured that the restorative imperative—creating space for as many potentially affected communities as possible to engage—was upheld.

Our research team observed one such conference held in a local community hall. Many tables had been set up, and each was staffed by a facilitator who was an EPA officer. It began with an initial town hall meeting phase of community consultation, where people had to register in advance so they could indicate if they wanted a speaking spot. Normally, most received

17 Although the new Conference of Interested Persons provided for under section 236 of the EP Act 2017 is expected to retain a similar diversity of formats, our research period did not extend to observations of this reincarnation. Accordingly, our discussion draws on observations of 20B conferences under the former Act, offering insights into both the restorative opportunities and limitations of such forums within the approvals process.

one—but only for three minutes. Facilitators helped moderate emotions beforehand, tempering anger and grandstanding by chatting with speakers before they spoke, reminding them that moderation and listening mattered on all sides.

The conference then proceeded to small group discussions at each table, with tables assigned to different concerns, such as noise or dust pollution. Each table had a facilitator actively jotting points on butcher's paper. A key question the facilitator would ask was: 'Have I captured this correctly?' Facilitators also encouraged forward-looking discussions, asking questions such as: 'Hypothetically, if we were to give approval, what restrictions would you like to see imposed on them—for example, monitoring, hours of operation, co-design?' One facilitator reinforced the importance of participation, telling us, 'This is not lip service; decisions are better when made this way'.

In reflecting on these conferences, EPA officers found that the community conference process was beneficial and worthwhile, although time-and resource-consuming. One officer remarked:

> It is an opportunity to find out what the community's interest is in the application and what their concerns are … We do not have the necessary local knowledge or historical knowledge that can really inform a good decision. We may go and do a site visit and everything will be fine, but then the next day the wind changes and everything stinks. The conference is an opportunity to tap into community knowledge.

EPA officers also commented approvingly on the fact that the community often suggested licensing conditions that addressed issues that would not have been raised without local knowledge and input. For example, in one community conference we observed, community members made highly practical suggestions about planting trees along the outside of the proposed industrial expansion to block its visual impact. While this may seem like a small concession, if it improves the amenity for the neighbours and increases biodiversity and air quality, it holds the seeds of a restorative beginning, leading to improved relationships and a better environment.

This act of listening and being willing to revise an initial stance provides a restorative start, but it is not a fix-all panacea. At the same conference, two disgruntled community members walked out, announcing they felt the approval decision had already been made—for them, a few screening trees failed to cut to the heart of the harmful issues their neighbourhood faced.

Another format described to us involved all parties sitting around a U-shaped table and the facilitator leading a formal conversation. It was attended by industry groups, Sustainability Victoria (another government agency), NGO opponents and community opponents.

Following the COVID-19 pandemic restrictions, many of these conferences shifted to an online format. We observed one virtual community conference, with various technical adaptations made to enable all participants to speak if they wished to.

In all these forums, sometimes the applicant would speak, and sometimes they would not. Sometimes key individuals would be present, and at other times, the applicant was represented by a community liaison officer or someone in a similar role.

Often, one of the key parties in attendance was the local council—sometimes more than one council—in recognition that environmental harm does not recognise borders. The council's presence is often important, ensuring that the different perspectives and solutions offered by those with roles and responsibilities for legal matters, planning and services at the local level are included. When we conducted our interviews, we were told that a proportion of EPA works approvals required planning approval (under the *Planning and Environment Act 1987*), and that a legislative option was available to convene the public notification and consultation process jointly with the relevant local council. This highlights the complexity of the approvals process and the range of actors involved.

During our 2019 interviews, EPA officers reported that major national and international environmental groups, such as Greenpeace, Friends of the Earth and the Australian Conservation Foundation, had not attended a works approval community conference since 2015. Major NGOs with a substantial Victorian state-level focus, notably, Environment Victoria and Environmental Justice Australia, attended, but irregularly. The latter organisations were, and still are, able to check the website of EPA Victoria, where they can now register to be updated on new development licences (formerly works approvals) through 'Engage Victoria'.[18] When they do make a strategic judgement to attend a conference, organisations like Environment Victoria and Environmental Justice Australia can be the most organised and effective repeat players in the room.

Local groups frequently attended the community conferences, as did practically oriented conservation organisations often known as 'Friends of' particular creeks or rivers, reflecting the more locally situated character of community participation.[19] These groups often bring invaluable local knowledge to bear on conversations, not only during the conference but also afterwards, when community members continue to engage in the respective group's activities. The EPA staff told us often that they wanted these 'insights into community interests' and appreciated the intelligence arising from 'concerns of local knowledge'.

Licence conditions requiring ongoing consultation with community groups are sometimes won as outcomes of an approval. In other cases, the relationship-building flows through to establishment of a new CRGs (discussed in the previous chapter) based around the identified environmental risks. Importantly, ongoing consultation with this type of group can become an enduring node of relational environmental justice. Some reference groups evolve into stable entities that look after the interests of their communities over the long-term (the BCRG discussed in the previous chapter being a prime example). However, many others tend to fall apart, sometimes due to serious breaches of trust with the permit or duty holder.

In the final stages of the community consultation process, EPA Victoria would receive an extensive report from the independent facilitator that summarised its outcomes. This would include summaries of the issues raised and, importantly, recommendations that emerged from the

18 See also Engage Victoria, 'EPA Development Licence Applications' (State Government of Victoria), accessed 15 February 2025, engage.vic.gov.au/epa-development-licence-applications. This site displays the applications the public can comment on ('Open for Feedback') and applications that are undergoing review ('Reviewing Feedback'). It further provides clarification as to which applications are in the process of reporting back or have completed their requirement to do so after feedback ('Reporting Back'). In each case, a timeline is provided indicating whether or not the application is open or closed for feedback. Engage Victoria is the State of Victoria's public engagement interface, where people can easily find all current and past consultations for projects.

19 An online search for the term 'friends of creeks Victoria' will provide a good snapshot of the types of groups we mean (such as Friends of Merri Creek, www.friendsofmerricreek.org.au/, and Friends of Stony Creek, www.geocities.ws/stonyck/. There is also the Riverkeeper organisation, originating in the United States, now with locally formed Riverkeeper associations across Australia, such as the Yarra Riverkeeper in Victoria (yarrariver.org.au/).

conference. While EPA Victoria is not legally bound by the report, the decision-maker is required to consider it, along with its recommendations, in their final decision. Recommendations often identify key concerns for the community and may include suggestions such that EPA Victoria request further information from the applicant, undertake its own assessment or commission independent peer reviews, or further request that the EPA impose strict conditions on any subsequent approval.

In some cases, a second follow-up information session took place. For example, a special information session was held when an independent hydrologist's report became available only after the initial conference. This second session enabled the hydrologist to make a public presentation and respond to community questions prompted by the new information and explore whether there is any possibility for further inputs by citizens. Such a process represents a shift away from the old regulator's framing of 'trust me, this is safe' towards a more multiparty restorative regulatory approach that channels anger into engagement and contestation into problem-solving. It can build or rebuild trust, and, notably, some reports make trust-building an explicit objective.

The Chair's conference report is published by EPA Victoria, adding a layer of objectivity, transparency and accountability to the process. It ensures that the EPA must, at the very least, justify how it has considered issues raised by the report and why it has chosen not to follow some or any of the recommendations.

Ultimately, an EPA development licence is a statutory document. It is published on EPA's Public Registers. The assessment report sets out the story of how the EPA evaluated the application and objectively reached its decision, including how it considered the issues and concerns raised in submissions and any conference report. This is sometimes made available on the Engage Victoria website used for consultation on the permission application. When this occurs, the approval process is transparent and accountable, ensuring that community input and regulatory considerations are clearly documented and accessible.

Nurturing restorative potential in the permissions process

So far, we have identified community conferences as incipient spaces of restorative regulation. But what would it take for them to truly thrive and fulfil their potential?

At present, the community conference format does not require the senior management team or company owners to be present. If the community is only able to interact with mid-level staff from an offending company, this can leave the impression in the public's mind that the company is not taking the matter seriously enough. This can erode relational trust and limit the potential for genuine debate.

Strengthening the restorative impact of these conferences requires clear guidelines for corporate participation, explicitly stating that top-level management attendance is expected. Given the significant time commitments and resource investment in these conferences, ensuring that senior management and/or site owners are present is not just a matter of good faith; it is also good business. Senior leaders have the authority to agree to commitments, allocate resources and enact real changes, with full awareness of company funds and liabilities. Their presence increases the likelihood of genuine, transformative outcomes.

In the best cases, the relationship-building arising out of a community conference flows through to the establishment of an ongoing CRGs for the site or industrial area, which maintains connectedness to community and facilitates continuous feedback. Sometimes, a condition is imposed on licences and permits that duty holders must consult with a community consultative committee. This is, in fact, made explicit in the EP Act 2017, where section 54(g) stipulates that permission may be made subject to a condition 'relating to consultation with the local community'.

Legislative authorisation for the requirement of community consultation is an important avenue for developing restorative regulation. Making ongoing relationship-building a condition of permissioning would help to foster a regulatory expectation on the part of both the permit holder (or duty holder) and the regulator to keep the community informed and engaged. Ideally, community participation and engagement could become a natural approach over time, with the respective company not needing to be told to act this way. Through experience and reflection, a relationally astute response would become second nature, and the company would simply include ongoing consultation as part of its socially responsible approach to responsive local community engagement, alongside a desire to maintain its social licence.

We suggest further that there is more scope for community conference organisers to proactively engage local environmental or other neighbourhood groups on a consistent, regular basis. Doing so would not only harness local expertise and insights, but also strengthen ongoing relationships with community, ensuring that community concerns and suggestions are fully captured and passed on to EPA Victoria. This approach is relevant for any regulator seeking to build trust and legitimacy in its interactions with communities. As one EPA officer told us:

> My experience is that they [the community] are better engaged with the issues that relate to the environment, and they understand to a significant degree the potential impacts of commercial and industrial operations that tend to directly impact them.[20]

To guide the development of a more restorative approach, the following suggestions may assist:

- Ask the question: 'On whose Country is this happening?'[21] And: Are the Traditional Owners of the affected area aware of the proposed activity? Has the application included a risk assessment of any impacts on Traditional Owner cultural values? What opportunity has there been for these values to be discussed?
- Encourage a format supportive of deep listening to, and by, all affected groups, as part of both initial consultations and more formal consultation processes.
- Ensure there is clarity of understanding by all parties as to the ways in which community ideas, suggestions and concerns will be used in the decision-making process.
- Ensure senior management or company owners are present at a conference. This will help to optimise the potential for developing relational trust and promote genuine debate.

20 Interview with an EPA officer.

21 In Australia, we say 'Country' when referring to land, waters, sky, e.g. Country, Sea Country, Sky Country. See Chapter 10 for more information about Indigenous and Traditional Owner culture and knowledges.

- Focus dialogue on avoiding or minimising future harm to the community and the environment. Consciously seek out answers to the question: What could be better here? Do this in a collaborative manner that encourages co-design.
- Set aside sufficient resources and time for community conferences. They are not the appendix of good regulatory governance; they are its beating heart.
- View the licensing or approvals process as an opportunity to build future relationships between all those involved. This also means establishing guidance materials on how to make this process a more restorative and relational one.
- Enable and value genuine debate and contestation through the creation of appropriate dialogue forums and facilitation.

In making these suggestions, we note that certain features of the permissions process make some of these aspirations challenging to operationalise. As noted above, the permissions process is essentially reactive, as it is triggered by applications. This means that regulators like EPA Victoria have limited scope in how they can respond, as they are dependent upon what is specified in legislation and regulations as allowable. This points to the need to have clear understandings about what scope for change might exist in facilitating restorative dialogue and feedback. In many development applications and licence approvals, room for substantive input may be limited to licence conditions, as discussed above.

More ambitiously, community participation in permissions approvals and licence reviews could contribute to the iterative cycle of standards creation. If structured to receive community input, this could give communities a meaningful role in helping to shape the outcomes of approval processes to prevent harm before it occurs.

It is to this possibility that we now turn.

Citizen empowerment through restorative standards-setting

Our final reflection on restorative harm prevention involves an area that is almost invisible but perhaps one of the most consequential: regulatory standards-setting. Regulatory authorities engage in standards-setting for multiple purposes, some to clarify expectations of regulatee conduct for specific activities or risks of harm, others to offer guidance for the regulator's operations and decision-making. Some standards are relevant for decisions regarding licences, permits and other forms of permission, while others inform decision-making around compliance approaches and monitoring of the health of the environment. At EPA Victoria, standards-setting has traditionally been based on scientific understandings of the state of the environment, and current and future risks, and has involved using quantitative measurements. However, this approach has gradually changed over time.

Involving community in standards-setting by and for regulators is not a recent practice—it has been recognised for a while now as an important aspect of inclusive and effective governance. Engaging communities in the standards-setting process is a helpful way to ensure that the standards are relevant and responsive to the needs of those affected. However, this important exercise in building trust and cooperation can be sidestepped by a regulator for various reasons, including limited resources, the complexity of balancing many perspectives, resistance to change, reliance on top-down, expert-driven approaches, or fear of losing control.

Once it is accepted that communities should be part of the standards-setting process, rather than it being seen as a purely technical exercise on the basis of scientific input, new opportunities for community involvement and consultation open up. This cultural shift often requires a shift of mindset within organisations. It requires proactive efforts to build relationships, provide sufficient resources and fully understand the benefits of community involvement. When meaningfully integrated, community participation and engagement in standards-setting can be transformative, promoting transparency, increasing trust and incorporating diverse perspectives that lead to more comprehensive and effective regulatory outcomes.

In one current example of stepping up to include community in standards-setting, EPA Victoria explicitly claims to set standards 'in consultation with Traditional Owners' and to take into account 'the aspirations of Traditional Owners and the community'.[22] A case in point is EPA's 2021 Environment

22 'Our Regulatory Approach' (EPA Victoria, 10 November 2022), www.epa.vic.gov.au/our-regulatory-approach (click on 'Set Standards'.)

Reference Standard (ERS),[23] which lists multiple environmental values across the different categories of ambient air, ambient sound, land environment and waters, and Traditional Owner cultural values in relation to water. These latter values are defined as:

> [w]ater quality that protects the cultural values of Traditional Owners, [with government] having recognised [their] primary responsibility for protecting the values of water for cultural needs, to ensure that Traditional Owner cultural practices can continue.[24]

The indicators for measuring these values are required to be developed in consultation with Traditional Owners.

This inclusion of cultural values has the potential to be transformative for EPA Victoria's approach to environmental protection. Since EPA officers must consider the ERS when making permissions decisions, traditional knowledge relevant to the landscape about which the decision is being made becomes integral to assessing the risk of harm to the environment. Consequently, that knowledge should inform the decision being taken. Additionally, some aspects of the environment are now recognised as having cultural values, both tangible and intangible, embedded within. This understanding grants permissions officers the authority to refuse an application if it risks causing unacceptable harm to a part of the environment where cultural values could be eroded.

To put this another way: a single tree located near a waterway might seem to be a replaceable single tree. But if it is part of a ceremonial area or is a traditional birthing tree or a scar tree, it embodies more than its physical presence. The tree and its surrounding landscape may hold cultural significance that not only makes it irreplaceable but also exposes the broader risk to the cultural values of that landscape. By embedding Traditional Owner cultural values into the water part of the ERS, regulatory decision-making can explicitly take account of the risks of harm posed to these values by activities that are the subject of permissioning decisions.

23 'Environment Reference Standard', Environment Protection Act 2017 no. S245 Gazette 26 May 2021, as amended by Environment Reference Standard No. S158 Gazette 29 March 2022, www.epa.vic.gov.au/sites/default/files/2025-05/consolidated-ERS.pdf, 19. See also Chapter 5 Part 5.2 of the EP Act 2017, which contains the sections relevant to environment reference standards.

24 'Environment Reference Standard', 2021: 19. There we also read: 'Values may include traditional aquaculture, fishing, harvesting, cultivation of freshwater and marine foods, fish, grasses, medicines and filtration of water holes.'

Standards may also evolve through an intentionally iterative process that actively involves community and incorporates built-in feedback loops. This means collecting input over time, to shape and adapt the standards accordingly. For example, pollution reporting or Open Houses can provide opportunities for communities to share concerns, to which regulatory agencies must respond. In this way, the regulatory response becomes both reactive—addressing immediate issues—and proactive—updating standards to prevent future harm. For instance, if repeated community complaints reveal that a 500-metre buffer around a new landfill is insufficient, the regulator may respond by expanding it to 1.5 kilometres. This adjustment acknowledges and incorporates lived community experience into the decision-making process.

A more direct avenue for community input is for regulators to actively invite community to provide input into significant changes to existing standards or help co-design new ones. This could involve reaching out to community liaison or environmental review committees in the regulator's network, making it clear that input to a standards review is welcome and valued. By extending an invitation for community input, the regulator not only acknowledges but actively seeks community expertise and diversity of perspectives for enhancing the standards. This is a restorative approach because it supports inclusiveness, fosters a sense of the community having a direct stake in the solution and reflects a shared responsibility for regulatory outcomes. Tapping into the collective wisdom of the community directly impacted by the standards can strengthen the standards' effectiveness and legitimacy.

Preventing harm, strengthening trust: The restorative advantage

This chapter has explored the restorative potential that may exist in permissioning decisions and standards-setting. Making the effort to nurture and grow the relational aspect of these regulatory processes is a vital project for the future, not just for EPA Victoria but for all regulators.

Three key takeaways for regulators emerge from this chapter.

We first suggested that incorporating restorative approaches in permissions and approvals can help prevent future harm through the integration of local expertise, knowledge and multiple perspectives in the decision-making process. Restorative approaches often lead to better decisions because they tap into in the long-term memory of community. Community members can help to identify risks that might otherwise be overlooked and can often offer creative solutions on how to reduce the chances of future harm.

Second, incorporating relational approaches into all regulatory interactions creates opportunities to build relationships between community, industry, regulators and other parts of government. Having strong relationships already in place can help regulators to navigate difficulties that may arise in the future and provide pathways to creative problem-solving. An additional benefit of building stronger relationships is the potential to lessen community resentment and anger if things do go wrong. Relational opportunities, such as community conferences, play a key role in building the communal trust norms discussed in the introduction, which are essential for fostering citizen trust in regulatory authorities.

These advantages are important for regulatory agencies to consider when making decisions about resourcing and automation. While community engagement processes require human interaction, which necessitates resources, the immediate and long-lasting advantages they provide should also be factored into the equation.

The third key point is that restorative approaches do not inherently necessitate collaborative decision-making, although they do emphasise the need for fair, transparent processes that define the scope for community input for everyone's understanding. Being clear and fair about process helps to ensure that people feel respected and validated even when they do not get the solutions they had hoped for.

In our next chapter, we explore what happens when inspections are conducted restoratively. We will shed light on why it is crucial to look beyond metrics and instead tap into the innate human need for connection and relationship-building.

5

Monitoring potential harm through restorative inspections

Source: Author.

The environment is where we all meet; where we all have a mutual interest; it is the one thing all of us share.

—Lady Bird Johnson[1]

1 Lady Bird Johnson was First Lady of the United States from 1963 to 1969.

Regulatory inspections are often seen as rigid, procedural, even adversarial —but what if they could be something more? This chapter explores how restorative approaches can transform inspections into opportunities for learning, trust-building and meaningful engagement. We first set out the benefits of incorporating restorative approaches, then discuss practical strategies for expanding the relational dimensions of inspections, drawing on both empirical findings and scholarly insights.

Approval—whether a licence, permit or other regulatory permission—is not an end stage. Rather, it marks the beginning of ongoing vigilance, requiring both regulator and regulated to constantly scout the horizon for potential harm, working together, where possible, to prevent it. As the previous chapter showed, a restorative approach to the permissions process ideally fosters a productive relationship between the regulatee, regulator and impacted community, establishing communication pathways and building trust. In this chapter, we examine how attentiveness to the relationships between regulator and regulatee can strengthen ongoing monitoring and reduce the risk of harm.

This chapter focuses on inspections, a key regulatory tool used to monitor compliance, carried out by delegated officers under legislative authority. Inspections play a proactive role in identifying hazards, assessing risks and detecting noncompliance before harm occurs. When issues are found, inspectors can enforce measures to rectify or mitigate harm, and prevent future risks in a timely and efficient manner. Restorative approaches do not replace inspections but complement them by facilitating cooperation, improving communication and strengthening long-term compliance outcomes.

A narrow interpretation of the inspector's role typically focuses on monitoring compliance with legislation, identifying noncompliance and imposing the appropriate sanctions. This approach generally involves only two parties—the inspector and the regulatee—and does not explicitly consider relational dynamics. In contrast, we conceive of inspections as part of a broader regulatory ecosystem, thus changing the conventional framing of regulatory inspections significantly. This perspective opens up the possibility of explicitly considering enduring relational engagement as a positive outcome and encourages the inclusion of other actors, such as other government agencies. We also suggest that inspections can do more than just minimise risks; they can also maximise the regulatee's ability to conduct their activities in a manner that benefits the impacted community and the environment.

Despite its potential value, the notion of a 'regulatory inspection' may not always be welcomed by either regulated entities or regulators. The regulated parties may view noncompliance as a cost-saving strategy or 'just the way things work around here' and may resist conversations aimed at improvement. Meanwhile, regulators may be disinclined to hang around chatting with uncooperative regulatees, preferring to inspect by rote and resort to formulaic responses backed by legal teeth.

While existing management, psychology and regulatory literature has explored why people take particular stances towards compliance mechanisms,[2] we focus on how regulators can more effectively leverage the relational aspect of inspections. We propose that embracing a restorative approach in the inspecting process can provide valuable opportunities to address common challenges, such as noncooperation, resistance, delays, lack of corrective actions and repeat violations, through relational strategies.

To this end, we ask:

- How can routine regulatory activities, such as inspecting premises, incorporate restorative practices?
- What are the potential benefits of doing so?

In investigating these questions, we seek to provide practical suggestions for regulators looking to innovate and increase the effectiveness of their regulatory inspections.

2 Valerie Braithwaite, Gerben Bruinsma, and David Weisburd, 'Defiance and Motivational Postures', in *Encyclopedia of Criminology and Criminal Justice*, eds. Gerben Bruinsma and David Weisburd (Springer, 2014).

Environmental inspection and restorative inspecting

While our focus is on environmental inspection, it shares many similarities with other regulatory inspections, making our suggestions broadly applicable across a range of regulatory areas. To illustrate this broader relevance, we include examples from other regulatory areas such as aged care.

An environmental inspection is a systematic, structured assessment of the environmental management practices of approval holders or duty holders to determine compliance with their obligations under environmental law. Accordingly, EPA Victoria refers to them as 'compliance inspections'. Environmental inspections may include on-site visits to a facility to review its processes and equipment, environmental audits or reviews, direct communications between the inspecting regulator and duty holder (casual conversations or formal interviews), document reviews, data collection and sampling, and other applied approaches.[3] Environmental inspections can occur regularly, sporadically, with or without notice, depending on the intended rationale motivating the regulator.

Whatever type of inspection the regulator uses, our interest lies in what we call 'restorative inspecting'.[4] Our perspective on restorative inspecting focuses upon the less formal, more relational and conversational aspects of the inspection process.[5] We seek to highlight how these aspects, often overlooked, can significantly increase the effectiveness of an inspection. Restorative inspecting emphasises the importance of the relationships between the regulator and the regulated, focusing on interactions such

3 Environmental policymaker Cynthia Giles notes that on-the-ground inspections, while reliable much of the time, must be supplemented by or, in some cases, replaced by other forms of inspecting, including document reviews, because on-site inspections alone do not necessarily reveal all the compliance issues. Thus, what constitutes inspecting must be viewed broadly to include both on-site and off-site investigatory methods. Cynthia Giles, *Next Generation Compliance: Environmental Regulation for the Modern Era* (Oxford University Press, 2022), 51, doi.org/10.1093/oso/9780197656747.001.0001.

4 Miranda Forsyth, 'Turning Up the Restorative Dial in Environmental Regulation with an Adaptive Learning Loop', in *The Palgrave Handbook of Environmental Restorative Justice*, eds. Brunilda Pali, Miranda Forsyth, and Felicity Tepper (Palgrave Macmillan, 2022), 147–69, doi.org/10.1007/978-3-031-04223-2_7.

5 Restorative inspecting remains applicable to off-site inspecting as well. When discoveries of noncompliance necessitate follow-up and queries, inspectors can still use restorative approaches. By being attentive to the relational dynamics and starting with an empathetic conversation, inspectors may elicit more information and cooperation than if they are strict or make assumptions.

as positive reinforcement, reassurance and open communication. These elements serve as a means for establishing cooperativeness, and for resolving challenges and concerns effectively.

Why do restorative inspecting?

Restorative inspecting offers the potential to support the expectation of continued improvement in compliance by regulatees.[6] It also underpins the potential for corporate culture change, particularly in the current climate of growing expectations that business will properly and transparently fulfil its environmental, social and governance (ESG) obligations.[7] In each instance, restorative inspecting is able to benefit all the parties involved. How is this so?

During an inspection of one factory with a past history of major compliance problems, the owner told us that when he thinks about the EPA Victoria people who had, in his mind, made a positive difference, and the ones who had made things worse, he considered that what made things worse was when inspectors did things ***to*** his business or did things ***for*** it. In his mind, those who improved his company's environmental stewardship were those who did things ***with*** him, his team and his business.

6 We view 'continued improved compliance' as a concept that not only ensures adherence to regulatory requirements but also promotes a broader shift towards continuous improvement as an operational model. This approach seeks to drive substantive improvements that not only benefit business efficiency but actively reduce and remove the potential for environmental harm. EPA Victoria supports this continual improvement approach. As part of the broader mandate under section 25 of the EP Act 2017, duty holders must implement the general environmental duty, and section 25(4)(b) requires duty holders to conduct 'environmental performance evaluations'. EPA Victoria, 'Implementing the General Environmental Duty for Licence Holders', 2 May 2025, www.epa.vic.gov.au/implementing-general-environmental-duty-licence-holders. The EPA advises duty holders as follows: '[C]ontinual improvement of your environmental performance is central to proactive environmental management. You will review the results of your environmental performance evaluation to identify opportunities to improve your future environmental performance'. EPA Victoria, 'Continual Improvement and Review', 9 March 2022, archived at the Wayback Machine, web.archive.org/web/20250428025229/https://www.epa.vic.gov.au/for-business/find-a-topic/environment-protection-laws-and-regulations/implementing-the-general-environmental-duty---a-guide-for-licence-holders/continual-improvement-and-review.

7 Despite the Trump administration 2.0 rollbacks concerning environmental regulation, ESG will likely continue to inform corporate practices. As international banker Samantha Barnes notes, ESG initiatives remain in place in the European Union, California and other jurisdictions globally. Samantha Barnes, 'Does ESG Stand a Chance in the Trump 2.0 Era?', *International Banker*, 23 January 2025, internationalbanker.com/finance/does-esg-stand-a-chance-in-the-trump-2-0-era/.

In the words of one EPA field practitioner, what mattered was that the duty holder:

> [u]nderstand[s] that [it is about environmental stewardship], [sees that the inspector is] interested in what [they are] doing, and [sees that] we're here together working out how to fix the issue that's impacting on the community together ... Sometimes it is hard to get the company in that mindset; sometimes it does involve court cases and all that, and punishment.

The EPA practitioner then outlined how he approached the duty holder:

> But I like to approach it from the start that no-one's deliberately trying to do anything wrong, which most of the time they're not ... Unless, of course, you go out there and they're just horrible—and then you go, well! That's when you do have to exercise that judgement, going yep, nope, this person's not interested, they're not going to respond until I really start to apply pressure and use these powers that I've got.
>
> I suppose that's the thing, having powers is one thing, knowing when to use them [is another]. I don't think you can necessarily be trained in that, I think that's your professional judgement that you develop over time.

We were struck by these observations—without invoking the word 'restorative', we noticed the presence of restorative principles within both the duty holder and the regulatory officer. Each of them had effectively summarised the core insight of the International Institute of Restorative Practices (IIRP), quoted in the previous chapter but repeated here due to its significance:

> [H]uman beings are happier, more cooperative and productive, and more likely to make positive changes in their behavior when those in positions of authority do things with them, rather than to them or for them. [8]

8 Wachtel, 'Defining Restorative', 3; see also Lindsey Pointer, 'Learning to Work "with" (the Social Discipline Window)', *Lindsay Pointer*, PhD (blog), 18 February 2018, lindseypointer.com/2018/02/18/learning-to-work-with-the-social-discipline-window/.

In 2003, restorative practitioners Ted Wachtel and Paul McCold proposed the concept of a social discipline window,[9] which has broad application across many settings. This concept, an adapted version of which is shown in Figure 5.1, is represented as a quartered square resembling a windowpane. It describes four basic approaches to maintaining social norms and behavioural boundaries, each defined by different combinations of high or low expectations of behaviour and high or low support:

- The top left pane represents ***doing to***, a punitive approach.
- The lower right pane represents ***doing for***, a permissive approach.
- The upper right pane represents ***doing with***, the restorative approach.
- The lower left pane represents ***not doing***, considered neglectful.

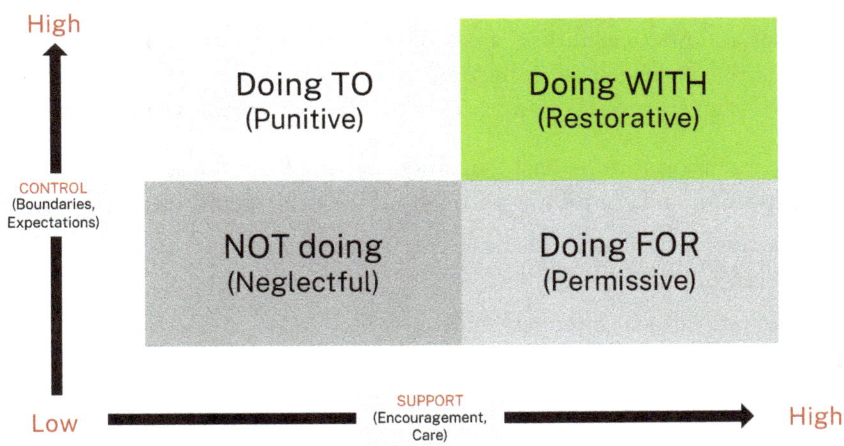

Figure 5.1. The Social Discipline Window in the restorative context

Source: Modified from Ted Wachtel and Paul McCold, 'Restorative Justice in Everyday Life'.

9 First discussed by Paul McCold and Ted Wachtel in a 2003 conference paper, 'In Pursuit of Paradigm: A Theory of Restorative Justice' (presentation at XIII World Congress of Criminology, Rio de Janeiro, Brazil, 12 August 2003); a detailed explanation is provided in Ted Wachtel and Paul McCold, 'From Restorative Justice to Restorative Practices: Expanding the Paradigm', *IIRP News*, 5 August 2004, www.iirp.edu/news/from-restorative-justice-to-restorative-practices-expanding-the-paradigm. See also Katherine Evans and Dorothy Vaandering, *The Little Book of Restorative Justice in Education: Fostering Responsibility, Healing, and Hope in Schools* (Good Books, 2016).

The restorative domain combines both high control and high support, emphasising doing things ***with*** people rather than ***to*** them or ***for*** them. The restorative approach allows regulators to address any problematic behaviour while practising empathy and maintaining strong relationships.

The benefits of working ***with*** people to achieve the desired regulatory ends have been empirically demonstrated across multiple studies.[10] Working with regulatees enables them to become part of the solution, allowing the regulator and the community as a whole to benefit from their unique insights, creative responses and resources.

How to conduct restorative inspecting

In what follows, we outline a set of 'how-to' suggestions for activating a restorative approach to inspection processes regardless of the regulatory area. We suggest seven key approaches to effective restorative inspecting:

- Pay attention to relational dynamics, starting from the outset of the inspection and continuing throughout the process and its outcomes.
- Consider holding an exit conference as a standard practice at the end of each inspection.
- Use motivational interviewing techniques.
- Regularly use positive reinforcement (e.g. praise) to acknowledge progress and improvements.
- Provide restorative assurances to increase cooperation and strengthen relationships.
- Focus on outcomes over outputs, considering opportunities for both improvement and risk mitigation.
- Leverage partnerships to build social capital and to serve as vital bridges for sharing resources, knowledge and perspectives.

10 John Braithwaite, 'Regulating Nursing Homes: The Challenge of Regulating Care for Older People in Australia', *British Medical Journal* 323, no. 7310 (2001), doi.org/10.1136/bmj.323.7310.443; Valerie Braithwaite, *Defiance in Taxation and Governance: Resisting and Dismissing Authority in a Democracy* (Edward Elgar, 2009), doi.org/10.4337/9781848449077; Margot Rawsthorne et al., 'Understanding Community-Led Disaster Preparedness', *Australian Journal of Emergency Management* 38, no. 2 (2023): 49–54.

We now discuss each of these approaches in turn, while emphasising that the most effective restorative inspecting will likely arise from implementing as many of them as possible, if not all, for each inspection. We recognise that there are many inspections, especially those in the high-risk category, that will require punitive measures to hold regulates to account. However, even in high-risk contexts, restorative approaches remain important for achieving long-term improvements in communication, understanding and trust.

1. Attentiveness to relational dynamics

Restorative regulation is inherently a relational process, making it the first order of business to signal attentiveness to the relationship involved. In fact, experienced EPA practitioners whom we interviewed emphasised that this is not just the first but also the second order of business during an inspection. First comes the relational greeting; second, a conversation that centres around the problem itself, rather than any alleged wrongdoing of the regulatee. This resonates with regulatory scholar Malcolm Sparrow's advice that a regulatory encounter should start with a conversation that is about the regulator seeking to understand the problem and eliciting the regulatee's perspective on it.[11]

One senior EPA officer interviewee told us:

> I'll usually say: 'This is why I am here.' But I think it's best to approach that from: 'I'm here not necessarily to crack the whip,' although there will be circumstances where that is more than appropriate—to go there and take a no-nonsense approach. But, mostly, you want to have a conversation and get them talking about what they do. I usually start … visits with: 'What is it you do here? Take me through your process.'
>
> And I think that's a very good way of understanding it because you can't really understand what action you want them to take or what you're going to do, or even what they might have done wrong, unless you understand what it is they do. So, you've really got to take that time to understand their process, so that later on, when you're actually going round the place and looking at things, you get an idea of what those sorts of things do.[12]

11 Malcolm K. Sparrow, *The Character of Harms: Operational Challenges in Control* (Cambridge University Press, 2008), doi.org/10.1017/CBO9780511753862; Malcolm K. Sparrow, *The Regulatory Craft: Controlling Risks, Solving Problems, and Managing Compliance* (Brookings Institution Press, 2011); Malcolm K. Sparrow, *Fundamentals of Regulatory Design* (published by author, 2020).

12 Interview with a Senior EPA officer.

This senior practitioner perceived that the move to preventive duties in the new EP Act 2017, especially the general environmental duty (GED, discussed in Chapter 2), facilitated an inspection strategy of understanding the problem first:

> And this is where I think that old approach of—you know, the big stick approach of what offence has occurred—is sort of going to fall out. It's going to be more aligned with: What isn't here? What is absent? What is missing from this site? What is—where is the process going wrong? Where is the preventive duty not taking effect?
>
> [For example, with] odour and air emissions, it's not always obvious that there's pollution that's occurred. Yes, you can trace odour in the field and interview the community, and get witnesses and possibly prosecute for pollution of air, which I've done so many times, but what is harder is, okay, going back to the plant [and asking:] 'How is this odour getting out of here?' 'What is missing?' 'What is best practice?' And 'What is not being applied here?'[13]

This reflection indicates the voice of experience, noting that taking a more relational approach can help elicit more cooperation in identifying risk and preventing harm.

Restorative scholar Lindsey Pointer sums up why having this curiosity is such a valuable part of a successful relational approach:

> What strikes me about the restorative strategy for addressing behavior issues is the humility it requires on the part of the teacher, facilitator, parent or other person of authority. Rather than thinking that we know best and approaching the problem with an already formed answer (as is the case in both the punitive and the permissive strategies), the restorative strategy approaches the issue by asking questions, with a humble and compassionate desire to better understand. It is the only strategy that allows us to actually get to the core of the issue.[14]

13 Interview with an EPA field officer.

14 Pointer, 'Learning to Work "with" (The Social Discipline Window)'.

Attentiveness to the relational dynamics starts with the greeting.[15] This serves as the relational entry point and sets the scene, providing an acknowledgement of respect that cannot be overlooked.[16] One seasoned EPA practitioner said, for example, that if he is visiting a local farmer, he might greet with: 'It's pretty dry. How are the crops looking? You know, I grew up on a farm.'

The practitioner drew on his own experience:

> I've seen some people, officers, junior officers or whatever else, they come, they get out of the car [and say] … 'I'm here because I've received a complaint that you've been burning or burying waste' … [If you start like that,] you've pushed someone straight off on the wrong side straight away.[17]

Relational work continues throughout an inspection beyond the 'greeting' and the stage of 'Can you help me understand the problem?' As one Environment Protection Officer (EPO) said during a field interview that in the later stages, 'Following through on your word is a big thing as well.' These 'later stages' include when there is no alternative left but to impose enforcement actions of one kind or another. And even when the toughest regulatory action is required, relationships continue to matter. Reflecting upon a case where EPA regulatory action resulted in the company becoming bankrupt, one EPO told us:

> You can still be a strong regulator or a strong officer and do it in a respectful way. And that's why they used to call me at [the now bankrupt firm] 'the smiling assassin'. But they'd still pick up the phone and they still answer my phone calls; they still call me. They wouldn't speak to a lot of others. Most other regulators … [they] wouldn't speak to, but they still will [speak to] me because at least I was respectful to them. If they ask me to do something for them in regards to, 'Look, we can't get in contact with anyone from [a particular government agency] about XYZ,' [I'll reply,] 'Not a

15 Restorative practices practitioner Lesley Parkinson notes: 'People initially think about the word "restorative" as meaning repairing harm or something that's gone wrong, when in fact we are all restoring very small elements of our relationships every day. You could even say that greeting someone with a "good morning" is restorative, as it's reminding us of the importance of our relationship.' Lesley Parkinson, *Restorative Practices at Work* (Crown House Publishing, 2023), 9.

16 Iris Marion Young, *Inclusion and Democracy* (Oxford University Press, 2002). Iris Marion Young developed the theory around greeting as a feminist practice for eliciting social justice conversations. See also Parkinson, *Restorative Practices*, 54.

17 Interview with an EPA officer at an observation.

> problem. Leave it with me. I'll make sure I join it all up.' Okay, so at times, it's just about going a little bit above and beyond or whatever else, to build that bit of a rapport.[18]

This comment illustrates that bringing the relational skills and social competence of the inspecting officers to the forefront of interactions can make or break the regulatee's responsiveness, even in a business mostly disinclined to cooperate. In short, relational skills are essential for effective regulation.

2. The exit conference: End-of-inspection reflection

An exit conference (also known as an exit interview or exit meeting) is a meeting that typically occurs at the end of an inspection process. It usually involves a discussion between the inspecting officers and the business being inspected.

The best workplace safety regulators and aged-care-home inspectors hold an exit conference at the end of major workplace inspections. These conferences are attended by the business or facility's management as well as worker representatives. In the case of aged care facilities, residents, their relatives and advocacy group representatives also attend.[19] During the exit conference, the inspecting officers share their initial findings, any concerns they have, areas where the business could improve and possible recommendations, depending on the specific situation. This gives the business a chance to understand the inspectors' observations before issuance of formal feedback and allows the business to start addressing any issues right away, if needed.

The exit conference can be conducted formally using elements of a restorative process. This might involve everyone sitting in a restorative circle together at the end of an inspection. The goal is to agree in a participatory way on the nature of the harms identified during the inspection and how to repair them.

The exit conference does not always have to be so formal, though. It can also happen in a more casual way at the conclusion of an inspection. This allows space and opportunity for everyone to provide reflections and feedback on the inspection process.

---

18 Interview with an Environment Protection Officer (EPO) at EPA Victoria.

19 John Braithwaite, *Restorative Justice & Responsive Regulation* (Oxford University Press, 2001), 17–18, 63, doi.org/10.1093/oso/9780195136395.001.0001.

Although EPA Victoria does not include restorative exit conferences as part of its inspection practice, incipient instances of this are evident. For example, we observed that EPA officers sometimes conducted informal exit conferences where no formal notice or enforcement action was issued. In these cases, there tends to be closure through the officer having a brief, informal chat, perhaps while standing outside or while they are leaving the premises and walking to the EPA Victoria car. Sometimes, they might offer a bit of praise for things that have improved and give cautions about things to watch out for to prevent problems getting out of hand if left unattended.

These casual interactions at the end of the inspection can deepen the relationality of the inspection process. They also provide the regulator with an opportunity for iterative information-gathering on the ground, with a mind to resolving the problem quickly and forging ongoing relationships.[20]

3. Unlocking behaviour change: Motivational interviewing

Motivational interviewing (MI) is a person-centred approach through which problems can be discussed and fixed cooperatively.[21] Rather than having an expert or person in authority tell someone to change their behaviour, MI is a collaborative technique that frames discussions about behaviour change as a 'conversation between two equals',[22] encouraging exploration of the person's reasons and motivations for wanting to change.

Motivational interviewing has been shown to be highly effective in a wide range of health contexts, such as when people quit smoking, reduce alcohol consumption or improve dietary habits, thus restoring their health.[23] The same techniques work in other settings, such as probation and parole. For example, probation officers can use MI techniques to have offenders

20 John Braithwaite, Toni Makkai, and Valerie Braithwaite, *Regulating Aged Care: Ritualism and the New Pyramid* (Edward Elgar, 2007), doi.org/10.4337/9781847206855.

21 David Burnes et al., 'RISE: A Conceptual Model of Integrated and Restorative Elder Abuse Intervention', *The Gerontologist* 63, no. 6 (2022): 966–73, doi.org/10.1093/geront/gnac083.

22 Donna S. Cross, Kevin C. Runions, Ken A. Resnicow, et al., 'Motivational Interviewing as a Positive Response to High-School Bullying', *Psychology in the Schools* 55, no. 5 (2018): 646–75, doi.org/10.1002/pits.22120.

23 Jennifer Hettema, Julie Steele, and William R. Miller, 'Motivational Interviewing', *Annual Review of Clinical Psychology* 1, no. 1 (2005): 91–111, doi.org/10.1146/annurev.clinpsy.1.102803.143833; Brad W. Lundahl, Chelsea Kunz, Cynthia Brownell, et al., 'A Meta-Analysis of Motivational Interviewing: Twenty-Five Years of Empirical Studies', *Research on Social Work Practice* 20, no. 2 (2010): 137–60, doi.org/10.1177/1049731509347850.

reflect on why they want to desist from illicit drug use, rather than simply ordering them to stop. The evidence from MI suggests that officers more effectively encourage desistance when they ask why the probationer wants to desist from drug use.

In a regulatory context, MI seeks to elicit and strengthen a wayward regulatee's motivation to make changes. The technique involves exploring and addressing postures of ambivalence, uncertainty or discomfort the regulatee may have, to enable them to make positive changes in their behaviour or circumstances. In the case of environmental protection, the aim is to reflect on the motivational postures of regulatees to help them accomplish high levels of environmental stewardship.

Motivational interviewing is not a replacement for traditional restorative practices but a valuable complementary approach that can help where behaviour change forms a central component of addressing harm or resolving conflicts. In the context of a restorative approach, MI can:

- **Facilitate open and honest dialogue**. Motivational interviewing involves an emphasis on active listening and empathy, and the creation of a non-confrontational space for the expression of opinions, concerns and motivations.[24] This helps promote respectful and constructive dialogue, part of which can include the regulatee's feeling comfortable about expressing ambivalence or their mixed feelings about making changes. A skilled motivational interviewer using open questions will help conflicted individuals to explore these mixed feelings constructively.[25]
- **Promote accountability**. Motivational interviewing encourages individuals to take responsibility for their actions and the consequences caused.
- **Increase care**. As John Braithwaite notes, MI 'can build motivation to care about nonviolence and non-domination of people or ecosystems'.[26]
- **Empower autonomy**. Motivational interviewing aims to support the individual's autonomy and self-directed problem-solving, giving them a say in how to resolve the harm and take ownership of the solutions.[27]

24 John Braithwaite, 'Motivational Interviewing and Restorative Justice Praxis', in *The Praxis of Justice: Liber Amicorum Ivo Aertsen*, eds. Brunilda Pali, Katrien Lauwaert and Stefaan Pleysier (Eleven International, 2019).

25 Braithwaite, 'Motivational Interviewing and Restorative Justice Praxis'; Burnes et al., 'RISE: A Conceptual Model'; Parkinson, *Restorative Practices at Work*.

26 Braithwaite, 'Motivational Interviewing and Restorative Justice Praxis'.

27 Cross et al., 'Motivational Interviewing as a Positive Response.

- **Change behaviour.** By enhancing intrinsic motivation and making the change meaningful, MI can motivate individuals to make amends and change their behaviour permanently.[28]
- **Build rapport.** MI can develop a relationship of trust and respect, aiding future interactions and collaborative problem-solving.

Motivational interviewing has a strong evidence base for its effectiveness, not least in the promotion of intervention goals.[29] When MI is used within a restorative framework, practitioners can help individuals find the motivation to resolve problems constructively and collaboratively.

One restorative inspection hypothesis is that experienced practitioners are expert at MI. The body of evidence discussed above supports the idea that regulatory actors who elicit, and are responsive to, regulatees' own motives for compliance are more likely to achieve it. A study by Lars Forsberg, Hans Wickström and Håkan Källmén specifically found MI to be helpful in improving environmental inspections.[30] Motivational interviewing, along with positive reinforcement such as praise (discussed next), are relational practices that contribute to achieving restorative justice within regulatory inspections.

4. The power of positive feedback: Boosting compliance with praise

We hypothesise that regulators who reflect on the 'motivational postures' of regulatees, a term coined by Valerie Braithwaite, have a better chance of achieving high levels of environmental stewardship.[31] By understanding the different attitudes and mindsets of regulatees, regulators can work to transform disengaged, resistant or game-playing corporate actors into engaged and committed environmental stewards.

One effective tool that regulators can use is to make a genuine effort to communicate positive reinforcement when environmental improvements are accomplished.[32] For example, a quantitative study of aged-care-home

28 Cross et al., 'Motivational Interviewing as a Positive Response'.

29 Burnes et al., 'RISE: A Conceptual Model'.

30 Lars Forsberg, Hans Wickström, and Håkan Källmén, 'Motivational Interviewing May Facilitate Professional Interactions with Inspectees During Environmental Inspections and Enforcement Conversations', *PeerJ* 2, no. e508 (2014): 14, doi.org/10.7717/peerj.508.

31 Valerie Braithwaite, *Defiance in Taxation and Governance*.

32 John Braithwaite, 'Motivational Interviewing and Restorative Justice Praxis'.

inspections found that inspection teams who were inclined to praise improvements achieved markedly greater compliance with quality-of-care standards in the two years following inspections of 410 aged care homes.[33]

It is surprising that in the training of inspectors across all regulators, so little is spoken about informal praise (as opposed to awarding certificates or anything more formal), when praise is such an effective enforcement tool.

As part of their published regulatory approach, both EPA Victoria and EPA South Australia have integrated 'recognition and reward' into regulatory policy.[34] This enables the regulator to draw on a range of approaches, including praise and recognition, to encourage and reward good practice and behaviour (Figure 5.2).

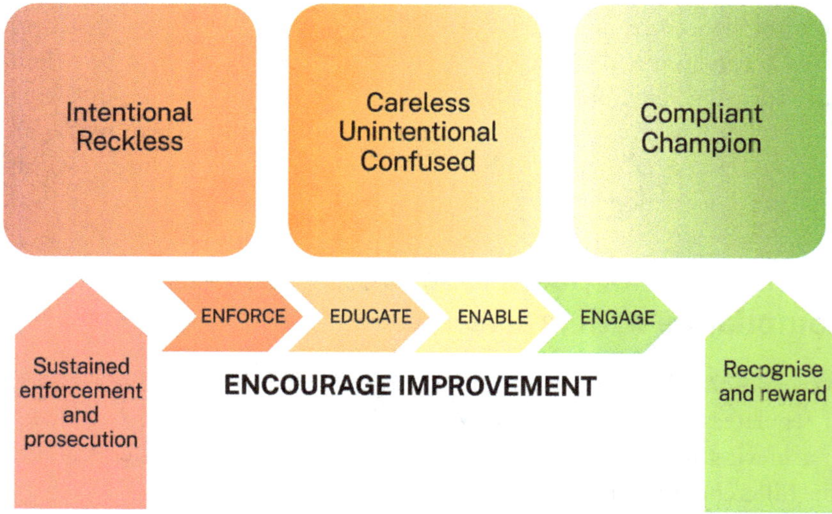

Figure 5.2. EPA South Australia's regulatory approach

Source: EPA South Australia, 'EPA Regulatory Approach: How We Interact and Intervene', last modified 4 February 2025, www.epa.sa.gov.au/business_and_industry/regulatory_approach.

33 Toni Makkai and John Braithwaite, 'Praise, Pride and Corporate Compliance', *International Journal of the Sociology of Law* 21, no. 1 (1993): 73–91.

34 EPA South Australia, 'EPA Regulatory Approach', last modified 4 February 2025, www.epa.sa.gov.au/business_and_industry/regulatory_approach; EPA Victoria, 'Support Business to Comply with the Law', last modified 25 May 2025, www.epa.vic.gov.au/node/43456#improve-practices-and-performance.

The key is for regulators to adopt a positive, motivational approach rather than a purely punitive one. By acknowledging and rewarding positive steps, they can help shift regulatees' mindsets and encourage a culture of environmental responsibility that drives meaningful, lasting environmental progress.[35] This stands in contrast to the mere imposition of penalties, which may breed resentment and resistance.

Formal acknowledgements of praise can help regulators showcase desired behaviours industry-wide and encourage similar outcomes. As former EPA CEO John Merritt says, there is value in 'spotlighting the good': 'You do need programs that recognise achievements … So, incentives, awards, we need the people who are raising the bars so we can say it's reasonable of us to expect you to aspire to that.'[36]

However, a restorative organisation will also go beyond formal forms of recognition to encourage informal praise as part of the relational approach to connecting with people, to enable them to feel seen, heard and understood.

Praise in action: A case study of a restorative joint inspection

This case study from our observation of a joint inspection under the EP Act 1970 illustrates the power of praise as a relational practice in regulatory enforcement. The inspection involved two EPA officers and a local government environment officer visiting an industrial area with a significant dust problem.

As we drove into the area, we observed many trucks emitting dust from uncovered loads on the roads leading to and from the industrial sites. This regular road traffic was a major contributor to the overall dust concentration in the area, rather than being limited to specific sites. At the time of our observation, EPA Victoria had limited powers to address dust emitted from loads on trucks when on public roads, as that fell under the regulatory jurisdiction of the Department of Transport.[37]

---

35 Research by the OECD shows that positive reinforcement can effectively encourage compliance and nurture a culture of responsibility. For example, OECD, 'Ensuring Environmental Compliance', accessed 23 February 2025, www.oecd.org/en/topics/ensuring-environmental-compliance.html.

36 Merritt, 'Incentivising Compliance'.

37 As noted above and in Chapter 2, the EP Act 2017 now includes a general environmental duty. This expectation may well expand the officers' ability to address off-site dust from truckloads.

This created a dilemma for the EPA, as Transport inspectors rarely visit the area, and the EPA was receiving community complaints about the dust. This led to the EPA feeling primarily accountable for preventing the much wider dust problem that was generated, in part, from trucks on these roads.

We asked EPA Victoria's authorised officers:[38] 'Is there is anything the EPA can do?' They told us that on site, they can and do perform multiple inspections as a response to trucks generating dust. This can lead to the officers issuing a site notice to undertake remedial works, such as installing a dousing bar and wheel washes to dampen loads and sealing surfaces on site with a hardstand. Off site, however, they told us all they could do was to ask the duty holder to warn the trucks that before they enter their site, they must cover loads to reduce the dust, perhaps by suggesting that Transport inspectors might be around. Then, if the authorised officers returned and saw the trucks entering sites with their loads now covered, they would praise the site owner for their cooperation and initiative.

Although we understand that the EP Act 2017 changes the way EPA Victoria can respond to such issues, this case study shows the regulators using the relational lever to persuade more generalised compliance beyond the site-specific regulatory tools they are legislatively empowered for. By praising the site owners for taking the initiative to address the broader community concern about dust, the inspectors were able to foster greater respect and buy-in for environmental stewardship, revealing that informal praise can be an effective complement to traditional enforcement tools.

5. Regulatory empathy: Building trust and reliance through restorative assurances

In general, we refer to 'restorative assurances' as those instances in which regulatory inspectors seek to reassure the regulatee, through statements and actions, with the intention of providing confidence, clarity, or support. They are not statements of fact or legality that bind the regulator. Rather, they are reassurances that strengthen the relational interactions between regulator and regulatee and provide support where appropriate.

38 The EP Act 2017 title for inspectors is 'authorised officers', a term also used by various other regulatory agencies in such jurisdictions as Australia, New Zealand and the United Kingdom.

Such restorative reassurances can foster a cooperative working relationship and may help with building or rebuilding trust, providing compliance guidance, promoting resilience, and encouraging growth and improvement. Restorative reassurances include acknowledgement of efforts already made by the regulatee. The regulator may use positive messaging that they are there to assist with information and knowledge to help the regulated entity better navigate the regulatory framework rather than making things more difficult.

During the inspections we attended as observers, we noted instances of these restorative assurances in action. We found them to be important in encouraging openness and trust between the parties. In one observation, for instance, we observed an authorised officer who, upon noticing a slump in the shoulders of a company representative bearing the brunt of the identified problems, reassuringly said, 'We are not trying to persecute you.'

Then an interesting thing happened. The corporate representative prefaced a revelation possibly more frank than their employer would have liked with, 'To be honest', suggesting that the EPO's kindly, supportive statement had emerged as an invitation for more frank and constructive conversation. It implied the cessation of playing the usual government-and-business games and instead focusing on being frank and getting things fixed.

This simple, empathetic encounter was relational. When it was learned that the corporate representative was keen to get to their toddler's birthday party on time, the EPO acknowledged this as important, with an ensuing warm and friendly discussion about their respective children. Referencing back to the party later in the inspection, the senior EPO twice repeated: 'We will get out of your hair now,' while also emphasising that early prevention will save time later: 'Coming up with a solution lessens the risk of anyone coming back to you.' The restorative assurances and relationality demonstrated in this particular case reveal what restorative practices of prevention can mean at the street level.

In many ways, the use of restorative assurances is innately human. But in a regulatory context, where regulatory enforcement officers sometimes feel constrained to maintain a serious and authoritative demeanour, they may feel less inclined to give such assurances. Yet, as the above observation reveals, reassurances are a valuable means of cultivating a constructive and supportive regulatory environment that both empowers the regulatee to learn, adapt and improve, and builds trust and relationality between the regulator and regulatee. Through empathy, guidance and honest communication, regulatory officers can reduce tensions and encourage cooperation, thereby promoting compliance and regulatory effectiveness without having to wield the stick.

6. Outcomes over outputs institutional support for positive inspections

A recurring issue raised by our interviewees concerned the ways in which Key Performance Indicators (KPIs), such as requirements to undertake a certain number of licence inspections, could dissuade officers from feeling they have the time and space, and the support of executive management, to undertake more restorative approaches. Retributive style enforcement outcomes (official warnings, orders, court matters, etc.) are reported on as achievements in annual reports, whereas restorative interventions are not.

In the context of environmental protection, outputs refer to the tangible, measurable results such as the number of inspections conducted within a period of time. Environmental outcomes, on the other hand, reduce the numbers of pollution incidents and even avert such incidents, increase cooperation and compliance, deepen the regulatee's environmental awareness and lead to a long-view consideration of environmental protection. There is a regulatory tension and a balance to be struck between ensuring that the regulator undertakes inspections of the premises to which it has issued licences and ensuring that there is time and space for being responsive.

A positive environmental outcome, for example, is when a polluter fully understands the consequences of the pollution they are responsible for, and commits to addressing it systemically, so that it never happens again—thereby ensuring a 'preventive outcome'.

The focus on regulatory *outputs* that can easily be counted risks undermining the advantages that come from a focus on environmental *outcomes*. 'Non-events' like *not* polluting and *not* destroying habitat often fail to be counted, recognised or rewarded in technocratic approaches to protecting the environment. This lack of recognition has a cumulative impact on the regulatory enforcement culture: opportunities for identifying and boosting preventive outcomes tend to be negated and practices that lead to preventive outcomes overlooked.

The risk-based approach has become standard across many regulatory agencies, and regulators tend to overlook the benefits of seeking out opportunities to improve. For this reason, we suggest that a focus on outcome over outputs should involve identifying and maximising these opportunities, not just mitigating risks.[39]

Many officers in the field are alert to the need to conduct 'beyond-inspection' site visits that emphasise prevention, rather than just issuing notices. One officer told us:

> I've been to many sites with my key stakeholders as an engagement piece just for information instruction, not to sit there and inspect the site because there's a site to inspect, but to go there and have conversations and talk about what might happen if you do this and this. We've got some senior leaders in this team [who think] that it's like our job to stop work from coming in. How you do that? You get engaged, you get out there and talk … I believe that there's a place for numbers, absolutely, it tells you that you are doing your work, and how you're tracking against targets, and that is important. There's also some strategic components to do. You work to protect the environment, human health, all that stuff, which, you might only get one number for, but you might spend 60 or more days on and it's more important to do that.[40]

Perfunctory inspections that amount to 'regulatory ritualism' are a major problem in many regulatory authorities.[41] John Braithwaite and Valerie Braithwaite testified to the Royal Commission on Aged Care that if we want to understand why 80 per cent of COVID-19 deaths occurred in aged care homes in Australia (with similar outcomes in some other countries),[42] we must understand the pathology of a long-term regulatory ritualism of hitting inspection targets, combined with a short-term unwillingness of public service leaders to put inspectors in the field to check infection-control compliance when it was most needed.

---

39 This challenge is not unique to regulation. Anthea Roberts discusses the need for integrative policy approaches that balance risk, reward and resilience in complex policy, business and regulatory systems. Anthea Roberts, 'Risk, Reward, and Resilience Framework: Integrative Policy Making in a Complex World', *Journal of International Economic Law* 26, no. 2, (2023): 233–265, 240, doi.org/10.1093/jiel/jgad009.

40 Interview with an EPA officer.

41 Braithwaite, Makkai and Braithwaite, *Regulating Aged Care*.

42 For percentages of aged care deaths due to COVID-19 in Australia, since 2020, see Department of Health, Disability and Ageing, 'COVID-19 Outbreaks in Australian Residential Aged Care Facilities', Australian Government, last modified 20 January 2026, www.health.gov.au/resources/collections/covid-19-outbreaks-in-australian-residential-aged-care-facilities.

The most committed frontline staff in any regulatory agency tend to have a deep understanding of what is required to achieve an objective like protecting the environment. Qualitative analysis of our data reveals resentment towards the required load of paperwork following inspections, compounded by KPIs that can get in the way of improving the environmental outcomes. Heavy reporting requirements following inspections were viewed by EPOs on inspections as strong disincentives to also visit licence holders nearby, particularly as that would mean being saddled with additional paperwork.

One private-sector legal practitioner we interviewed held the view that KPIs that are focused on hitting targets for more formal enforcement actions can sometimes undermine a commitment to environmental stewardship. The following quote reflects a concern that prioritising the meeting of targets could weaken prevention because focusing on targets punishes active stewardship:

> I'll give you an example of that. A client that owns or operates an industrial site will identify a particular historical issue to do with an aspect of their site, where they might identify that there's an issue that needs to be addressed, some kind of contamination, whatever it might be. The client has identified it, and the client proactively communicates with EPA about it and says to EPA, 'This is what we've found, this is what we're going to do about it. Are you happy with that?' The EPA say, 'Yes, that sounds great. Thanks for doing that.' Then they issue a pollution abatement notice, which formalises, in a statutory instrument or in a statutory notice, what the client's said they're going to do. The client will often get grumpy about that because a pollution abatement notice is effectively public. The fact that you've been issued with one is public, and you're required internally to notify it up through senior management ranks. It's the sort of thing that will go into your corporate sustainability report or your public environmental reporting in relation to your performance.[43]

An unintended—and perverse—consequence of an over-reliance on targets is that it is not a measure for addressing risk. There are times of crisis (such as the Hazelwood Mine fire) when KPI pressure drives responsiveness to environmental stewardship in a counterproductive direction. As one EPA officer put it:

43 Interview with a private sector lawyer.

> Or we've got [a risk monitoring system], and they just come up with a number each year that we have to hit for our licence compliance inspections. When a Footscray fire hits and something else hits, we still have to do the same number … [We] always ended up doing it, and it affects the wellbeing of our staff. They get burned out; they move jobs because they have so much to do and they still have to hit that number … For the licence inspections, we actually have a checklist that we take with us when we do licence inspections. It's a behavioural-based checklist … It asks questions like, do you have an environmental management plan? Do you have an environmental statement for your site? Do you have health and safety procedures? Do you have all these things? Are you aware of your obligations? … It's difficult because, on one hand, I would like … us to not be so focused on numbers, but on the other hand, I know there are ways that you can measure behaviour change at work.[44]

While we acknowledge that this is just one viewpoint and does not necessarily reflect the views of many others we interviewed, it nonetheless goes to the heart of the broader concern that compliance systems may overly focus on easily quantifiable metrics.[45] This over-reliance has the potential to undermine relational, outcomes-focused approaches, for, as author Seth Godin points out, '[M]etrics (and methods) don't work for human interactions, insight, or innovation'.[46] He further notes:

> What actually separates thriving organizations from struggling ones are the difficult-to-measure attitudes, processes, and perceptions of the people who do the work. Culture defeats strategy, every time. Measurable skills without productive attitudes aren't worth much.[47]

One way to respond to these concerns is at an institutional level. It involves developing alternative metrics that can be used to measure and incentivise better environmental outcomes following restorative inspections. One good suggestion was made by an EPA officer who stated, 'There's other ways to measure than statistics. It's all about narrative …' As we noted in previous chapters, in restorative justice, stories are acknowledged as powerful forms

44 Interview with an EPA officer.

45 There is a natural human tendency to try to simplify problems by focusing on the most easily measurable elements. But what is most easily measured is rarely what is most important, indeed sometimes not important at all. That is the first source of metric dysfunction.

Jerry Z. Muller, *The Tyranny of Metrics* (Princeton University Press, 2018), 23, doi.org/10.2307/j.ctvc77h85.

46 Seth Godin, *The Song of Significance: A New Manifesto for Teams* (Penguin Random House, 2023), 41.

47 Godin, *Song of Significance*, 112.

of communicating. Stories tap into our emotions as well as our thoughts, recalling Kate Gavens' prompt to win hearts and minds.[48] They can provide reassurance that behavioural change, and healing of environment and communities is possible.[49]

It should be a priority for regulators to find ways to use stories to encourage restorative inspections that result in avoidance of harm, through the sharing of valuable insights and lessons from experience. Regulators could achieve this, for instance, by regularly sharing case studies between inspecting officers, having a dedicated intranet space featuring exemplary stories and outcomes, incorporating storytelling into training programs and developing an internal community of practice. To embed this outcomes-oriented approach in the regulator, it is important that senior management sets the tone by actively supporting and promoting such sharing of stories, confirming its value in staff learning and development in restorative practices. We discuss some of these suggestions in more detail in Chapter 10.

7. Restorative inspection through partnerships

One final way to do restorative compliance is through co-regulatory models or partnerships. We came across three examples of these during our research that had restorative potential: the Officers for the Protection of the Local Environment (OPLE), the Environment Protection on Country (EPOC) pilot program and the Build Aware program. We discuss the EPOC program in Chapter 9; the other two examples are discussed here.

The first example is the OPLE program.[50] This is a co-regulatory partnership with municipal or rural council environmental inspectors. OPLE officers were typically located at either the council or EPA offices, depending on the local arrangements, and are now only in EPA offices. Their role is to assist local councils in managing smaller pollution reports (e.g. concerning

48 Kate Gavens, 'Incentivising Compliance'; Miranda Forsyth et al., 'A Future Agenda for Environmental Restorative Justice?', *The International Journal of Restorative Justice* 4, no. 1 (2021): 17–40, doi.org/10.5553/tijrj.000063.; see Chapter 1 for a discussion on winning hearts and minds.

49 Miller, 'The Importance of Storytelling'.

50 'Officers for the Protection of the Local Environment', EPA Victoria, last modified 17 December 2024, www.epa.vic.gov.au/officers-protection-local-environment.

litter, dust, odours and noise), provide environmental monitoring and assessment support, and offer environmental education to business and the community.[51]

The OPLE program is a great example of 'smart regulation'. It effectively combines the enforcement tools and the relational capital available to both EPA Victoria and the local council in joint inspection teams.[52] Planning orders are one example of enforcement tools available to councils that are not available to the EPA. Our research suggests OPLE is a valuable regulatory innovation, extending access to inspection know-how and resources particularly in rural and regional communities that are often underserved compared to larger towns and cities, where most regulators tend to concentrate their efforts. Neglected rural communities have warmed to the program for this reason, with one local media outlet even describing their OPLE as a 'new gem' enriching the Gippsland (Latrobe City and Baw Baw Shire Councils).[53]

The OPLE program was developed to enable the EPA to focus its resources more on the biggest environmental issues, as a way of targeting sites and problems. As the OPLE is place-based, it leaves more room for taking a restorative, humanised and relational approach. In 2022, the OPLE program was reviewed and expanded to cover all local government areas across Victoria.

We can theorise the potential of the OPLE program as building bridging social capital in a world of rural disadvantage, where people often feel that the only political voice they have is through their elected local council member.[54] All too often, rural residents are easily forgotten, leaving them feeling that no-one in either state or federal governments is listening to them. Even if municipal officers in their shire council do not appear to listen to environmental concerns, the OPLE program at least provides a pathway for these voices to be heard because the regulatory conversation now includes a

---

51 Environment Protection Authority Victoria, 'Officers for the Protection of the Local Environment (OPLEs)'.

52 For more details on what smart regulation consists of, refer to Neil Gunningham, Peter N. Grabosky and Darren Sinclair, *Smart Regulation: Designing Environmental Policy* (Clarendon Press, 1998), doi.org/10.1093/oso/9780198268574.001.0001; Neil Gunningham and Darren Sinclair, 'Smart Regulation' in *Regulatory Theory Foundations and Applications*, ed. Peter Drahos (ANU Press, 2017), 133–48, doi.org/10.22459/rt.02.2017.08.

53 'OPLE to Shine in Gippsland', *Mirage News*, 28 August 2019, www.miragenews.com/ople-to-shine-in-gippsland/.

54 Robert D. Putnam, *Bowling Alone: The Collapse and Revival of American Community* (Simon & Schuster, 2000).

local officer who is attuned to the shire and its issues. When EPA Victoria listens to its OPLEs, it is in turn listening to the bridges of social capital that connect to rural voices. This includes the voices of its own staff, who are rural people themselves, inspecting in rural spaces.

The most frequent focal areas of OPLE inspections are water, noise and illegal waste, with other issues-—such as air, odour, general waste and septics—being less common. This suggests the program is responsive to the specific environmental challenges faced by rural and regional communities.

The second example of a co-regulatory model or partnership involves the Build Aware program, which takes regulators as a whole out of their silos.[55] In the region around Wodonga, for example, three times a year since 2016, the Victorian Building Authority, WorkSafe Victoria, Energy Safe Victoria, Consumer Affairs (Victoria) and EPA Victoria join forces to conduct five days of targeted inspections of around 200 building sites.[56] Each agency visits only a selection of these sites (40 out of 200 for the EPA). Not all agencies deploy locals with rural relational capital, but enough of them do for the bridging capital to work, and for each agency to be eyes and ears for issues to which other agencies should, in fact, be responsive.

This program provides a working example of the way in which different agencies can work alongside each other to provide an educational campaign about environmental responsibilities for an industry sector (construction and building). It allows inspectors to share inspection stories and ideas, and gives EPA officers a chance to raise awareness of the new GED under the EP Act 2017. It can also showcase, for public viewing, the willingness and collegiality of different government agencies working together to prevent environmental harm. It is relational at both the workplace and community levels, as a form of 'relational agency' in which '[r]elational agency shifts the focus from the system to joint action and the impact on those who engage in it between and across systems'.[57]

55 'Meeting your obligations', EPA Victoria, last modified 15 May 2025, www.epa.vic.gov.au/meeting-your-obligations.

56 'Build Aware Shows High Compliance in Wodonga', *Mirage News*, 17 September 2019, www.miragenews.com/build-aware-shows-high-compliance-in-wodonga/. See also 'The Build Aware campaign,' Environment Protection Authority Victoria.

57 Anne Edwards, 'Relational Agency: Learning to Be a Resourceful Practitioner', *International Journal of Educational Research* 43, no. 3 (2005): 174, doi.org/10.1016/j.ijer.2006.06.010.

These examples from the context of EPA Victoria exemplify what is possible through the development and implementation of a partnership-oriented or co-regulatory approach. Such partnerships, combined with the local deployment of larger numbers of regulatory staff and the formation of networks with local councils, other regulators and Traditional Owner organisations, and supplemented by a pivot towards a more place-based and regional focus (as we saw happening with EPA Victoria), can provide a more restorative approach—one that is inclusive, participatory and transparent.

Towards a restorative approach to inspections

This chapter has demonstrated a range of practicable, realistic and valuable possibilities for taking a more restorative route to regulatory inspections in all regulatory spheres, including the environmental domain, aged care and work safety. Our observations of inspections and interviews with EPA Victoria's field officers have revealed a range of different understandings, viewpoints and hopes as to the way inspections currently work, along with pertinent stories and reflections for how they might work more restoratively in the future.

The tension between the desire to promote good relationality in inspection work and the requirement to fulfil all the paperwork in a timely and comprehensive manner is a challenge faced by many regulatory organisations across Australia and around the world. While valuable, KPIs cannot be the sole measure by which we judge the effectiveness of inspections and compliance. As John Braithwaite says, 'They have a place but must be kept in their place' or we risk 'the more measurable driving out the more important'.[58] A broader focus on seeking better environmental outcomes and fostering cooperative, responsive regulatory relationships supports both continuous improvement and the integration of restorative practices. Restorative practices practitioner Lesley Parkinson sums this up well:

58 John Braithwaite, 'Responsive Excellence', Working paper (University of Pennsylvania, 2015), 1–12, 7–8.

> [F]or restorative practices to become the new norm, a key and significant finding … is that when leading and enabling a culture of continuous improvement, relationships count' [and organisations] 'should pay as much attention to the social side of change … as the technical side.[59]

From MI and restorative assurances to encouraging praise and reflection, the seven approaches we have highlighted provide a good foundation for restorative inspecting. With its emphasis on working with the innate human desire to connect and relate, restorative inspecting can help reduce tensions and strengthen cooperativeness. This builds positive relationships between inspecting officers and inspected regulatees, relationships that go to the heart of supporting compliance, improving environmental performance and fostering a culture of responsible stewardship.

In our next chapter, we explore the application of restorative approaches to emergency situations. We discuss how these approaches can provide effective ways to respond to unexpected challenges; first, by drawing on locally contextual knowledge as events unfold, then by harnessing the community's collective wisdom and resilience to shape a more connected and sustainable recovery.

59 Parkinson, *Restorative Practices*, 25.

6

Restorative responses to reports of harm

Source: Author.

> *[T]rue restorative justice goes to the issue of community of impact and talking to that community of impact about what they see as restorative. What would they like to see happen?*
>
> —Cheryl Batagol[1]

1 Interview with Cheryl Batagol, former Chair of EPA Victoria, 16 October 2020 at EPA headquarters, Melbourne.

This chapter explores how regulators can adopt a restorative, relational first response to harm, particularly during and after emergency events. We look at best practices for prioritising the needs of affected communities to ensure they are acknowledged and addressed promptly and empathetically. We also offer suggestions for handling community reports, complaints and concerns in a way that builds trust and supports long-term relational engagement.

Things go wrong, even with the best-laid plans. A factory accident releases toxic chemicals, a pile of stored rubbish catches alight, or a sewage pipe bursts. When these incidents occur, citizens expect to be able to report the matter to the state and receive a quick and effective response to their concern. When we first talk to someone about an issue, their initial response is critical—this we are increasingly learning from research into the role of first responders in contexts such as mental health incidents and sexual assault. The first point of contact can either establish trust and confidence or leave people feeling disappointed and frustrated, asking why they bothered reporting the incident at all.

In this chapter we discuss ways in which incorporating restorative elements into regulators' responses to citizen concerns and alarms is beneficial, and how these elements can be nurtured. While initial encounters between citizens and regulators are rarely considered in need of a restorative focus, we argue that they should be. In fact, early encounters can build a solid relational foundation for helping affected individuals and communities recover from harm and build resilience.

The concept of 'path dependency', a principle studied by complexity scientists, sheds light on why these initial moments matter.[2] The evidence on path dependency shows that complex systems are highly influenced by early events, suggesting that initial encounters can disproportionately

2 'Path dependence is a dynamic theory assuming that initial events can increasingly constrain present and future choices.' Jochen Koch, Martin Eisend, and Arne Petermann, 'Path Dependence in Decision-Making Processes: Exploring the Impact of Complexity Under Increasing Returns', *Business Research* 2, no. 1 (2009): 67–84, 67, doi.org/10.1007/bf03343529.

set the tone for a relationship.[3] A brief reflection on your own relational network will likely remind you how first encounters often determine which relationships you embrace and which you walk away from.

The chapter first examines public incident reporting before turning to emergency response. Drawing on our research in EPA Victoria, we use case studies of environmental regulation to illustrate these interactions, but our analysis applies as well to other regulators that rely on reports from the public. While incident reports and emergency response may seem to exist at opposite ends of a spectrum of seriousness, we argue that a restorative approach improves the outcomes of both, for similar reasons.

Heeding what members of the public or community have to say about what is going on is vital.[4] Whether facing immediate crises or slow-burning environmental degradation, community members are often the first to detect changes in their surroundings. Their daily observations of shifts in what is normal in their environs offer the first clues that something is not right. Community is often the first to witness an eruption of problems and call it in. When regulators fail to value this input—when public reports and complaints go unheard—frustration and disengagement follow.[5] A regulatory system that listens, acknowledges and responds effectively can harness community willingness to help and reassure citizens that their concerns are getting fixed.

Incident reporting by the public

Incident reporting presents an important opportunity for the regulator to establish a good relationship with members of the public. Much of the dynamic of that relationship is set the first time a person calls to report a pollution event. On the one hand, the caller may not get the response they

3 Celeste A. Kettaneh, William T. Chung, and Kevin C. Chung, 'First Impressions: Setting the Stage for Better Relationships', *Plastic and Reconstructive Surgery* 152, no. 4 (2023): 693–98, doi.org/10.1097/PRS.0000000000010661; Robert B. Lount Jr. and Nathan C. Pettit, 'The Social Context of Trust: The Role of Status', *Organizational Behavior and Human Decision Processes* 117, no. 1 (2012): 15–23, doi.org/10.1016/j.obhdp.2011.07.005.

4 Cary Coglianese, *Listening, Learning Leading: A Framework for Regulatory Excellence* (The Penn Program on Regulation, 2015).

5 Susan Biggar, Louisa M. Lobigs, and Martin Fletcher, 'How Can We Make Health Regulation More Humane? A Quality Improvement Approach to Understanding Complainant and Practitioner Experiences', *Journal of Medical Regulation* 106, no. 1 (2020): 7–15, doi.org/10.30770/2572-1852-106.1.7.

are after or get any response at all. Conversely, they may receive a response that affirms the importance of their communication, validating the effort they have taken to bring it to the attention of the regulator.

Clearly, ensuring that a regulator's reporting mechanism makes members of the public feel heard is essential. We tend to trust people who take the time to understand what we are saying in the context in which we want to situate it.[6] Whether the regulator ultimately agrees with their perspective is often less important than the experience of having been genuinely understood. Active listening and attuned responsiveness not only build trust in the regulatory process but also reinforce a sense of procedural fairness.[7]

From an operational standpoint, it is imperative for a regulator to actively promote and encourage public reporting. Citizen reports of pollution events are a crucial way to bring harm to the regulator's attention. Members of the public who care enough to make the effort to report are the 'eyes, ears and noses' of their communities. In the case of EPA Victoria, public reports can cover a wide range of pollutants, including noise emissions, illegal waste dumping, smoke in the air or from vehicles, foul, abnormal or offensive odours, waste or chemical spills into creeks and rivers, littering and more.[8]

Reporting harm is a form of citizen empowerment. It is a means for the public to monitor and hold to account those responsible for local environmental harm. It also plays a role in protecting community wellbeing, especially since many pollution events have far-reaching effects when contaminants disperse through air or water. From the perspective of the environment—an interest without a voice—citizen reporting becomes a means of advocacy that gives nature a voice while reinforcing that protecting the environment is in everybody's interest.

6 This trust is heightened by 'meeting community members *where they are at*' [and] 'looking at community members as whole people, not just someone with a problem that must be fixed'. Amy E. Lansing et al., 'Building Trust: Leadership Reflections on Community Empowerment and Engagement in a Large Urban Initiative', *BMC Public Health* 23 (2023): 1–25, 9, doi.org/10.1186/s12889-023-15860-z.

7 Edward Kass, 'The Power of Nice: Active Listening, Procedural and Interpersonal Fairness Perceptions and Prosocial and Antisocial Negotiation Behaviors', *Organization, Leadership, and Communications* 6 (2010), repository.usfca.edu/olc/6.

8 For EPA Victoria's online pollution reporting portal, see, 'What Pollution and Waste You Can Report', EPA Victoria, last modified, 9 january 2025, www.epa.vic.gov.au/what-pollution-and-waste-you-can-report.

How does incident reporting work in EPA Victoria?

Within the context of EPA Victoria's reporting framework, calls from the community reporting pollution, or complaining about management of an environmental harm, are handled by a contracted Melbourne call centre. There is, in addition, a small permanent staff who manage customer service.

The involvement of a contract to a precariat of call centre workers has both negative and positive effects. On the one hand, commitment to and knowledge of EPA values may be truncated, potentially jeopardising the relationship between community and regulator. On the other hand, when a disaster event occurs, all available EPA staff are rightly focused on managing the event itself and are working long hours. This is obviously the appropriate priority for restoring the environment and assuring human health.

Still, empathetic initial response is not the same as feedback being provided directly from knowledgeable staff after the fire is extinguished. The ability to provide feedback on actions taken, measures to be put in place to prevent recurrence, and assistance available to aid the recovery of those still suffering the aftereffects of the incident, is a vital regulatory function that cannot be avoided or outsourced.

Building a restorative approach to incident reporting

> *[I]ncident responses must be conceived within a relational as well as a regulatory framework, and … this—a restorative response—has the potential to radically shift the focus, conduct and outcomes of investigative processes.*[9]

Regardless of the mechanisms in place for answering calls from the community, both those who are receiving calls and any staff providing follow-up can help ensure that the experience for members of the public is a restorative one.

A restorative approach to pollution reporting goes beyond simply logging complaints; it requires thoughtful and proactive engagement with civic reporters. We identify three key restorative approaches to guide responsiveness to incident reporting:

9 Jo Wailling et al., 'Humanizing Harm: Using a Restorative Approach to Heal and Learn From Adverse Events', *Health Expectations* 25, no. 4 (2022): 1193, doi.org/10.1111/hex.13478.

1. demonstrating deep listening and empathy
2. providing meaningful feedback
3. ensuring there is a 'no-wrong-door' policy.

Below, we explore what each of these entails in practice.

1. Practise deep listening and empathy towards civic reporters

The regulator's response to a civic reporter should demonstrate deep listening and an expression of empathy, even more so where there is a likelihood of disagreement. As discussed in Chapter 1, deep listening is a core restorative practice. In this context, it means careful, attentive listening to the civic reporter, with an awareness of the potential impacts of the incident or issue being reported. Since these interactions will almost always occur over the phone, the medium itself imposes certain limits on what is possible.

Deep listening is both an innate capability and a trainable soft or real skill. An organisation attentive to empathy as a capability will seek to integrate it into the core of its operations—for example, by hiring individuals with a natural inclination for connection and for understanding others, encouraging empathetic leadership to set the tone for the whole organisation and recognising employees who demonstrate such leadership in the course of their work.[10] As a soft or real skill, empathy can be developed through training programs that teach fundamental techniques—such as deep listening, emotional validation, open-ended questioning and perspective-taking—while also offering advanced strategies for managing complex interactions, such as responding effectively to an angry or distressed civic reporter.[11] Role-playing exercises and real-life case discussions can help staff gain insights and refine their approach. Additionally, training can support employees in managing the emotional toll of these interactions, equipping them with strategies for enhancing their emotional regulation and resilience.

One regional EPA Victoria manager reflected that they would not typically expect a private call centre, governed by contract, to deliver a flexible and relational response. However, we were given an unexpected example of just that. A woman, distraught over the death of her cat the previous night, was referred to the local regional office. In Australia, where 'feral' (non-domestic)

10 Coglianese, *Listening, Learning Leading.*

11 Biggar et al., 'Health Regulation More Humane?'.

cats pose a severe threat to native fauna, a dead cat could never rate on EPA Victoria's risk metrics that guide enforcement triage. Yet, to maintain trust, the EPA must respond to more than just risk. This means not only expressing empathy but also acknowledging the extent to which pollution impacts affect individual community members, even when the impact may only be perceived.

The complaint staff and system had the wisdom to prompt a call of deep concern to the complainant, responding to the impact of the odour complaint on both the community member and her cat—a call made by a reasonably senior EPA staff member. Why was it important to escalate the complaint? It was not only because the complaint was formally made regarding the odour but also because it acknowledged the complainant's personal experience in a holistic way. Her cat had fallen ill on a cold winter's night, and the putrid smell from a nearby waste disposal site was so overpowering that it forced her to keep the home heater off—she refused to circulate the tainted air inside. The complainant believed that her cat died because it was shivering so severely. For her, this was a matter for EPA Victoria because it converged with the ongoing harm caused by foul odours affecting her and her entire neighbourhood.

The deep listening demonstrated in this incident report allowed all aspects of the pollution impact to be recognised. She was given information about the steps EPA Victoria was taking to prevent a similar incident from ever happening again. Additionally, she was invited to join the CRGs for the odour-causing site—a chance to transform her experience as a wounded member of the community into an opportunity to become a healer of the environment. Her story serves as a valuable example of how a regulator can ensure that a citizen not only receives a sincere apology for the failure to prevent the incident but also learns about the corrective actions being taken, and experiences attentive care and empathy. Because the responders did not apportion blame, shirk responsibility or dismiss the caller's experience as 'trivial', both the process and the outcome displayed restorative values and practice.

A restorative organisation can effectively use a call centre to handle enquiries and complaints, as EPA Victoria currently does, provided that appropriate structures are in place. Training those receiving calls to be attentive to restorative reporting should not be challenging. In fact, the existing quality assurance process already incorporates some restorative criteria when calls are reviewed. Feedback questions such as, 'Actively listened to customer?', 'Rapport building?', and 'Clear communication?' are examples of how restorative values can be integrated into call centre operations.

In other words, we are suggesting that some small but key changes to the process for responding to calls, incorporating more explicitly restorative criteria, will make this process more robustly restorative. These small changes will require a response to criteria such as:

- Showing a sense of urgency to solve the customer's issue
- Acknowledging the importance of the issue to the customer
- Expressing empathy.

It is entirely reasonable to expect a regulator to engage a call centre that has well-trained and empathetically responsive staff. In fact, any reputable call centre should prioritise a high standard of empathic care in their interactions. Environmental and other regulators can impose terms in their contracts with customer service providers that make this an expectation. A clause could also be included to require regular surveys of citizens who call in, eliciting their responses after the call to statements like:

- I felt the EPA's response showed it was an authority that genuinely listened to citizens.
- I was satisfied with the timeliness of the response to my call.
- I was satisfied with the quality of the response to my call.
- EPA Victoria's response made me feel that it took my complaint seriously.

Continuous improvement in independently audited results over the years, reflecting high satisfaction levels, might help secure a response to pollution and complaint reporting that is increasingly restorative. The regulator's leadership needs to ensure, however, that not only is the call centre it contracts accountable for a more restorative response; ultimately, frontline and regional staff, and the board, are also accountable to the community for their interactions with them in times of distress, urgency and problems.

2. Provide meaningful feedback to civic reporters

Citizens lose trust in government when they make what they believe is a serious report or complaint and hear nothing back. In most instances, where substantive feedback is required, it cannot come from a call centre. It must come from the regulator's experts who have been at the frontline.

When we first started our research, EPA Victoria was responding to this challenge with a KPI requiring that all reports and complaints receive a reply within three days. Although this KPI seemed to promise increased engagement, its time constraint meant that it failed to have a restorative impact because few environmental problems can be resolved in just three days. As a result, the overwhelming majority of people who made an environmental report to the pollution hotline only received initial advice about the status of their report over those three days, stating little more than that EPA Victoria was working on the issue (or sometimes, not working on it). In many cases, that was the last communication the complainants heard.

One EPA officer told us they would say to people: 'Please keep reporting if the issue persists.' She continued: 'We'll give them a spiel of how important it is to us for them to keep reporting, but that's not an update to them. It's a useless KPI.' The call centre is a business, so it met the KPI, but little more, to fulfil its contract.

Since conducting our interviews, the model has changed somewhat, with the three-day response time extended to five days to provide increased scope for information-gathering. Citizens will be told that their issue has been 'triaged' (assessed to determine its urgency and the next steps). The notification will say that either it has gone to the next step or the incident has been closed after being assessed through a triage process. When the report made does not fall within the purview of the EPA, it is sent on to the correct agency with a 'warm transfer' (a direct, assisted handover).

The need for a meaningful response raises a tricky distinction between providing a response that satisfies the civic reporter and addressing the full scope of what the regulator is able to achieve. One EPA officer we interviewed explained:

> Most community members who are complaining about, for example, a landfill … would [resolve to] close the landfill, which in most cases, 99 per cent of the time, isn't going to happen.

She said this limitation on what EPA Victoria can do makes it difficult for the people calling back to report on progress, because:

> [E]ven though [the company may have] done everything to comply, from the people she's spoken to, that's not good news. That's still not good news, because they want blood … They want [the] EPA to suspend them, fine them through the roof, whereas [the business] complying with our demands isn't a good news story for them.

She further commented that the combination of community frustration and strict adherence to legal boundaries requires EPA Victoria to come in with what she called 'the education piece'. This approach ensures the community is made aware that established processes are in place to manage the situation and that it is the EPA's responsibility to make sure the previously offending business remains in compliance with the set of rules that permit its continued operation.

A 'restorative piece' can also help to ease the tension and soften the unresolved hope that the company will have the book thrown at it or be permanently shut down. As we know from restorative justice research in other domains, after a restorative dialogue has occurred, when people feel listened to and have had the opportunity to engage with different perspectives on the issue, they are far less likely to insist on highly punitive responses to harm.

If the complainant continues to feel that the EPA's response in relation to an offending business is insufficient, a restorative piece might entail turning the 'education piece' into more than the mere imparting of information. As well, it could mean acknowledging the complainant's ongoing grievance and taking steps to restore trust by communicating the changes the business operator has implemented, along with details on how these adjustments have reduced or prevented harm to people and the environment. The process may extend further by connecting the complainant with the business operator for an open day-style tour or similar site visit, to allow the community member to witness the improvements firsthand and directly ask questions of the operator.

This effort can result in good relational outcomes for both the complainant and the regulator. The acknowledgement and detailed communications outlined above demonstrate both attentiveness to the complainant's concerns and the facilitation of appropriate direct engagement, two important factors in strengthening the regulatory process. As lawyer Natasha Danson explains:

> [I]f the representative of the regulator demonstrates compassion, empathy (without showing favouritism), respects the dignity of the complainant … listens to them, and treats their concerns seriously, the complainant … will respond more cooperatively and favourably and will have a more positive view of the regulator.[12]

12 Natasha Danson, 'The Case for Empathy by Regulators', *Grey Areas: A Commentary on Legal Issues Affecting Professional Regulation*, no. 248 (2020), Steinecke Maciura LeBlanc Barristers & Solicitors, www.sml-law.com/wp-content/uploads/2020/07/Greyar248.pdf.

It is also beneficial for the regulator to view the unresolved complaint as 'free feedback' that potentially highlights ongoing discontent within the community. This feedback can signal the need for broader engagement, such as through community forums like the Open House or a Q&A at the next CRGs meeting.

3. Implement a policy of 'no wrong door' for reporting

Environmental regulation is a complex institutional ecology that can confound even its insiders. For instance, if someone calls EPA Victoria's call centre about an incident such as a fire—whether at a factory, involving chemicals, or even piles of tyres—the EPA will usually not be the appropriate responder. If the call relates to the immediate fire emergency, the Metropolitan Fire Brigade (now known as Fire Rescue Victoria) would likely be the first responder. If the call concerns chemicals released by the fire flowing up Stony Creek after a fire incident, Melbourne Water would likely be the relevant responder. In other cases, it may be Maribyrnong Council, WorkSafe Victoria or EPA Victoria. Essentially, which agency is responsible for responding will depend on the aspect of the problem causing trouble and the stage of its lifecycle in which it occurs.

Given the diversity of potential responders, one restorative practice that might ensure genuine listening and a voice for citizens is to adopt a 'no-wrong-door' policy. We previously discussed this in Chapter 3 in the context of communities seeking information from regulators. For high-impact incidents, emergency protocols across response agencies already incorporate a no-wrong-door approach: whichever agency receives the initial notification triggers notifications to the appropriate response agency. For non-emergency situations, this policy would require agencies to structure it into their approach and procedures.

An idea of what this would look like in practice was outlined to us by an EPA officer:

> [T]he No Wrong Door principle is not a bad restorative principle, because it's to say, 'We'll support you even though you've come to the wrong door. This is not the complaint line you should have called, you should have called Melbourne City Council or Aboriginal Victoria, or whatever.' For the line to be able to say, 'We can help you, but one of the main ways we will help you is getting you in contact with the relevant City of Melbourne contact person for this matter.'

When civic reporters voice their concerns and provide information about a pressing harm like a factory blaze or a burning pile of tyres, having a no-wrong-door policy in place ensures that their information reaches the right agencies. It also reassures the civic reporters that their efforts are worthwhile and are being acted upon. Moreover, the civic reporter can be given directions as to which agency will follow up with them when the incident has been dealt with. This not only streamlines the work of the regulators involved but also helps the citizen understand which agency is the right one to contact for follow-up or any future issues.

The no-wrong-door policy is restorative in both intent and outcome. It unites agencies, communities and industry under a common goal: to fix the problem and safeguard people and the environment. Much like restorative justice, it is forward-looking, collaborative and focused upon shared responsibility.

Pollution reporting and environmental priorities

While responsiveness to the direct citizen voice is unequivocally important, enforcement resources are always scarce in regulatory agencies. Some EPA officers we interviewed noted a concern that sometimes too many resources were devoted to responding to the 'squeakiest wheels'. They thought this happened because it seemed the 'politically safe' thing to do, even when it was unclear if community complaints were legitimate.

The volume of complaints, the feedback from a restorative conference or reports from a CRGs of citizens living near a waste disposal site may direct attention to issues such as foul odours or intermittent backyard-burning haze. These nuisances, while unpleasant, are generally less harmful to human and environmental health than some more hazardous issues that might lack odours or visibility yet do not raise sensory ire. This reaction makes sense: as embodied beings, we are primed to respond most actively to pollution that affects our senses immediately—odours, noise, dust and smoke, since these alert us to possible danger and prompt us to seek safety quickly. However, what confronts the human senses immediately does not always accord with a scientifically valid prioritisation of harms that a regulator would or should respond to. For example, hazards such as chemical contamination, excess carbon emissions or water pollution may not be easily sensed, yet they are measured in parts per million and represent significant risks that warrant a stronger regulatory response.

Responding each day to the different contours of the sensory problems affronting a local community, such as issues relating to shifts in wind direction, can be extremely labour-intensive for EPA Victoria. If the EPA were to chase every minor incident—a localised rotten smell, roadside litter, a non-hazardous spill—it would divert efforts from addressing higher-risk issues, such as hidden storage of toxic chemicals, radiation, or airborne and leaching chemicals. In an ideal world, an exceptionally well-resourced regulator could be suitably responsive to every pollution report and complaint while also dedicating adequate resources to fixing all the biggest problems. Unfortunately, that perfect scenario does not exist, and we have yet to encounter a regulator in any regulatory domain with enough resources to do that.

From a restorative perspective, one partial answer to this conundrum is to emphasise good communication and transparency between regulators and their communities. Once the immediate crisis of an emergency has subsided and the phase of issuing urgent directives has passed, regulators must make the effort to talk *with* communities, not solely *to* them.[13] Regulators need to explain both their scope of responsibility and their priorities.[14] To escape the trap of low trust that our data suggests EPA Victoria often faces, spaces are needed for more honest conversations with citizens about what EPA Victoria can—and cannot—achieve. This dialogue is essential for building a foundation of trust that is the basis for all effective public engagement—a trust that, as mentioned earlier, is currently diminishing for all regulatory agencies.

Consider the Australian Competition and Consumer Commission (ACCC) as an instructive example. The ACCC is widely respected for being tough and effective in its enforcement, probably more so than any other Australian business regulator. However, since the 1980s, the ACCC had a philosophy that can be summed up as: 'Don't let your enforcement priorities be overly ruled by the mailbag' (the ebb and flow of complaints). The ACCC resolved this dilemma by bringing representatives of the organised consumer

13 Coglianese, *Listening, Learning Leading*.

14 Biggar et al. assert that this must occur early in the process to address 'expectation gaps' as a way of potentially improving 'confidence in the process and acceptance of the outcome'. Biggar et al., 'Health Regulation More Humane?', 13.

movement (like *CHOICE* magazine, itself a recipient of a massive volume of consumer complaints) into the deliberative processes that set enforcement priorities. Furthermore, the highest level of enforcement decision-makers in the ACCC were present at each meeting.[15] The ACCC has an impressive record of pursuing litigation cases that offer the greatest potential to transform industry practices. It also does not hold back in requesting ministerial support to conduct participatory public inquiries into addressing major structural challenges in a multidimensional way. This is evident in its current collaborative efforts with the Australian Securities and Investment Commission (ASIC) to tackle greenwashing and to promote honesty in ESG reporting.[16]

The other part of a restorative answer to this conundrum is to be understanding. Even if a complaint appears trivial from a scientific perspective, the fact remains that the individual complainant is authentically suffering in some way, and their concerns deserve acknowledgement and reassurance. While it may not be feasible to respond to every minor incident, especially not at the expense of tackling more serious problems, it is imperative to respond respectfully by centring connection and humanity. Kate Gavens, Chief Conservation Regulator in Victoria, expresses the importance of this clearly:

> As a regulator, I think sometimes you can get lost in the powers, duties, functions part of our role. Really at the end of the day, we're here to deliver outcomes for the community. Certainly, our powers, duties and functions really help us on that journey, but I often encourage staff to go back and look at the Acts we administer, the outcomes in that legislation, the objectives in the legislation and really think about what matters and how do we effectively make a difference.
>
> Understanding human nature, understanding what drives human behaviour, why are people doing the things that they're doing, I think that is one of the most fundamental things a regulator can do to be effective and deliver a good outcome.[17]

15 For more details on one current method through which the ACCC brings together consumer groups, community organisations and relevant government agencies, see 'National Consumer Congress', Australian Competition & Consumer Commission, www.accc.gov.au/about-us/conferences-and-events/national-consumer-congress. This yearly event provides a forum for discussing issues affecting consumers and for collaborating on strategies aimed at improving consumer justice and welfare.

16 Ayman Guirguis et al., 'Australia Greenwashing: Half-Yearly Review of ASIC and ACCC Prosecutions—and ACCC Position on Environmental Collaborations', *K&L Gates Hub*, 21 October 2024, www.klgates.com/Australia-Greenwashing-Half-Yearly-Review-of-ASIC-and-ACCC-Prosecutions-and-ACCC-Position-on-Environmental-Collaborations-10-21-2024.

17 Kate Gavens, 'Incentivising Compliance'.

The challenge for regulators is to structure systems and processes so they allow this perspective to shine through more clearly. In chapters to come, we discuss how restorative reporting can be complemented with more macro-level restorative regulation processes, such as restorative inquiries and community conferencing. For example, restorative inquiries can tackle the bigger, more complex issues like reducing greenhouse gas emissions or avoiding waste creation. Another macro-level process with restorative implications could be the creation of mechanisms to aggregate data from community-driven pollution reports. This data can inform more situated and targeted policy development within the regulator. By having these restorative, big-picture approaches on standby—ready to be activated as resources permit and urgent needs arise—a more holistic response can be achieved to restoratively address priorities in environmental, health, safety, and other regulatory challenges.

Restorative incident response: Emergency and recovery

The role of regulatory agencies in incident and emergency response is necessarily oriented to addressing an imminent public threat. The way emergency response agencies engage and communicate with directly affected communities plays a crucial role in shaping recovery from what can often be deeply traumatising events. Although the immediate priority for a regulatory agency is to remove the harm, the actions taken to achieve this can at times perpetuate existing issues or even create new ones.

While these challenges are acknowledged, a restorative approach can be embedded into the response process that follows an incident of environmental harm. We divide this response process into two time periods—the immediate emergency response and the subsequent recovery that spans the days, weeks and sometimes even years that follow. Restorative approaches are immensely relevant during periods of both response and recovery, especially in their ability to address impacts suffered by the network of relationships due to the harm and to build trust through interpersonal communication and rapport.[18]

18 Restorative approaches can help restore social cohesion and resilience, rebuild trust between neighbours, and between community and authorities, and address the emotional bonds and connections to place that are often disrupted by disaster events. See, for example, Rubinia Celeste Bonfanti et al., 'The Role of Trust in Disaster Risk Reduction: A Critical Review', *International Journal of Environmental Research and Public Health* 21, no. 1 (2023): 1–21, doi.org/10.3390/ijerph21010029; Kelly Bergstrand and Brian Mayer, '"The Community Helped Me:" Community Cohesion and Environmental Concerns in Personal Assessments of Post-Disaster Recovery', *Society & Natural Resources* 33, no. 3 (2020): 386–405, doi.org/10.1080/08941920.2019.1709002.

The accountabilities of agencies responsible for emergency response and recovery are clearly defined and specific, the priority being to prevent immediate injury and harm. At the same time, it is important, as far as possible, to consider the very real impacts experienced by members of the public during and after an emergency. Therefore, we propose the following guidance checklist for regulators seeking to follow a restorative approach to emergencies and their aftermath, noting that the feasibility of these measures will depend on the specific context.

Restorative engagement checklist for emergency events

- **Be present**. Show up in person in communities affected by the aftermath of emergencies.
- **Speak with those affected**. Where appropriate and safe to do so, ask people how they have been affected. Speak with as many people as possible and ask, 'Who have we not heard from yet?'
- **Gauge feelings**. Ask people about their current feelings and emotional state. Ask 'How are you feeling now?'
- **Genuinely listen**. Listen sincerely to their responses and ensure that interruptions are minimised (especially when things are busy).
- **Orient people towards the future**. Ask them what they think needs to happen next for them to move forward.
- **Involve community**. Listen to their responses and find ways to meet them where possible. Explore ways to involve affected people in shaping future plans.
- **Make apologies**. Apologise if your agency's actions have contributed to worsening the situation.
- **Do regular check-ins**. Follow up regularly to see how recovery is going, for as long as your agency continues to have a role.

This checklist outlines actions that can generate an authentic and responsive approach to affected citizens, one of active accountability and relational care. The suggested approach reflects the restorative aim to 'encourage, enable and maintain *caring* relationships' and to 'striv[e] to observe the principles and obligations of care in the way [the regulator] operate[s]'.[19]

19 Marshall, 'Justice as Care'.

It is also consistent with counselling and psychiatric scholarship that demonstrate how a small amount of early, well-targeted intervention can be far more effective than attempting to resolve issues after they have escalated, affecting relationships and other institutions.[20]

The actions in the checklist are straightforward, and it is neither difficult nor unreasonable to build them into emergency protocols as guidance to regulatory staff. Following the checklist 'enables and empowers both parties and … affirms the equal worth of each'.[21] For regulatory agencies and government leaders, a key challenge during an unfolding incident that affects the community is ensuring that systems and protocols are in place to support deep listening throughout the recovery phase. This means reflecting a genuine understanding of the impacts on those affected. Yet this is rarely straightforward: emergencies arrive without warning, and they often draw in a range of agencies whose usual work lies outside emergency response as their primary function.

Consider two recent examples from Melbourne—unrelated to EPA Victoria—that illustrate failures to be responsive during and after emergencies, providing valuable context for our discussion.

The first example occurred during one of the outbreaks of COVID-19 in Victoria that led to a state shutdown lasting many months. Inquiries revealed that the outbreak was exacerbated by a failure to translate vital COVID-19 information sheets into languages spoken by many migrant communities. Additionally, there was a lack of coordination between the government and multicultural and ethnic organisations experienced in working directly with these communities, and both the communities and organisations struggled to access current, relevant information in their languages.[22] Such an oversight might have been minimised or even avoided if part of the regulatory response had consistently addressed the question, 'Who are we not including?'

---

20 Amy B. Stapleton et al., 'Effects of Medical Crisis Intervention on Anxiety, and Posttraumatic Stress Symptoms: A Meta-Analysis', *Psychiatric Quarterly* 77, no. 3 (2006): 231–38, doi.org/10.1007/s11126-006-9010-2.

21 Marshall, 'Justice as Care', 178.

22 James Houghton, *Communicating About COVID-19: Health Literacy and Language Services During the Pandemic*, Ethnic Communities' Council of Victoria, October 2020, 7, eccv.org.au/communicating-about-covid-19-health-literacy-and-language-services-during-pandemic/; Yara Murray-Atfield, 'Melbourne Public Housing Tower Resident Says Community Is Being "Treated Like Criminals" Amid Coronavirus Lockdown', *ABC News*, 5 July 2020, www.abc.net.au/news/2020-07-05/coronavirus-lockdown-melbourne-public-housing-residents-speak/12423170.

The second example also originates from the pandemic context. It involves a decision in 2020 by the Victorian Government's Crisis Council of Cabinet that resulted in residents of several public housing towers being forced into sudden lockdown.[23] The former premier announced at a press conference:

> There will be no one allowed in … and no one allowed out. If you're in one of these towers … you will not be allowed to leave your unit, your dwelling within that tower, for any reason.[24]

Without warning, more than 3,000 residents of nine housing towers in Flemington and North Melbourne, 'home to some of the country's most vulnerable people', suddenly found themselves unable to leave their homes, detained against their will.[25] Many residents were unaware of the incredibly swift lockdown until they saw police standing outside their buildings.[26] A considerable number of residents reported that they felt like prisoners, and for some residents who had previously felt targeted by police, the police presence triggered past trauma.[27] Disgruntled residents later filed a class action against the government. It was settled for A$5 million in May 2023. However, these residents later publicly stated that what they really wanted from the government was an apology rather than financial compensation,[28] a call echoed by the Victorian Ombudsman in its inquiry into the incident.[29] In fact, the first recommendation of the investigation was that the government '[a]pologise publicly to residents of the Flemington and North Melbourne public housing estates for harm or distress caused by imposition of the immediate lockdown on 4 July 2020'.[30] The government has not issued an apology but instead released a statement acknowledging that its 'immediate response was not perfect' and outlining what it had learned.[31]

23 Victorian Ombudsman, *Investigation into the Detention and Treatment of Public Housing Residents Arising from a COVID-19 'hard lockdown' in July 2020*, (State of Victoria, 17 December 2020), www.ombudsman.vic.gov.au/our-impact/investigation-reports/investigation-into-the-detention-and-treatment-of-public-housing-residents-arising-from-a-covid-19-hard-lockdown-in-july-2020/.

24 Morgan Liotta, 'Tower Lockdown "Confusion and Distress" Could Have Been Prevented: GP', *NewsGP*, 6 August 2020, www1.racgp.org.au/newsgp/clinical/tower-lockdown-confusion-and-distress-could-have-b.

25 Liotta, 'Tower Lockdown'.

26 Australian Associated Press, 'Melbourne Public Housing Tower Residents Offered $5m Payout Over Covid Lockdown', *The Guardian*, 9 May 2023, www.theguardian.com/australia-news/2023/may/09/melbourne-public-housing-tower-residents-win-5m-payout-over-covid-lockdown.

27 Murray-Atfield, 'Tower Resident'.

28 Australian Associated Press, 'Melbourne Tower Residents'.

29 Victorian Ombudsman, *Investigation into the Detention and Treatment*.

30 Victorian Ombudsman, *Investigation into the Detention and Treatment*, 'Opinion', www.ombudsman.vic.gov.au/our-impact/investigation-reports/investigation-into-the-detention-and-treatment-of-public-housing-residents-arising-from-a-covid-19-hard-lockdown-in-july-2020/#opinion.

31 Premier of Victoria, *Statement on Victorian Ombudsman Housing Report* (State of Victoria, 17 December 2020), www.premier.vic.gov.au/statement-victorian-ombudsman-housing-report.

On a more positive note, the recovery effort following the Hazelwood mine fire stands out as an example of how post-emergency review can provide the basis for reforms and rebuilding of community trust. The post-emergency response included multiple public inquiries that focused on hearing from the community and identifying how government communications and community engagement during emergency response and recovery phases could be improved.[32]

One of the key community concerns during the emergency was the communication of air quality risks due to the Hazelwood Mine fire and the way official warnings were provided to those affected.[33] While communication about the reduced air quality had involved official warnings, social media and community-led discussions, analysis of the event revealed problems with official communication. A critical issue was that standard air filters protect only against particulate matter (tiny particles in the air, such as dust or soot) and are ineffective against gases like carbon monoxide, meaning that evacuation was the only safe option for vulnerable people in highly contaminated areas.[34] Feedback from affected communities showed that people needed faster, clearer and more accurate information through multiple channels.[35] Such communication also needed to be delivered empathetically, including through trusted local spokespeople.

Following the fire, reforms were introduced to improve public communication and warning systems. These included the launch of the VicEmergency app and the establishment of a community co-designed air-monitoring network in the Latrobe Valley.[36]

32 The first inquiry was held in 2014 and was reopened in a 2015–2016 inquiry, followed by a series of progress reports, with the Inspector-General for Emergency Management publishing the final progress report in 2022. Inspector-General for Emergency Management, *Hazelwood Mine Fire Inquiry—Progress Report 2022*, www.igem.vic.gov.au/publications/publications/hazelwood-mine-fire-inquiry-progress-report-2022. For government responses to the inquiries, see State Government of Victoria, *Hazelwood Mine Fire Inquiry: Victorian Government Implementation Plan* (Department of Premier and Cabinet, June 2016), www.healthassembly.org.au/wp-content/uploads/2024/08/Hazelwood-Mine-Fire-Inquiry-Implementation-Plan.pdf.

33 State Government of Victoria, *Hazelwood Mine Fire Inquiry Report 2014;* Yell and Duffy, 'Community Empowerment and Trust'.

34 Michelle Duffy, Sue Yell, Larissa Walker, et al., 'The Social Justice Issues of Smoke Im/Mobilities', *Australian Geographer* 54, no. 4 (2023): 573-87, doi.org/10.1080/00049182.2023.2256595.

35 State Government of Victoria, *Hazelwood Mine Fire Inquiry Report 2014.*

36 Premier of Victoria, 'New App to Put People First During Emergencies', State Government of Victoria, 16 November 2016, www.premier.vic.gov.au/new-app-put-people-first-during-emergencies; Premier of Victoria, 'Strengthening Air Monitoring in the Latrobe Valley', State Government of Victoria, 7 December 2017, www.premier.vic.gov.au/site-4/strengthening-air-monitoring-latrobe-valley.

These stories underline that those making the policy and regulatory calls in an emergency context need to ask, in a timely and respectful way, who should be included in the communication of decisions about emergency response, and who to apologise to and check in with after the impact. These questions need to be a standard part of any regulators' response to emergency events. As we said at the outset of this chapter, things will almost certainly go wrong, and mistakes will be made, because emergency events involve many unknowns and uncertainties. However, a restorative approach can help people to heal and move forward from incidents of harm by nurturing stronger relationships that facilitate early and ongoing engagement.

Restorative emergency response: Two stories from Victoria

We anchor our reflections on opportunities for taking a restorative approach to emergencies with two case studies. The first concerns the 2018 factory fire in the western suburb of Tottenham in Melbourne, and the second involves the Hazelwood Mine fire in the rural township of Morwell, Victoria. Each of these stories resulted in significant environmental impacts and required a multi-agency response under the 'command-and-control' legislative framework, in which EPA Victoria serves as a 'support agency' in the State command structure. These two stories highlight the significance of clear, timely and inclusive communications with affected community members and groups, which is all the more important during such large-scale emergency events.

The Tottenham industrial fire, 2018

The Tottenham industrial fire was one of several fires in Melbourne that resulted from warehouses being used to unlawfully store hazardous waste.[37] The fire took the Metropolitan Fire Brigade (MFB, now known as Fire

37 Illegal storage of chemical stockpiles was occurring in seven warehouses across suburbs in Melbourne's North, four sites in Epping and three sites in Campbellfield. See also Jack Kerr and Dan Oates, 'Chemical Stockpiles Found at Melbourne Warehouses Linked to West Footscray Inferno', *ABC News*, 2 January 2019, www.abc.net.au/news/2019-01-02/illegal-chemicals-stored-in-melbourne-warehouses-epa-claims/10678258; Melbourne Water Corporation, *Stony Creek Rehabilitation Plan 2019–2029*, Melbourne Water Corporation, 8 September 2019, 6, www.melbournewater.com.au/about/what-we-do/publications/stony-creek-rehabilitation-plan.

Rescue Victoria)[38] several days to fully control. It emitted a large plume of toxic black smoke, visible across Melbourne, that extended over a number of suburbs to the south-east of the fire.[39] In the hours after the fire began, authorities issued a 'community advice warning' for local residents, urging them to close their windows and doors, while childcare centres, schools and businesses were closed.

Despite the message of precaution, many residents reported headaches and nausea from exposure to the black smoke.[40] Representatives of the organisations Anti-Toxic Waste Alliance and Friends of Stony Creek would later testify to the impacts, with one resident remembering 'waking to the sound of explosions and watching a black plume of smoke billow over [her] home' and how she 'witnessed [their] creek being turned into a cocktail of chemicals that day'.[41]

As in so many emergencies, multiple government agencies, including EPA Victoria, were involved in responding to the fire.[42] The MFB was the lead agency, as required under the Victorian Emergency Framework and the State Emergency Command Team.[43]

The firewater the MFB used to put out the fire soaked up the chemicals stored in the warehouse, which then leaked into the nearby waterway, Stony Creek. Long before this incident, the local community had affectionately called their creek an 'oasis' and 'a haven to escape to'.[44] The chemicals that leached into it during the incident included hydrocarbons, acetone, herbicides and heavy metals.[45] Within hours of the fire, fish, eels, birds

38 For more on Fire Rescue Victoria, see FRV [Homepage], www.frv.vic.gov.au/.

39 Victorian Government Inspector-General for Emergency Management, *Report into the West Footscray Industrial Fire (August 2018)* (State of Victoria, 2020), www.igem.vic.gov.au/publications/report-into-the-west-footscray-industrial-fire-august-2018; Melbourne Water Corporation, *Stony Creek Rehabilitation Plan*.

40 Mark Santomartino, 'Melbourne Factory Fire: 30 Million Litres of Toxic Water Pumped from Creek As Smoke Rises', *9 News*, 31 August 2018, www.9news.com.au/national/fire-melbourne-tottenham-footscray-exacuation-factory-chemicals/62fc9b76-2b13-43fe-b764-2d4a6c234a17.

41 Benjamin Millar, 'Community Highlights Toxic Tottenham Fire Impact', *Star Weekly*, 14 August 2019, maribyrnonghobsonsbay.starweekly.com.au/news/community-highlights-toxic-tottenham-fire-impact/, citing Sue Vittori, Chair of the Anti-Toxic Waste Alliance.

42 Melbourne Water Corporation, 2019, *Stony Creek Rehabilitation Plan*.

43 For more on the distribution of responsibilities under Victoria's emergency management planning framework, see 'Victoria's Emergency Management Planning Framework', Emergency Management Victoria, accessed 17 February 2025, www.emv.vic.gov.au/responsibilities/emergency-management-planning/emergency-management-planning-resource-library-0/victorias-emergency-management-planning-framework.

44 Melbourne Water Corporation, *Stony Creek Rehabilitation Plan*.

45 'The Tottenham Industrial Fire', EPA Victoria, last modified 12 May 2025, www.epa.vic.gov.au/tottenham-industrial-fire.

and other wildlife were washing up dead on the banks of Stony Creek.[46] Black sludge remained on the banks, rocks and vegetation afterwards, with a strong chemical odour permeating the area for months to come.

Local activist residents in the affected community later discussed the event with us. On recounting the impact on someone the first community member knew, they said:

> Her husband was so worried. He had the kids at home. He looks out that day and he sees guys in hazmat suits and gas masks down by the creek. This was Melbourne Water, as they were trying to manage what was coming down that creek and work out what to do. He lives 50 metres from the creek. He's looking over his back fence, seeing guys in hazmat suits, and no-one's knocking on their door, no-one's telling him.
>
> He went down there and he said, 'What the hell is going on? And why isn't someone telling me what's going on? Is it safe for my family to be here? You're wearing suits. What's going on with us?' At any point in that immediate one and a half to two months afterwards, there was no doorknocking. There was [*sic*] some calls made to some strategic schools and preschools and what have you, and businesses and that, but there was no doorknocking.
>
> As a community engagement practitioner, I felt that we were really let down by our authorities. I was also thinking on the side of the authorities as well, because you're creating a problem for yourselves here guys, because I knew what was going to happen if they didn't get out and actually engage. That's exactly what did happen. Residents just started getting more and more angry and more and more frustrated.

In responding to what the first community member had just related, a second community member said: 'Because the messaging was, "We've measured the air. It's safe. You've got nothing to worry about." But people are getting sick and getting nosebleeds.' Then the first community member picked up the story:

46 Simone Fox Koob et al., 'Scores of Dead Fish, Eels Wash Up After Melbourne Factory Fire', *The Age*, 31 August 2018, www.theage.com.au/national/victoria/scores-of-dead-fish-eels-wash-up-after-melbourne-factory-fire-20180831-p500z5.html. Several of our interviewees also related the range of devastating effects during our interviews.

> 'And I'm getting asthma!' [Community members say] these sorts of things. So it's completely at odds with ... the community's experience. It just undermines the trust you have in the authorities. [People say things like,] 'I'm living in a different world here. I'm experiencing something different to what I'm being told. Is it safe for my nose to be bleeding? Is it safe to be having asthma or headaches as a result of this?'

The second community member responded:

> I could see it all this time, so at that public meeting, it was only a week after the fire, I went around afterwards and spoke to each of the different stores, because they had their talking heads for a while and then a few questions. No-one asked [the EPA senior officer] what would have happened if the smoke cloud had ... grounded. I really wish we had. On the way out, one of our group members did. Her [the EPA senior officer's] response was [that] she shook her head and ... said, 'You don't want to know. Serious stuff.'[47]

Emergency situations, from fire to chemical spills, are difficult situations that require a fast response. Communication is paramount, both between agencies, and from agencies to communities that have been impacted. At the time of the emergency, clear hierarchies are needed, and everyone has a designated function.

Yet, once the emergency subsides and the recovery phase begins, without clear, open and honest communication with the affected community, trust in the authorities will quickly drop, as the interview excerpts above have revealed. To build and sustain trust with those directly affected, the communication approach must quickly shift away from a top-down command-and-control model to one that actively involves community in a two-way exchange of trusted information between the authorities and the affected community. This exchange should be conducted in ways that are sensitive to the emotional context in which knowledge is being shared. Understanding the emotional context can help avoid inadvertently disrespecting the community, as former CEO of EPA Victoria John Merritt notes can sometimes happen:

47 Interview with local activists.

> But people are not stupid, they just want to be taken seriously and treated with respect. And so much of what we do is that we inadvertently disrespect people. We've lost before we start.[48]

The best way to build trust and respect is to leverage existing relationships between the regulator and trusted local individuals or groups. These people can give the regulator access to community wisdom, providing valuable insights into both the specific characteristics of the place and situated knowledge about the emotional landscape of the community. The stronger these connections are, the more effectively the regulator can stay in touch with, and accurately assess, community needs. Ideally, a regulatory officer should be able to say, for instance, 'Has anyone contacted [the Friends' Group]? If not, someone should,' and this follow-through should be seen as an imperative within the agency.

During the first part of our research, the then Chair of EPA Victoria, Cheryl Batagol, made it clear that these imperatives mattered. She told us it was critical to:

> begin a process of engaging the community so that they could see a future. Not just to stay the protests, but to actually have the community understand that we won't abandon them. [49]

The choice of the word 'abandon' is particularly telling, emphasising the need for the regulator to understand the emotional valence of the community and their deep fears, fears that the affected community members quoted above clearly felt.

In emphasising this priority, Batagol said that not only did EPA Victoria need to talk about what had happened to respond to the community's protests but also to send its officers to walk along the creek with locals who regularly used both the waterway and surrounding amenity, and to run what she described as 'like a pop-up', talking to people at local shopping centres.[50] These actions were designed to build trust by demonstrating a genuine, two-way commitment to listening to and addressing community concerns.

48 John Merritt, 'Incentivising Compliance'.

49 Interview with Cheryl Batagol.

50 Interview with Cheryl Batagol. For a range of other activities involving community and carried out by other agencies, such as a community information day, live Facebook chats and doorknocks, see Melbourne Water Corporation, *Stony Creek Rehabilitation Plan*.

In reflecting on how to approach an emergency response from a restorative angle, Batagol observed:

> [T]o my mind, restorative justice in this case is to understand the impacts of the event, understand that during the emergency we have to be able to do things like close off waterways, warn everybody and determine what the impact [on] that waterway is … [t]hen to move into recovery where it's cleaned up enough to move into rehabilitation.

One community activist illustrated what restorative emergency response means when she described a meeting that was held with local community members in the aftermath of the fire. She related the following:

> I stood up at that meeting. Andrea Hinwood, the chief scientist at the EPA spoke at that. She was the only person that, I think, spoke genuinely with a sense of genuine frankness and acknowledging that it was a major issue, and she actually apologised. She actually said, 'I'm really sorry this has happened.' No, not saying it was her fault, but just saying, 'I'm really sorry this has happened.' She was the only person in the whole meeting who spoke—Melbourne Water spoke, Council spoke— [who] said that. I actually messaged her the next day and thanked her for saying that, for apologising to the community and … acknowledging what a serious thing had happened.[51]

This interviewee's poignant account of the value of the apology cannot be overlooked. Restoratively, an apology is essential for healing, restoring relationships and resetting what has been broken—the very embodiment of the 'relational justice of care'.[52] However, the hierarchical structure and dispersed responsibilities within bureaucracies often leave staff at a disadvantage when it comes to delivering this much-needed relational justice.

Yet, the relational turn is neither unrealistic nor out of reach. When senior officers in EPA Victoria can share the pain of ordinary citizens—mums and dads, grandparents and children—they create the prospect for empathy that, through relational connection, can extend into an organisational commitment to relational justice. This example shows that it is crucial for senior regulators to engage empathically in listening to affected communities—'[E]mpath[et]ic engagement with the public, after all, is an essential ingredient of any responsive, responsible governmental

51 Interview with a local environmental activist.

52 Marshall, 'Justice as Care'.

authority.'[53] The involvement of senior regulators sets the tone for the entire organisational culture, liberating all officers to respond in more relational and caring ways. In turn, this relational feedback loop helps the community feel genuinely heard and acknowledged, and may also help them to accept that not all regulatory actions can be immediately visible or fully implemented.

The story of Stony Creek's repair will continue for some time, having now entered its long-term recovery phase. A rehabilitation plan for the creek, covering the years 2019 to 2029, was formed in consultation with local community members and organisations, along with various government agencies, including EPA Victoria.[54] Both the water corporation and the government agencies involved have made it clear that they intend, as far as possible, to meet the community's aspirations for rehabilitation and future protection of the creek during this timeframe. The community's aspirations include the transformation of Stony Creek into:

> Australia's best protected, connected and respected urban waterway … a showcase for how community, government and business can partner to achieve enduring physical, social and ecological health benefits. The final outcome will connect communities to each other, communities with nature, and allow life to thrive in and along Stony Creek for generations to come.[55]

Apart from the desirable outcome of having a healthy creek again, this collaborative rehabilitation has the potential to showcase enduring relationships, a rebuilding of trust and a shared commitment to healing. It is to be hoped that as Stony Creek revitalises, so, too, will the spirit of restoration, echoing the notion that resilient recovery is not just about the physical outcomes but also reflects strengthened interconnections between community, industry and regulators.

The Hazelwood Mine fire, Morwell, 2014

Our next case study returns us to the story we opened with at the start of this book, the 2014 Hazelwood Mine fire and its effects on the Morwell community. To recap, the local community was adversely affected by what was initially a bushfire but that went on to ignite the brown coal in the open-

53 Cary Coglianese, 'Empathy in an Automated State', *The Regulatory Review*, 10 January 2022, www.theregreview.org/2022/01/10/coglianese-empathy-automated-state/.

54 Melbourne Water Corporation. *Stony Creek Rehabilitation Plan*, 2.

55 Melbourne Water Corporation. *Stony Creek Rehabilitation Plan*, 3.

cut mine near Hazelwood power station. Smoke and ash covered Morwell, generating enormous alarm and anxiety among residents. Subsequent health problems, both actual and potential, affected the residents. There was major disruption of everyday life: children could not play outside, residents were worried about the safety of their pets, and outside visibility was so bad it frightened the locals. While the bushfire produced a fast-moving crisis, the burning coal turned the crisis into a long-running ordeal for Morwell's community, becoming what disaster management practitioners now often refer to as a 'long emergency'.[56]

A Board of Inquiry for the Hazelwood Mine Fire Inquiry (the Inquiry) was critical of the mine owners for not having processes in place for managing the fire. It was also critical of government authorities for their poor communication throughout the emergency. (We will return to this Inquiry in Chapter 8, to explore its restorative nature in more detail.) A number of state government authorities were implicated, including the Department of Health, the Country Fire Authority, the Metropolitan Fire and Emergency Services Board, and EPA Victoria.

Resilience scholars Susan Yell and Michelle Duffy, who studied the social media communications at the time through Facebook, pointed out the benefits of people being able to share their experiences through social media.[57] They noted that horizontal networking, a form of building connections and relationships between individuals of a similar level of power who have common interests or challenges, was vibrant through the crisis. They point out, however, that while residents are excellent sources of information on flooding, roads that are cut, and even how much rain is falling, they were not equipped to assess the danger of the smoke that they were breathing in day and night over the 45 days that the burning continued and in the weeks following, when ash was still in the air.

The Inquiry recommended greater involvement by authorities in social media communications. In particular, it found that having authorities participate actively in social media was vital for intervening to correct misinformation. Although this recommendation may no longer seem novel over a decade later—given that governments and response agencies now regularly use

56 This term is especially apt in the context of climate change. See also Ann Florini, Gordon LaForge, and Anne-Marie Slaughter, 'Democratic Governance for the Long Emergency' in *Democracy in a Hotter Time: Climate Change and Democratic Transformation*, ed. David W. Orr (MIT Press, 2023), 160–75, doi.org/10.7551/mitpress/15122.003.0016.

57 Yell and Duffy, 'Community Empowerment and Trust'.

social media as a communications tool—the underlying point remains vital. Regulators must assess the full range of communication options, including potentially novel approaches such as those enabled by AI, that facilitate two-way communication between them and the community.[58]

Furthermore, from the point of view of accessibility, timeliness, reach and effectiveness, regulators should use two-way communication mediums that the public use most commonly. Social media is not only valuable for updating and correcting information but also serves as a useful means for gathering feedback, addressing concerns and maintaining an open dialogue with the community. That said, it is important not to assume that everyone uses, wants to use, or can access social media or AI-informed tools. Traditional forms of media, such as pamphlets, radio messages, door-to-door engagement and community meeting hubs should also be employed to ensure that all segments of the community are reached.

Arguably, the most important restorative moment for EPA Victoria was listening directly to the affected Morwell community during a visit organised by authorities to Morwell in the form of an open meeting with the community. At this meeting, the Chair and the CEO (at that time) personally represented the EPA. Coming face-to-face with the fears, doubts and worries of the residents proved to be a transformative experience for the Chair Cheryl Batagol—a moment she publicly acknowledged. This instance showcased an EPA Chair living restorative values and setting a compassionate tone for the whole organisation. Beyond social media, websites and leaflets, the meeting clearly demonstrated that what really counts for restorative communication is having senior officers in positions of authority turning up in person, authentically facing the crowd and taking responsibility for their part in the response and recovery.

58 For a range of possibilities using AI to improve communications during emergency events, such as for speedy dissemination of information and for obtaining feedback from residents to improve understanding of community needs and concerns, see Nitin Liladhar Rane, Saurabh P. Choudhary, and Jayesh Rane, 'Artificial Intelligence for Enhancing Resilience', *Journal of Applied Artificial Intelligence* 5, no. 2 (2024): 1–33, doi.org/10.48185/jaai.v5i2.1053.

Best practices for a restorative and relational first response to harm

Bringing these ideas together, we close this chapter with a focus on practical guidance for implementing a restorative and relational first response to harm. Here, we outline best practices for incident reporting, response and recovery, as well as key considerations for regulators to ensure a relational and effective process over time.

So, how do we best implement a restorative response to harm?

Throughout this chapter, we have outlined a range of possible options. Here, in the following two lists, we summarise what we consider to be best practices for achieving a restorative, relational first response to harm. These suggestions are intended for regulators to consider as part of the training, processes and protocols that guide how agencies and their staff respond to citizen reports and emergencies. We note that the specific opportunities will vary depending on the nature of the emergency; the following suggestions offer general guidance.

A. Incident reporting

- Acknowledge that incident reporting is a form of citizen empowerment and a source of free feedback for the regulator.
- When reporting is partially or wholly outsourced, ensure that performance metrics for contracted call centres include qualitative scores for empathetic approaches.
- Develop processes to establish positive relationships with members of the public from the moment a report is made. Use deep listening, provide meaningful feedback and adopt a 'no-wrong-door' approach.
- Make it clear that the first report is not the end of the matter. Reassure the civic reporter that there will be follow-up about outcomes from the appropriate staff or agency.[59]

59 Biggar et al., 'Health Regulation More Humane?'. The authors note that '[r]egulators need to place greater emphasis on communicating the possible outcomes that can be achieved and the processes by which an outcome is reached', 13.

- Establish and maintain strong ties and feedback systems with other relevant regulatory agencies likely to consistently be involved with your agency's regulatory work.
- Use restorative processes, such as listening circles, when community grievances persist even after a report is resolved. Recognise that ongoing concerns may signal deeper structural issues requiring attention. On occasions, this may require complementing restorative reporting with more macro-level restorative processes (e.g. restorative inquiries) (see Chapter 8) and community conferencing (see Chapter 4).
- Keep the focus on shared responsibility between the regulator, its co-regulators, industry and community. Remember: the community has agency as much as it has needs.

B. Response and recovery

- Implement the Restorative Engagement Checklist for Emergency Events (above) as a guide for first response: show up, ask questions, listen, apologise, include and follow up.
- Re-establish or create a relationship between the regulatory agency and the affected community as early as possible. This may include giving apologies, if needed, quickly and meaningfully.
- Shift promptly to a two-way communication approach that consistently builds and sustains trust, ensuring that the flow of information is maintained without interruptions.
- Carefully consider who should be involved. Ensure that factors such as culture, age, gender, language, health and other specific needs are addressed in a timely, inclusive and participatory way. Acknowledge that the community is neither a monolithic concept nor an object to be acted upon.
- Aim to uphold the principles and obligations of care in responding to affected community. Lack of understanding, low thresholds of tolerance for perceived inaction, and frustration are always likely to accompany community engagement. A caring, empathetic approach can help reassure individuals, even when all actions may not be immediately possible.
- Check back in regularly. Follow-through requires having in place systems of triggers or reminders so that regulatory staff stay connected, ensuring that all commitments—both small and large—are fulfilled.

Defining your community

In thinking about who comprises the community, it is essential to be as inclusive as possible, actively reaching out to individuals and groups who might otherwise remain disconnected. This inclusivity should extend to Traditional Owners, minority communities, isolated rural residents and recent arrivals. A community can be large or small, often comprising multiple subcommunities within one community of place, and may be intersectional across various communities.[60] Recognising these diverse networks and groups is critical.

The physical presence of regulatory staff—combined with efforts to work through established community-based networks—helps create clear channels of communication. It is even better to establish these connections *before* an incident occurs, so that the relationships are already strong and everyone knows who to reach out to, and where they are, in times of need. This builds community resilience through connection and trust, reassuring community members that support will be there when needed.[61]

Once these connections are established, when 'sudden and unexpected changes' occur, 'information can be obtained by using social relationships maintained for other purposes'.[62] For instance, support could be leveraged through CRGs and similar two-way information-sharing groups that are already meeting regularly. Although social media has grown in importance as a means for disseminating information and updates, the physical presence of regulatory officers must remain the key relational way of staying genuinely connected, making these community connection points essential.

Three restorative questions

In terms of what needs to be communicated during response and recovery, we suggest that regulators ask three restorative questions:

60 See Chapter 3, 'On what community means'.

61 Ann Dadich et al., 'Building Resilient Australian Communities', *JMI Policy Insights* (2025), James Martin Institute for Public Policy; Mateus Kambale Sahani et al., 'Engaging Communities as Partners in Health Crisis Response: A Realist-Informed Scoping Review for Research and Policy', *Health Research Policy and Systems* 22, no. 1 (2024): 1–15, doi.org/10.1186/s12961-024-01139-1.

62 Russell R. Dynes, 'Social Capital: Dealing with Community Emergencies', *Homeland Security Affairs* 2, no. 2 (2006): 1–26, 2, 5. See also our discussion in Chapter 4 on proactive and consistent engagement with community groups and Chapter 3 for community empowerment methods.

- What happened?
- Who is being/was affected, and what did that feel like to them?
- What needs to happen to make it better?

Healing community after a disaster entails more than restoring the environment, supply chain networks and infrastructure. It also means focusing on building or rebuilding relationships between the regulator and the affected communities in a meaningful and enduring way.

Staff experience and perspectives

When a regulatory organisation endeavours to embrace a restorative approach towards its regulatory processes, senior management needs to recognise the experiences and perspectives of staff as they navigate the complexities of addressing complaints and managing emotional input. Staff at the frontline and in the field who deal directly with community emotions, and office staff who handle schedules, deployment and responsiveness during incident response and recovery, all face significant challenges. Responding to complaints and managing emotional input is not an easy process.[63] This work can be a tiring, frustrating and, at times, troubling experience for staff—especially when they hail from the same affected communities themselves and have deep connections within them. We interviewed several EPA officers who lived in the same area as the community facing the environmental challenges.

A restorative organisation must therefore support and acknowledge its staff's emotional and professional investments.[64] This support is integral to fostering an environment of empathy, shared responsibility and collaborative problem-solving. As the regulatory agency responds to community concerns, it must equally provide mechanisms to help staff manage the

63 Victorian Ombudsman, 'Good Practice Guide: Managing Complex Complainant Behaviour', 2 February 2022, www.ombudsman.vic.gov.au/learn-from-us/practice-guides/managing-complex-complainant-behaviour/; Kathryn Mulhan, 'Managing the Costs of Emotional Labor in Emergency Ambulance Call-Taking', *The Journal of Emergency Dispatch*, 22 July 2020, www.iaedjournal.org/managing-the-costs-of-emotional-labor-in-emergency-ambulance-call-taking.

64 Victorian Ombudsman, 'Good Practice Guide'. Research shows that it is important to provide frontline staff with emotional awareness training to strengthen their resilience and self-restoration, which are essential for maintaining effective responses in emotionally demanding contexts; see, for example, Emily Jacobs and Richard J. Keegan, 'Sustaining Optimal Performance When the Stakes Could Not Be Higher: Emotional Awareness and Resilience in Emergency Service Personnel (With Learnings for Elite Sport)', *Frontiers in Psychology* 13 (2022): 1–15, doi.org/10.3389/fpsyg.2022.891585.

intricacies of balancing connections with community and their regulatory responsibilities. (We discuss this in more detail in Chapter 10 in relation to supporting the efforts of restorative champions.)

It's about time

Finally, while our focus here has been on *responding* to harm, a restorative approach operates across a temporal spectrum. A restorative approach is equally able to look back in time, fully consider the present and aim to create a better future. The holistic nature of the emergency preparedness cycle thus requires a restorative incident response to consider actions that can be taken:

- before emergencies occur, by establishing and nurturing community connections
- at the time of the incident, through a prompt and caring response
- in the long term, by co-designing with community a future that prioritises mitigation and prevention to avoid the recurrence of the problems.[65]

Our next chapter moves us into the phase of repairing harm. Although we have touched on recovery and renewal in this chapter, we next detail the processes and frameworks needed to support the restorative regulatory approach to repairing harm during the recovery phase.

65 For example, community-based emergency management could be one approach to call upon in creating partnerships with communities. See Emergency Management Victoria, *Community Based Emergency Management: Better Connected, and Working Together—Before, During and After: Overview 2023*, (Emergency Management Victoria, 2023), www.emv.vic.gov.au/how-we-help/community/community-based-emergency-management/community-based-emergency-management-overview.

7

Repairing harm and ensuring active accountability

Source: Author.

> *By actively investing in the well-being of their communities, businesses can foster social cohesion, equality, and sustainable development, thereby creating a more stable and prosperous environment for their operations and the community alike.*
>
> —Kirk Feller[1]

1 Kirk Feller, 'Giving Back Is a Business's Moral Responsibility', *Rolling Stone*, 1 August 2023, www.rollingstone.com/culture-council/articles/giving-back-is-good-business-1234797862/.

In this chapter, we explore restorative remedies—innovative tools that ensure genuine accountability while repairing harm. We explore how these approaches build trust, encourage voluntary commitments and pave the way for sustainable, mutually beneficial relationships. We examine the role of restorative justice conferences: what they are, when they work best and what outcomes they can achieve. We address some of the challenges involved and reveal a few strategies for overcoming them. The chapter finishes with a look at additional restorative solutions regulators can draw on to support those making amends, to ensure that harm is meaningfully and effectively repaired.

Unlike traditional regulatory models that rely primarily on sanctions after harm has occurred, restorative approaches also seek to meet the needs of victims and ensure active accountability for repairing harm. One important way to achieve this is by strengthening relationships between those harmed and those who caused harm, primarily through dialogue-based processes. Restorative approaches are based on the insight that, as inherently social beings, humans derive meaning and fulfilment through our relationships. By resolving conflict through connection and understanding, we can restore and strengthen these essential bonds.[2]

Many practices have been developed to advance these restorative objectives, including restorative justice conferences, victim-offender mediation and healing circles. In this chapter, we examine how such practices might operate within a regulatory cycle that incorporates restorative approaches. Some practices, like the restorative conference—which we detail extensively below—may be familiar to many readers. Others represent more innovative strategies, opening the door to creative, restorative adaptations of traditional sanctioning processes. Two examples are restorative sanctions and restorative enforceable undertakings, which we describe towards the end of this chapter.

These processes can lead to various outcomes. Sometimes, they produce an apology by the wrongdoer, or an acknowledgement of the impacts caused by their hurtful actions. In other cases, the wrongdoer may make an offer or commit to concrete reparative actions, such as restoring a local park, organising a tree-planting event, or launching a new community project.

2 Marshall, 'Justice As Care'.

Ideally, these outcomes will lead to fully addressing what Emeritus Professor Chris Marshall calls the victims' 'needs for repair'. Writing about what victims really want, he notes:

> As well as truth telling and accountability, they crave recovery, and all three requirements feed a primitive drive for a justice that restores their wellbeing. Offending has injured them at their spiritual and relational core; it has denied their inherent dignity and trampled on their rights and feelings, as though these things do not really matter. Justice therefore *requires* the mending or healing of these visceral injuries, otherwise it remains partial at best and re-victimising at worst.[3]

To understand what restorative remedies offer in the regulatory process, we start by examining why they deserve the regulator's attention, exploring their benefits for building trust, activating accountability, encouraging cooperation and achieving more effective, long-term compliance.

Why use restorative remedies for regulatory offences?

While restorative justice is increasingly accepted as a more holistic approach within criminal justice, its application to regulatory offences is relatively new. This raises important policy questions, such as:

- When is a restorative justice process appropriate?
- What should its relationship be with conventional sanctions?
- Should restorative processes be available for serious offences, recalcitrant offenders, or only for minor or first-time violations?

We argue that, while there will always be some offenders who are unwilling or unable to engage in restorative processes, requiring more coercive approaches, it is essential to genuinely consider restorative paths before resorting to punitive options for *all* regulatory offences.[4] Rather counterintuitively, the evidence is clear that restorative approaches are often more effective for serious offences than for minor ones.[5]

3 Marshall, 'Justice As Care', 179.

4 John Braithwaite, 'Types of Responsiveness', in *Regulatory Theory: Foundations and Applications*, ed. Peter Drahos (ANU Press, 2017), 117–32, doi.org/10.22459/RT.02.2017. In particular, see Part 3, 'Pyramidal Responsiveness', 118–21.

5 Jacqueline Joudo Larsen, *Restorative Justice in the Australian Criminal Justice System* (Australian Institute of Criminology, 2014), www.aic.gov.au/publications/rpp/rpp127; Braithwaite, 'Types of Responsiveness'.

Our call to proactively identify and pursue restorative responses reflects the most up-to-date research and practitioner insights, which highlight their potential to achieve better, longer lasting outcomes. While the prevailing economic model of the rational actor has come to dominate our thinking about compliance, with its presumption that a person will comply when the costs of noncompliance outweigh the costs of compliance, recent literature demonstrates that restorative processes are highly effective and often result in significant transformation and reduced recidivism.[6]

One explanation is that restorative processes allow the offender to gain insight into the impact of their behaviour and take responsibility for repair, meaning that compliance is self-generated rather than having to be imposed by an authority.[7] That said, we stress that restorative approaches are **not** suitable in cases where the offender is not willing to take responsibility for the harm caused.[8]

In building trust and commitment, restorative processes can also encourage voluntary cooperation, inspiring offenders to go beyond minimum compliance. By harnessing the willingness of the offender and the positive problem-solving creativity that is generated by the restorative process, the regulator can both expect and set new, better and more sustainable

6 Lawrence W. Sherman et al., 'Are Restorative Justice Conferences Effective in Reducing Repeat Offending? Findings from a Campbell Systematic Review', *Journal of Quantitative Criminology* 31, no. 1 (2014): 1–24, doi.org/10.1007/s10940-014-9222-9; Fulham et al., 'The Effectiveness of Restorative Justice Programs; Ministry of Justice, 'Policy Name: Restorative Practice (Incorporating Restorative Justice Services) Policy Framework', Ministry of Justice and HM Prison & Probation Service (UK), 6 February 2023), assets.publishing.service.gov.uk/media/63e12cb3e90e076264193957/restorative-practice-incorporating-restorative-justice-services-policy-framework.pdf; Shahid Kahn and Mia Lucas, 'The Effectiveness of Restorative Justice Programs in Reducing Recidivism', Department of Public Health, Yale University.

7 Meredith Rossner and Helen Taylor, 'The Transformative Potential of Restorative Justice: What the Mainstream Can Learn from the Margins', *Annual Review of Criminology* 7 (2024): 357–81, doi.org/10.1146/annurev-criminol-030421-040921; Mark Umbreit and Marilyn Peterson Armour, *Restorative Justice Dialogue: An Essential Guide for Research and Practice* (Springer Publishing Company, 2010), doi.org/10.1891/9780826122599.

8 The offender's taking responsibility is essential for the process to be productive and to avoid retraumatising the victim(s). As restorative justice scholar Mara Schiff explains: 'In an adversarial model, we are generally trained not to take responsibility rather than to take responsibility. And restorative process is grounded in taking responsibility and being honored for that.' Dr. Mara Schiff, 'Taking Responsibility: A Conversation on Restorative Justice and Youth', interview by Sarah Schweig (23 October 2012), Center for Justice Innovation, www.innovatingjustice.org/publications/taking-responsibility-conversation-restorative-justice-and-youth. See also John Braithwaite, 'Accountability and Responsibility Through Restorative Justice', in *Public Accountability: Designs, Dilemmas and Experiences,* ed. Michael Dowdle (Cambridge University Press, 2006), 33–51.

operating standards.[9] A recent meta synthesis of qualitative research on restorative justice found that the emotional exchanges that often occur in restorative processes help participants to see each other as 'human' rather than as labels or rigid categories (e.g., 'victim' or 'offender'), a shift that encourages empathy and understanding.[10] In addition, restorative justice is often experienced as personally transformative, altering the participants' perspectives, fostering personal growth and encouraging accountability while helping them to find closure.[11]

Restorative justice also delivers a range of benefits beyond deterrence that extend to victims and the wider community. Criminologist Larry Sherman and his team, in their systematic review in 2015, found that restorative approaches in the criminal context led to increased victim satisfaction, greater perceptions of procedural fairness and a decreased desire for revenge among the persons harmed, particularly for those involved in violent crime.[12] Additional benefits include:

- the pooling of diverse perspectives and knowledge of everyone impacted (e.g., victim[s], community, regulator, environment) to develop more informed and holistic solutions for moving forward together
- the strengthening of relationships and communication channels between participants
- an increase in public trust in the regulator through the provision of a voice for victims in the process.

In some contexts—such as environmental, workplace and family situations—a restorative justice process may be particularly useful where there is an ongoing and future relationship between the offending party and impacted individuals or communities. This is often the case where community and industry are co-located. In such situations, the party taking responsibility

9 For foundational insights into ways in which a regulator might harness regulated entities' creative problem-solving to bolster compliance, see Ian Ayres and John Braithwaite, *Responsive Regulation: Transcending the Deregulation Debate* (Oxford University Press, 1992), doi.org/10.1093/oso/9780195070705.001.0001; Edward L. Deci and Richard M. Ryan, 'The "What" and "Why" of Goal Pursuits: Human Needs and the Self-Determination of Behavior', *Psychological Inquiry* 11, no. 4 (2000): 227–68, doi.org/10.1207/S15327965PLI1104_01; and Christopher Ansell and Alison Gash, 'Collaborative Governance in Theory and Practice', *Journal of Public Administration Research and Theory* 18, no. 4 (2008): 543–71, www.jstor.org/stable/25096384.

10 Masahiro Suzuki and Xiaoyu Yuan, 'How Does Restorative Justice Work? A Qualitative Metasynthesis', *Criminal Justice and Behavior* 48, no. 10 (2021): 1347–65, doi.org/10.1177/0093854821994622.

11 Rossner, 'Restorative Justice In the 21st Century'.

12 Sherman et al., 'Are Restorative Justice Conferences Effective?'

for repairing environmental harm might agree to commit financial, human and/or expertise resources to projects that benefit the affected community, such as creating eco-friendly infrastructure, establishing a wildlife corridor or developing a community garden. They might also support community events, community-led restoration projects, cultural exchanges or public art installations that raise awareness of environmental issues.

Rather than the usual cycle of end-of-story payment of fines, reputational damage and a return to 'business as usual,' these innovative approaches can start a new story—one in which the offender actively collaborates with the community. In the context of repairing environmental harm, this means corporate offenders not only take responsibility but also work alongside the community to restore the environment. Through these efforts, they can rebuild relationships and regain their social licence to operate. In turn, this increases community agency; as John Braithwaite notes, 'Restorative justice [is] partly about community building by encouraging citizens who are not offenders to assist in righting wrongs that offenders have caused.'[13]

With this in mind, we now discuss key restorative practices that regulators can use to respond to harm.

Restorative justice conferences

In this section, we explore restorative justice conferences—their purpose, process and impact. We begin with an overview of what they entail and discuss a New Zealand example to illustrate the steps involved. We then assess their effectiveness and consider when they might be appropriately integrated into the regulatory process. To bring this to life, we discuss one of our four main case studies—the Hampton Park Landfill—where EPA Victoria held a restorative justice conference. This story reveals several important insights about the value of the restorative justice conference for building relationships, ensuring transparency and facilitating knowledge-sharing. We finish by addressing the challenges and limitations regulators may encounter when implementing restorative conferences.

13 Braithwaite, 'Accountability and Responsibility', 42.

What are restorative justice conferences?

Restorative justice conferences are among the most widely recognised and commonly used forms of restorative justice. They have been applied across various domains, including criminal justice, education, health care, workplaces and, more recently, environmental regulation.[14]

A restorative justice conference brings together the individuals or representatives of entities who have caused harm and the victims affected, whether individuals or groups, together with supporters and other interested parties, for a structured, facilitated dialogue. A trained facilitator takes responsibility for creating and maintaining a safe space for open dialogue. While the victim(s) may or may not be physically present, these conferences typically involve a face-to-face meeting. Either before or at the beginning of the meeting, the person who caused harm takes responsibility for the harm caused. This acceptance of responsibility is a precondition of the conference occurring, which differentiates it from mediation processes.[15]

The dialogue generally covers three broad themes or stages, which are approached in a relatively structured manner. These three stages involve asking:

1. What happened?
2. How have people been affected?
3. What needs to happen to make things better? And: Who is responsible for making that happen?

The dialogue itself can last many hours, sometimes even the whole day.[16] It may involve a number of breaks, while some conferences may be adjourned and then reconvened at a later date to complete the process. A distinctive feature of restorative justice conferences is how they are structured to guide participants as they openly feel and express emotions, moving away from

14 Restorative justice conferences have been used more regularly in environmental regulation in New Zealand than in any other jurisdiction. They have been used occasionally in Australia in the environmental context.

15 Refer to 'Respectful Restorative Dialogue' in Chapter 1 for more details.

16 By way of example, in the story of the Hampton Park Landfill, which we discuss below, the conference lasted for almost five hours.

anger towards understanding and hope. At the end, many participants describe the experience as a shared journey, a dynamic that criminologist Meredith Rossner refers to as 'emotional entrainment'.[17]

While the conference itself is important—especially the work that occurs through the emotional group dynamics—significant preparatory work takes place beforehand. Facilitators meet with victims, offenders, their families and support people, and, where relevant, representatives from broader groups (such as civic organisations or cultural and faith-based groups). Not surprisingly, the evidence suggests that the better prepared the parties are, the better the outcomes that arise from the conference.[18] Throughout the process, parties often become less punitive in their outlook and instead focus more on constructively determining how to move forward.[19]

There are multiple theoretical explanations for why restorative conferences are effective.[20] In the provision of opportunities for meaningful dialogue, and when participants are encouraged to consider different perspectives on the issue, victims experience decreased feelings of vengefulness, while the wrongdoer often gains insights into the impact of their behaviour on the victim. These shifts in perspective help each participant move towards healing and recovery.

The Karapiti Incident – An example of a restorative justice conference

From Aotearoa New Zealand, the Karapiti incident provides a good example of a restorative justice conference in the environmental regulatory context. This incident concerned the Wairakei Geothermal Power Station located in *Te Ika-a-Māui* (North Island of Aotearoa New Zealand). The power station is operated and managed by a large power company, Contact Energy. In February 2019, a holding pond at the power station containing geothermal fluid unexpectedly broke its banks and discharged into the Waikato River (*Waikato Te Awa*), turning the river brown from the

17 Meredith Rossner, *Just Emotions: Rituals of Restorative Justice* (Oxford University Press, 2013), doi.org/10.1093/acprof:oso/9780199655045.001.0001.

18 Mark W. Lipsey, 'The Primary Factors that Characterize Effective Interventions with Juvenile Offenders: A Meta-Analytic Overview', *Victims & Offenders* 4, no. 2 (2009): 141–42, doi.org/10.1080/15564880802612573.

19 Rossner, 'Restorative Justice'.

20 Rossner, 'Restorative Justice'.

resulting sediment. The pollution incident attracted considerable publicity, particularly as it had a significant effect on a national iconic site, the Huka Falls and the greater Waikato Te Awa (Waikato River).

Contact Energy was prosecuted under New Zealand's *Resource Management Act 1991*. The company pleaded guilty and eventually paid a fine.[21] But rather than going straight to sentencing, the company opted to enter a restorative justice process.

The restorative justice conference was facilitated by an experienced restorative justice practitioner. The practitioner initially met with all the parties to assess their motivation for participation, what they hoped to achieve, and what kinds of remedies the offenders were able to offer. They also discussed who else needed to be in the room. The conference brought members of the *Tūwharetoa* Māori Trust Board, representatives of the First Nations peoples on whose land the spill had occurred, into dialogue with the Waikato Regional Council, the regulatory authority responsible for bringing the prosecution, and senior representatives from Contact Energy.

The Karapiti restorative justice conference went through the three stages outlined above: (1) What happened? (2) Who was impacted and how? and (3) What needs to be done to move forward? The conference was an opportunity for Contact Energy to be made aware of the full impact the incident had had on the local Māori iwi (tribe), particularly from a cultural perspective. This deeper understanding enabled the formulation of a staged process to develop a holistic response to the harm, one that ultimately enabled the building of far more significant connections between Contact Energy and the local iwi.

At the first restorative conference, held in October 2019, one of the agreed outcomes was for Contact Energy to commission a cultural impact assessment on the spill.[22] The assessment identified actions that Contact Energy should take to remediate and restore the damage caused by the spill, grounded in overarching values that should guide the restoration: *whakapapa* (genealogy/descent), *mana whakahaere/kaitiakitanga* (leadership/governance and stewardship) and *mauri* (life force/spiritual essence of the Māori people

21 *Waikato Regional Council v Contact Energy Limited* [2020] NZDC 24794.

22 Tūwharetoa Māori Trust Board Waikato River Committee, *Karapiti Incident: Waipuwerawera/Waikato River Cultural Impact Assessment* (Tūwharetoa Māori Trust Board, September 2020).

and place).[23] A second restorative justice conference, held in October 2020, focused on determining how and when Contact Energy would implement the recommendations from the cultural impact assessment.

Several projects were chosen collaboratively, including the development of a cultural values/*mātauranga* and *tikanga* (protocols) measurement framework for the Waikato Te Awa and related tributaries. Other projects included a cultural training module for Contact Energy staff and Wairakei site induction, as well as ongoing planning for the Waipuwerawera Stream (a tributary of the Waikato Te Awa) restoration works. All projects were to be undertaken according to a 'whole of catchment approach'.[24]

At this second restorative meeting, the leaders of Contact Energy made a formal apology to the local Māori iwi about the harm that had been caused. The second-in-charge at the national office attended, along with the local manager of the site. Reflecting on the apology, one conference participant stated:

> I was waiting for the apology. And I thought, you can stand up and say sorry. It would be easy to say we are sorry and shake hands and walk out of [the] room. But I felt they were genuine. I thought they actually meant it.[25]

The participant also noted that, at an emotional level, the restorative justice conference was different from being in court:

> [We] would have sat and listened in court—it has a formal nature. This, while it had an agenda, was still relatively informal. People could say more in this setting than in a courtroom.

At the time of writing, the response to the incident and the relationship-building is ongoing, with Contact Energy having established a specific role within its structure to maintain direct contact with the local iwi. As detailed in the company's 2024 *Annual Report*, significant progress continues with the Wairakei Relationship Group and other community-focused initiatives.[26] Had a standard prosecution pathway been pursued, it is highly unlikely that these relational, healing and ongoing repair-focused outcomes would have

23 See, for example, Manaaki Whenua Landcare Research, 'Key Māori Principles, 1996–2025'.

24 Tūwharetoa Māori Trust Board, *Position Description* (2021), www.tuwharetoa.co.nz/app/uploads/2021/07/Kaiawhina-Karapiti-JD.pdf.

25 Interview with a conference participant.

26 Contact Energy, *2024 Integrated Report* (2024), contact.co.nz/investor-centre/reports-and-results/integrated-report. See 'Commitment to the Wairakei Environment', 50, and 'Building Relationships', 51.

been achieved. As one participant concluded: 'If it [the restorative justice conference] hadn't … happened, we would have gone to court; Contact Energy would have been fined. That would have been the end of it.'

In place of such an abrupt end, the restorative justice process enabled interpersonal interactions that both healed ruptured relationships and created possibilities for future collaboration.

How effective are restorative justice conferences in achieving compliance?

The evidence, particularly—but not only—from criminal law enforcement, shows that restorative justice conferences are effective in improving compliance with the law.[27] One reason for this is that, unlike criminal trials, from which offenders may emerge with a comparatively reduced fear of future prosecution, restorative processes maintain that deterrence effect by leaving participants more attuned to the consequences of their actions, including the potential for prosecution.[28] In other words, restorative justice can sharpen future deterrence, whereas overuse of criminal prosecution can blunt it.[29]

Beyond deterrence, restorative justice offers a deeper relational connectedness and is of therapeutic value. The emotional expression that results from a restorative justice process humanises all participants, allowing the wrongdoer to truly understand the impact of their actions. This insight fosters behavioural change to avoid causing future harm—something that the ritualised and performative distancing nature of conventional courtroom proceedings cannot replicate.

27 Jeff Latimer, Craig Dowden, and Danielle Muise, 'The Effectiveness of Restorative Justice Practices: A Meta-Analysis', *The Prison Journal* 85, no. 2 (2005): 127–44, doi.org/10.1177/0032885505276969; William Bradshaw, David Roseborough, and Mark S. Umbreit, 'The Effect of Victim Offender Mediation on Juvenile Offender Recidivism: A Meta-Analysis', *Conflict Resolution Quarterly* 24, no. 1 (2006): 87–98, doi.org/10.1002/crq.159; Jennifer S. Wong, et al., 'Can At-Risk Youth Be Diverted From Crime?; Braithwaite, 'Street-Level Meta-Strategies', 205–25; Jeff Bouffard, Maisha Cooper, and Kathleen Bergseth, 'The Effectiveness of Various Restorative Justice Interventions on Recidivism Outcomes Among Juvenile Offenders', *Youth Violence and Juvenile Justice* 15, no. 4 (2017): 465–80, doi.org/10.1177/1541204016647428; David B. Wilson, Ajima Olaghere, and Catherine S. Kimbrell, *Effectiveness of Restorative Justice Principles in Juvenile Justice*.

28 Braithwaite, 'Minimally Sufficient Deterrence'.

29 Larsen, *Restorative Justice*.

Studies have shown that undertakings agreed to at a restorative justice conference (such as compensation payments or attendance at rehabilitation programs) are more likely to be completed than if ordered by a court.[30] Research into the use of restorative justice in white-collar or corporate crime, which have the closest relevance for regulatory offences, has found significant efficacy arising from employing restorative justice. This research notes that it is particularly effective when both extrinsic motivations (such as a desire to preserve public trust and reputation) and intrinsic motivations (such as socio-ethical awareness) are at play to encourage corporations to participate.[31]

In essence, restorative justice conferences are a powerful mechanism to facilitate the active accountability of those who have caused harm and to heal affected communities. They yield a wide range of outcomes that support the repairing of harm, such as apologies, reparations, donations to environmental or community groups, restoration and interpretation projects, and commitments to better relationships moving forward.[32] Given this potential, there is increasing recognition of the value of restorative justice conferences as a complementary enforcement approach. For instance, in a recent Sentencing Advisory Council report urging the inclusion of restorative justice into sentencing for occupational health and safety cases, researchers Octavian Simu, Paul McGorrey and Melanie Hull note:

> Given the significant support we heard during preliminary consultation, in survey responses, in written submissions, and in subsequent consultation on our draft recommendations, we are firmly of the view that there is a need to enable restorative justice conferences to occur alongside OHS [occupational health and safety] prosecutions.[33]

30 Jeff Latimer, 'A Meta-Analytic Examination of Youth Delinquency, Family Treatment, and Recidivism', *Canadian Journal of Criminology and Criminal Justice* 43, no. 2 (2001): 237–53, doi.org/10.3138/cjcrim.43.2.237.

31 See Katherine Beaty Chiste, 'Retribution, Restoration, and White-collar Crime', *Dalhousie Law Journal* 31, no. 1 (2008): 85–121, 3, canlii.ca/t/t12s; Zvi D. Gabbay, 'Exploring the Limits of the Restorative Justice Paradigm: Restorative Justice and White-collar Crime', *Cardozo Journal of Conflict Resolution* 8, no. 2 (2007): 421–85.

32 Mark Hamilton, *Environmental Crime and Restorative Justice: Justice as Meaningful Involvement* (Palgrave Macmillan, 2021), 135–37, 147, 150, doi.org/10.1007/978-3-030-69052-6.

33 Octavian Simu, Paul McGorrery, and Melanie Hull, *Sentencing Occupational Health and Safety Offences in Victoria: Report and Recommendations* (Sentencing Advisory Council, 2025), 18, www.sentencingcouncil.vic.gov.au/sites/default/files/2025-02/sentencing_ohs_offences_report_and_recommendations.pdf. The support mentioned in this quote came from a wide range of stakeholders, including regulators, employer associations, the Law Institute of Victoria and justice research centres, with 77% of survey respondents supporting the introduction of restorative justice conferences, Simu et al. *Sentencing*, 20.

This reinforces the important role restorative justice can play in regulatory enforcement, offering both accountability and repair.

Restorative justice scholar Mark Hamilton, who has studied several of these conferences, notes in relation to one that he observed:

> Apart from the obvious environmental and cultural benefits of conferencing, there were other benefits. It provided the opportunity for the offenders and victims to meet face-to-face, talk about the offending, its causes and its consequences, offer and accept apology and work collegiately to resolve the harm caused by the offending. This has benefits over traditional prosecution where offender and victim roles are minimal, where victim needs are not always met and offenders not always made accountable for their offending and where punishment can leave an offender stigmatised [references removed].[34]

For those interested in international examples, environmental lawyer Femke Wijdekop provides a more detailed exploration of restorative justice conferences in her writings.[35]

The value of apology

Apology is a valuable element of the restorative process (as discussed in Chapter 1). Many victims find receiving an apology essential to their healing, and research shows that offenders who participate in restorative justice processes are more likely to offer an apology to their victims than offenders sent to criminal courts.[36] An apology not only helps the victim heal but also signals contrition from the harm-doer, assisting in the mending of broken relationships.[37] An apology is often important for the victim to

34 Mark Hamilton, 'Restorative Justice Conferencing in Australia and New Zealand: Application and Potential in an Environmental and Aboriginal Cultural Heritage Protection Context', *International Journal of Restorative Justice* 4, no. 1 (2021): 81–97, 85, doi.org/10.5553/tijrj.000064.

35 Femke Wijdekop, 'Reconnecting with the Living Earth Through Restorative Justice', *KOSMOS*, 10 April 2019, archived at the Wayback Machine, web.archive.org/web/20231123071740/https://www.kosmosjournal.org/news/reconnecting-with-the-living-earth-through-restorative-justice/; Femke Wijdekop, *Restorative Justice Responses to Environmental Harm*, (IUCN, 2019), files.harmonywithnatureun.org/uploads/upload864.pdf.

36 Lawrence W. Sherman et al., 'Effects of Face-to-face Restorative Justice on Victims of Crime in Four Randomized, Controlled Trials', *Journal of Experimental Criminology* 1, no. 3 (2005): 367–95, doi.org/10.1007/s11292-005-8126-y.

37 Masahiro Suzuki, 'Possibility of Sincere Apology in Restorative Justice: When and How?', *International Journal of Offender Therapy and Comparative Criminology* 68, no. 13–14 (2022): 1342–56, doi.org/10.1177/0306624x221132238.

re-establish self-respect in relation to the harm-doer.[38] In turn, an apology is an important means for eliciting forgiveness from the victim.[39] Apologies can also help offenders demonstrate their morality as law-abiding citizens, supporting their reintegration into society.[40] Failure to apologise, however, 'can lead to strained relationships, grudges and vengeance'.[41]

Beyond words, the restorative process can create a 'shift in energy', as moments of recognition, small gestures, or shared laughter signal a transformation in relationships. Restorative scholar Meredith Rossner describes how turning points emerge in conferences through subtle cues—smiling, nodding or small talk over a coffee break—forming what she calls a 'subtle energy of forgiveness'.[42]

A restorative conference provides an opportunity to ask whether there is anyone to whom an apology is owed for the incident. This question may well be directed at a regulatory authority, either as the harm-doer or as a party taking responsibility for the harm. As Simu et al. state: '[A]n apology can be an incredibly meaningful outcome of restorative justice conferences […] and can go a long way towards recovery and healing.'[43]

38 Peter H. Rehm and Denise R. Beatty, 'Legal Consequences of Apologizing', *Journal of Dispute Resolution*, no. 1 (1996): 116–30, scholarship.law.missouri.edu/jdr/vol1996/iss1/7.

39 It is important to note that, as Richard Dening, the Director of the ACT's Restorative Justice Unit, says, forgiveness cannot be forced, as '[f]orgiveness […] only comes up if it is important to the person who has been harmed—it can never be pressed on them'. Cited in Julia Baird, *Bright Shining* (HarperCollins Australia, 2023), 155. For more on the role of forgiveness, see: Brad R. C. Kelln and John H. Ellard, 'An Equity Theory Analysis of the Impact of Forgiveness and Retribution on Transgressor Compliance', *Personality and Social Psychology Bulletin* 25, no. 7 (1999): 864–72, doi.org/10.1177/0146167299025007008; Harry M. Wallace, Julia Juola Exline, and Roy F. Baumeister, 'Interpersonal Consequences of Forgiveness: Does Forgiveness Deter or Encourage Repeat Offenses?', *Journal of Experimental Social Psychology* 44, no. 2, (2008): 1446–58, doi.org/10.1016/j.jesp.2007.02.012; Shike Li, Ivana Radivojevic, Kriti Jain, et al., 'When Apologizing Hurts: Felt Transgression and Restoration Efforts', *Journal of Organizational Behavior* 44, no. 1 (2023): 42–63, doi.org/10.1002/job.2672.

40 Prue Vines, 'The Value of Apologising Within a Moral Community: Making Apologies Work. *Oñati Socio-Legal Series* 7, no. 3 (2017): 370–89.

41 Rehm and Beatty, 'Legal Consequences', 116; Prue Vines, 'Apologising to Avoid Liability: Cynical Civility or Practical Morality?' Sydney Law Review, 23 (2005): 483–505.

42 Baird, *Bright Shining*, citing Professor Meredith Rossner, 157.

43 Simu, McGorrery, and Hull, *Sentencing*, 19.

Apologies, however, are not always straightforward. There is often considerable fear about the potential legal or insurance repercussions an apology might trigger. Many, especially executives of companies, worry that it could be treated as an admission of guilt for legal purposes. However, in the case of restorative justice processes, this fear is often unsubstantiated for the following reasons:

- It may reduce the desire to resort to litigation: 'An apology, properly given and accepted, diffuses anger and helps avoid litigation.'[44]
- It may serve as the best way to openly show understanding of the victims' pain and hurt. An apology for harm caused by an organisation is not an admission of criminal responsibility but an important relational gesture to validate the affected person's or group's feelings and experiences.[45]
- If a matter does reach court, there is a possibility that the apology may be viewed by a court as a relevant form of showing willingness to learn from the mistake, behave differently in the future and cooperate with the harmed party. Studies in the Netherlands suggest that, at least within the civil system, apologies rarely lead to negative legal consequences and may even offer legal benefits from the judge's perspective.[46]

---

44 Rehm and Beatty, 'Legal Consequences', 116.

45 See also the arguments of Prue Vines, who views apologies in the civil liability context as a form of 'corrective justice' that achieves, at the very least, the aim of acknowledging responsibility for harm as well as being an 'equaliser of the relationship'. 'In terms of general social culture this is important for creating the ability of two parties to continue on in their social roles.' Vines, 'Apologising to Avoid Liability', 503.

46 Lianne Wijntjens, 'The (Non-Existent) Legal Risks of Apologising: Courts Do Not See Apologies as a Way to Accept Civil Liability', *Journal of European Tort Law* 13, no. 3 (2022): 271–301, doi.org/10.1515/jetl-2022-0014. In Australia, Prue Vines notes that 'the evidence is that, for negligence at least, a court will not accept that an apology of itself demonstrates liability … It is for the court to determine.' Prue Vines, 'The Power of Apology: Mercy, Forgiveness or Corrective Justice in the Civil Liability Arena?', *University of New South Wales Law Review* 1, no. 1 (2007), doi.org/10.5130/psjlsj.v1i1.535.

An apology may also be a means for allowing the incorporation of human surrogates who might appropriately speak on behalf of non-human victims of the incident, such as rivers, forests, non-human animals and landscapes. Suitable surrogates may include First Nations peoples, river-keepers, Friends of 'X' River, Landcare volunteers, bushwalking clubs, sometimes farmers or fishers, environmental advocacy organisations and others who have firsthand knowledge of, and care for, land, water and the associated living beings.[47] As Djambawa Marawili, Yolngu Madarpa clan leader wisely sums up: 'Land and sea can't talk; we have to talk for them.'[48]

Providing space for multiple perspectives

In the assessment of impact and harm, another key reason for the effectiveness of the restorative conference is that it creates opportunities for different forms of knowledge and multiple perspectives to be shared and valued. Importantly, it enables the sharing of diverse perspectives on what constitutes harm, a subject on which there are often many very different opinions.

For instance, if a creek is polluted, perspectives on the harm may be varied and may include:

- **The local community's perspective**: the loss of enjoyment of a local amenity
- **Indigenous peoples' perspective**: disruption to their spiritual connection to waters or lands integral to cultural beliefs
- **Farmers and animal welfare/rescue practitioners' perspective**: injuries and deaths of non-human animals under their care
- **Local schoolchildren's perspective**: the end of their science visits and local learning opportunities

47 Felicity Tepper, 'La cuestión animal en la restauración de los ecosistemas: Poner en primer plano la familia animal a través de la justicia restaurativa medioambiental (JRM) [The Animal Question in Ecosystem Restoration: Foregrounding Animal Kin Through Environmental Restorative Justice (ERJ)]', *Revista de Victimologia [Journal of Victimology]* 15 (2023): 99–146, www.huygens.es/journals/index.php/revista-de-victimologia/article/view/248; Felicity Tepper, 'Amplifying Edge-Awareness: Socio-Ecological Restorative Approaches to Human-Wildlife Coexistence' in *Criminología verde: alternativas a la impunidad y al punitivismo ante los daños bio-socio-ecológicos [Green Criminology: Alternatives to Impunity and Punitivism Facing Bio-Socio-Ecological Harms]*, ed. Gema Varona (Dykinson, 2025), 41–81; Felicity Tepper, 'Koala Perspective of a Restorative Circle Facilitation' in *Justicia Restaurativa Medioambiental y Animal*, ed. Gema Varona (Dykinson, 2024), 125–35.

48 Djambawa Marawili and Annette Kogolo with Christina Balcombe Davidson, 'The Land and the Sea Can't Talk: We Have to Talk for Them', *Artlink* 36, no. 2 (2016): 26–33.

- **Environmental scientists' perspective**: the degradation of ecosystems and longstanding environmental impact
- **Tourism and recreation industry's perspective**: loss of revenue due to environmental damage affecting tourist activities
- **Government and regulatory bodies' perspective**: legal and policy implications, public health concerns or costly long-term resource management.

Multiple perspectives are essential for an effective and responsive restorative justice conference. In deciding who to include, it is important to ask: Who has the knowledge that needs to be respected, shared and learned from? This may include First Nations peoples' knowledge about Country or intangible cultural heritage, scientific knowledge about pollutants, or local and place-based knowledge about the impacts and solutions at community level. It is only by actively seeking out and incorporating these various perspectives that the conference attendance reflects a holistic understanding of harm and its impacts.

The regulatory cycle: Timing the restorative justice conference for best effect

A restorative justice conference may be used at various stages of the regulatory cycle. When we looked at community conferences in Chapter 4, such as the Conference of Interested Persons, we discussed restorative conferences in the context of approvals and licensing. While useful in that scenario, restorative conferences are most commonly used *after* harm has occurred. In this context, a conference can be held at one of either of two points in time. The first is before a state authority determines the sanction, to provide input into what the sanction will be, including any mitigating factors. The second point in time is when the sanction is handed down, which itself may contain a requirement to hold a restorative justice conference. In particular, this may help determine how a certain dimension of the sanction will be enacted, such as distributing monetary orders to community organisations, funding restoration works or other similar beneficial reparative outcomes.

Legislative examples across various jurisdictions

In Victoria, the EP Act 2017 enables the court to adjourn civil or criminal proceedings so that a restorative justice process may be conducted. This may be done at the court's own motion or by parties to the proceeding.[49] The provisions enabling a Conference of Interested Persons, explored in Chapter 4, also provide a mechanism by which EPA Victoria can explore the instigation of restorative justice processes outside of formal legal proceedings.

In 2015, New South Wales amended the legislative framework applicable to the Land and Environment Court, a specialist court for environment and planning matters, to incorporate restorative justice processes as part of its suite of possible orders.[50] Since then, while the court has encouraged the use of restorative justice processes in a number of cases through the adjourning of sentencing hearings to allow restorative justice conferences to take place, to date, restorative justice conferencing has predominantly been used by the court for cases involving Aboriginal heritage rather than for environmental crimes.[51]

In New Zealand, restorative justice outcomes have been officially endorsed since 2002. This came about with the passing of the *Sentencing Act 2002* that applies to all crime, including environmental prosecutions under the *Resource Management Act 1991*.[52] Under the Sentencing Act, parties must be offered the option of a restorative justice conference, an approach that is more structurally embedded into the system than the Australian examples. This is one factor that helps to explain why the use of restorative conferencing is so much more common in New Zealand than in Australia. In New Zealand, to date there have been close to 70

49 Part 11.6, Division 5, section 336(1), EP Act 2017.

50 Section 250 (1A) of the *Protection of the Environment Operations Act 1997* (NSW), which states: '(1) The court may do one or any more of the following—(a) order the offender to take specified action to publicise the offence (including the circumstances of the offence) and its environmental and other consequences and any other orders made against the person', legislation.nsw.gov.au/view/html/inforce/current/act-1997-156#sec.250. See also 'Guidelines for Seeking Environmental Court Orders', NSW EPA, last modified 26 March 2025, www.epa.nsw.gov.au/licensing-and-regulation/regulation/policies-and-guidelines/guidelines-for-seeking-environmental-court-orders.

51 See Nicola Pain, Rachel Pepper, and Millicent McCreath, 'Restorative Justice for Environmental Crime: An Antipodean Experience', *Australian Environment Review* 31, no. 8 (2016): 286, search.informit.org/doi/abs/10.3316/agispt.20171125; Nicola Pain, 'Encouraging Restorative Justice in Environmental Crime', *The Newcastle Law Review* 13 (2018): 29. Brian J. Preston, 'The Use of Restorative Justice for Environmental Crime', *Criminal Law Journal* 35, no. 3 (2011): 136, papers.ssrn.com/sol3/Delivery.cfm/SSRN_ID1831822_code1005507.pdf?abstractid=1831822&mirid=1.

52 Fred W. M. McElrea, 'The Role of Restorative Justice in RMA Prosecutions', *Resource Management Journal* 3, no. 7 (2004): 1.

restorative justice conferences held for environmental crimes.[53] In addition, a local government body, Environment Canterbury, created an Alternative Environmental Justice scheme, which diverts environmental offenders who accept responsibility and actively seek to make amends from prosecution towards a supervised restorative response.[54] Environment Southland Regional Council and West Coast Regional Council also operate similar schemes in New Zealand.[55]

If, and when, to hold a restorative justice conference: Limitations and considerations

Several factors limit the range of circumstances in which a restorative justice conference can and should be held.

For example, as we discussed in Chapter 1 in the context of voluntariness, a restorative justice conference can only proceed when the parties agree to participate. Before the conference can proceed, the offender must be prepared to accept that they have caused harm. In fact, the willingness of the offender to participate is often a key indicator of whether a restorative justice conference should be initiated.

53 There were 69 conferences as at the end of 2022, as depicted in Mark Hamilton and Ellie Stanton, 'Characteristics of Restorative Justice Conferencing in a New Zealand Environmental Offending Context', *New Zealand Law Review* 32, no. 4 (2024): 585–616; see also Mark Hamilton, 'Restorative Justice Conferencing in an Environmental Offending Context: The Role of Legislation', *Asia Pacific Journal of Environmental Law* 25 (2022): 51–76, 58, doi.org/10.4337/apjel.2022.01.03.

54 Bryan Jenkins, 'Environmental Restorative Justice: Canterbury Cases' (presentation, 38th Annual Conference of the International Association for Impact Assessment, Durban, South Africa, May 2018).

55 For example, see Environment Southland Regional Council, 'Environment Southland Diversion Scheme', in Environmental Southland Regional Council, Diversion Policies (October 2017), www.es.govt.nz/repository/libraries/id:26gi9ayo517q9stt81sd/hierarchy/about-us/plans-and-strategies/policies/compliance-policies/documents/ES%20Compliance%20Policies.pdf, 23, West Coast Regional Council, *Compliance and Enforcement Policy*, March 2018, www.wcrc.govt.nz/repository/libraries/id:2459ikxj617q9ser65rr/hierarchy/Documents/Services/Consents%20and%20Compliance/Forms/Compliance%20Forms/Compliance%20and%20Enforcement%20Policy%20March%202018%20Final.pdf. For an instance of usage, see West Coast Regional Council, 'Alternative Justice Outcome Reached for Westland District Council', media release, 20 May 2019, www.wcrc.govt.nz/repository/libraries/id:2459ikxj617q9ser65rr/hierarchy/Documents/Council/News%20and%20Announcements/News%20%28media%20releases%29/2019/Media%20Release%20-%20WDC%20-%20Alternative%20Justice%20Outcome.pdf.

So, why would an offending party voluntarily agree to participate? In the environmental context, many businesses strive to be seen as environmentally aware and committed to doing the right thing.[56] Restorative justice offers an opportunity to rebuild trust and improve their reputation with the community, and among their consumers. Some businesses may be dependent upon permits to operate, issued either by local councils or permissions given by local landowners, so a process that enables them to engage proactively with those in charge of issuing further permits may be attractive. This was certainly one motivation in the Karapiti incident discussed above, where Contact Energy is in the position of having to continually renegotiate permissions to use the land its power station is situated on.

A less self-interested motivation can be seen in the changing, growing recognition of the value of a healthy environment for human health, economic prosperity and ecosystem services integrity, emergent in both businesses and communities. Increasingly, people—and a growing number of companies—are now more inclined to view environmental protection as equally important, if not essential, to future prosperity, and feel genuine remorse for causing environmental damage.[57]

In other regulatory contexts, businesses often want to maintain their social licence to operate. After an offence for which the business is responsible, and where trust has been broken, this desire can often be more successfully brought about through participation in a restorative justice conference because it provides an opportunity to reset and rebuild relationships with

56 This is due to a variety of factors, not all of them altruistic. Businesses may pursue sustainability to strengthen corporate reputation, attract top talent, improve productivity or respond to consumer and investor demand. See Talal Rafi, 'Why Sustainability is Crucial for Corporate Strategy', *World Economic Forum*, 9 June 2022, www.weforum.org/stories/2022/06/why-sustainability-is-crucial-for-corporate-strategy/. Of course, the extent of commitment to environmental responsibility varies widely, influenced by such factors as regulatory, consumer and financial pressures.

57 In the case of companies, this is so even if the turn to nature originates from a place of self-interest, by 'putting a dollar value on nature' to treat it as 'natural capital' through initiatives such as 'nature positive' or 'nature-based' solutions. For companies that recognise the importance of caring about the environment and taking environmental responsibility, 'nature is a financial asset, and damage to it becomes a liability'. Linda J. Bilmes, 'Putting a Dollar Value on Nature Will Give Governments and Businesses More Reasons to Protect It', *The Conversation*, 11 May 2021, theconversation.com/putting-a-dollar-value-on-nature-will-give-governments-and-businesses-more-reasons-to-protect-it-153968. When companies experience genuine remorse, this often arises from a combination of factors: executives who live in the same affected communities, an awareness of the value of keeping their social licence to operate, and, in some cases, leadership by far-sighted CEOs committed to being good environmental citizens. For example, Yvon Chouinard, founder of outdoor gear company Patagonia, transferred ownership of the company to a trust to ensure all future profits are used to combat the climate crisis. Yvon Chouinard, 'Earth is Now Our Only Shareholder', Patagonia.com, 14 September 2022, www.patagonia.com/ownership/.

the affected community. Participating in a restorative justice process, including the giving of an apology and commitments to repair, may also help a company restore its reputation with its wider community of customers, media viewers and investors.

On the other hand, a restorative justice conference will not be appropriate where the harm is egregious and the harm-doers are unrepentant, uncooperative and disengaged, continuing to commit harm, or simply cannot be found. For example, in cases like the Tottenham industrial fire in 2018 and the Campbellfield toxic waste fire in 2019, what was needed more than restorative justice was an emphasis on prevention, incapacitation, good intelligence and surprise raids on a criminal syndicate.[58] As one of our interviewees stated:

> I don't think sitting down with a biker gang member is really going to help anyone in this community [laughter]. I think that having our concerns heard by the authorities and heeded and acted upon by the authorities, so that they don't happen again, is the best way to go towards providing restorative justice. We want preventive justice, we don't want restorative justice. We don't want things to be destroyed so they have to be restored. We want [it] prevented.[59]

What is more, restorative justice conferences are relatively time-consuming, requiring sufficient human and financial resources to be effective. Given the financial constraints within the regulatory enforcement cycle, a strategic approach could involve directing resources towards cases with the potential to yield substantial and meaningful transformation. This would enable these cases to serve as powerful signals to the relevant industry, emphasising both a firm stance against harm and a commitment to comprehensive restoration of both harm and relationships, an approach that transcends the typical confines of legal obligations and penalties.

---

58 In case of the Campbellfield fire reviewed in the Victorian Parliament's 2019 *Interim Inquiry into Recycling and Waste,* the Committee noted:

> The Committee has heard that the EPA has conducted many unannounced inspections following the discovery of significant illegal storage of chemical waste. However, the Australian Workers' Union—Victorian Branch told the Committee in a submission that, according to their members, 'recyclers are given adequate notice of an intended EPA visit that allows the dodgy operators to move products off-site or allow it to be hidden from sight and we understand this also happened at the Campbellfield site'.

This highlighted the value of unannounced visits as a deterrent for egregious breaches. Parliament of Victoria, *Inquiry into Recycling and Waste Management Interim Report,* Legislative Council Environment and Planning Committee (Victorian Government Printer, August 2019), 12, www.parliament.vic.gov.au/get-involved/inquiries/inquiry-into-recycling-and-waste-management/reports.

59 Interview with an environmental group.

Of course, another consideration must be the affected community. Prioritising cases must be paralleled with a sensitive appraisal of the community's needs, concerns and expectations. By way of example, a restorative justice conference could be earmarked for use when a culturally sensitive site or an area of high biodiversity is involved.

In addition to situations where the participants are willing to engage in the process, one consideration is whether the incident took place on lands owned by First Nations groups. Our research has revealed that in numerous instances within Australia and New Zealand, the use of restorative justice conferences has coincided with the imperative to address the interests, and facilitate the involvement, of First Nations peoples and groups. Restorative justice conferences provide an important opportunity for the inclusion of Indigenous voices and perspectives in ways that are broader than a formal court process, which is constrained by rules of relevance, standing and other unalterable protocols.[60]

Finally, a restorative justice conference will often ensure that parties leave the negotiations on far better terms with each other and more attuned to the other party's perspective than a traditional sanctioning process can achieve. This is because, unlike the traditional justice process, the restorative justice conference provides the opportunity for dialogue, deep listening and storytelling, helping every participant to share their impacts, grievances, suggestions for solutions and hopes for the future. Even for offenders who may initially have been reluctant to engage, the conference's positive outcome is summed up by one restorative justice facilitator's observation: '[B]y the time they get into the conference room, in general they have "got it"'.[61]

---

60 Chief Executive, *Office of Environment and Heritage v Clarence Valley Council* [2018] NSWLEC 205 (Land and Environment Court of New South Wales) and *Garrett v Williams, Craig Walter* [2007] NSWLEC 96 are two examples of prosecutions following the destruction of sites of significance to Traditional Owners. In each case, the NSW LEC facilitated a restorative justice conference. In both instances, the conferences brought together local First Nations communities impacted by the destruction of their cultural heritage and the responsible entities, including senior representatives and employees, in a conferencing circle to discuss what had happened, its effects and how to move forward.

61 Interview with a restorative justice practitioner.

An EPA restorative conference in action: The case of Hampton Park Landfill at Hallam Road

This case study involves EPA Victoria's first, and only, experiment with a restorative justice conference, the Hampton Park Landfill at Hallam Road in south-east Melbourne, one of our four major stories.[62]

Of special interest in this story is its additional innovative element, an enforceable undertaking—an accountability mechanism that also holds the potential for a restorative dimension, as we discuss further below. An enforceable undertaking is a legally binding promise to the regulator that allows individuals or companies facing the threat of prosecution to avoid prosecution by instead proposing a set of undertakings to fix the problems they are responsible for. If the regulator agrees to the proposal, the promisor's entering into the undertaking will avoid or defer the prosecution for the duration, to allow it to improve its compliance.[63] Along with having to remedy the noncompliance, undertakings tend to include a range of possible actions, including apologies, community donations, sharing knowledge gained with peer businesses, commissioning of studies, investment in repairing harmed environments, and practical measures to stop reoffending and prevent future harm.[64] Restorative actions such as these form part of what Andi Cross, business strategist and co-founder of Edges of Earth, calls 'businesses giving back', as a way to 'engage appropriately with local communities, foster inclusivity and promote conservation as part of the business model … to contribute directly and effectively to a more

62 The landfill site has been managed over time by a company that has changed its name several times. At the time of this offence, the company was known as SITA, then SUEZ, and it is currently operated by Veolia. Veolia refers to the site variously as 'Hampton Park Landfill Station', 'Hallam Road Landfill' and 'Hampton Park Outlook Transfer Station'. Veolia, 'Hallam Road Landfill', www.anz.veolia.com/our-facilities/landfills/hallam-road-landfill; Veolia, 'Hampton Park Outlook Transfer Station', accessed 20 February 2025, www.anz.veolia.com/our-facilities/transfer-stations/hampton-park-outlook-transfer-station. EPA Victoria refers to the site as either Hampton Park Landfill or Hallam Road Landfill; we have chosen to use the term 'Hampton Park Landfill' to reflect the suburb within which the landfill is situated, acknowledging its connection to the wider community.

63 The effect of an enforceable undertaking depends on the specific provisions of the enabling legislation. For example, under the EP Act 1970, an enforceable undertaking was required to be an 'alternative to prosecution', meaning that investigations had to be completed to a standard sufficient to support charges, but no charges would be laid. In contrast, under the EP Act 2017, enforceable undertakings are more flexible and can be entered into for any matter within the EPA's powers or functions under the Act, rather than being strictly an alternative to prosecution. In some other jurisdictions, charges may be laid and prosecution commenced but deferred, provided the enforceable undertaking is complied with.

64 Andi Cross, 'How Businesses Can Give Back to the Environment and Their Communities', *Forbes*, 3 April 2024, www.forbes.com/councils/forbesbusinesscouncil/2024/04/03/how-businesses-can-give-back-to-the-environment-and-their-communities/.

sustainable future'. Cross argues that '[t]hese efforts not only bolster a brand's reputation but also create a ripple effect that encourages others to follow suit'.

Everyone has grown sick and tired of the 'big stink' surrounding the Hampton Park Landfill. Located in south-east Melbourne, it is run by French transnational company Veolia, formerly Suez Recycling and Recovery.[65] In giving their impressions of the big stink, residents were far from complimentary:

> 'Smells like sewerage.'
> '[T]he methane was so bad it gave me an asthma attack.'
> '… like rotting fish.'

These comments represent just a small sample of the complaints made about the landfill by local residents in recent times. A local resident summed up the widespread sentiment: 'I can't understand why nothing is being done to stop it […] they need to shut the tip down.'[66]

The situation today reflects an ongoing problem that first began back in 2010, when pungent odours from the same, then much younger landfill started infiltrating the lives and workdays of local residents, workers and EPA officers. Back then, emerging from a long drought, Melbourne experienced wetter-than-usual conditions during a record-breaking La Niña that caused a rapid breakdown of organic matter in the landfill. This resulted in unpleasant smells regularly pervading the surrounding neighbourhood, seeping into people's houses and apartments.

People of modest means reside here. In a climate of increasingly competitive high house prices in a rapidly ballooning city, the option to sell and move elsewhere was not open to most of the affected residents. Even those who developed a hypersensitivity to the smell could not overcome the realities of rising housing costs. Yet, even if they could sell up and leave, not only were the residents' dwellings more affordable than elsewhere, but they were also part of both a community and a place. Overwhelmed and frustrated, their only recourse was to wearily lodge complaint after complaint with EPA Victoria.

65 Veolia merged with Suez Recycling and Recovery in early 2022.

66 Eleanor Wilson, 'Landfill Causing a Stink for Locals'.

The avalanche of complaints arrived at a particularly innovative time within EPA Victoria. The 2011 *Compliance and Enforcement Review* by Stan Krpan (the Krpan Review discussed in Chapter 2)[67] had proposed interesting new compliance tools, and a number of officers within the EPA were eager to try them out. The Hampton Park Landfill case seemed like the perfect opportunity.

The first regulatory innovation to be trialled was an enforceable undertaking. A relatively new regulatory tool, especially in the environmental regulation space, the enforceable undertaking had been used by EPA Victoria just a few times previously and by only two other environmental regulators at the time—one in New South Wales and the other in the Commonwealth. As such, it was still 'finding its feet' as an environmental regulatory enforcement process.[68] (We explore this restorative remedy in greater detail towards the end of this chapter.)

What made this particular use of an enforceable undertaking unique and exciting was its restorative nature. Part way through the negotiations for the enforceable undertaking, EPA Victoria decided to trial another regulatory innovation—the inclusion of a restorative justice conference—to help determine the terms of the enforceable undertaking. Historically, enforceable undertakings had only been negotiated directly between the enforcing regulator and the organisation undertaking the agreed commitments. It was a significant change to include the community affected by the environmental harm. The restorative conference was intended to provide the opportunity for residents to give their own input by answering the three key questions: What happened? How have people been affected? What can be done to improve the situation?

In May 2012, 17 EPA staff, including an EPA community liaison officer, did a two-day training workshop on restorative conferencing. This created both a knowledge base and an appetite to try it out in practice. The Hampton Park Landfill case appeared to be the excellent opportunity—it had a besieged community significantly impacted by foul odours, and the negotiations to produce the enforceable undertaking were progressing well.

67 Stan Krpan, *Compliance and Enforcement Review: A Review of EPA Victoria's Approach* (Environment Protection Authority Victoria, Publication 1368, February 2011 [The Krpan Review]).

68 Miranda Forsyth and Felicity Tepper, 'Environmental Enforceable Undertakings: An Innovative Tool to Repair and Prevent Environmental Harm', *Journal of Environmental Law* 36, no. 3 (2024): 385–411, doi.org/10.1093/jel/eqae021.

The community liaison officer was appointed as the conference organiser. He reached out to a seasoned restorative justice practitioner, David Moore, to assist with the facilitation. It should be noted that what was required in this context differed significantly from a traditional restorative justice conference that typically involves about four to 12 participants. In this instance, entire neighbourhoods needed to be authentically represented. Moreover, the conference was occurring midway through negotiations, meaning that legal teams on both sides were still heavily involved—and thus able to throw a spanner in the works at any moment.

The community liaison officer ran a series of meetings with community members, generally held in locations close to the offending landfill. In talking through the process with the residents, he came to understand their key concerns and was in a good position to determine questions of group representation. The meetings were intense, and in some ways may have served to release some of the pressure and frustration building prior to the conference. Selection of representatives was to some extent political, especially when one group of residents appointed a strident and vocal 'community advocate' who came from outside the residents' odour-affected area to represent them. This severely irritated other groups, many of whom considered this advocate to be a noisy intruder.

On the grey midwinter evening of 2 August 2012 in Melbourne, the conference took place in a mid-level hotel situated in the local area. The participants, about 30 overall, consisted of the community liaison officer and David, the community representatives, both the CEO and Chair of EPA Victoria, and senior management staff of the landfill operator. All were seated in an inclusive circle. In a clear indication of the significance and magnitude of the process to everyone involved, it started at 5.30 PM and continued nonstop for almost five hours, finally winding up at 10.20 PM.

Just before the conference started, lawyers for the landfill operator had announced they required the participants to sign non-disclosure agreements in relation to what transpired during the conference. This was new information for almost everyone, and it got the conference off to a very shaky start. It further compounded the simmering distrust among many of the community representatives who expressed concerns that the enforceable undertaking's terms had already been partially negotiated. Even worse, the terms negotiated thus far had not been revealed to the participants. While this made sense from a legal perspective, given that the undertaking was being evaluated as an alternative to prosecution proceedings, it appeared disingenuous to the community. Notwithstanding the careful preparation, it was starting to seem as if Hampton Park was, after all, far from being a perfect opportunity to test a restorative justice conference.

Despite these real and significant problems, the conference did go ahead. Looking back now, it can be viewed as a successful trial of restorative justice in a regulatory context. Most of our interviewees focused on the emotional energy released in the room when the community was discussing how the landfill issues had impacted on them. They voiced emotions, such as concerns about serious health impacts, not feeling safe, feeling let down by authorities, feelings of loss, feelings of being victims of a catastrophe. They asked questions that reflected their emotional uncertainty, like 'Who do I believe?' and 'Are we second class?' While some voiced ongoing distrust at the end of the conference, others remarked: '[Y]ou get a feeling from the company representatives that they finally saw the impact of what they were doing to the community.' There were also many community participants who noted the feeling that the regulator was listening too: 'I think the EPA was genuinely concerned about the distress of affected residents.'

In an interview in October 2020, the then Chair of the EPA, Cheryl Batagol, observed that:

> when you sit in a circle, as I did that night, and listen to the pain and the harm that it causes people … I was moved, so moved that we had to develop a better way of communicating with community … and of connecting communities with perpetrators.

Her comments highlight another theme we have explored throughout the book: the personal experience of hearing directly from those impacted by harm. This provides a powerful motivation for those who have created the harm, and for those responsible for regulating the harm, to invest in solutions to repair and prevent future harm.

The most concrete outcome of the conference was the inclusion in the enforceable undertaking of terms considered important to the community. These included a public statement of regret, the operation of an environmental report hotline, and improved environmental management systems targeted at addressing compliance, such as infrared drone monitoring of odour hotspots. Funding was also provided for two community benefit projects, covering an upgrade to a local park, tree planting, and restoration of the nearby River Gum Creek Reserve. There were also extra community-led outcomes that included an independent study into the health effects of odour and landfill gas[69] and improved reporting of the operator's commitments through the Hallam Road Community Reference Group, which continues to operate a decade later. We explored community reference groups (CRGs) in earlier chapters, particularly in Chapter 3, where we recounted the case of the Brooklyn Industrial Precinct CRG (BCRG). It is worth reiterating the immeasurable value they hold as bridges connecting the community, industry and regulatory bodies. Community reference groups play a pivotal role in enhancing relationships and outcomes, not only benefiting the environment but also fostering long-term community engagement, even when differing viewpoints arise among members. In the words of one long-term participant, 'There has been a genuine ability for community to have voice through it.'

The public health study initiated by the undertaking was a significant outcome. It was required to be undertaken in a manner that opened the doors of communication between the scientific experts and the community. This participatory approach encouraged dialogue and enabled community questions to be voiced and answered. Principal among those questions were: 'Is the area safe?', and 'Does the odour signal a health concern?'

There is often a chasm between the scientific evidence provided by regulatory bodies and technical experts, and the information that community members need in order to better understand and accept the truthfulness of what they are being told. For example, scholars Lynn Frewer and Brian Salter observed that during the bovine spongiform encephalopathy (BSE) health crisis in the United Kingdom in the 1990s—a time when public trust in scientific advice informing regulatory decision-making plummeted dramatically—'the longstanding decline in the public's trust in science has passed a threshold point where the legitimacy of scientific judgement is regularly questioned'.[70] They further noted that UK regulatory culture was 'dominated … by rationalist interpretations of scientific evidence', a stance they considered 'encouraged élite groups to dismiss … public reactions as inappropriate and irrelevant'.[71]

---

69 This was updated by the EPA in 2016, with further evidence: Environment Protection Authority Victoria, 'Air Emissions from Non-Hazardous Waste Landfills—Update of 2013 Literature Review', (Victoria State Government, December 2016, cleanaway2stor.blob.core.windows.net/cleanaway2-blob-container/2019/11/Air-Emissions-from-Non-Hazardous-Waste-EPA2016.pdf.

70 Lynn Frewer and Brian Salter, 'Public Attitudes, Scientific Advice and the Politics of Regulatory Policy: The Case of BSE', *Science and Public Policy* 29, no. 2 (2002): 138, doi.org/10.3152/147154302781781092.

71 Frewer and Salter, 'Public Attitudes', 139.

In response to evidence that experts claimed the public could not handle scientific uncertainty, the authors pointed out that contrary evidence revealed quite clearly that the public was familiar with the concept of uncertainty and even expected to be engaged on it. They concluded that scientific advice from regulators must be disseminated in a way that considers both the 'impact of science on society and the quality of life of citizens', while also being transparent and easy to understand.[72] Moreover, involving the public through consultation and engagement is essential in order to prevent citizens from becoming suspicious of the motives of both the scientific community and government.[73]

Restorative justice processes provide a way of bridging this chasm and helping to shift 'to a more pluralistic form of regulatory governance'.[74] This can be achieved through facilitating the engagement with diverse forms of knowledge and knowledge production among the scientific experts, the regulatory officers and citizens. This entails not only providing clear explanations of the conventional scientific methodologies employed by regulators, but also actively incorporating insights from knowledge sources such as citizen science, Indigenous science and lived experiences in two-way exchanges of knowledge. By providing opportunities for dialogue in a trusted, facilitated space, the full story can emerge, along with co-designed solutions.

In reflecting on the conference process, the community liaison officer commented that he saw it as a way to bridge the regulator's role to be objective with the fact that people have individual experiences of harm, experiences as worthy of consideration as the focus on objectivity in working through the challenge. 'This is the great thing about the restorative justice approach,' he told us: '[T]here is a bit of magic, a ritualised process that is important.'

We view the range of new restorative spaces that emerged from this milestone restorative conference as a diffusion of restorative practices, akin to seeds carried by the wind, sprinkled widely and taking root to flourish in fertile soil. Indeed, throughout this book, we have explored this theme of organic growth. In the Hampton Park Landfill case, this diffusion took root in two key outcomes. First, the relationships forged through direct and personal engagement strengthened connections between individuals. Second,

72 Frewer and Salter, 'Public Attitudes', 144.
73 Frewer and Salter, 'Public Attitudes', 144.
74 Frewer and Salter, 'Public Attitudes', 143.

the regulator's public attempt to act differently emboldened community members to demand and propose more relational and participative forms of engagement. For example, following the conference, a group called Friends of River Gum Creek was formed, receiving funding from SITA Australia (a waste management company) for tree planting and landscape work in the local reserve. The group continues today, regularly organising tree planting and community activities around the reserve.[75]

There are also cautionary tales and disappointments following this restorative justice conference, and these are equally important, to balance our broader argument in this book. When the landfill was taken over by a new company, its corporate memory was, in some ways, reset. A persistent challenge for relational processes like restorative justice is maintaining momentum for connectedness and relationality with community over long time periods, especially where corporate structures and the exigencies of time mean people move on and institutional memories are lost. In the case of Hampton Park Landfill, as earlier noted, a reemergence of the odours in recent years, although not as extreme as in 2010–11, has caused renewed community frustration.[76] This indicates the ongoing need for both industry and regulators to stay attentive and committed to community concerns.

From the perspective of EPA Victoria's innovatory approaches, this pilot was seen as a great 'good news' story. The biggest disappointment by far, however, is that the restorative conference pilot has not been repeated. Why this was so piqued our curiosity, given it was a highly effective event that is still spoken about positively in the EPA to this day and remembered by community members more than a decade afterwards.

We believe that several factors have contributed to this failure to repeat the experience. First, doing restorative justice well can be very hard, as it requires emotional vulnerability from everyone involved. Doing new things is hard, too—initial discomfort, and challenges that accompany novelty,

75 Friends of River Gum Creek, 'About', Facebook, accessed 20 February 2025, www.facebook.com/groups/764577273553660/.

76 As of 3 September 2024, the EPA advice to the public on its website about Veolia's Hampton Park Landfill noted that the EPA's officers had investigated pollution reports about odour from the landfill and confirmed that the odour source was the landfill. Remedial notices were issued, and the EPA continues to monitor compliance, noting that it would take the appropriate regulatory action to ensure that the landfill operators comply with their obligations. See EPA Victoria, 'Hallam Road Landfill', last modified 19 December 2025, www.epa.vic.gov.au/hallam-road-landfill.

often derail sustained progress. Prosecution, by contrast, may appear more straightforward because it is a familiar tool with clear, quantifiable metrics on paper, while restorative outcomes can be more difficult to measure.

Additionally, we think it is also about the sustained need to support restorative approaches so that they become embedded in the regulator's way of being. For these approaches to become a regular part of regulatory practice, the entire system must be intentionally considered, to accommodate and allow restorative practices to take root, grow and thrive. This is why we argue throughout this book for the exploration and nurturing of incipient and new restorative spaces—without an intentional approach to unearthing and valuing restorative practices, they will not be sustainable.

While restorative conferencing holds inherent value as a practice, it alone cannot drive transformational change within the regulatory context. What is required is the seeding and flourishing of restorative practices and values across many different regulatory spaces—a shift that can eventually lead to some change at a systems level. We will return to our suggestions for achieving this in Chapter 10.

Addressing challenges regulators might encounter with restorative justice conferences

While restorative justice conferences offer valuable opportunities for dialogue and resolution, they also have some drawbacks or limitations that must be understood so that any potential scepticism or genuine concerns can be addressed. By understanding these challenges, regulatory staff can identify what may hinder the use of restorative justice conferences in their own organisation, develop strategies for responding constructively to criticism and find ways to maximise both their potential and appeal.

First, the restorative justice conference can entail a lengthy process. It requires considerable preparation in advance and often then proceeds at a timeframe dictated by the parties. This may involve an adjournment for some time. In the Karapiti example above, the adjournment lasted for a year, to enable the development of a comprehensive cultural impact assessment. Delays like this can lead to challenges such as diminished momentum, difficulties with resource allocation and the risk of perceptions of regulatory inertia, which may reduce trust in the regulator's commitment to taking action. Overcoming these challenges requires regular, clear and updated messaging that the delays or adjournments are a vital part of ensuring the conference process remains sound and reflective of all parties' needs, and that the regulator is firmly committed to its continuance.

There are also cost considerations for the restorative justice conference. These include payment of the facilitator for preparation, hiring a suitable venue for the conference, providing refreshments, conducting the conference and writing up an outcomes report. In New Zealand, these costs are borne by the government for cases that use restorative justice under the *Sentencing Act 2002*, but this is not the case more broadly. Costs could be reduced if the regulator's premises are used or an affordable community venue hired, if a total cost is negotiated with the facilitator upfront, if the offending industry covers the costs either completely or partially, and if community volunteers are engaged to assist with logistical tasks. Moreover, while upfront costs are a consideration, research suggests that restorative justice conferences can offer significant cost benefits in the long term. As Simu et al. note:

> The general consensus from research on restorative justice conferences for individuals (though none yet involving corporate offenders) is that they can also offer significant cost benefits due to their potential to reduce future offending by participating offenders.[77]

Given that individuals within corporations—such as CEOs or senior managers—are often prosecuted for regulatory breaches, it is reasonable to consider whether similar benefits might extend to corporate leadership. If participation in a restorative process helps shift individual attitudes towards compliance, it may also influence broader corporate culture, potentially reducing the likelihood of future breaches.

Restorative justice conferences are also emotionally demanding for all participants. Unlike court proceedings, which have well-defined protocols and roles, the format and outcomes of restorative justice conferences may be less predictable. For some regulators, the unfamiliarity of the restorative process, concerns about managing emotions or unease about relinquishing some control over the proceedings might lead them to feel that engaging in it will be a potentially uncomfortable experience, making them hesitant to commit to such conferences. The provision of training and support

77 Simu et al., *Sentencing*, 19.

for participating regulatory staff can help build confidence in the process and ensure the emotional dynamics are properly managed, making the experience more predictable and psychologically safer.[78]

Restorative justice conferences may be seen as new and innovative in the regulatory context, which can lead some regulators to perceive them as too risky to proactively endorse and promote. As we note in Chapter 10, it is essential for the executive level to set the prevailing tone and establish an authorising environment. This is why clear organisational support for restorative endeavours is so crucial. Additionally, clear pathways for implementation must be meticulously developed to facilitate both the use and successful execution of restorative conferences. One regulator we spoke with suggested the need for developing a 'restorative justice button' and to have that built into the operating procedures or regulatory workflow. The idea behind this metaphor is to make organising restorative justice conferences relatively straightforward—and hence a more attractive and accessible option for regulators.

Finally, many restorative justice facilitators have an impression that it is hard to get high-quality participation in the restorative circle once it reaches 40 or more people. At the Hampton Park Landfill restorative conference, this impression led to an attempt to restrict the circle numbers to 30, though it may have reached nearly 40. With so many key EPA players, corporate duty holders, representatives from local councils and other government agencies, only a dozen community members were selected by EPA Victoria to attend. According to the Dandenong EPA Office, there had been 2000 community complaints about the landfill over a 15-month period, suggesting that many more community members would have wanted to be involved if the opportunity had been made accessible.

78 Effective facilitation and preparation are crucial to managing emotional dynamics, helping participants feel more comfortable and supported throughout the process. Formal restorative justice conference training courses offered across many jurisdictions help facilitators become competent and confident in managing these dynamics to enable participants to fully engage in the process. See further Meredith Rossner, *Just Emotions: Rituals of Restorative Justice* (Oxford University Press, 2013), doi.org/10.1093/acprof:oso/9780199655045.001.0001; Meredith Rossner, 'Emotions and Interaction Ritual: A Micro Analysis of Restorative Justice', *The British Journal of Criminology* 51, no. 1 (2011): 95–119, doi.org/10.1093/bjc/azq075; Nathan Harris, Lode Walgrave, and John Braithwaite, 'Emotional Dynamics in Restorative Conferences', *Theoretical Criminology* 8, no. 2 (2004): 191–210, www.ojp.gov/ncjrs/virtual-library/abstracts/emotional-dynamics-restorative-conferences; 'Facilitating Listening Circles: Advanced Training and Essential Skills for Facilitators', International Institute for Restorative Practices Graduate School, accessed 20 February 2025, www.iirp.edu/professional-development/facilitating-listening-circles; Gale Burford, John Braithwaite and Valerie Braithwaite eds., *Restorative and Responsive Human Services* (Routledge, 2019), doi.org/10.4324/9780429398704.

This limitation highlights a democratic challenge inherent in traditional restorative justice circles: when the number of participants grows too large, it can hinder meaningful engagement and exclude important voices, undermining the process's ability to fully address community concerns. Restorative justice after mass civil-war atrocities could offer instructive lessons here. Particularly in Colombia, experiments are under way with new models in this macro-focused area of restorative justice to scale up participation to accommodate much larger numbers of participants. We should keep an open mind, therefore, to learn from this evolving experience.[79] The Truth and Justice Reconciliation process in South Africa is another example of how such an approach can engage more broadly.[80]

Finally, when community concerns are widespread, providing broad involvement of all interested community members is not only restorative but fair. David Moore and Alikki Vernon assert that '[a] larger group sets relations right—not simply between the person or people-directly-harmed and those-formally-responsible, but across their social network'.[81] This offers a compelling reason to experiment with ways to involve more community participants while maintaining a manageable process. Approaches such as subgroup circles, rotating participation in and out of the circle based on topics being discussed, facilitator assistant, and using interactive technology tools like polling and digital discussion boards or themed circles can all contribute to more inclusive engagement without compromising the effectiveness of the restorative approach.

Beyond conferences: Other restorative remedies

EPA Victoria has already been using various alternative restorative sanctions for a considerable period, demonstrating a longstanding commitment to restorative approaches. One such restorative sanction has involved directing the monies from a successful prosecution to be allocated to local communities instead of going towards State revenue. Another sanction has involved what we view as a restorative twist on enforceable undertakings. To explore these two restorative remedies available to regulators, we first

79 John Braithwaite, 'Scaling Up Crime Prevention and Justice', *Crime and Justice* 50, no. 1 (2021): 247–99, doi.org/10.1086/716093.

80 Lucy Allais, 'Restorative Justice, Retributive Justice, and the South African Truth and Reconciliation Commission', *Philosophy & Public Affairs* 39, no. 4 (2011): 331–63, doi.org/10.1111/j.1088-4963.2012.01211.x.

81 Moore and Vernon, *Setting Relations Right*, 60.

look at restorative payment awards and, examining a case study, show how a fine payment can be used to develop relationships with local Indigenous peoples through collaborative restoration projects. Then, we look deeper into the restorative twist on enforceable undertakings, which orients these agreements towards not only improved compliance but also the repair of relationships and increasing community engagement.

Restorative payment awards

After a prosecution, penalty monies are typically paid into State revenue. However, for many years, EPA Victoria has availed itself of a discretionary alternative approach, one that is far more restorative. Known as a section 67AC scheme after the section authorising it under the former EP Act 1970, this scheme allows penalty monies to be allocated to local communities instead of being paid into the standard revenue coffers. Section 67AC(2)(c) of the EP Act 1970 allowed for an environmental project that was:

- restorative or enhanced the environment in a public place; or
- for the public benefit, even if the project is unrelated to the offence.

Projects were sourced through the Inspiring Environmental Solutions program.[82] This was a program that invited Victorian communities to submit community and environment-based projects for funding that would restore or revitalise the local environment.[83] When a prosecution suitable under section 67AC was identified, a small number of proposal-holders were invited to submit a detailed project plan. Project proposals were assessed using established criteria available on EPA Victoria's website.[84]

82 See also 'Inspiring Environmental Solutions', EPA Victoria, last modified 9 September 2021, archived at the Wayback Machine, web.archive.org/web/20250521144033/https://www.epa.vic.gov.au/about-epa/our-programs-and-projects/inspiring-environmental-solutions; and *Inspiring Environmental Solutions: EPA's Community Funding Program,* Program Guidelines, Environment Protection Authority Victoria, 2011, archived at the Wayback Machine, web.archive.org/web/20250414050624/https://www.epa.vic.gov.au/-/media/epa/files/publications/1419.pdf.

83 The EPA retains the procedures in place under the new EP Act 2017 to enable restorative projects. It 'has been established to implement and oversee' restorative project orders made under section 332 of the EP Act 2017. See also Environment Protection Authority Victoria, 'Inspiring Environmental Solutions'.

84 'Applicants can submit a registration form anytime during the year.' EPA Victoria, 'Inspiring Environmental Solutions'.

According to EPA records, during the time it was used, around 56 per cent of prosecutions resulted in sentencing made under section 67AC, with varying sums allocated.

Further, a court can also require an offender to take specific actions instead of, or in addition to, any penalty. This order might include publicising the offence, completing a project to restore or improve the environment, or conducting an environmental audit. EPA Victoria has routinely sought publication of environmental offences and a public apology as part of any court order. The EPA may also encourage offenders and victims to meet as part of a restorative justice conference.

The purpose of section 67AC's approach was to link the enforcement of environmental offences to the restoration of the harm caused to the communities and environments affected. However, unlike the thrust of most restorative justice initiatives that encourage the participation of those directly impacted, section 67AC tended to be a primarily redistributive response to environmental harm. It was initiated by allocating funds to incorporated community organisations.

The outcome of this process, for most of its life, was that restoration of harm was typically abstract, disconnected from those directly impacted and the specific environmental harm. The process took the form of community development for the local environment. In addition, there was no victim involvement in the process.

An example of the section 67AC order in practice comes from the Brooklyn Industrial Precinct, an area of Melbourne discussed in Chapter 3. The suburb of Brooklyn faces significant socio-economic disadvantage and is heavily industrialised. As the Precinct story related, its proximity to multiple industrial sites exposes its residents to dust, noise, and chemical pollutants.

Our example revisits Australian Tallow Producers (ATP), the Brooklyn manufacturer that renders perishable meat by-products, first introduced in Chapter 3.[85] At the time of our research for this story, ATP had been fined three times, with escalating severity, for ongoing pollution-related offences. Through creating a liaison group (the BCRG) involving community, industry, the local councils and regulators, EPA Victoria had developed

85 See also Australian Tallow Producers, [Homepage], accessed 20 February 2025, www.austal.com.au/.

social capital in the Precinct. The existence of social capital enabled the EPA to identify several restorative project options ready to proceed with in the event of any future infringements. After further complaints about ATP's polluting, the EPA prosecuted the company in 2015. The court heard victim impact statements from a number of witnesses. Ultimately, the court ordered that ATP pay AUD$200,000 to the Hobsons Bay City Council towards building a recreation area near the community centre, to benefit the affected Brooklyn community. This sentencing money allowed the Council to accelerate a previously planned park upgrade, bringing community benefits sooner than expected. As we detailed in Chapter 3, this also helped ATP to start rebuilding its relationship with the community.

The section 67AC scheme was reformulated in the EP Act 2017 to place greater emphasis on being restorative. Now called a 'restorative project order', it grants courts the discretion under section 332(1) to order a person to carry out a project for the restoration or enhancement of the environment in a public place or for the public benefit.[86] The scheme also enables:

- penalty monies to be allocated directly to local communities and the environment to achieve a restorative outcome.
- a link to be made between the sanctioning of environmental offences and restoration of the harm caused to the communities and environments affected. As in the previous arrangements, EPA Victoria may invite Traditional Owners and other suitable organisations or parties to prepare a proposal.
- the participation of those directly impacted, where appropriate, by allocating funds in the form of community development for the local environment.

86 In full, section 332 reads as follows: '**Restorative project orders.** The Court may order the person to carry out a project for the restoration or enhancement of the environment in a public place or for the public benefit, whether or not the project is related to the offence or contravention. (2) Without limiting subsection (1), an order under that subsection may require the person to pay an amount of money, for the carrying out of a project for the restoration or enhancement of the environment in a public place or for the public benefit, to (a) a specified person or organisation; or (b) the Restorative Project Account.' EP Act 2017. See also *Sanction Powers Policy*, EPA Victoria, June 2021, 10, www.epa.vic.gov.au/sites/default/files/epa/publications/1814.pdf.

In addition, a new provision (section 332(2b)) empowers the court to direct funds into a restorative project account for environmental restoration or enhancement in a public area or for public benefit. This provision ensures that a restorative project can be established later, even if one is not immediately available at the time of sentencing or penalty, allowing for a purposeful timeframe for project development.

When combined with an adjournment to conduct a restorative justice process, these innovative provisions give Victorian courts and the regulator significant scope to involve victims actively in determining how penalty money should be spent and allocated. This restorative approach encourages the exploration of creative avenues to mend the harm, facilitate the rebuilding of relationships, and devise innovative solutions for repair. It is a model that other regulators may wish to explore.

The new section 332 orders provide a compelling example of a space where the seedlings of a restorative approach have taken root, with the potential to be nurtured and grown. This is an apt point to introduce our case study on how this approach can support First Nations peoples to be part of a healing-focused regulatory response.

Case study: Restorative penalties and Traditional Owner groups

> *Our Ancestors looked after this Country and we are duty-bound to look after it for the next generation—including the water that falls on and flows through Country.*[87]

Australia's historical treatment of First Nations people by European settlers is deeply regrettable, involving punitive, retributive, paternalistic and alienating policies, interactions and attitudes.[88] Until 1992, the Australian legal system failed to recognise the pre-existing rights of First Nations peoples, maintaining the legal fiction of 'terra nullius'—that the land was

87 Rodney Carter, CEO of the Dja Dja Wurrung Group, cited in Giovanni Torre, 'Dja Dja Wurrung Clans Call for Water Rights and Greater Say in Water Management'.

88 Australian Law Reform Commission, *Changing Policies Towards Aboriginal People*; Veronica Matthews et al., 'Justice, Culture, and Relationships: Australian Indigenous Prescription for Planetary Health', 636–41.

'empty'—on British arrival in 1788.[89] Aboriginal and Torres Strait Islander peoples were denied the right to vote in federal elections until 1962, and in 1967, a referendum amended the Australian Constitution to recognise them in the national census (i.e., as part of the Australian population) and allow the federal government to legislate for them.[90] Today there is a significant gap in life expectancy, and First Nations people continue to be the most disadvantaged sector of Australian society.[91] Australia as a whole still has a long way to go in regard to ensuring full justice and respect for its First Nations people.

This general Australian context may in some way explain why it has taken Australia's regulators such a long time to come around to understanding that working collaboratively with First Nations people is a moral imperative rooted in fundamental principles of basic fairness, respect and good governance. Both historical and current injustices give impetus to the necessity for

89 In 1835, the Governor of New South Wales, Richard Bourke, used the legal principle of terra nullius to justify British settlement. This principle means that certain land 'belongs to no-one'. The principle endured but was finally changed in 1992 with the High Court of Australia's Mabo decision, which recognised Aboriginal and Torres Strait Islander peoples' continuing connection and rights to land through Native Title. A summary of the Mabo case can be found here: Australian Institute of Aboriginal and Torres Strait Islander Studies (AIATSIS), *Overturning the Doctrine of Terra Nullius: The Mabo Case*, 27 September 2008, aiatsis.gov.au/sites/default/files/research_pub/overturning-the-doctrine-of-terra-nullius_0_3.pdf.

90 The National Museum Australia explains this as follows:

> The *Commonwealth Electoral Act 1962* received assent on 21 May 1962. It granted all Aboriginal and Torres Strait Islander people the option to enrol and vote in federal elections. Enrolment was not compulsory for Aboriginal and Torres Strait Islander people, unlike other Australians. Once enrolled, however, voting was compulsory [...] It was not until 1984 that Aboriginal and Torres Strait Islander people gained full equality with other electors under the *Commonwealth Electoral Amendment Act 1983*. This Act made enrolling to vote at federal elections compulsory for Indigenous Australians.

'Indigenous Australians' Right to Vote', National Museum Australia, last modified 27 May 2025, www.nma.gov.au/defining-moments/resources/indigenous-australians-right-to-vote. AIATSIS staff further explain that:

> [w]hile many people think that the Referendum gave Aboriginal and Torres Strait Islander peoples the right to vote, this wasn't the case. Aboriginal people could vote at the state level before Federation in 1901; Queensland and Western Australia being the only states that expressly prevented Aboriginal and Torres Strait Islander peoples from voting ... On 27 May 1967, Australians voted to change the Constitution so that like all other Australians, Aboriginal and Torres Strait Islander peoples would be counted as part of the population and the Commonwealth would be able to make laws for them. A resounding 90.77 per cent said 'Yes' and every single state had a majority result for the 'Yes' vote. It was one of the most successful national campaigns in Australia's history.

AIATSIS, 'The 1967 Referendum', last modified 16 March 2026, aiatsis.gov.au/explore/1967-referendum.

91 Australian Institute of Health and Welfare, *Aboriginal and Torres Strait Islander Health Performance Framework: Summary Report* (AIHW: Australian Government, August 2024), www.indigenoushpf.gov.au/report-overview/overview/summary-report; Elizabeth Jane Macpherson, *Indigenous Water Rights in Law and Regulation: Lessons from Comparative Experience* (Cambridge University Press, 2019), 11, doi.org/10.1017/9781108611091; Matthews et al., 'Justice, Culture, and Relationships'.

regulatory engagement with Aboriginal and Torres Strait Islander peoples to prioritise the establishment of trust as a foundation upon which to build ongoing relationships and collaboration.[92] This also means that regulatory staff need to be trained in cultural competence, to ensure respectful and culturally appropriate engagement. Further, there is a need to acknowledge the active agency that Aboriginal and Torres Strait Islander peoples bring to any collaboration, noting that their leaders have been actively working since the early 1900s to establish organisational frameworks aimed at enhancing engagement with the state.[93] This enduring effort continues to this day and emphasises their commitment to representing their self-management preferences and promoting collaborative and partnership efforts for mutual outcomes.

Historically, EPA Victoria had limited formal engagements with Traditional Owner groups, despite their profound and enduring linkages with Country, something we elaborate on in Chapter 9.

Significant engagement with the Dja Dja Wurrung (or Djaara), the Traditional Owners of the Country in central Victoria, began in the aftermath of a 2016 sewerage spill. The EPA prosecuted the water corporation responsible, Coliban Region Water Authority (Coliban Water). The Djaara people refer to this area as 'upside-down Country' due to the prominence of mounds created by old tailings heaps from centuries of mining, particularly during the Victorian gold rush in the mid-1800s.

92 The Australian Human Rights Commission highlights that since colonisation, First Nations peoples have resisted state-sanctioned injustices, including mass killings, displacement, and cultural suppression, leading to deep-seated mistrust towards governmental institutions. Australian Human Rights Commission, 'The History of Aboriginal and Torres Strait Islander Peoples Advocating for the Right to Be Heard', accessed 20 February 2025, humanrights.gov.au/our-work/aboriginal-and-torres-strait-islander-social-justice/history-aboriginal-and-torres-strait. Additionally, the Victorian Public Sector Commission notes that European colonisation subjected Aboriginal and Torres Strait Islander communities to massacres, violence, disease and loss, further eroding trust in regulatory bodies. 'Aboriginal and Torres Strait Islander Culture and History', Victorian Public Sector Commission and State Government of Victoria. To address this mistrust, the Australian Institute of Health and Welfare emphasises that effective engagement requires governments and organisations to work collaboratively with Indigenous communities, fostering trust through sustained commitment and culturally informed practices. Janet Hunt, 'Engaging with Indigenous Australia—Exploring the Conditions for Effective Relationships with Aboriginal and Torres Strait Islander Communities', Closing the Gap Clearinghouse Issues Paper no. 5 (Australian Government—Australian Institute of Health and Welfare, Australian Institute of Family Studies, October 2013), www.aihw.gov.au/getmedia/7d54eac8-4c95-4de1-91bb-0d6b1cf348e2/ctgc-ip05.pdf?v=20230605181119&inline=true.

93 Josephine Bourne, 'Indigenous Organisation Leaders: Balancing Tensions Between Achieving Political Goals and Regulatory Requirements' (ANZSOG, 16 August 2022), anzsog.edu.au/news/indigenous-organisation-leaders-balancing-tensions-between-achieving-political-goals-and-regulatory-requirements/; Marcia Langton and Aaron Corn, *First Knowledges Law: The Way of the Ancestors*, First Knowledges series (Thames & Hudson Australia, 2023).

As Traditional Owners, Djaara have long felt excluded from management decisions around water and Country, despite this being an ancestral and intergenerational duty. Rodney Carter, the CEO of the Dja Dja Wurrung Clans Aboriginal Corporation, and descendant of Dja Dja Wurrung and Yorta Yora peoples, said recently:

> Since colonisation, management decisions have caused irreparable damage to our rivers, lakes and swamps. We have been unable to fulfil our cultural obligations to care for waterways, because we have been excluded from participation in water management. We have limited opportunities to contribute our lore and our knowledge to heal waterways. We are also prevented from participation in the water economy.[94]

Rather than Coliban Water paying a fine to the government as would usually occur, the EPA successfully argued for use of the section 67AC mechanism to fund a local land rehabilitation project. This was one of three prosecutions resulting in orders under section 67AC that supported the healing of upside-down Country.

The first order was made to the local council, the City of Greater Bendigo, which partnered with the local catchment management authority and the Dja Dja Wurrung Clans Aboriginal Corporation (Dja Dja Wurrung) to implement the order. The rehabilitation project focused on creating frog ponds as a restorative measure to ensure the ongoing survival of the threatened growling grass frog species. Through this collaboration, the Dja Dja Wurrung reimagined the project in line with their 20-year Country plan, significantly expanding its impact and scope.[95] This included planting a broader range of culturally and environmentally significant species than initially envisioned, as well as constructing the frog ponds in a way that revived the food and fibre plants important for cultural revitalisation.

Crucially, this project strengthened Dja Dja Wurrung's growing capacity and reputation for successfully delivering complex restoration projects and has led to further funding from a number of other state agencies. In our interviews, the Dja Dja Wurrung described the incident as a catalyst for growth, independence, reconciliation and restoration. One of our EPA interviewees further added that the restorative justice benefits were 'cascading' to better collaborative relationships and better environmental health.

94 Torre, 'Dja Dja Wurrung Clans Call for Water Rights'.

95 Djaara, *Dhelkunya Dja: Dja Dja Wurrung Country Plan 2014–2034*, Dja Dja Wurrung Clans Aboriginal Corporation, 2014, djadjawurrung.com.au/wp-content/uploads/2021/04/Dhelkunya-Dja-Country-Plan-2014-2034.pdf.

From a restorative justice perspective, this project demonstrated that, in addition to healing Country, initiatives like these can go some way to healing relationships between the regulator and community groups affected by the state's historic failure to protect both humans and urban ecosystems from damage. As several of our EPA interviewees noted, where an imbalance in regulating has caused harm to communities and the environment, when done right, restorative orders like the former section 67AC can 'give something back', with outcomes going back to the community and fostering a sense of ownership over the solution.

The second order involved a direct payment of AUD$100,000 to the Dja Dja Wurrung Clans Aboriginal Corporation for undertaking an Aboriginal Waterway Assessment of Post Office Creek and relevant areas of the nearby Campaspe River. [96] This was the first time a project of this type had been awarded by courts to a Traditional Owner group under the EP Act 1970.[97] This is an example of a restorative initiative giving rise to a further restorative initiative.

The third section 67AC order occurred following an incident in 2019, when Coliban Water discharged treated wastewater into the Campaspe River. EPA Victoria prosecuted the authority again and in 2021, another order resulted in the payment of AUD$150,000 to the Biolinks Alliance project to restore Snipes Creek. Biolinks Alliance teamed up with the Dja Dja Wurrung and local community to fulfil the stream restoration project.[98]

Both Dja Dja Wurrung and Coliban Water maintain an ongoing relationship at the time of writing this book. For example, Coliban Water worked with the Dja Dja Wurrung to ensure that cultural heritage was included in the company's business case for modernising its water distribution network aimed at increasing regional water supply.[99] In addition, Coliban Water has made a reconciliation plan, the *Innovate: Reconciliation Action Plan 2023–2025*, to acknowledge the Traditional Owner custodians, their connection and history to the land, water and Country the company works on, and

96 EPA Victoria, 'Coliban Region Water Corporation (ABN: 96 549 082 360), last modified 3 October 2023, www.epa.vic.gov.au/coliban-region-water-corporation-abn-96-549-082-360.

97 EPA Victoria, 'Coliban Region'.

98 Biolinks Alliance, '$150,000 Funding Granted to Biolinks Alliance in Coliban Water vs. EPA Court Case', 2023, biolinksalliance.org.au/coliban-water-epa-funding.

99 'Business Case to Examine Efficiency of Key Murray Water System' (Coliban Water, 25 August 2023), coliban.com.au/business-case-examine-efficiency-key-murray-water-system.

to strengthen relationships with Aboriginal peoples.[100] The participatory intent is summed up in the words of the Managing Director Damian Wells and Chairperson Bob Cameron:

> We commit when working with Aboriginal peoples to empower them wherever our actions impact their lives by firstly coming to them. We will not form a view until we have heard their view. We will ensure that the aspirations of Aboriginal peoples are embedded in our business. We recognise we have much work to do to make this a reality. We hope this Innovate RAP [reconciliation action plan] shows our commitment to reconciliation and helps us progress our journey towards healing and equality.[101]

Restorative enforceable undertakings

> *An enforceable undertaking can be a constructive alternative to prosecution or civil penalty proceeding. It may contribute positively to the delivery of restorative justice outcomes.*[102]

Earlier in this chapter, in the context of restorative justice conferences, we shared the story about the application of an enforceable undertaking in the Hampton Park Landfill case. In this section, we expand on the specifics of the enforceable undertaking to highlight its restorative potential as a regulatory tool.

If an enforceable undertaking is not complied with, the court may enforce it. Moreover, under some legislation, the court can impose the same penalties that would have been available for the original offence.[103] Enforceable undertakings are, in most cases, negotiated by regulators like EPA Victoria. However, they share much in common with the more familiar concept of deferred prosecution agreements (DPAs), in which cases the prosecutor announces an intent to prosecute but then pauses that intent while observing how sincerely the defendant cooperates with future prevention. If a restorative conference is used, then the prosecutor will be looking for an apology, accountability, healing of victims, environmental protection

---

100 'Innovate Reconcilation Action Plan: July 2023 – July 2025', Coliban Water, August 2023, last modified 23 January 2026, coliban.com.au/about-us/reconciliation-action-plan.

101 Coliban Water, Reconcilation Action Plan. A 'RAP' is a Reconciliation Action Plan, set up by organisations and businesses in Australia to strengthen their commitment to justice for First Nations people.

102 EPA Victoria, *Compliance and Enforcement Policy*, 29 January 2025, www.epa.vic.gov.au/about-epa/publications/1798-2.

103 For example, in the Victorian jurisdiction, see EP Act 2017, section 300.

and reparations. The United States Department of Justice corporate crime prosecution guidelines have encouraged DPAs in cases where the company has a credible compliance program that has succeeded in:

- uncovering offences
- uncovering which individuals were responsible for them
- conducting a root cause analysis of offences
- reporting the offending actions to the Justice Department; and
- has taken appropriate reparative and preventive reforms (so long as they are not a recidivist).[104]

John Braithwaite argues that both enforceable undertakings and DPAs share the empirical virtue that they can sharpen deterrence, while overuse of prosecution can blunt it.[105]

Enforceable undertakings and DPAs share another common deterrent aspect: although they may be less punitive than fully fledged prosecutions, they can occasionally lead to larger financial penalties, greater executive accountability—including dismissals, demotions or lost bonuses—and more substantial improvements to preventive measures through strengthened corporate compliance systems. That is not true with all regulators, as the Banking Royal Commission pointed out in 2018 in comparing the enforceable undertakings of ASIC and the Australian Prudential Regulation Authority (APRA) unfavourably to those of the ACCC.[106] Columbia Law School professor John Coffee has discussed the imperative for DPAs to be 'truly earned'.[107] Often they are not, as is also often the case with restorative justice, when the principle of 'earned redemption' is frequently neglected.

104 Miriam H. Baer, 'Designing Corporate Leniency Programs', in *The Cambridge Handbook of Compliance*, ed. D. Daniel Sokol and Benjamin van Rooij, Cambridge Law Handbooks (Cambridge University Press, 2021), doi.org/10.1017/9781108759458.025.

105 Braithwaite, 'Deterrence'. See also Marina Nehme et al., *The General Deterrence Effects of Enforceable Undertakings on Financial Services and Credit Providers* (Centre for Law, Markets and Regulation UNSW, 2018), download.asic.gov.au/media/4916053/18-325mr-deterrence-effects-of-enforceable-undertakings-on-financial-services-and-credit-providers.pdf.

106 We discussed the ACCC in Chapter 6. Each of these corporate 'watchdogs' have enforceable undertakings as an available sanction under the appropriate conditions.

107 John C. Coffee, Jr., *Corporate Crime and Punishment: The Crisis of Underenforcement* (Berrett-Koehler, 2020), 147. The concept of 'earned redemption' in the context of restorative justice signifies that the offender will be held accountable for their behaviour and will be facilitated to 'earn their way back into the trust of the community'; Lesley Wexler and Jennifer K. Robbennolt, '#METOO and Restorative Justice', *GP Solo*, July/August, 2020, 69, files.webservices.illinois.edu/9316/me-too-restorative-justice.pdf.

Generally, enforceable undertakings and DPAs are speedier, more flexible and tend to consume fewer legal and investigations staff resources than prosecutions.[108] Of course, these benefits are dependent upon how the undertaking is administratively organised within a regulator. By way of example, DPAs and enforceable undertakings can cut out the often considerable number of preliminary appearances at court that are associated with a major prosecution. This means regulators that devote a decent amount of resources to enforceable undertakings should be able to take decisive enforcement action of some kind against more culpable licensees or duty holders than regulators restricted solely to prosecutions. Considering the evidence indicates that certainty of enforcement is more important to deterrence than is the severity of punishment, this presents an additional rationale for regulators to allocate greater resources to enforceable undertakings.[109]

The most fundamental reason for using enforceable undertakings more often, demonstrated both by the Hampton Park Landfill case and as argued by restorative justice scholar Christine Parker, is their enormous potential to leverage restorative justice.[110] This rationale for their use has also been recognised in the United States, where Richmond School of Law professor Andrew Spalding has conceptualised the United States Sentencing Guidelines as encouraging a restorative justice approach for corporations through the promotion of deferred corporate prosecution agreements.[111]

Enforceable undertakings, as EPA Victoria has clarified, offer a constructive alternative to prosecution and civil penalty proceedings. They embody the potential for a restorative approach in regulatory matters and hold promise as an instrument of positive, future-oriented change. As our case study revealed, these undertakings have the ability to be conducted in a manner aligned with restorative principles and processes, placing the focus on mending relationships, enhancing compliance and fostering community engagement. Beyond these tangible outcomes, enforceable undertakings possess an inherent capacity to amplify deterrence, exemplifying how regulatory measures can be both remedial and proactive.

108 Forsyth and Tepper, 'Undertakings'.

109 Braithwaite, 'Deterrence'.

110 Christine Parker, 'Restorative Justice in Business Regulation? The Australian Competition and Consumer Commission's Use of Enforceable Undertakings', *Modern Law Review* 67, no. 2 (2004): 209–46, doi.org/10.1111/j.1468-2230.2004.00484.x; see also Forsyth and Tepper, 'Undertakings'.

111 Andrew Brady Spalding, 'Restorative Justice for Multinational Corporations', *Ohio State Law* 76, no. 2 (2015): 357–408, doi.org/10.31228/osf.io/2ez96.

Nurturing future-oriented, enduring repair

Under the EP Act 2017, the key regulatory policies, the *Compliance and Enforcement Policy* and *Sanctions Policy*, make it clear that the use of alternative measures to provide restorative outcomes may be more appropriate for meeting the needs of the public interest than a prosecution and can provide 'restorative justice opportunities particularly for the involvement of communities affected by a contravention'.[112] For all regulatory agencies, incorporating restorative conferences and restorative remedies into the regulatory spectrum broadens the methods available for repairing harm and rebuilding relationships. Most importantly, a restorative approach expands the range of victims whose hurt can be addressed.

Repairing harm in the regulatory context includes a focus on preventing future noncompliance. Restorative regulation is a way of honing in on this focus, orienting harm-doers towards being harm-preventers and better neighbours. Through restorative conferences, the direction of fines towards community projects, and the implementation of enforceable undertakings that address both the harm and the systemic problems, restorative approaches connect licensees or duty holders to their communities. This raises the stakes for respectful and authentic engagement with the individuals and communities, including First Nations groups, who are impacted by their activities.

The next chapter, the final in our exploration of ways to address harms restoratively in the regulatory context (Chapters 4 to 8), builds the case for centring those directly impacted. We explore how actively involving those who are often sidelined in the aftermath of harm generates new insights and strengthens harm prevention as a shared responsibility. We examine how learning from past incidents of harm, and embracing the rise of citizen participation and co-production, are vital elements in the effort to shape a regulatory future that is not just reactive but actively restorative.

112 EPA Victoria, *Sanction Powers Policy*, 7. EPA Victoria further states: 'Public interest—where EPA believes there is a reasonable prospect of conviction, we will consider whether prosecution in a criminal court or proceedings in a civil court is in the public interest. An alternative or complementary measure may be more appropriate to provide restorative outcomes.' (9); EPA Victoria, *Compliance and Enforcement Policy*, 9.

8

Learning from harm and rebuilding

Source: Andrew Wright (IM&T, Lucas Heights), CSIRO CommsHub

> *The world that regulators inhabit, and the societies they serve and the industries they oversee, are constantly changing. To be truly excellent, regulators must be constantly striving to listen, learn, and lead.*
>
> —Cary Coglianese[1]

1 Coglianese, *Listening, Learning Leading*, 6.

How can regulatory processes promote trust and learning, and generate meaningful repair? This chapter explores *restorative enquiry* as a practice for building relationships and understanding, as well as how *public inquiries* that apply restorative approaches can effectively address systemic harms. We examine whether a *restorative public inquiry* approach should be more widely adopted by regulators, drawing on the Hazelwood Mine fire case study. Beyond formal processes, we also consider collaborative learning and repair through citizen participatory activities that actively involve those impacted in shaping the way forward.

Accidents and mistakes are a universal aspect of human endeavour. While they may sometimes be attributed to the actions of a single individual, in our interconnected world they often result from a combination of factors and actors. Ideally, as well as repairing the harm caused by specific incidents, individuals and institutions should also learn from these events to stop them happening again.

This chapter builds the case that active involvement of those impacted by the harm—voices often excluded from conventional justice processes—contributes to better learning and creates opportunities for harm prevention. It also offers a chance to rebuild trust in regulatory institutions, especially in situations where inadequate responses to incidents of harm have cast long shadows over the affected communities striving to rebuild their lives and create a more resilient future.

The potential for learning and repair following harm depends largely on the regulatory context. In environments where the focus is on assigning blame and punishment, encouraging open conversations about what went wrong can be a daunting challenge. People may feel hesitant to acknowledge their mistakes or collaborate on refining solutions to prevent future harm. In such contexts, people often retreat to their respective corners, and where financially feasible, may 'lawyer up' to prepare for an adversarial battle in which one side emerges triumphant and the other is defeated.

A retributive approach to investigating harm can also send ripples through the entire regulatory system, potentially stifling progress. As former EPA CEO John Merritt observes, when regulators are driven by fear and preoccupied with avoiding mistakes, they tend to 'just shrivel up and just become inward looking'.[2] This risk-averse mindset can stall experimentation and creativity—key qualities needed to respond to the myriad regulatory challenges in our increasingly complex world.[3]

Typical investigative responses following harm have a tendency to readily assign culpability to those most proximate to the actual incident and to bring in the 'experts'. This tends to ignore systemic factors that may have contributed to the harm, as well as sideline the experiences and voices of those impacted by the harm, rarely acknowledging their experiences, let alone inviting their insights.

Restorative responses, in contrast, take a fundamentally different approach—one rooted in relationships. They recognise that human connection lies at the heart of how we experience harm and healing, as well as what causes it in the first place. A restorative enquiry begins not with blame or assumptions, but with a simple yet profound question: What has this harm meant for those involved? This shift creates space not only for understanding what happened but also for cultivating trust and healing as essential elements of growth. Those impacted are not pushed to the margins; instead, they play a central role in exploring what went wrong and shaping a path towards restoration and future prevention. This approach stems from appreciating that those harmed are often best placed to explore what happened and offer insights on how to promote restoration and mitigate future risks.[4]

While restorative approaches place a strong emphasis on identifying who needs to take responsibility for repairing harm, it is often necessary to look at factors and structures beyond the actual incident that occurred. In addition, responsibility for repair is assumed within a process designed to sustain or restore relationships and trust, not fracture them further. Even in the

2 John Merritt, 'Incentivising Compliance'.

3 Research suggests that creative individuals are more inclined to take 'good' risks that bring about innovation. If the regulatory institution is risk-averse, this regulatory caution can limit the ability of individual employees who are comfortable with ambiguity, flexibility and unfamiliar situations, and who undertake creative problem-solving that might generate new ideas and more effective practices. See Michele Wucker, 'The Surprising Link Between Creativity and Risk'; Maura Crepaldiet et al., 'The Bidirectional Relationship Between Risk and Creativity: A Systematic Review', *TPM—Testing, Psychometrics, Methodology in Applied Psychology* 31, no. 1 (2024): 41–57, doi.org/10.4473/TPM31.1.3; Anthony D. Fredericks, 'Why Taking Risks is Critical for Creativity', *Psychology Today*, 21 January 2022, www.psychologytoday.com/au/blog/creative-insights/202201/why-taking-risks-is-critical-creativity.

4 Wailling et al., 'Humanizing Harm'.

wake of profound harm and suffering, the potential for adaptation, learning and growth is most likely to emerge from relational connection and shared problem-solving (referred to in this chapter as 'co-production').[5]

This chapter explores how restorative approaches can deepen learning from incidents of harm. Rather than attempting to cover the entire field of restorative learning opportunities, we build on our previous discussions of restorative justice conferences, enforceable undertakings and community projects—each of which, in its own way, creates opportunities for learning from harm. Here, we highlight two proactive restorative learning approaches: restorative enquiry and citizen participatory activities, both of which offer pathways for transforming harm into understanding and collectively tilling the soil from which more just and resilient futures can grow.

Restorative enquiry

In this section, we discuss the concept of *restorative enquiry* as a general process focused on facilitating learning, relationship-building and collaborative problem-solving across regulatory agencies, industry and communities. We use 'enquiry' in its general sense—an act of asking questions, seeking information and exploring issues, as a restorative practice. On a larger scale, we examine the more formalised process of a *public inquiry*—a structured public event designed to address systemic social, economic and environmental issues.[6] To maintain this distinction, we refer to large-scale public investigations that address harm affecting entire communities or groups as a *restorative public inquiry*.

While this distinction between 'enquiry' and 'inquiry' follows Australian English conventions, in North America, 'inquiry' is commonly used for both.[7]

5 The National Collaborative for Restorative Initiatives in Health, *He Maungarongo Ki Ngā Iwi*.

6 For example, Restorative Inquiry Council of Parties, *A Journey to Light: A Different Way Forward*, Final Report of the NSHCC Restorative Inquiry (Province of Nova Scotia, 2019), restorativeinquiry.ca/report/Restorative-Justice-Inquiry-Final-Report.pdf.

7 In British, Australian and New Zealand English, 'enquiry' is often used for general questioning, while 'inquiry' refers to formal, often legal or political investigations, such as public, police and Royal Commission inquiries. North American English does not typically distinguish between the two. Dean Koorey, 'Q&A: Inquire vs Enquire', *Australian Writers' Centre*, 18 February 2015, www.writerscentre.com.au/blog/qa-inquire-vs-enquire/; Kevin Eldridge, 'Is It Enquiry or Inquiry?—Australian Spelling', 2024–25, www.australian-dictionary.com.au/dictionary/is-it-enquiry-or-inquiry.php.

What is restorative enquiry?

Restorative enquiry is an important, often structured, practice within the restorative justice process. It is a way of seeking understanding and promoting dialogue, drawing upon the congruent principles of appreciative enquiry.[8] Appreciative enquiry is a method of gradually unearthing the strengths and positive attributes of organisations and actors through a participatory approach that engages stakeholders in conversations and activities to explore what is needed to create a positive and constructive environment for change and improvement. Similarly, restorative enquiry seeks to 'find a different way forward and to be an essential part of the journey … the restorative approach [being] essential to the way forward'.[9]

Even though restorative justice is often thought of as being an interpersonal process that works on a micro-scale, its principles can be applied to address broader, deeper societal problems that both impact and are impacted by regulatory regimes. After this section, we explore how it can also inform formal, structured public processes, including public inquiries such as Royal Commissions.

Restorative justice is based on the assumption that moving forward requires a full and honest understanding of what has happened in the past.[10] For this reason, as we have noted in various chapters, restorative justice enables those involved to ask broad questions about what happened, why, and how people have been impacted. By creating a space for the voices of those who have been—and continue to be—affected, and for stories often overlooked or dismissed as irrelevant, such as those stemming from colonisation or discrimination, restorative justice can catalyse a transformative shift. This shift includes not only the acknowledgement of lived experiences but also the cultivation of understanding, empathy and a shared commitment to rebuilding what has been broken.

8 Antonio Sandu and Simona Damian, 'Applying Appreciative Inquiry Principles in the Restorative Justice Field', *Postmodern Openings* 3, no. 2 (2012): 37–52, postmodernopenings.com/wp-content/uploads/2012/06/3-Applying-Appreciative-Inquiry-Principles.pdf.

9 Restorative Inquiry Council of Parties, *Journey to Light*, Chapter 2.

10 Howard Zehr, *The Little Book of Restorative Justice*; Anne Maree Payne and Heidi Norman, *Coming to Terms with the Past? Identifying Barriers and Enablers of Truth-Telling and Strategies to Promote Historical Acceptance*, Research report of Indigenous Land and Justice Research Group, School of Humanities & Languages, University of NSW (UNSW and Reconciliation Australia, 2024), www.reconciliation.org.au/wp-content/uploads/2024/04/Barriers-and-enablers-to-truth-telling-report.pdf.

Reflecting on why restorative approaches are so effective, restorative practitioners David Moore and Alikki Vernon emphasise how the restorative structure facilitates emotional shifts from a backwards looking, blame-oriented stance to a forward-looking, collaborative approach:

> Experienced practitioners familiar with the practical theory for facilitating group conferences know that when group members work together to paint a fuller picture of *how we got here*, and *where we are now*, it is far easier to reach consensus on *where we wish to go*, and on *how we can get there*. Increasing the size of the group amplifies the shift in understanding and in feeling.[11]

In practice, enquiry in the restorative context involves asking questions 'that facilitate understanding and promote empathy and perspective-taking'.[12]

Scholar Jo Wailling and colleagues, who have explored the use of restorative responses to harm in medical contexts, created a restorative enquiry framework that sets out four steps, each based on a question: [13]

1. Who has been hurt and what are their needs? (*past focus*)
2. Who is responsible for meeting needs and what are their obligations? (*present focus*)
3. How can harms and relationships be repaired? (*future focus*)
4. How can we prevent it from happening again? (*future focus*).

Restorative enquiry thus focuses upon unconditional, non-judgemental listening, storytelling and relational repair, which restorative justice scholars Mark B. Scholl and Christopher B. Townsend explain as follows: [14]

> Unlike the retributive inquiry process designed to determine whether the individual is guilty, restorative inquiry provides the individual with opportunities to reflect, problem solve and take accountability.

---

11 Moore and Vernon, *Setting Relations Right*, 60. This recalls the discussion in Chapter 7, in which restorative justice scholar Meredith Rossner is cited in reference to turning points that create a shift in energy.

12 Mark B. Scholl and Christopher B. Townsend, 'Restorative Justice: A Humanistic Paradigm for Addressing the Needs of Victims, Offenders, and Communities,' *Journal of Humanistic Counseling* 63, no. 3 (2023): 4, doi.org/10.1002/johc.12204.

13 Wailling et al., 'Humanizing Harm'.

14 Scholl and Townsend, 'Restorative Justice', 4.

When practised at its most restorative levels, restorative enquiry seeks to put those who have been harmed, and those responsible, into positions where they have agency over generating change moving forward. In other words, whereas more traditional fact-finding enquiries—such as regulatory reviews and internal organisational or workplace investigations—often separate the impacted group from the group conducting the enquiry and the group responsible for implementing recommendations, a restorative enquiry seeks to blend these groups together.[15] A restorative approach embodies co-production, in which authority figures such as policymakers or leaders collaborate with citizens and those likely to be impacted by the changes, sharing power, risk and the opportunity to co-design and deliver transformative measures. When viewed as a sociopolitical practice, restorative enquiry supports citizen involvement and participatory democracy, empowering citizens to play an active and collaborative role in shaping or supporting governance and regulation.[16]

Restorative enquiry can take place at all stages of the regulatory cycle. It may be conducted on a small, localised scale or expanded into a formal restorative public inquiry at a broader level, encompassing a region, nation, state or province. At the smaller end of the spectrum, restorative enquiry creates a safe space for members of local communities to share their experiences and articulate what they need in order to restore or strengthen wellbeing, relationships and trust. Participants then use this information to co-design a way forward. When scaled up, as we discuss next, this same approach can be applied to systemic harm, enabling collective reflection and action on a much larger scale.

The public inquiry as a restorative process

A public inquiry, such as a royal commission, board of inquiry, parliamentary inquiry or ombudsman inquiry, extends beyond individual cases to examine widespread issues.[17] A public inquiry can be considered restorative when it actively engages public participants in dialogue and/or intentionally applies

15 See, for example, Jennifer Llewellyn et al., *Nova Scotia Home for Colored Children Restorative Inquiry: Council of Parties Third Public Report* (Dalhousie University, 2018), digitalcommons.schulichlaw.dal.ca/reports/64/.

16 Sandu and Damian, 'Appreciative Inquiry Principles', 46.

17 Llewellyn, 'Responding Restoratively'; Darlene Lawrence, 'The Pursuit of Social Justice by the Care-leavers from the Nova Scotia Home for Coloured Children and the Production of Knowledge' (MA diss., Mount Saint Vincent University, 2019), ec.msvu.ca/server/api/core/bitstreams/34c03b71-b4a6-4252-a01e-dd99440aa26c/content.

the restorative approaches discussed in the previous section. A key feature of a public inquiry as a restorative process is its provision of a structured space for collectively uncovering truths, enhancing accountability and creating a more just response to harm.

A restorative public inquiry—our term for formal, large-scale public inquiries based on restorative principles—builds on the principles of restorative enquiry to address systemic or interconnected harms, especially those affecting entire communities or creating regulatory challenges. [18] As a structured, large-scale form of narrative enquiry, a restorative public inquiry provides a forum for far more people to gather together and engage in collective storytelling and problem-solving than is possible with restorative justice conferences or circles.

We view public inquiries as restorative when they go beyond mere fact-finding and top-down recommendations to create spaces for collective reflection, amplify the voices of impacted communities and engage citizens in shaping solutions. Rather than focusing solely on accountability, a restorative approach to a public inquiry also prioritises healing, restoration and systemic repair. A public inquiry that seeks to root its outcomes in justice and transformation is inherently restorative and can play a proactive role in identifying and addressing potential harms before they escalate, thereby foregrounding prevention and strengthening community resilience.

One of the key proponents of the restorative public inquiry at this broad level is scholar Jennifer Llewellyn, who writes that it can be used:

> to recognize and respond to the relational nature of the harms, and their legacy, by focusing on the contexts, causes, and circumstances, including the institutions, systems, and structures that shaped, facilitated, and contributed to the history and experience [of those harmed].[19]

This perspective positions the restorative public inquiry as a distinct and deeply relational method of investigating and resolving harm that addresses both the immediate effects and the broader systemic and structural factors that contribute to the perpetuation of harm.

18 The Canadian Restorative Inquiry into the Nova Scotia Home for Colored Children was the first ever public inquiry to be called and established as a 'Restorative Inquiry'. We consider this as an important example that demonstrates the value of restorative approaches as a public inquiry model. For more details, see Restorative Inquiry Council of Parties, *A Journey to Light*, 6.

19 Llewellyn, 'Responding Restoratively', 6.

A restorative public inquiry may follow a government apology, for example, to atone for harms that have negatively impacted particular groups or communities in society. The harm to the public or communities may be a one-off event, such as a large-scale wildfire destroying homes. It may also be an ongoing harm, such as continual groundwater contamination from a landfill or persistent noise pollution from an airport. When harm is widespread or built into a system, a restorative public inquiry can help identify and rectify problems that affect entire governments, regulators and/or industries. This approach acknowledges issues that continue unabated or have ongoing impact into the present and addresses the varying degrees of harm caused to particular groups in society or communities. Affected groups or communities can include persons in care, Indigenous peoples, consumers purchasing finance and security products, communities and neighbourhoods, and—in a forward-thinking jurisdiction—even the community of nature in its own right.[20]

A restorative public inquiry can be proactive in identifying potential future harms through deepening our understanding of the dynamics behind historic social and political injustices. Restorative practices are inherently proactive in terms of developing relationships, fostering a sense of community and seeking to ensure the wellbeing and flourishing of participants.[21] By emphasising the proactive nature of restorative justice and practices, the restorative public inquiry can—and should—play a significant preventive function. Ideally, through including a wide diversity of voices in the process

20 John Braithwaite, Toni Makkai and Valerie Braithwaite, *Regulating Aged Care: Ritualism and the New Pyramid* (Edward Elgar, 2007); John Braithwaite, 'Regulating Nursing Homes: The Challenge of Regulating Care for Older People in Australia', *BMJ* 323, no. 7310 (2001): 443–46, doi.org/10.1136/bmj.323.7310.443; National Emergency Management Agency, '2019–2020 Royal Commissions and Inquiries', a webpage listing State and federal inquiries into the 2019–2020 bushfires, accessed 2 March 2025, knowledge.aidr.org.au/resources/2019-20-royal-commission-and-inquiries/. Recognition that the community of nature is eligible to be included in its own right is growing globally. For example, in Victoria, the *Yarra River Protection (Wilip-Gin Birrarung Murron) Act 2017* became the first statute in Australia to recognise a river as a living entity. *Wilip-Gin Birrarung Murron* means 'keep the Birrarung alive'. It is also the first English/Aboriginal language statute in Australia. Anne Poelina et al., *Declaration of Peace for Indigenous Australians and Nature: A Legal Pluralist Approach to First Laws and Earth Laws* (Springer, 2024), vii, doi.org/10.1007/978-981-99-9327-7.

21 The International Institute for Restorative Practices asserts that 80 per cent of restorative practices are intended to be done proactively. Gina Baral Abrams, Mary Jo Hebling, and Beth Smull, 'Proactive Restorative Practices: Creating the Conditions for Individuals and Communities to Flourish', Slide Presentation, International Institute for Restorative Practices, 25 October 2018, accessed 02 March 2025, www.iirp.edu/images/conf_downloads/FoqHEZ_Proactive_RP_Creating_the_Conditions_for_Individuals_and_Communities_to_Flourish.pdf.

from the start, the restorative public inquiry process generates a sense of collective responsibility for repairing the harm and encourages collective efficacy to stay involved in ongoing collaborative prevention.

Canada has taken the innovative lead in using the restorative public inquiry. It has held restorative public inquiries across various domains—for instance, in relation to Canada's equivalent of Indigenous Stolen Generations,[22] sexual assault in universities and the abuse in institutions for children.[23] In particular, we have gleaned many insights from the first public inquiry in the world to purposefully adopt a restorative approach, the 2019 Restorative Inquiry into the Nova Scotia Home for Colored Children (Nova Scotia Restorative Inquiry).[24] Healing and prevention of unsafe future risks of harm are central restorative values in these Canadian restorative public inquiries. So, too, is deep listening to survivors and stakeholder communities, along with their active participation in an open process. This approach can help to uncork the previously bottled-up awareness among experts—whether in communities, institutions or government—of major risks that have gone unaddressed. By creating space for open participation and deep listening, it allows these concerns to be aired and acted upon by multiple regulators, law enforcers and political leaders.

In Australia, there has been consideration of using a restorative public inquiry for prevention and healing in response to harms experienced during and after bushfires.[25] Similarly, in Victoria, the Yoorrook Truth and Justice Commission has been established to investigate injustices experienced by the First Peoples of Victoria.[26] While it is not formally termed

22 The term 'Stolen Generations' is specifically associated with Australia. It refers to the policies and practices of Australian governments and church missions between approximately 1910 and 1970, which resulted in the forced removal of Aboriginal and Torres Strait Islander children from their families. These children were often placed in institutions, foster homes or adopted by non-Indigenous families with the stated goal of assimilating them into settler society. The Australian Human Rights and Equal Opportunity Commission wrote a report in 1997 entitled 'Bringing Them Home', which popularised the term 'Stolen Generations'. Australian Human Rights and Equal Opportunities Commission, *Bringing Them Home,* Report (Commonwealth of Australia, 1997), humanrights.gov.au/our-work/projects/bringing-them-home-report-1997.

23 Lawrence, 'The Pursuit of Social Justice'.

24 Restorative Inquiry Council of Parties, *Journey to Light.*

25 Michael Eburn, 'Looking to Courts of Law for Disaster Justice', in *Natural Hazards and Disaster Justice: Challenges for Australia and Its Neighbours*, ed. Anna Lukasiewicz and Claudia Baldwin (Springer, 2020), doi.org/10.1007/978-981-15-0466-2_7.

26 'About Yoorook', Yoorook Justice Commission, accessed 2 March 2025, yoorrookjusticecommission.org.au/about/.

a restorative public inquiry, it has adopted a method that aligns closely with restorative values and practices, as it emphasises healing, storytelling and truth-telling outcomes.[27]

The aim of a restorative public inquiry is to hear many people's stories—whether across a community, society, state or nation—to listen to their suggestions for repair and making things right, which also means helping those who have been harmed to find a better way forward.[28] As was noted in the report of the Nova Scotia Restorative Inquiry, in this way the restorative public inquiry becomes 'part of the larger journey to light' and 'a different way forward', able to support 'a complex understanding of what happened, who was involved and affected, and the nature of the harms and their legacies, including the historical, social, and political context'.[29]

A restorative public inquiry shares some features with a traditional public inquiry such as a royal commission. However, unless such inquiries purposefully adopt restorative approaches, they will differ from the restorative public inquiry in the following ways:

- Traditional public inquiries typically concentrate on uncovering facts and assigning blame—or sometimes sidestepping accountability altogether.[30] The restorative public inquiry deliberately moves away from a retributive, risk-averse approach, focusing instead on healing, understanding and shared responsibility for moving forward.

27 Truth-telling has 'multiple dimensions, including a foundational requirement for healing and reconciliation, a form of restorative justice, a process for First Nations peoples to share their culture and history with the broader community, to build wider understanding of the intergenerational trauma experienced by Aboriginal and Torres Strait Islander people and to strengthen awareness of the relationship between past injustices and contemporary issues', Anne Maree Payne and Heidi Norman, *Findings from the Literature Review,* (Indigenous Land and Justice Research Group, School of Humanities and Languages, University of NSW, 2024), 8, www.reconciliation.org.au/wp-content/uploads/2024/03/Coming-to-terms-with-the-past-Literature-review.pdf.

28 Llewellyn, 'Transforming Restorative Justice'; Llewellyn, 'Responding Restoratively'; Sandu and Damian, 'Appreciative Inquiry Principles'.

29 Restorative Inquiry Council of Parties, *Journey to Light*, 6, 19.

30 For example, journalist Simon Jenkins documents what he calls 'postponing blame' in the Grenfell Tower fire inquiry in London, a fire that killed over 70 people and injured as many. Costing over £200m and taking seven years, he felt that the (non-restorative) judge-led public inquiry into this disaster heightened feelings of revenge, underlined that 'Britain is obsessed with prison' and that delays partly occurred from the hope that those who should be held responsible 'had passed out of sight'. He considers that a judge-led inquiry is more about letting those who should have taken responsibility 'off the hook' and that '[r]eform is not to be found in interminable lawyer-led inquiries, nor in the primitivism of the jail cell. Reform can only lie in an intelligent and sensitive government.' Simon Jenkins, 'Want Justice for the Victims of Grenfell? It's Now Clearer Than Ever That Public Inquiries Are Not the Answer', *The Guardian*, 6 September 2024, www.theguardian.com/commentisfree/article/2024/sep/05/justice-victims-grenfell-public-inquiries-not-answer.

- A traditional public inquiry might involve community consultation, but this is often only one component of its overall process. In contrast, a restorative public inquiry actively engages community throughout every phase of the repair and healing work—building relationships, supporting learning, increasing understanding and collaboratively developing and implementing plans for action (see Figure 8.1).
- A restorative public inquiry is focused on understanding not only what happened, but also on exploring *why* it happened, with an emphasis on the root causes and systemic factors. It seeks to connect individual harm to broader social, cultural or institutional issues, revealing how the harm fits into a larger pattern and why it matters, not just to those directly involved but to everyone affected by these systemic issues.[31]
- A restorative public inquiry process is shaped by restorative principles: a commitment to doing no further harm, the proactive prevention of future harm, and the inclusion of all voices. It also seeks to build healthy and just relationships, enabling us to learn and act together.
- Similar to a traditional inquiry, a restorative public inquiry looks at the past in order to learn how to prevent future harms. However, with its emphasis on participation at every stage—including the participation of those with the power to make change—the restorative public inquiry aims to create meaningful change, driven by the insights and active involvement of the public. It seeks to shape a more equitable, informed and collectively determined path forward.

Figure 8.1 illustrates a distinctive feature of the Nova Scotia Restorative Inquiry: the community's or public's integral role in every facet of the investigative process. At its heart, the restorative public inquiry process is a collaborative journey characterised by three pivotal elements: building relationships, learning and understanding, and planning followed by action. These elements intersect continuously, mirroring the active engagement of the community.

Each of these elements was addressed across various stages during the Nova Scotia Restorative Inquiry. It began with a strong emphasis on relationship-building, moved into a middle phase focused on learning and understanding, and culminated in planning and action for the final phase. While these three phases were conceptually distinct, the process was not strictly linear. Instead, it entailed interconnected, cyclical layers of activity that 'built on and continued the work from the one before'.[32]

31 Restorative Inquiry Council of Parties, *Journey to Light*, 6.

32 Restorative Inquiry Council of Parties, *Journey to Light*, 57.

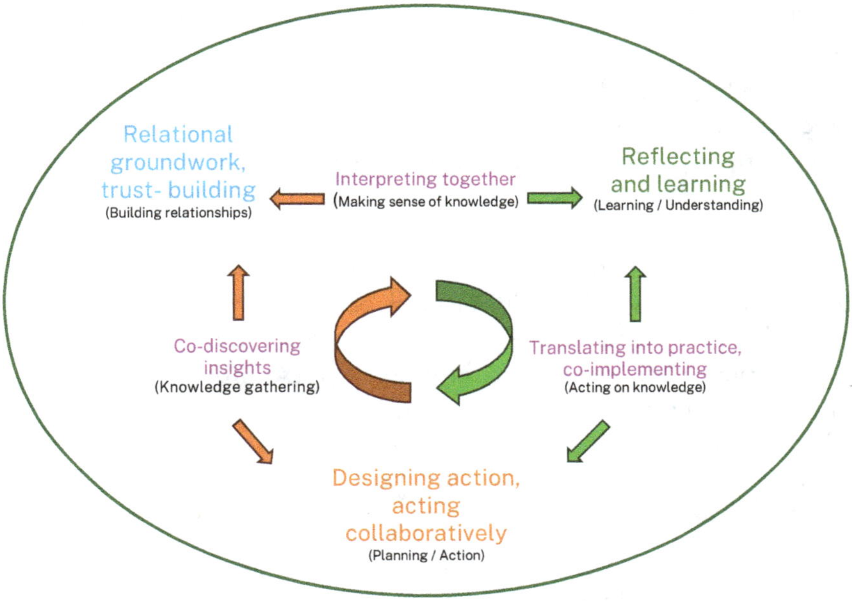

Figure 8.1. Involving the community in all phases of the public inquiry process

Source: Modified from Restorative Inquiry Council of Parties, *Journey to Light*, 57.

The approach taken in the Nova Scotia Restorative Inquiry epitomises what we see as mattering most for the future of public inquiries. Whether it is a dedicated restorative public inquiry model like Nova Scotia's, or any public inquiry incorporating restorative practices, its investigative, truth-telling and relationship-building processes must always centre the collective wisdom of the community, guiding progress and outcomes at an organic pace. Restoratively led inquiries should be structured to enable participants to develop a sense of shared responsibility for both the processes and the results.

Any public inquiry that adopts restorative practices, be it a royal commission, a parliamentary inquiry or ombudsman investigation, will move beyond simply establishing what happened to probing why it happened and how it might recur if the collective wisdom is ignored. The future effectiveness of public inquiries will, in many cases, depend on integrating the public and affected communities to inform the investigatory process and to help shape and implement its outcomes. This, in turn, will ensure that public inquiries benefit those directly affected while helping to prevent future harms that could impact society as a whole.

Building on that foundation, when harm extends to the environment and nature, a restorative public inquiry opens up additional avenues not traditionally captured by conventional justice systems or investigatory processes. It provides an innovative opportunity to use our imaginations and creativity to find ways to hear nature's representatives in discussions about the harms done, not only to human communities but also to rivers, forests, the air, ecological communities and other-than-human animals. This includes the exploration of multispecies approaches to preventing future harm, in which the wellbeing of all species—human and non-human alike—becomes central to the process.[33] Traditional justice systems in our present time often struggle to incorporate these broader, cross-species impacts, making a restorative public inquiry process, particularly one with a bioregional focus, well suited to supporting more inclusive and forward-thinking solutions that address the need for harmonious coexistence between all species.

To explore the practical potential of a restorative public inquiry and its transformative possibilities for addressing harm and healing, we now turn to look at what it might mean for EPA Victoria to adopt this approach. We will also look at one of our four main case studies, the Hazelwood Mine fire, to examine the emergent restorative elements that suggest it could serve as a precursor to a *public restorative inquiry*.

Is there a role for a restorative inquiry in EPA Victoria?

While our conceptualisation of a restorative public inquiry has not yet become part of the EPA's practice in Victoria, nor has it found its place within regulators' enquiry practices more broadly, it could inspire future shifts in regulatory practice. In this light, we offer an exploration or a thought experiment as to how it could be realised in practice. We use the EPA's experience as a promising starting point, particularly given the holistic emphasis in the EP Act 2017 on prevention, the general environmental duty (GED) and shared responsibility.

33 Felicity Tepper, 'Amplifying Edge-Awareness: Socio-Ecological Restorative Approaches to Human-Wildlife Coexistence' in *Criminología verde: Alternativas a la impunidad y al punitivismo ante los daños bio-socio-ecológicos* [*Green Criminology: Alternatives to Impunity and Punitivism Facing Bio-Socio-Ecological Harms*], edited by Gema Varona (Dykinson, 2025), 41–81.

The EP Act 2017 allows EPA Victoria to establish advisory panels to provide advice to the EPA on any matter, and these panels may accept public submissions.[34] One possible way to make these panels more effective would be to explore their reconceptualisation as a restorative public inquiry.

One senior EPA officer suggested that this provision in the new Act could also be used to invite an advisory panel to convene a citizens' jury on a 'knotty problem' or to receive advice on a complex, systemic problem requiring a multifaceted response. However, the terms of reference for an advisory panel would be limited to matters within EPA Victoria's regulatory responsibility, such as issues requiring a regulatory decision by the EPA. This would constrain the ability of an advisory panel to recommend broader legislative or structural reforms. That said, if participants raised wider systemic issues, suggested legislative or regulatory changes, the panel could still convey these public aspirations to the Victorian Government, highlighting areas where reform may be needed.

As we noted earlier, a restorative public inquiry is well suited to addressing big-picture, systemic environmental problems.[35] If adopted by EPA Victoria, it could help unearth new opportunities for boosting collaboration between regulatory agencies, particularly where the multiple connections between causes and drivers have previously not been made or were perhaps misunderstood or insufficiently explored.

For example, organised crime activities, such as illegal dumping and dangerous waste stockpiling, cause direct harm to both the environment and the wider community. A restorative public inquiry could help demonstrate the value of having all Australian police forces taking this environmental harm more seriously, while also providing strong supporting evidence for more direct and closer collaboration with environmental regulators to stamp out environmental crime. An approach grounded in shared responsibility, multi-agency cooperation and collaborative law enforcement

34 Part 8.5, section 235 of the EP Act 2017 sets out the procedure that enables the EPA to establish advisory panels. They can be established to provide advice to the EPA on any matter relevant to administering the Act and its regulations. The EPA controls each panel's terms of reference, the scope of its inquiry and any conditions relating to it. Panel members are appointed based on their having the appropriate expertise and qualifications. At the time of writing this book, the EPA was yet to establish an advisory panel. Environment Protection Authority Victoria, 'Register of Advisory Panels', last modified 29 June 2001, www.epa.vic.gov.au/about-epa/public-registers/advisory-panels.

35 This kind of high-level deliberation across government was flagged by the 2016 Inquiry into the EPA as something needing to be addressed (particularly in recommendations 7.1 and 7.3). However, to date, the recommendation has not been implemented. Armytage et al., Independent Inquiry (the MAC Review, discussed in Chapter 2).

could potentially put a stop to harmful organised environmental crime by revoking the relevant waste management licences as well as putting some dangerous people in prison.

John Braithwaite recounts a story involving the Australian Taxation Office (ATO) that further illustrates the stakes in tackling organised environmental crime. According to Braithwaite, the ATO was unaware a decade ago that tax evasion was rife in the underground waste disposal market, and that sometimes the ATO might actually be the regulator with the best capacity to put dangerous players in prison, almost in an Al Capone-style manner.[36]

The rationale for conducting a restorative public inquiry on an issue like waste disposal (legal or illegal) moves beyond merely connecting the silos of different regulators' capabilities. It tackles fundamental questions of justice, such as: Who gets to live near waste? Who does not? And how much power do residents have to demand relocation of the activities or even their own homes? If we cannot deploy the 'avoid, reuse and recycle' waste options, and if we can no longer dump waste in the backyards of communities in places such as China or Indonesia,[37] only a restorative public inquiry—one that looks into the complexities of the entire waste management cycle—can reveal innovative, equitable locational solutions for waste disposal.[38] Standard regulatory enforcement tools, which are so often incapable of delivering a systemically informed solution, repeatedly fall short, as evidenced by the EPA's having to spend huge resources on attempting to mop up crooked attempts at disposal.

---

36 Al Capone was a notorious gangster from the 1920s and early 1930s in the United States of America. Despite his being involved in numerous criminal activities, American authorities were only able to convict him on charges related to failing to pay taxes on his illicit income. The Federal Bureau of Investigation, 'Al Capone', accessed 1 March 2025, vault.fbi.gov/Al%20Capone.

37 Around 2018, countries such as China began to restrict the importation of recycling waste, an arrangement that many developed countries had relied upon for decades to reduce recyclable waste stockpiles. Alana Semuels, 'Is This the End of Recycling?', *The Atlantic*, 5 March 2019, www.theatlantic.com/technology/archive/2019/03/china-has-stopped-accepting-our-trash/584131/; Monique Retamal et al., 'Here's What Happens to Our Plastic Recycling When It Goes Offshore', *The Conversation*, 30 January 2019, theconversation.com/heres-what-happens-to-our-plastic-recycling-when-it-goes-offshore-110356.

38 The location of waste is a significant environmental justice issue. Equitable waste site selection involves considering the needs of affected communities, environmental impacts and the overall public good, rather than merely managing waste through reactive cleanup efforts. An equitable, restorative approach to waste disposal locations ensures that waste is not disproportionately placed near vulnerable communities. Brad Jessup, 'Environmental Justice as Spatial and Scalar Justice: A Regional Waster Facility or a Local Rubbish Dump Out of Place?', *McGill International Journal of Sustainable Development Law and Policy* 9, no. 2 (2013): 69–107, www.jstor.org/stable/24352643; Environmental Defender's Office, *Implementing Effective Independent Environmental Protection Agencies in Australia* (EDO, January 2022), www.edo.org.au/wp-content/uploads/2022/01/Implementing-effective-independent-EPAs-in-Australia-Report.pdf.

A further advantage of the restorative public inquiry is its capacity to pave the way for improved understandings between diverse knowledge systems, such as First Nations knowledges and Western or technical bodies of knowledge. This can contribute to deeper, collective eco-literacy among all individuals and increase awareness of our shared responsibilities towards our environment.[39]

As we discussed in the previous chapter, every regulator, including the EPA, must ensure that the technical and scientific information it deals with daily is both transparent and intelligible to the public. This information should also be enriched by incorporating other forms of knowledge, including insights from the custodians of Country, waters and landscapes, as well as from local communities. These perspectives are essential because they reflect the cultural significance of the environment and provide firsthand accounts of environmental harm impacting homes, workplaces and cultures, as well as insights into the preventive measures needed.

In line with our exploration for the restorative regulatory spaces worthy of nurturing, we now examine an example of a public inquiry that followed the Hazelwood Mine fire incident, one of our four key stories, to uncover its restorative dimension.

The Hazelwood Mine Fire Inquiry: An incipient restorative public inquiry

Following the Hazelwood Mine fire, the Victorian Government commissioned several public inquiries (described collectively as the 'Hazelwood Mine Fire Inquiry', here 'the Inquiry') into the causes of the persistent fire in the mine and its health impacts. Among its responsibilities, the Hazelwood Mine Fire Inquiry Board was tasked with reporting on short, medium and long-term options for rehabilitating the land on which the mining activities had occurred. The Inquiry's process involved a number of potentially restorative elements, including its use of structured community consultation. The consultation questions were initially framed in a quite restrictive manner:

39 Nicole M. Ardoin, Alison W. Bowers, and Mele Wheaton, 'Leveraging Collective Action and Environmental Literacy to Address Complex Sustainability Challenges', *Ambio* 52 (2022): 30–44, doi.org/10.1007/s13280-022-01764-6.

1. What long-term infrastructure needs of the Latrobe Valley could this/ these mine site(s) fill?
2. What should be done towards these desired ends while this/these mine(s) are still operating?

These questions directed participants to think primarily in terms of future economic utility and infrastructure needs. In doing so, they failed to open up space for expressing grief, concern for long-term environmental and cultural harm, or alternative visions for restoration and care. This narrow framing arguably limited the scope of community input and the restorative potential of the process.

However, the summary of the feedback received indicates that there was, in practice, room for members of the community to express their concerns in a more expansive way—for example, by sharing their stories about how the fire had affected them both individually and as part of the community.[40] This suggests that even if the aim is to restrict the community's engagement to questions about what to do next, it is very difficult—and many would argue, unwise—to do so without first providing an open-ended period for sharing personal and communities stories about the impacts of what has happened.

A restorative approach in which the discussion is based on the standard sequence of restorative questions provides a useful structure for the steps that could be incorporated into public inquiry processes like this one. The first questions are: 'What happened?' and 'Who was impacted?' These lead into an open discussion: 'What needs need to be met, and by whom?' followed by 'How can relationships and harms be repaired?' and, finally, 'How can we prevent it happening again?'

The Hazelwood Mine Fire Inquiry also contained, to a limited but important extent, the restorative dimension of collective responsibility. Collective responsibility is the concept that a group—whether a restorative circle or an organisation like a corporation or a regulatory body—shares responsibility for the process, actions, decisions and outcomes of its members.[41] This stage

40 Hazelwood Mine Fire Inquiry, 'Mine Rehabilitation Community Consultations – 4 & 5 August 2015: Summary of Discussion', (State Government of Victoria, 2015), hazelwoodinquiry.archive.vic.gov.au/wp-content/uploads/2015/08/Summary-of-Mine-Rehabilitation-community-consultations-PDF-383KB.pdf.

41 Kay Pranis, 'Individual and Collective Accountability in a Restorative Framework', online presentation, 12 November 2018; Howard Zehr, *The Little Book of Restorative Justice*.

is often reached in restorative dialogues after participants have collectively passed through the emotional stages of anger, hurt and confusion that typically characterise the discussions around the first set of restorative questions in the sequence. Once past this stage, participants become emotionally ready to explore the future and show a willingness to assume responsibility for initiating positive changes.[42] Scholars and practitioners refer to this as the process of emotional alignment.[43] Moore and Vernon further note that '[m]aking sense of a shared situation together gradually rebuilds sufficient trust for people to invest in a subsequent agreement for action'.[44]

At this point, the expectation is that participants will collectively decide on the next steps to be taken.[45] A strong message emerging from the Inquiry was the local residents' concern about air-quality monitoring, and their loss of faith and trust in the EPA to monitor and report in a fair manner. In the spirit of collective responsibility, this message was heard not only by the Inquiry but also resulted in the establishment of community co-designed air-monitoring network—including a smoke-sensor sub-network—led by the EPA. This network aimed to improve data collection, display and communication.[46]

Next, we explore this co-production aspect, one brought to the fore by the Inquiry.

42 Moore and Vernon, *Setting Relations Right.*

43 Meredith Rossner, *Just Emotions: Rituals of Restorative Justice*, Clarendon Studies in Criminology (Oxford University Press, 2013), doi.org/10.1093/acprof:oso/9780199655045.001.0001.

44 Moore and Vernon, *Setting Relations Right*, 44.

45 Long et al., 'Community Engagement'.

46 This air monitoring network is known as the 'Latrobe Valley ambient air monitoring network'. EPA Victoria was responsible for leading the community co-design process, which involved regular reporting to the co-design panel, providing recommendations and seeking feedback from panel members on the findings. In 2020, the EPA advised that it would 'continue to engage with the community to better understand its changing needs and to determine what future configurations of the air monitoring network might look like'. Inspector-General for Emergency Management Victoria, *Hazelwood Mine Fire Inquiry Progress Report 2021*, State Government of Victoria (February 2022), 20, last modified 19 August 2024, www.igem.vic.gov.au/publications/publications/hazelwood-mine-fire-inquiry-progress-report-2021. For whole report, see Inspector-General for Emergency Management, *Hazelwood Mine Fire Inquiry: Implementation of Recommendations and Affirmations. Progress Report 2021*, State Government of Victoria, 2021, issuu.com/igemvic/docs/hazelwood_mine_fire_inquiry_-_progress_report_2021.

Collaborative learning and repair: Co-production, citizen science and civic ecology

Key terms

Co-production and co-design[47] are often described as collaborative, user-centred approaches to problem-solving and designing innovative solutions that involve all stakeholders (regulators, industry and communities).[48] While there is no single shared definition, common elements include the coming together of individuals with diverse perspectives, a willingness to collaborate and an emphasis on equal contribution of expertise—whether professional or experiential—aimed at tailored outcomes to meet community needs, and shared decision-making and power.[49] Co-design may focus mainly on the design phase (planning and problem-solving), while co-production may occur during the production or delivery phases (collaboratively delivering and implementing solutions). However, this distinction is not hard and fast.

Citizen science involves non-professional individuals and groups participating in scientific research, data collection and environmental monitoring to raise awareness of environmental issues and foster collaboration between volunteers and professional scientists. This supports more comprehensive, community-informed research and knowledge bases.[50]

47 These aspects of co-production are common elements. However, as we will discuss in Chapter 9 in relation to Indigenous co-production, there is no single definition of co-production, and understandings of it vary.

48 Elke Loeffler and Tony Bovaird, eds., *The Palgrave Handbook of Co-Production of Public Services and Outcomes* (Palgrave Macmillan, 2021), doi.org/10.1007/978-3-030-53705-0. Loeffler and Bovaird note that co-production contains the 'elements of both citizen action and citizen voice' to achieve 'publicly-created values', 5, 42.

49 Elinor Ostrom, 'Crossing the Great Divide: Coproduction, Synergy, and Development', *World Development* 24, no. 6 (1996): 1073–87, doi.org/10.1016/0305-750x(96)00023-x; Elizabeth B.-N. Sanders and Pieter Jan Stappers, 'Co-Creation and the New Landscapes of Design', *CoDesign* 4, vol. 1 (2008): 5–18, doi.org/10.1080/15710880701875068.

50 Rick Bonney et al., 'Citizen Science: A Developing Tool for Expanding Science Knowledge and Scientific Literacy', *BioScience* 59, no. 11 (2009): 977–84, doi.org/10.1525/bio.2009.59.11.9; Artemis Skarlatidou et al., 'How Can Bottom-up Citizen Science Restore Public Trust in Environmental Governance and Sciences? Recommendations from Three Case Studies', *Environmental Science and Policy* 160, 103854 (2024): 1–10, doi.org/10.1016/j.envsci.2024.103854.

> **Civic ecology** is the practice of community members actively engaging in environmental stewardship, restoration and sustainable management — such as habitat restoration, community gardening and urban farming — to create more resilient and sustainable communities while strengthening social bonds and civic participation.[51]

In an environmental context, collective responsibility can be restoratively harnessed through engaging with community expertise. This refers to both existing expertise and the motivation of community members to acquire relevant skills through active civic engagement. For interested community members, co-production and co-design, citizen science and civic ecology initiatives provide valuable participatory means for collaborative repair and learning in the aftermath of environmental disasters.

A key gift of restorative practices to regulatory governance is the combination of the diversity and passion of local expertise. This combination motivates intense local observation and brings forth the local wisdom that restorative practice is well placed to capture. In a report commissioned for the United States Environmental Protection Agency in 2018, the National Advisory Council for Environmental Policy and Technology noted that disaster response and recovery is one area in which citizen science can play an invaluable role for environmental protection. It cited Water Research Foundation's Research Manager, Djanette Khiari, who expressed the concern that '[i]important information can be overlooked if the public is not involved'.[52] The community members in the factory fire case study (discussed in Chapter 6) were at the frontline of environmental inspection. They had a presence in the field 24 hours a day and were ready to tell a neighbour who let their dog swim in the creek: 'The creek is still not safe; take your dog home straight away and hose him down.'[53]

The Hazelwood Mine Fire Inquiry led to a significantly expanded investment in co-designing citizen science initiatives at EPA Victoria. While citizen science at the EPA had mainly involved citizen monitoring and citizen

51 Marianne E. Krasny and Keith G. Tidball, *Civic Ecology: Adaptation and Transformation from the Ground Up* (The MIT Press, 2015), doi.org/10.7551/mitpress/9780262028653.001.0001.

52 National Advisory Council for Environmental Policy and Technology (NACEPT), *Information to Action: Strengthening EPA Citizen Science Partnerships for Environmental Protection*, National Advisory Council for Environmental Policy and Technology (April 2018), 10–13, www.epa.gov/sites/default/files/2018-04/documents/nacept_2018_citizen_science_publication_eng_final_v2_508_0.pdf.

53 Interview with a community member.

action research, the Inquiry prompted the decision to make a much larger effort to involve the community directly in designing the air-monitoring system. One participant described the process as follows:

> They followed a number of different workshops, where you sat down and said, 'Okay, here's a group of people.' People from EPA and others would have been there more for clarity, to assist them: 'Here's the wind pattern. This is genuinely what we've got. This is what we said. If you're going to monitor for this, this is what you need to monitor, right? What are the impacts?' Then people sat around, and they had maps, and they put stickers on where they thought that monitoring places had to go and what they had to monitor.[54]

This quote shows how citizen science connects to the important restorative values and practices of healing, accountability, safety, deep listening, citizen empowerment and relational justice, with a focus on sites of wrongdoing and the prevention of future harm. In referring to the purposeful outreach undertaken by the EPA following the Hazelwood Mine catastrophe, one EPA Victoria officer told us:

> It is one way to work with a community who has been impacted by something, to help them get a better understanding about what that impact really means, what they can do to help make things better.[55]

The citizen science co-design process was heavily contested. Residents had deep distrust of both EPA Victoria and industry, which led to intense debates over where to place the air monitors controlled by the citizens. For instance, discussions centred on whether citizen science air monitors should be placed next to industry monitors to check the accuracy of industry's data or positioned elsewhere to add extra value and extend the data collection. Moreover, the boundary between industry and community interests was not cleanly drawn. At times, these interests overlapped, such as when shared local concerns and personal affiliations aligned. At other times, tensions surfaced within the community itself, with differing priorities emerging between residents as some sought to prioritise individual over collective interests. The following exchange in one of our interviews reflects some of this discussion:

54 Interview with an EPA Victoria air quality specialist.

55 Interview with an EPA Victoria officer.

> EPA officer: One guy was claiming that his [alpacas] … had weeping eyes because of the sulphur dioxide … Alpacas were weeping because of the SO2 levels which, jeez, that's a big call. They were the things you had to consider, I think. The group then sat down and said, 'OK.' Like any community group, you'll always have some people that are louder than others, and they tend to influence people, and, I think in that region, they may have decided to think about putting [in] a sensor.
>
> Interviewer: Then they were able to put a sensor near where his alpacas were?
>
> EPA officer: Yes. That's what I'm saying. Because a lot of it was driven by the community. It was all about, 'What's the purpose of it? Where do you want it? Do you want it where people live, or do you want it in farm areas?'[56]

The key lesson from the citizen voice method of the citizen science process following the Hazelwood Mine fire was the same as the lesson we discussed earlier with EPA Victoria's move to Open House meetings:

> One of the things that was really evident was the need to … have tables and have ways of communicating one-on-one with people … Standing up there and lecturing people doesn't work.[57]

By engaging in two-way knowledge-sharing, all participants have a role in continuing to improve the understanding of what works best to mend the damage and prevent future harm. It is a practice that embodies care, collective responsibility and collective efficacy—a shared belief in the community's capacity to enact change.[58] Direct involvement of citizens, residents, Indigenous groups and communities in shaping, learning from,

56 Interview with an EPA Victoria officer.

57 Interview with an EPA Victoria officer, Morwell.

58 Repair as a practice of care is closely linked to everyday acts of maintenance and kindness that often go unnoticed but contribute significantly to enhancing community resilience in urban spaces. Some individuals engage in small but meaningful acts of repair that help sustain their communities, quietly but effectively building the scaffold for everyone in the community to feel a sense of connection and understand the value of shared responsibility. These ongoing, often informal efforts reflect a broader ethic of care, one that demonstrates 'how we care for each other around here' and reinforces the social fabric, creating mutually experienced everyday acts of urban kindness. Of course, this applies not only to the urban context, but to wherever people associate. What matters most is to acknowledge and support those who are proactively inclined towards acts of care that help mend and restore harm. Tom Hall and Robin James Smith, 'Care and Repair and the Politics of Urban Kindness', *Sociology* 49, no. 1 (2015): 3–18, doi.org/10.1177/0038038514546662.

and implementing repair and recovery initiatives is paramount for building community resilience and fostering active relationships with regulators and industry.

In some respects, citizen science may also address declining trust in the expertise of authorities. Scholar Artemis Skarlatidou and colleagues note that citizen science has the potential to 'promote epistemic trust', but this depends on the presence of a clear framework that recognises and supports its trust-building role. When citizen science is designed to ensure meaningful and inclusive participation, it reinforces democratic engagement in environmental governance and supports citizen scientists in developing 'well-informed, rational trust' in regulatory expertise. Ensuring inclusivity and representativeness is critical, as trust is shaped not only by the accuracy of scientific knowledge but also by perceptions of fairness, legitimacy and transparency.[59]

When co-production is actively promoted and supported, its collaborative endeavours have the potential to significantly improve communication and transparency between citizens and regulators, strengthen trust, and help citizens to contribute directly to the effectiveness of repair efforts within their own neighbourhoods, community spaces and local environments.

Information and transparency: Key to effective restorative practices

To enable effective participation in regulatory processes, including both restorative enquiry and restorative public inquiry, it is essential to commit to ensuring that the public has access to accurate information and tools for building trust in its sources.

Supporting the synergy between regulators and communities involves equipping hands with tools—from spades and hoes to air-quality monitoring devices and environmental sensors—along with comprehensive guidance and unwavering support. This holistic approach empowers communities and provides tangible support for 'reparative follow-through'—the sustained practical action needed to repair harm and restore relationships after environmental damage. Participatory mechanisms such as citizen science, civic ecology and community monitoring amplify repair efforts

59 Skarlatidou et al., 'Bottom-up Citizen Science', 10.

while heightening vigilance and precaution. These practices contribute to restorative regulation by enabling citizens to actively repair the harm and cultivate local best practices, instilling a sense of community ownership. By having the community's hands on the tools alongside regulators and companies, this collaboration increases the likelihood that citizens will remain vigilant about reporting and taking actions to prevent future harm.

Valuable support and guidance can come from the regulator (and industry, where appropriate) by providing publicly accessible and easy-to-navigate online tools that are well resourced and frequently updated. These tools help citizens independently access scientifically reliable information regarding issues like potential land and groundwater contamination. For example, the Victoria Unearthed map provides a platform with geographical information that citizens can click on to discover what is known about sites of concern to EPA Victoria and other regulators in their locale.[60] It is an example of an informative and best-practice EPA and whole-of-government regulatory transparency initiative for enabling citizen science. In addition, a multitude of other relevant interactive websites and applications (apps), including air quality apps, crowdsourced mapping, and dataset aggregators such as the impressive Atlas of Living Australia, can be used by citizens.[61] These valuable platforms and tools enable citizen scientists and civic ecologists to freely and easily increase their participation and engagement. Regulators might consider promoting such external initiatives, where applicable to their regulatory domain, in their own materials for citizen engagement.

Along with promoting data transparency, regulators and industry must facilitate involvement by providing guidance sessions on using participatory tools effectively. They should also be open to synthesising diverse knowledge systems with traditional scientific methods, including local and Indigenous knowledge. Achieving this will require significant effort, including finding respectful and supportive ways to engage existing networks of expertise, managing associated costs and developing co-production approaches that enable participatory citizen repair work. In particular, '[a] system is also needed that integrates citizen and traditional science with outputs that feed

60 State Government of Victoria, 'Victoria Unearthed', mapshare.vic.gov.au/victoriaunearthed/.

61 For example, see the Atlas of Living Australia, which enables anyone to search records and datasets, explore local and adjacent areas, and use maps and coding tools for accessing, using and analysing biodiversity information. See the Atlas of Living Australia website at www.ala.org.au/, accessed 2 March 2025.

into response networks and enforcement.'[62] The prospect of a system that seamlessly integrates citizen science, Indigenous knowledge and traditional science offers the potential to repair past harms while laying the foundation for a resilient and relationally attentive future.

Co-production is still viewed by many in government as a '"black box" and a novel approach'.[63] This means that not all public service staff will welcome it, as some may fear losing control over decisions or even losing a job.[64] While sympathetic to such concerns, scholar Sanna Tuurnas does not see its novelty or the associated concerns as a barrier. Instead, she views them as opportunities for skill-building and encouragement to help shift the 'logic of service production … from [the] traditional idea of delivering public services *for* the public towards the idea of delivering public services *with*, or even, *by* the public'.[65] This, of course, recalls the restorative approach of doing things *with* people rather than to them or for them, as discussed in Chapter 5. Tuurnas further notes that '[t]his logic requires a new relational approach between citizens and staff in public service organisations', thereby also incorporating the restorative value of relationality.[66]

As a restorative practice, co-production deserves to be nurtured by regulators. Tuurnas suggests that preparing staff for effective co-production is most successful when it helps staff to understand their role as stimulators of 'active citizenship'. This preparation involves not only interaction training but also empathy training.[67] However, Tuurnas emphasises that what matters most is *learning by doing*—giving staff the chance to experiment and find out for themselves what works best.[68]

Our final thought is that, given the decline in trust we addressed at the outset of this book, these restorative participatory practices can play an invaluable role in building trust between citizen participants and those facilitating them.[69] When civic participants are empowered with data, resources and skills, they gain the capacity to witness real-time changes, analyse them,

62 Kieran Hyder et al., 'The Role of Citizen Science in Monitoring Small-Scale Pollution Events', *Marine Pollution Bulletin* 120, no. 1 (2017): 51–57, doi.org/10.1016/j.marpolbul.2017.04.038.
63 Sanna Tuurnas, 'Skilling and Motivating Staff for Co-Production', in *The Palgrave Handbook of Co-Production of Public Services and Outcomes*, eds. Elke Loeffler and Tony Bovaird (Palgrave Macmillan, 2021), 491, doi.org/10.1007/978-3-030-53705-0_25.
64 Tuurnas, 'Skilling and Motivating', 491.
65 Tuurnas, 'Skilling and Motivating', 492.
66 Tuurnas, 'Skilling and Motivating', 492–93.
67 Tuurnas, 'Skilling and Motivating', 501–02.
68 Tuurnas, 'Skilling and Motivating', 502.
69 Skarlatidou et al., 'Bottom-up Citizen Science'.

provide constructive feedback, and raise pertinent questions of operators and regulators to hold them to account. A regulator who embraces these participatory practices will promote increased trust and ignite a renewed sense of transparency and accountability, as well as reinforcing a shared sense of responsibility within their communities.

The restorative possibilities inherent in recovery

In this chapter, we have reflected on the restorative possibilities of learning and recovery after harm. Our focus has been on the period following the initial response phase—when the attention shifts towards learning from what went wrong, preventing its repetition in the future and sustaining long-term engagement with the affected citizens and communities, both human and ecological.

Restorative justice values and practices assume a vital role in this recovery phase, contributing to the ongoing accountability and safety of all concerned. They help establish mechanisms that build trust, facilitate the timely exchange of information and tap into a diverse range of skills and knowledge to support meaningful and effective repair. By incorporating community involvement, restorative approaches extend capacities beyond what government can achieve alone, making it more likely that recovery efforts are better informed and adapted to the needs of those most affected.

Furthermore, restorative values and practices support staff by acknowledging that, despite their best efforts, mistakes are sometimes inevitable in the regulatory process.[70] A restorative regulator empowers its staff to view errors as valuable learning opportunities. Staff are encouraged to engage the community in setting things right and to continuously improve practices collaboratively with those they serve, potentially gaining important allies in monitoring, reporting and evaluating.

70 Cary Coglianese tells us: 'As the American football coach Vince Lombardi said when urging his players to achieve perfection, in the end "perfection is not attainable." The excellent regulator will, and must, always strive for perfection and never be truly satisfied with anything short of it. Nevertheless, the reality is that mistakes inevitably will happen – and perhaps some of them could possibly be quite tragic if not catastrophic. The regulator is, after all, overseeing the behavior of others, and a mistake that arises within the operation of a regulated entity may at times be beyond what would be possible for even the most excellent of regulators to have prevented.' Coglianese, *Listening, Learning, Leading*, 26.

In particular, this chapter has illustrated how both restorative enquiry and a restorative public inquiry can adeptly frame and guide deliberative dialogue, enabling systemic reflection on what went wrong. This reflection, in turn, creates room for productive learning. Such framing is essential when a regulator is faced with complex environmental and other regulatory challenges, as it transforms great harm into fertile ground for regeneration and growth.

As with all restorative regulatory approaches explored in this book, there is a spectrum of 'restorativeness' in the regulatory response. This chapter has shown how this spectrum ranges from a restorative public inquiry to more traditional public inquiries, such as a royal commission, which may integrate or reveal incipient restorative elements. For regulators aiming to embed restorative enquiry into their daily regulatory practices, or to hold a *restorative public inquiry* to address the more complex web of systemic influences, we see the following elements as essential:

- **Ensure all voices are heard and valued**. Officially recognise and embed the inclusion of all voices—and the importance of actively listening to everyone—as a critical requirement in the response to harm.
- **Create psychologically safe spaces for dialogue and relationship-building**. These spaces must be suitable for encouraging open, non-judgemental conversation, so that people feel safe to speak freely. To achieve this, regulators can:
  - invest in a trained facilitator
  - provide psychosocial peer, family and cultural support
  - choose a neutral venue
  - use clear, restorative language without blame or judgement (also in associated promotional and support materials)
  - encourage the use of feedback loops for expressing concerns and suggesting improvements
  - incorporate community-building activities to strengthen relationships.
- **Give those impacted by harm a voice in shaping the format of the restorative enquiry/restorative public inquiry**. This involves asking key questions:
  - Who should be involved in the process?
  - Where should the event be situated? (physical space—company's or regulator's premises, community hall, online, hybrid, etc.)

  - How can all participants be encouraged to tell their stories? How can deep listening be encouraged in turn?
  - Who needs to listen to what community members have to say? Additionally, what steps should be taken to ensure the right people are involved in decisions about reparative orders or actions?
- **Ensure co-production of recovery pathways.** Give those who have been harmed the opportunity to be involved in co-producing the pathways forward. As outlined above, co-production is only effective when regulatory staff are trained, sufficiently resourced and supported to facilitate participatory processes, including the ability to experiment and adapt as needed (more on this in Chapter 10).

The practice of restorative enquiry invites all stakeholders to engage in a collective journey of discovery. Through this transformative process, communities and regulators move beyond being passive recipients of information to becoming active co-creators of recovery. As this restorative approach takes root, it nourishes a growing sense of accountability, trust and shared responsibility—cultivating both the incipient restorative elements and purposefully integrated restorative practices that are needed for a just and sustainable future.

As restorative practices take root and begin to grow, however, they cannot be fully realised without an acknowledgement of the depth and breadth of wisdom and expertise that exists within Indigenous communities. At various points in our chapters so far, we have touched upon the profound significance of Indigenous wisdom, embodied ways of being, knowing and doing, and deep-time narratives around harm, healing and restoration. In the following chapter, we expand upon the compelling reasons why it is essential to include Indigenous voices, knowledge and expertise to fully achieve restorative regulation.

9

Indigenous-led restorative and regenerative regulation

Source: Author.

We have our eye on the same destination—a sustainable future where Indigenous people are recognized for their wisdom and honoured for their culture—there is no problem taking a different path to reach that place.

—Kirstie Parker[1]

1 Claire Torina Coulthard, 'The Land is Sacred: Bunji', *The Oxford Blue Student Newspaper CIC*, 13 November 2022, theoxfordblue.co.uk/the-land-is-sacred-bunji/, citing Kirstie Parker. Kirstie Parker is a Yuwaaliyaay journalist, Aboriginal Australian activist and a Co-chair of Reconciliation Australia. 'Reconciliation Australia Board: New Co-Chairs', *News*, Reconciliation Australia, 16 December 2024, www.reconciliation.org.au/changes-to-reconciliation-australia-board/.

First Nations peoples' approaches to regulation provide essential insights for developing restorative and regenerative regulation. They emphasise deep interconnections, collective stewardship, and the integration of traditional and contemporary knowledge systems. The chapter shows how meaningful Indigenous participation in regulatory bodies—through initiatives like EPA Victoria's Environment Protection on Country pilot and strategic employment—can move beyond tokenistic consultation to transform environmental protection and community healing. Using examples like mosaic burning, cultural flows and yarning, we illustrate how Indigenous wisdom and practices offer holistic solutions that benefit both Country and community, while emphasising that authentic restorative regulation requires First Nations people to be equal partners in shaping, guiding and implementing regulatory approaches.

What might happen when we seek to transform the regulatory mindset to think beyond harm, to focus not only on the healing of harm but also on the regeneration of communities and environments? This transformative journey invites us to adopt what we call a regenerative mindset. Former head of regenerative design, Josie Warden, explains that the regenerative mindset:

> is one that sees the world as built around reciprocal and co-evolutionary relationships, where humans, other living beings and ecosystems rely on one another for health, and shape (and are shaped by) their connections with one another. It recognises that addressing the interconnected social and environmental challenges we face is dependent on rebalancing and restoring these relationships.[2]

For many people worldwide, regeneration is an evolving story of healing the separation between humanity and nature, a divide deepened by the long reach of industrialisation and its extractive, unidirectional relationship to nature.[3] However, for others, particularly Indigenous peoples and communities, such a rift is incomprehensible. Indigenous peoples, especially, have never felt this separation, as their way of life is characterised by profound interconnectedness and relationship with and within the natural

2 Josie Warden, cited in Christopher Smith, 'Reparative Readings', *Anatomies of Power* (blog), 20 December 2021, anatomiesofpower.wordpress.com/2021/12/20/reparative-readings/.

3 Jaime Ojeda et al., 'Reciprocal Contributions Between People and Nature: A Conceptual Intervention', *BioScience* 72, no. 10 (2022), doi.org/10.1093/biosci/biac053.

world.[4] Yet, they and their cultures bear the weight of industrial activities that, at times, inflict wounds on this interconnectedness and leave scars upon landscapes, with land and waters sick and in need of healing.

We therefore look to Indigenous approaches to regulation for guidance on pathways towards regeneration. Our focus is principally on the continent now known as Australia, home to the world's oldest continuing cultures—sources of deep knowledge and resilience, deserving of recognition and celebration.[5] Yet, Australia as a nation still has a long way to go in ensuring that its regulatory frameworks enable the First Nations people of Australia to take leadership in caring for Country.[6] Instead of sidelining the First Law of First Nations people, as has happened for over 200 years, we need to have both First Law[7] and Australian Western law '*working in tandem*', coexisting, as this is far more likely to 'deliver a regenerative Country, a regenerative economy and a regenerative humanity'.[8]

4 This is reflected in expressions of interconnectedness found around the world. Examples include *Kaitiakitanga*, *Pachamama*, *Ubuntu* and *Buen Vivir* (*sumak kawsay*). See also Te Ara, 'Kaitiakitanga—Guardianship and Conservation', *Te Ara: The Encyclopedia of New Zealand*, 2007, teara.govt.nz/en/kaitiakitanga-guardianship-and-conservation; Daniela di Salvia, 'Pachamama', in *Encyclopedia of Latin American Religions*, ed. Henri Gooren (Springer International Publishing, 2019), doi.org/10.1007/978-3-319-27078-4_65; Robin Wall Kimmerer, *Braiding Sweetgrass: Indigenous Wisdom, Scientific Knowledge and the Teachings of Plants* (Penguin Press, 2020); United Nations Environment Programme (UNEP), 'Indigenous Peoples and the Nature They Protect', *News, Stories & Speeches*, 8 June 2020, www.unep.org/news-and-stories/story/indigenous-peoples-and-nature-they-protect; Thaddeus Metz, 'Ubuntu: The Good Life', in *Encyclopedia of Quality of Life and Well-Being Research*, ed. Filomena Maggino (Springer International Publishing, 2024), doi.org/10.1007/978-3-031-17299-1_4029; Oliver Balch, 'Buen Vivir: The Social Philosophy Inspiring Movements in South America', *Sustainable Business Blog, The Guardian*, 4 February 2013, www.theguardian.com/sustainable-business/blog/buen-vivir-philosophy-south-america-eduardo-gudynas; 'Indigenous People and Nature: A Tradition of Conservation', *News, Stories & Speeches*, United Nations Environment Programme (UNEP), 26 April 2017, www.unep.org/news-and-stories/story/indigenous-people-and-nature-tradition-conservation; Vandana Shiva, *Staying Alive* (Indraprastha Press, 1988).

5 Reconciliation Australia, 'We Need to Celebrate Success', news release, 25 February 2013, www.reconciliation.org.au/we-need-to-celebrate-success/; Matthews et al., 'Justice, Culture, and Relationships.

6 Terri Janke et al., 'Indigenous: National and international Frameworks That Support Caring for Country', in *Australia State of the Environment 2021*, Australian Government Department of Agriculture, Water and the Environment, Canberra, 2021, soe.dcceew.gov.au/indigenous/management/national-and-international-frameworks-support-caring-country. We discuss both Country and the concept of caring for Country in this chapter.

7 By First Law, we mean the collective body of law of the First Peoples of the continent now called Australia—law grounded in the land as its source, guiding life since the time of the Creation time/the Dreaming and continuing to do so today.

8 Anne Poelina et al., *Declaration of Peace for Indigenous Australians and Nature: A Legal Pluralist Approach to First Laws and Earth Laws* (Springer, 2024), 100, doi.org/10.1007/978-981-99-9327-7; see also Langton and Corn, *First Knowledges Law*.

For clarity, we use the term 'Country' as many First Nations people use it, to reference their relationship and enduring connection to land, sea, waters, sky, fire and landscapes for all time.[9] We discuss what Country is about in the next section.

Our intent is to identify how First Nations perspectives and practices can inform the shaping of fully inclusive restorative regulation. In many ways, this chapter is a starting point in thinking through what is needed to open up and foster a restorative regulatory space, one that recognises Indigenous knowledge and values as a critical part of regulation.

A more radical aim is that in this way, Indigenous knowledges and practices will be transformative to future approaches to regulation. It is our contention that restorative regulation will only be fully achieved where Indigenous perspectives are included as part of the regulatory framework, acknowledging that '[m]any Indigenous worldviews have the power to radically transform environmental management by inscribing values of connectivity, reciprocity, and trust in ethical relationships with all species'.[10] For all forms of regulation, these Indigenous worldviews are equally important for holistic understanding and inclusion. Where this occurs effectively, Indigenous perspectives have the ability to enrich restorative regulation by emphasising the cultural, ecological and social dimensions that exist alongside the legislative and bureaucratic requirements.

In writing this chapter, we are deeply mindful that we are not First Nations people. We acknowledge the long history of misappropriation of Indigenous knowledge and are committed to avoiding inadvertently contributing to or perpetuating that legacy. In the spirit of mutual learning and reconciliation, what we seek to do is to identify lessons from our exploration of First Nations Australians' perspectives and approaches, particularly within the context of our research on environmental and restorative regulation.[11]

9 The term Country is complex, as will be discussed in this chapter. It refers not only to the physical places, lands and waters, but also contains 'complex ideas about lore, place, custom, language, spiritual belief, cultural practice, material sustenance, family, and identity': Tegan Shields et al., 'Creating an Authorizing Environment to Care for Country', *Conservation Letters* 18, no. 1 (2025): 1–6, 3, doi.org/10.1111/conl.13075.

10 Samantha Muller, Steve Hemming, and Daryle Rigney, 'Indigenous Sovereignties: Relational Ontologies and Environmental Management'. *Geographical Research* 57, no. 4 (2019): 399–410, 403, doi.org/10.1111/1745-5871.12362.

11 This chapter includes many direct quotes from Indigenous scholars and commentators, to honour and amplify the voices and insights of First Nations people.

We hope these insights will have resonance with regulators seeking to adopt more holistic and inclusive regulatory approaches that honour and respect First Nations' knowledge.

Our examples draw from environmental regulation; however, the principles, ethos and practices we discuss are broadly relevant to other regulatory domains—whether in child protection, health care or financial systems. We have structured the following discussion around a set of principles that we see as central to both Indigenous-led regulatory approaches and regenerative regulation. Our intention is not to provide an exhaustive overview but rather to offer a selection of insights that open up dialogue. We do this to help guide regulators in their efforts to engage with Indigenous approaches in future regulatory practices attuned to restorative regulation. We also hope these insights may be of value for First Nations people who would like to contribute to shaping the direction and content of restorative regulation.

This chapter is, therefore, an attempt to open up an intercultural conversation about Western and Indigenous-led regulatory possibilities, in recognition that 'these two systems now must find ways of working together for all Australians'.[12]

We would like to acknowledge the First Nations people who participated in interviews as part of our research. They generously shared their time and knowledge to help us better understand their perspectives in the regulatory space. We trust that our chapter reflects, to the best of our ability, the wisdom they shared with us.

Our modest effort to describe a few elements here is intended as a tribute to the small portion of Indigenous-led regulatory approaches we have learned about through our research, while we fully acknowledge that our interpretations are our own. Ultimately, First Nations people must decide how to define, shape and use Indigenous-led regulatory approaches, and what is, and would be, meaningful for them in the context of restorative regulation.

12 Langton and Corn, *First Knowledges Law*, 1–8, 1.

Recognition of interconnectedness

> *Country is central to everything Aboriginal: it is a continuum, without beginning or ending. In this worldview, everything is living—people, animals, plants, rocks, earth, water, stars, air and all else. There is no division between animate and inanimate.*[13]

Understanding the profound interconnection between people, place and spirit is foundational to thinking about how Indigenous perspectives find voice and recognition within regulatory systems.[14] In Australia, this interconnectedness is most clearly expressed through the Indigenous worldview of 'Country'. Country is not simply land or place. Country holds profound cultural and spiritual meaning—it is a relationship, a fundamental identity and worldview, and a way of being.[15] First Nations people often speak of Country as they would a person, a living entity consisting of water, air, fire, soils, people, animals, plants and spirituality. For instance, authors *tebrakunna* country,[16] Emma Lee and Robyn Eversole describe the Indigenous concept of Country as reflecting 'connections to land, sea and sky arising from unheralded lengths of occupation',[17] often expressed in specific terms like 'Sky Country' and 'Sea Country', as well as the overarching term 'Country'. They further describe Country as 'a relational concept in which the region itself is a regional development actor, and relationships are inclusive, reciprocal and focused on the long term'.[18] Kinship links each person to Country; this relationship endows each individual with purpose and a duty to care for Country, which creates

13 Bill Gammage and Bruce Pascoe, *First Knowledges Country: Future Fire, Future Farming*, First Knowledges series, ed. Margo Neale (Thames & Hudson, 2021), 1–8, 1.

14 'Land Is Our Future: Caring for Country', in '"Taking Care of Culture": State of Victoria's Aboriginal Cultural Heritage Report' (Victorian Aboriginal Heritage Council, November 2020), www.aboriginalheritagecouncil.vic.gov.au/sites/default/files/2021-01/Taking%20Care%20of%20Culture%20Discussion%20Paper_04012021_2.pdf; Faisal Moola et al., 'The Potential for Indigenous-Led Conservation in Urbanized Landscapes in Canada', *Frontiers in Human Dynamics* 6 (2024): 1–18, doi.org/10.3389/fhumd.2024.1340379; Teagan Goolmeer et al., 'Indigenous-Led Designation and Management of Culturally Significant Species', *Nature Ecology & Evolution* 8 (2024): 1623–31, doi.org/10.1038/s41559-024-02466-w; Rona Glynn-McDonald, 'First Nations Systems Thinking', *Common Ground*, 14 July 2021, last modified 20 October 2022, www.commonground.org.au/article/first-nations-systems-thinking.

15 Glynn-McDonald, 'First Nations Systems Thinking'.

16 Here, *tebrakunna* country is named as an author in recognition of Country's agency as a living being and source of knowledge, understood as informing through the life, stories and beings connected with it.

17 *tebrakunna* country, Emma Lee, and Robyn Eversole, 'Rethinking the Regions: Indigenous Peoples and Regional Development', *Regional Studies* 53, no. 11 (2019): 1510–19, 1513, doi.org/10.1080/00343404.2019.1587159.

18 *tebrakunna* country et al., 'Rethinking the Regions', 1516.

a deep sense of belonging.[19] Forced separation from Country severs the ties between individuals and these vital relationships, while the use of dismissive labels such as 'nomadic' and 'empty land' to justify this separation have caused deep harm for centuries.[20]

In discussing the 'Aboriginal worldview' of land as the law, Kombu-merri and Wakka Wakka philosopher Mary Graham further summarises the importance of Country for maintaining relationships between people: [21]

> The two most important kinds of relationship in life are, firstly, those between land and people and, secondly, those amongst people themselves, the second being always contingent upon the first. The land, and how we treat it, is what determines our humanness. Because land is sacred and must be looked after, the relation between people and land becomes the template for society and social relations. Therefore all meaning comes from land.[22]

Country in this conception is alive and has a 'consciousness'.[23] Moreover:

> [w]hen Indigenous nations 'speak as Country', they speak as part of a living body; they speak lawfully through their rights and sovereignties to Country as part of a living whole.[24]

19 Pat Dudgeon et al., *Connection Between Family, Kinship and Social and Emotional Wellbeing*, (Australian Institute of Health and Welfare [AIHW], 2021), www.indigenousmhspc.gov.au/getattachment/e129c621-58a4-4966-8730-dcf6e3a533a8/dudgeon-et-al-2021-family-kinship-20210802.pdf.

20 Bruce Pascoe, *Dark Emu, Black Seeds: Agriculture or Accident?* (Magabala Books, 2014); Australian Human Rights Commission, *Wiyi Yani U Thangani (Women's Voices): Securing Our Rights, Securing Our Future Report*, (2020), 9 December 2020, humanrights.gov.au/our-work/aboriginal-and-torres-strait-islander-social-justice/publications/wiyi-yani-u-thangani.

21 Mary Graham is one of Australia's leading Aboriginal philosophers and authors. See David Rutledge, 'Stability, Security and Survival: A Conversation with Mary Graham', *The Philosopher's Zone* (radio broadcast), 8 December 2023, www.abc.net.au/listen/programs/philosopherszone/the-philosophers-zone/102961342.

22 Mary Graham, 'Some Thoughts About the Philosophical Underpinnings of Aboriginal Worldviews', *Worldviews: Global Religions, Culture, and Ecology* 3, no. 2 (1999): 105–18, 106, doi.org/10.1163/156853599X00090, also available at Mary Graham, 'Some Thoughts About the Philosophical Underpinnings of Aboriginal Worldviews', *Australian Humanities Review*, accessed 7 March 2025, australianhumanitiesreview.org/2008/11/01/some-thoughts-about-the-philosophical-underpinnings-of-aboriginal-worldviews/.

23 Deborah Bird Rose, *Nourishing Terrains; Australian Aboriginal Views of Landscape and Wilderness* (Australian Heritage Commission, 1996). See also Bhiamie Williamson, '"Although We Didn't Produce These Problems, We Suffer Them": 3 Ways You Can Help in NAIDOC's Call to Heal Country', *The Conversation*, 5 July 2021, theconversation.com/although-we-didnt-produce-these-problems-we-suffer-them-3-ways-you-can-help-in-naidocs-call-to-heal-country-163362.

24 Muller et al., 'Indigenous Sovereignties'.

As a holistic, living entity, Graham says that Country is:

> *the* great teacher; it not only teaches us how to relate to it, but to each other; it suggests a notion of caring for something outside ourselves, something that is in and of nature and that will exist for all time.[25]

Country suffuses every action and decision taken by First Nations people, embodying complex layers of 'law, place, custom, language, spiritual belief, cultural practice, material sustenance, family and identity'.[26] The interconnectedness with Country as 'family, kin, law, lore, ceremony, traditions, and language … has been this way since the dawn of time'. [27] For all First Nations people, Country is a whole, a past, a present and a future, the continuum integral to Indigenous culture and beliefs.[28]

Central to this relationship is reciprocity—a commitment to mutual respect, balanced interaction and caring stewardship that ensures human beings take only what they need. The reciprocity approach preserves natural resources and honours the entire environment—both its living and inanimate elements—that all depend on them. This principle is often summed up as 'healthy Country, healthy people'.[29] As one Djaara leader told us, 'If we can get Country right and healthy, we can get people right and healthy.'

Australian (Western positivist) law recognises that Aboriginal and Torres Strait Islander people have rights and interests in Country that arise from their traditional First Law and customs, reflected in the term 'Traditional Owners'.[30] Traditional Owners of different local regions and varied languages across Australia have voice and authority to speak on behalf of Country, and to speak to Country's health and wellbeing.

---

25 Graham, 'Some Thoughts ', 108.

26 'Welcome to Country', Australian Institute of Aboriginal and Torres Strait Islander Studies (AIATSIS), last modified 25 May 2022, aiatsis.gov.au/explore/welcome-country.

27 NSW Government, Health Sydney Local Health District, 'Heal Country, Heal Our Nation', NAIDOC Week 2021, Heal Country! 4–11 July 2021, www.slhd.nsw.gov.au/pdfs/NAIDOC-Week-2021.pdf.

28 Bird Rose, Nourishing Terrains, 7.

29 Evolve Communities, 'Connection to Country—Why is Country Important to Aboriginal and Torres Strait Islander People?', *Sites at Scale* (blog), accessed 7 March 2025, www.evolves.com.au/connection-to-country/; Jessica K. Weir, Claire Stacey, and Kara Youngetob, *The Benefits Associated with Caring for Country, Literature Review*, Caring for Our Country, Australian Institute of Aboriginal and Torres Strait Islander Studies (AIATSIS, June 2011), aiatsis.gov.au/sites/default/files/research_pub/benefits-cfc_0_2.pdf; Doc Reynolds and Liz Cameron, 'Yarning Up with Doc Reynolds: An Interview About Country from an Indigenous Perspective', *Wildlife Research* 52, WR24104 (2025): 1–7, doi.org/10.1071/WR24104.

30 *Mabo v Queensland (No 2)* [1992] HCA 23, (1992) CLR 1, see aiatsis.gov.au/ntpd-resource/742; *Aboriginal Land Rights (Northern Territory) Act 1976*, www.austlii.edu.au/cgi-bin/viewdb/au/legis/cth/consol_act/alrta1976444/; 'Engaging With Traditional Owners' (Australian Institute of Aboriginal and Torres Strait Islander Studies [AIATSIS], 23 December 2020), aiatsis.gov.au/publication/94688.

Country has its own agency:

> [Its places] speak, and the ancestral beings within them are agents in the spiritual encounters that living people have with them. Typically, it is tradition for senior Indigenous people to call out to their ancestors and speak to them. Places have an energetic presence that holds all manner of information available to traditional owners, especially elders. Knowledgeable elders have relationships with special places that are imbued with remembered qualities.[31]

The relational ideas inherent in the concept of Country, together with the ability of Traditional Owners to speak truths about Country's health and wellbeing, hold the potential to shift how the concept of landscape-and-waterscape is understood: as a distinct and interconnected entity, intimately connected to local First Nations people. In particular, this lends itself to the inclusion of landscape-and-waterscape, as understood by First Nations people, as an active participant with a voice in the practice of restorative justice.

In other words, when a human being feels a deeper personal connection with the natural world, with Country, then they have the potential to heal themselves more profoundly by contributing to restoring and healing the parts of the Earth system with which they identify. Indigenous justice emphasises this interconnectedness, going beyond the essentialising of conventional justice as reconciliation solely between an offender, their victim, their state and their community.[32] Rather, it urges us to acknowledge our moral responsibilities towards the other-than-human beings and ecosystems at the same time as restoring human relationships.[33] This holistic approach to justice enhances the healing process.

31 Langton and Corn, *First Knowledges Law*, 45.

32 Chris Cunneen and Juan Tiari, 'Indigenous Criminology', in *The Routledge Companion to Criminological Theory and Concepts*, eds. Avi Brisman, Eamonn Carrabine, and Nigel South, (Routledge, 2018), 306–10, doi.org/10.4324/9781315744902; Larry Chartrand and Kanatase Horn, *A Report on the Relationship Between Restorative Justice and Indigenous Legal Traditions in Canada* (Department of Justice Canada, October 2016), www.justice.gc.ca/eng/rp-pr/jr/rjilt-jrtja/rjilt-jrtja.pdf.

33 In speaking about the *Maturwarra* Fitzroy River, Anna Poelina explains that 'First Law' is a collective of 'moral laws', and that the River goes well beyond being viewed as a resource or geological feature, as it 'is the basis of our spirituality, our Law, our home, our ancestral estate'. The River, says Poelina, 'is a living ancestor serpent and sacred giver of a holistic system of law, leadership and governance, which we were born into and are bound to by a moral contract, a law of obligations to nurture and protect *Maturwarra*'. Minority Rights Group, '"Just-Us for All": Indigenous Wisdom for Human and Planetary Well-being', Minority and Indigenous Trends 2023—Focus on Water, 20 June 2023, minorityrights.org/resources/trends2023-just-us-for-all-indigenous-wisdom-for-human-and-planetary-well-being/; Reynolds and Cameron, 'Yarning Up'.

For regulators, the crucial takeaway is that just as one form of harm can trigger another, so can one kind of restoration lead to another, provided that these interconnections between challenges and solutions are sufficiently understood. Therefore, it is essential to identify mechanisms that facilitate such interconnections, strengthening efforts to restore both landscapes and communities.

One effective approach is through inclusive restorative justice processes, which offer the possibility to explore regulatory issues from many perspectives. Restorative approaches create a context in which different worldviews can be present and contribute.

Moreover, restorative justice is a means of reckoning with deeper historical and social contexts that shape the regulatory approaches to restoration of harms and are inseparable from holistic restoration of Country, communities and relationships. As Veronica Matthews and colleagues note:

> From an Aboriginal and Torres Strait Islander perspective, there is a need for restorative justice—a reflective process of understanding and acceptance by the Australian population of the harm created by colonization, and commitment to address that harm and its intergenerational consequences.[34]

Through these restorative approaches—open dialogue, deep listening and collaborative problem-solving—a space opens for the diverse narratives of harm and healing to be shared, understood and woven together into a more holistic understanding of what needs to be done to repair Country. In this way, regulators do not just become attuned to the local Indigenous context—they actively create spaces where multidimensional worldviews can be acknowledged and engaged with, balancing out the bureaucratic technical, rational worldview, 'to work together in fashioning new forms of "pluriverse", or of "multivocality", embracing a full recognition of Indigenous First Law'.[35]

34 Matthews et al., 'Justice, Culture, and Relationships', 3.

35 Poelina et al., *Declaration of Peace*, 129.

Indigenous approaches to regulation

> *Indigenous people have a culture that relates to the land and sea in a holistic way that also includes connections to powerful and significant places. However, the emphasis that is now put on management of discreet sites can overlook and diminish Indigenous connections to the environment as a whole.*[36]

Key to any understanding of First Nations approaches to law, broadly understood to include regulation and governance, is the immutable fact that all three—law, regulation and governance—are fully embedded in culture. As has been powerfully expressed by authors Marcia Langton and Aaron Corn: 'Law and culture are inseparable—one is the other. And country holds all knowledge as an integrated whole, not compartmentalised into separate disciplines.'[37] Additionally, the body of First Law is complex, multifaceted and nuanced. It is important for us to acknowledge at the outset that there is no singular definition of Indigenous-led approaches to regulation—this will depend upon context, cultural expectations and the self-determined approach of the respective First Nations people towards a specific regulatory matter:

> There are hundreds of dreaming stories and a law for the place is the truth for that one place. … [T]here are multiple truths, there's not one truth. So there's no absolutism in Aboriginal thinking. And in multiple truths, there's multiple perspectives. So all perspectives are valid and reasonable.[38]

Given this diversity of perspectives, we aim to point to some of the features that are commonly shared across many of them.[39]

---

36 Citation from a participant in an Indigenous Working Group Workshop, Melbourne, 8 November 2002, in Australia National Oceans Office, *Sea Country: An Indigenous Perspective: The South-east Regional Marine Plan Assessment Report* (National Oceans Office, 2002), 39, www.dcceew.gov.au/sites/default/files/documents/indigenous.pdf.

37 Langton and Corn, *First Knowledges Law*, 2.

38 Christian Eva et al., '"It's Self-Determination. Blackfullas Making Right Decisions for Blackfullas": Why Indigenous-Owned Businesses Create Better Indigenous Employment Outcomes', *Australian Journal of Social Issues* 59, no. 1 (2024): 29–56, 38, doi.org/10.1002/ajs4.292.

39 'Aboriginal and Torres Strait Islander Australia is made up of many different and distinct groups, each with their own culture, customs, languages and laws. They are the world's oldest surviving culture; cultures that continue to be expressed in dynamic and contemporary ways.' Australian Institute of Aboriginal and Torres Strait Islander Studies (AIATSIS), 'Map of Indigenous Australia', last modified 28 March 2025, aiatsis.gov.au/explore/map-indigenous-australia.

Indigenous-led regulatory approaches prioritise holistic, place-based and community-focused ways of regulation, centring the interconnectedness of all living beings and the need for sustainable, regenerative practices.[40] Relationality and relationships are foregrounded in any interactions seeking to address conflict, negotiate changes, obtain or provide guidance and implement collaborative efforts:

> Relationships are central to Aboriginal people, and it is the wholeness of these relationships rather than the abstract nature of each component that is key to wellbeing and lived experience.[41]

Additionally, Indigenous-led regulatory approaches emphasise the valuing of local wisdom, self-governance and self-management, and respect for the environment; they embody collaborative and participatory decision-making, sometimes called 'co-regulation'.[42]

In the following story about Mumma Doris Shillingsworth, a respected Gandugari Elder of the Murrawarri Nation, Indigenous scholar Dr Tyson Yunkaporta describes the essence of an Indigenous-led regulatory approach and its strained relationship with the typical bureaucratic approach:

> What we had found was a broad, common description of Indigenous ways of valuing, ways of being, ways of knowing and ways of doing. These things had a widespread order, a sequence in all cultural activities in which people were sharing or producing knowledge on Country. We had our own personal metaphors for describing this process of induction. I referred to it as spirit, heart, head and hands. Mumma Doris knew it as **Respect, Connect, Reflect, Direct**. She insisted on that order. She also identified that non-Aboriginal people seemed to work through the same steps but in reverse.
>
> She has observed interventions and programs imposed on her community for over half a century, noticing that they always begin with the last step—**Direct**. Government agents come into the

40 Neil M. Dawson et al., 'The Role of Indigenous Peoples and Local Communities in Effective and Equitable Conservation', *Ecology and Society* 26, no. 3 (2021), doi.org/10.5751/ES-12625-260319; Kawika B. Winter et al., 'Indigenous Stewardship Through Novel Approaches to Collaborative Management in Hawai'i'.

41 Michael Wright et al., 'Co-Designing Health Service Evaluation Tools That Foreground First Nation Worldviews for Better Mental Health and Wellbeing Outcomes'; Glynn-McDonald, 'First Nations Systems Thinking'.

42 Renee Henry and Edward Swann, 'The Regulatory Approach—QLD Indigenous Councils Challenges in Drinking Water Services, Water Supply Regulation, Department of Regional Development, Manufacturing and Water' (Queensland Government, December 2022).

> community with a plan for change and they direct activities towards this change immediately. When it all fails, they go backwards to the next step, **Reflect**. They gather data and measure outcomes and try to figure out what went wrong. Then they realise they didn't form relationships with community, so belatedly go to the next step, **Connect**. Through these relationships they discover the final step (which should have been the first), finding a profound respect for members of the community they ruined. They cry as they say farewell and return to the city, calling, 'Thank you, I have learned so much from you!'[43]

This story tells us that Indigenous approaches to regulation are grounded in relationship-building. These relationships require careful reflection and respect before problems are named or actions directed.[44] In contrast, non-Indigenous approaches often begin with someone directing action—only later do those involved come to recognise the value of the foundational steps they initially skipped. This is the all-too-common reality of bureaucratic endeavours with First Nations Australians.

Can non-Indigenous actors avoid this repeated pattern of failure to direct, reflect and connect by identifying and seeking opportunities to create practice around Indigenous regulatory approaches?

We believe the answer, in part, lies in a shift in approach—one that moves beyond fragmented and imposed frameworks towards governance that is regenerative, inclusive and grounded in shared responsibility. This means we need to reconsider the ways in which Indigenous legal and regulatory approaches are engaged: not as peripheral contributions within Western systems, but as integral to shaping governance and its outcomes.[45] As we turn from principle to application—going from knowing to being and doing—the way Indigenous-led regulatory approaches are engaged becomes crucial. They are not a mere adjunct or insertion within existing regulatory frameworks but involve '*working in tandem*' to support a pluralistic, restorative regulatory approach focused on regenerative outcomes. [46]

---

43 Tyson Yunkaporta, *Sand Talk: How Indigenous Thinking Can Save the World*. Emphasis added by authors.

44 Janet Hunt, 'Engaging with Indigenous Australia—Exploring the Conditions for Effective Relationships with Aboriginal and Torres Strait Islander Communities', Issues paper no. 5, October 2013, www.aihw.gov.au/getmedia/7d54eac8-4c95-4de1-91bb-0d6b1cf348e2/ctgc-ip05.pdf.

45 Indigenous governance includes Indigenous ways of knowing, being and doing, diverse perspectives and knowledge, respectful relationships and Indigenous-led action.

46 Poelina et al., *Declaration of Peace*; Eva et al., '"It's Self-Determination"'.

The following sections explore how regulatory practices that embrace a shared responsibility to protect are oriented towards healing and regeneration, and how the inclusion of multiple perspectives can contribute to this meaningful shift. We also consider ways to ensure First Nations people have genuine voice with power and are supported in leading co-production endeavours.

Shared responsibility to protect

Country suffers harm when its rivers are filled with refuse and pollution, its trees are chopped down to make way for transport corridors, its native vegetation is cleared for resource extraction and its native species are endangered through habitat loss. Land-use changes, waste disposal and urban encroachment all have profound impacts on Country. Negative consequences follow when careful, inclusive planning is neglected—particularly planning that considers impacts on Country, Indigenous culture and native wildlife.

We speak about healing of Country, but prior to healing, Traditional Owners have a responsibility—sometimes expressed as a cultural duty—to protect their Country. Traditional Elder Gheran Yarraman Steel of the Kulin Nation in Victoria explains that Traditional Owners do not just think about Country as a physical space, but about all the things that have occurred on that Country and all the things that will occur into the future. As such, there is a responsibility to protect it from those who cause harm and will not respect and honour the laws that exist in relation to it.[47] Furthermore, sick Country must be cared for and restored to health: 'If Country is unwell, it needs to heal. We must listen to Country and what it needs.'[48]

Significant obstacles currently prevent many Traditional Owners from carrying out this duty, including the separation from Country we referred to above, as well as systemic barriers to meaningful inclusion in regulatory

47 'Gheran Yarraman Steel: Welcome to Country for John Mawurndjul', *Bunjil Place*, YouTube, 24 November 2020, www.youtube.com/watch?v=2O_qj2h24Xc.

48 Evolve Communities, 'Connection to Country'.

formulation and implementation. Fortunately, there are positive signs of change, in both the shaping of policies to better fit Indigenous perspectives and management practices, and in strengthened support for the duty of caring for Country.[49]

The idea of a shared responsibility to protect our environment—and our communities and future generations—is a regulatory value that some regulators are already acting upon. In Victoria, for instance, the EP Act 2017 heralded a profound shift from being 'consequence based' and 'managing pollution' to being 'prevention based' and seeking to avoid pollution altogether.[50] In the Act, this preventive approach is called the 'principle of primacy of prevention' (section 15) and it is enabled by a new general environmental duty (GED) (section 25, Part 3.2), which we introduced in Chapter 2 and discussed in Chapter 5 in the context of inspections.

The GED is a positive duty to proactively identify and manage environmental risk and is a shared responsibility of all Victorians (the principle of shared responsibility in section 16 supports the GED).[51] The GED is intended to be enduring and flexible, and to provide regulatory officers with the power to fill regulatory gaps where no specific requirement exists in current legislation. For example, licence holders are required to meet the GED in addition to the specified terms of their licence. This has potential for CRGs or other affected groups to initiate ongoing dialogue about a licensed site. Aside from the GED's immediate regulatory value, it could theoretically become particularly significant during a licence review, introducing a powerful new dynamic for protecting Country as a shared responsibility.

The success of a general statutory duty to prevent harm from pollution and waste will depend on many factors, including the extent to which it can drive a cultural change of mindset in the population. This means broad acceptance of a cultural shift, moving towards support for a more active stewardship approach to protecting the environment and community. A stewardship approach exists in many Indigenous-led regulatory frameworks, often

49 Dr Josephine Bourne notes that 'change is happening right now', resulting from 'learning from others … and being humble'. ANZSOG, 'What Is Culturally Responsive Regulation?'.

50 EPA Victoria, 'What We Do', last modified 14 February 2025, www.epa.vic.gov.au/what-we-do.

51 The GED is contained in Part 3.2 of the EP Act 2017. The GED states that '[a] person who is engaging in an activity that may give rise to risk of harm to human health or the environment from pollution or waste must minimise those risks, so far as reasonably practicable'.

referred to as 'caring for Country'.[52] This care ethos is a 'way of being in the world' that reflects interconnectedness and shared responsibility.[53] It is relational and includes care for

> all of the values, places, resources, stories, and cultural obligations associated with that area, as well as associated processes of spiritual renewal, connecting with ancestors, food provision, and maintaining kin relations.[54]

First Nations stewardship of Country benefits environment and landscape on the one hand and the cultural, emotional, health-related, sociopolitical and economic wellbeing of First Nations people on the other.[55]

In discussing the governmental agencies and the NGOs that work in environmental protection, conservation and land management, Bush Heritage's National Aboriginal Engagement Officer Cissy Gore-Birch makes an important point:

> The current organisations working within the land, sea, conservation and environment sector need to work in collaboration and not in *competition.* We are working towards the same goals—let's reflect, rethink and re-adjust why we work in this field and to re-check what our Traditional Owners are saying and how we are really making changes within and influencing others. This industry should not be taken for granted, each and everyone of us have a responsibility to look after Country and speak the truth.[56]

52 The phrase 'caring for Country' refers broadly to the First Nations 'approaches to land and water management' that are contextualised to local conditions and 'based in the laws, customs and ways of life that Indigenous people have inherited from their ancestors and ancestral beings'. Weir et al., *Caring for Country*, 1.

53 Muller et al., 'Indigenous Sovereignties', 403.

54 Jon Altman, Geoff Buchanan, and Libby Larsen, 'The Environmental Significance of the Indigenous Estate: Natural Resource Management as Economic Development in Remote Australia', Centre for Aboriginal Economic Policy Research Discussion Paper no. 295/2007 (ANU College of Arts & Social Sciences, 2007), 37, caepr.cass.anu.edu.au/research/publications/environmental-significance-indigenous-estate-natural-resource-management.

55 Weir et al., *Caring for Country*; Emma Woodward et al., *Our Knowledge Our Way in Caring for Country.*

56 Woodward et al., *Our Knowledge Our Way*, 82.

Her recognition of our shared responsibility for looking after Country, as well as the need to work together to achieve this goal, reinforces that environmental protection and cultural protection are shared tasks. These tasks require us to listen deeply to the First Nations custodians of Country and to pursue this shared responsibility in the spirit of working together and continuously learning from one another, 'with an aim … to develop trust in, and acceptance of, the reciprocal value of "two-way knowledge".'[57] In such a vision, everyone will see themselves as responsible for ensuring that regulatory objectives are achieved, rather than placing the onus solely on the regulator, First Nations custodians, a single community group, or an NGO. The shared responsibility to protect is *everyone's* business.

Resonance with restorative regulation

In the previous chapter, we examined restorative enquiry as a process that can help to ensure that future healing germinates from past harm. But, as we noted at the start, there is also a possibility of rethinking regulation as fundamentally geared towards healing and caring, to inform a regenerative form of regulation that is more holistic, better adapted to our world of complex living systems, and inclusive of collective wisdom.

Dr Tyson Yunkaporta's 'Australian Indigenous ways of learning' diagram, shown in Figure 9.1, summarises other key dimensions of the Indigenous approach that are applicable to restorative regulation. Many of these learning ways, such as story sharing, community links, non-linearity and non-verbal communication are equally valued aspects of the restorative regulatory approach discussed throughout this book. Others, such as learning maps and deconstruct/reconstruct, have equivalences through restorative justice's emphasis upon learning and its future-oriented focus on collaboratively shaping improved pathways for the future.

57 Sarah Martin, *Bush Heritage Australia: Restoring Nature Step by Step*, 1st ed. (NewSouth, 2016), 202; Woodward et al., *Our Knowledge Our Way*.

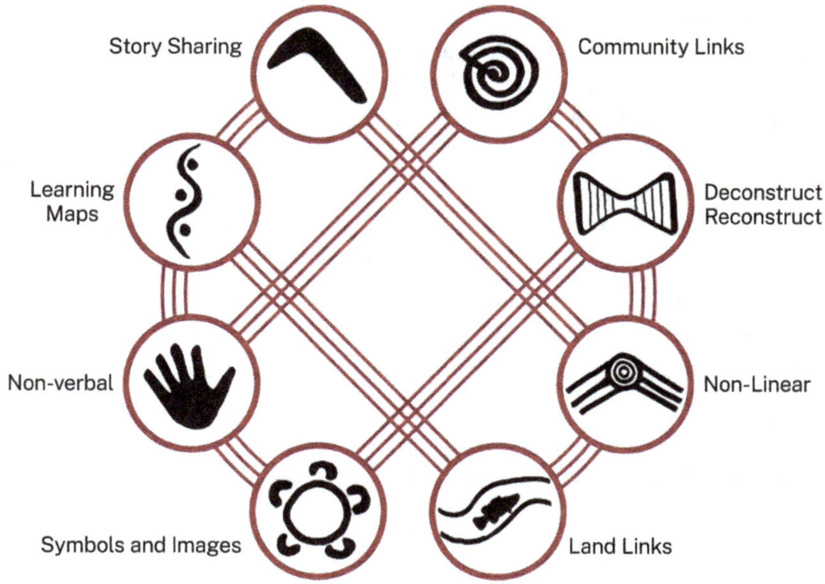

Figure 9.1. First Nations Australians' ways of learning

Source: Tyson Yunkaporta, 8ways Framework, originally in *Aboriginal Pedagogies at the Cultural Interface* (PhD dissertation, 2009: 46). researchonline.jcu.edu.au/10974/21/JCU_10974_Yunkaporta_2009_thesis.pdf, shared by NSW Department of Education as 'Eight Indigenous Ways of Learning'.

The concept of '*Makarrata*' as interpreted in the *Uluru Statement from the Heart* as 'the coming together after a struggle' also resonates with restorative justice.[58] *Makarrata* is a Yolŋu Matha word and is focused upon justice, conflict resolution and peacemaking.[59] Indigenous lawyer and activist Noel Pearson sees *Makarrata* as embodying the idea of:

58 'Makarrata is the culmination of our agenda: **the coming together after a struggle**. It captures our aspirations for a fair and truthful relationship with the people of Australia and a better future for our children based on justice and self-determination.' 'Uluru Statement from the Heart', The Uluru Statement, 2024, accessed 08 March 2025, ulurustatement.org/the-statement/view-the-statement/. *Makarrata* is a term widely understood in Australia since its adoption in the 1980s by the National Aboriginal Conference as an alternative word for 'treaty' to show the intention to form an agreement 'within Australia, between Australians'. Daniel McKay, 'Uluru Statement: A Quick Guide', *Parliamentary Library Research Paper Series* 2016–17, 19 June 2017, 1, parlinfo.aph.gov.au/parlInfo/download/library/prspub/5345708/upload_binary/5345708.pdf. In 2017, the Uluru Statement from the Heart requested the establishment of a Makarrata commission for truth-telling and treaty-making. This proposal was defeated in the referendum of 2023.

59 Victoria Grieve-Williams, 'Makarrata: The Aboriginal Healing Process We Should All Know About', *SBS Voices*, 4 July 2019, last modified 09 July 2019, www.sbs.com.au/voices/article/makarrata-the-aboriginal-healing-process-we-should-all-know-about/8nd8avji8.

> two parties coming together after a struggle, healing the divisions of the past. It is about acknowledging that something has been done wrong, and it seeks to make things right.[60]

Like restorative justice, *Makarrata* is embodied as both values and practice. It requires a coming together to talk and reflect on what has happened, to stop avoiding or denying the harm. In its most literal meaning of 'a spear penetrating' a person to stop them from hunting, running or walking away, and as a peacemaking concept, *Makarrata* asks the wrongdoer to slow down, stop and reflect on what they have done (or keep doing) that creates harm.[61] It seeks to understand both sides of a conflict, with the ultimate aim being to 'call accusers to account' and restore wellbeing through healing wounds and using ongoing dialogue to address contestations, again akin to restorative justice.[62]

For Australia as a whole, *Makarrata* is concerned with healing the deep wounds caused by unresolved colonial history. It acknowledges that the First Nations Custodians of Australia's diverse landscapes hold an equal and indispensable place in Australian history. More than this, it requires settler Australians to acknowledge the existence of First Law, which both exists and has always endured, connected to all 'life across time, space and place'.[63] It calls for removing the Australian state's ability to perpetuate harm, empowering First Nations people to speak on their own behalf.[64] This acknowledgement has strong resonance with the principles of restorative justice, emphasising healing, inclusion and equitable recognition for a more harmonious future.

60 McKay, 'Uluru Statement', citing Noel Pearson, 1.

61 Adrian Little, 'The Politics of Makarrata: Understanding Indigenous-Settler Relations in Australia', *Political Theory* 48, no. 1 (2020): 30–56, 42, doi.org/10.1177/0090591719849023; Luke Pearson, 'What is a Makarrata? It's More Than a Synonym for Treaty', *ABC News*, 10 August 2017, RN, www.abc.net.au/news/2017-08-10/makarrata-explainer-yolngu-word-more-than-synonym-for-treaty/8790452.

62 Marcia Langton, 'Personal Perspectives', in Langton and Corn, *First Knowledges Law*, 9–21, 15. As discussed in Chapter 1, key elements of restorative justice—dialogue, deep listening and multiple perspective-taking—are essential for addressing ongoing contestations between and within communities, and supporting respectful, open-minded engagement that strives to collaboratively resolve contestations over time. In this way, restorative justice can, in part, respond to *Makarrata's* call for undoing the broader injustices perpetuated by the state, offering a framework for healing and transformation that respects First Nations voices and sovereignty.

63 Langton and Corn, *First Knowledges Law*, 1; see also Marcia Langton, 'Personal Perspectives', 16 and Langton and Corn, *First Knowledges Law*, 32–61.

64 This understanding contrasts with the way non-Indigenous commentators often perceive or interpret Makarrata, as discussed in Little, 'The Politics of Makarrata', 42.

Voice with power

Across multiple countries, Indigenous movements emphasise that repairing past wrongs and achieving meaningful healing require systemic change that restores power and voice to those who have been historically silenced.[65]

Structural reforms that empower historically marginalised voices are required across all of government, including in regulatory authorities at the federal, state and local levels. All the measures discussed below, such as employing more First Nations staff as regulators, will only be fully enabled and effective if supported by the right structural, policy and financial frameworks. The regulatory ecosystem in which regulators operate must be structurally geared to support these initiatives, including recognition of the necessity for First Nations people to have direct input into shaping structural transformations so they are both adequate and reflective of their needs.

Recognition also sits at the heart of restorative approaches, emphasising that individuals, including those within Indigenous communities, are more likely to achieve positive changes when those in positions of authority work *with* them, acknowledging their perspectives and lived experiences, rather than doing things *for* or *to* them.

The importance of voice for empowerment can be illustrated using the example of environmental regulation. In the context of managing and protecting Australia's environment, First Nations people continue to seek 'greater management, involvement, and empowerment ... over Country'.[66] Critically, however, more than consultation is needed to ensure that this happens. It also requires:

- collaboration, mutual exchange of knowledge and ecological understanding.
- the inclusion of First Nations Australians as employees, managers and directors in government entities that are responsible for working with Country. This requires that cultural competency, as a core, ongoing organisational value, deeply embeds cultural awareness and practices throughout the organisation.

65 Jaclyn Silbernagel, 'Systemic Change—Indigenous People and the Legal System', podcast, episode 12 in series Let's Talk Poverty, *enough for all*, 1 June 2022, enoughforall.ca/podcasts/systemic-change-indigenous-people-and-the-legal-system; Tom Johnson, Tanya Allport, and Amohia Boulton, 'Te Ruru: Co-creating an Indigenous Systems Change Framework', *Journal of Awareness-Based Systems Change* 4, no. 1 (2024): 49–75, doi.org/10.47061/jasc.v4i1.7006.

66 NAIDOC, '2021 Theme: Heal Country', 2021, accessed 8 March 2025, www.naidoc.org.au/get-involved/2021-theme.

- deep listening.
- redress for historical injustices.

All too often, First Nations people have felt that regulatory approaches to managing the environment, including the co-management of parks and heritage places, has involved a power imbalance, information asymmetry, interpretations of objectivity to meet Eurocentric ends, and overwhelming expectations to attend complex meetings with little to no support. Scholar Justin O'Brien calls this '[t]he disingenuous nature of the application of bureaucratic power'.[67] In many cases, state actors relegate First Nations communities to the role of 'the consulted'. Speaking about co-management of Kakadu National Park with Bininj landowners, O'Brien observes the following:

> [The] busy application of a seemingly mundane set of land management policies and practices in the park inadvertently denies Bininj separateness, and (ironically) such denial of difference drives the marginalization of Bininj from decision-making.[68]

Assumptions in regulatory decision-making processes that dismiss Indigenous worldviews and lifeworlds deny First Nations people their agency.[69] Moreover, when state actors view First Nations people through 'the lens of a deficit model' because of a presumed reticence to conform to imposed epistemologies, the policymakers and regulators risk treating First Nations people as disengaged, not interested, or lacking in good governance.[70] These assessments are, however, misplaced and reveal a lack of will to understand or engage with Indigenous perspectives. Frustration and dismay arise when directives are issued before respect is shown and meaningful consultation takes place—when there is no conversation, no asking what First Nations communities want, and no genuine listening, as discussed earlier.

---

67 Justin O'Brien, 'Creating Space: Comanagement Considerations in Kakadu National Park', in *Reclaiming Indigenous Governance: Reflections and Insights from Australia, Canada, New Zealand, and the United States*, ed. William Nikolakis et al. (University of Arizona Press, 2019), 287, doi.org/10.2307/j.ctvqc6jwv.15; Muller et al., 'Indigenous Sovereignties'.

68 O'Brien, 'Creating Space', 286.

69 Muller et al., 'Indigenous Sovereignties'.

70 O'Brien, 'Creating Space', 289; Jacqueline McGowan-Jones, in ANZSOG, 'What Is Culturally Responsive Regulation?'.

Regulatory systems must recognise the legitimacy of Indigenous worldviews to break patterns of exclusion and ensure meaningful engagement. In talking about culturally responsive regulation, Jacqueline McGowan-Jones, Western Australia's Commissioner for Children and Young People and an Arrente/Warramungu woman, argues:

> [Regulators] have to change the narrative from a deficit approach and work collaboratively with those we regulate to get the right outcomes. Keep these discussions going. Understand the challenges and the concerns and discuss the barriers with a solutions focus. Work out what is a 'must' and what is a 'nice' and what is urgent and important. And urgent and important, I believe in a regulatory sense … is about recognising strengths in our communities; it is about recognising that we need to do this in partnership … It is about understanding who are the partners in this, and the partners are those you're regulating. And doing this in partnership rather than an oversight, punitive approach to what we do. How do we work in partnerships for better outcomes?[71]

Dr Josephine Bourne, a Gumulgal woman of Mabuiag Island, explains that this is also about needing to reframe the narratives that 'support the healing of the Indigenous-State relationship':

> The emergence of a new narrative is necessary at this point in the relationship. A better way of working together grounded in mutual respect for each other's governance knowledge and systems. Growing an appreciation for understanding the systems of governance that mean 'good governance' in both worlds and the possibility of redesign in the space between our worlds.[72]

Healing and protecting Country and First Nations communities is therefore about moving beyond the imposition of solutions, approaches and attitudes. It concerns 'the historical, political, and administrative landscapes adapting to successfully empower and celebrate Aboriginal and Torres Strait Islander communities, nations, and heritage'.[73] This entails stepping back and taking the time to actively engage First Nations people, creating space for different worldviews and seeking to understand alternative approaches to

71 McGowan-Jones, in ANZSOG, 'What Is Culturally Responsive Regulation?'.

72 Josephine Bourne, 'Indigenous Organisation Leaders: Balancing Tensions Between Achieving Political Goals and Regulatory Requirements', *News and media*, Australia and New Zealand School of Government (ANZSOG), 16 August 2022, anzsog.edu.au/news/indigenous-organisation-leaders-balancing-tensions-between-achieving-political-goals-and-regulatory-requirements/.

73 NAIDOC, '2021 Theme: Heal Country.'

governance. It requires identifying the Indigenous regulatory approaches they themselves determine are needed, and to ask first what they see as being the problems in need of addressing. This is a better way forward than assuming the problems, imposing predetermined solutions and merely seeking First Nations people's support for implementation:

> Indigenous people are telling us there is an expectation mob are part of the process from the problem location to the evaluation of it's [*sic*] success.[74]

Later in this chapter, we will think more about genuine, relational engagement with First Nations communities through co-production.

Voice with power: Employment of First Nations people in regulatory agencies

An interview with an Indigenous officer at a regional office of a sister state regulator, at the time known as Aboriginal Victoria, yielded insights that have sharpened our vision for the possibilities for justice as recognition, justice as restoration of cultural heritage, and ways to honour ancestors.[75] The Indigenous officer told us:

> We're very fortunate in this region. We have a core group of Aboriginal employees in key land departments and agencies that are particularly clued in to not only the Aboriginal community, but what's going on, on the ground. That process of discovery is often very close to those key individuals. It's known, it gets reported quickly. It's managed with a very high degree of Aboriginal involvement really, which may be quite different, I would imagine, from other states. We are quite unique, I think, potentially in that space.[76]

We asked if the officer thought this high level of Aboriginal involvement was key to increasing awareness, or if Indigenous engagement was just one part in a whole set of factors:

74 Marnee Shay and Grace Sarra, '"Co-design" Is the Latest Buzzword in Indigenous Education Policy. Does It Live Up to the Hype?', *The Conversation*, 4 September 2023, theconversation.com/co-design-is-the-latest-buzzword-in-indigenous-education-policy-does-it-live-up-to-the-hype-212194. 'Mob' is a First Nations term for First Nations groups or peoples in Australia.

75 This agency is now known as 'First Peoples—State Relations'. See also The Victorian Government, 'First Peoples – State Relations', www.firstpeoplesrelations.vic.gov.au/.

76 Interview with an Indigenous EPA officer.

> I would say it was key. I think having those key individuals on the ground keeps everybody on it. It puts ancestral remains front and centre in terms of the management of those lands. I don't think that it would have such a high profile if those key individuals weren't in those positions.

Meriam man Richard Weston, the Chief Executive Officer of Maari Ma Health, says that Indigenous staff 'have great cultural connections to communities' and that they are best placed to help find 'ways into those conversations' that discover the Indigenous community's priorities.[77] The local knowledge and insights of First Nations people are crucial for context-specific regulatory approaches affecting Country and Indigenous communities, and:

> [i]n the public sector, it's really critical because the public sector is obviously there to provide services and provide policy and, in a sense, it reflects … the Australian community.[78]

However, in Australia, First Nations people experience lower levels of employment than non-Indigenous people, and, while a steady increase in Indigenous employment has occurred since 1994, this has been mainly in the private sector.[79] Systemic barriers (often subtle), historical legacies and a lack of cultural safety contribute to the challenges facing First Nations Australians in many workplaces, in both the private and the public sector.[80]

---

77 ANZSOG, 'What Is Culturally Responsive Regulation?'.

78 Nigel Gladstone and Cameron Gooley, 'Government Says "More Work Required" to Boost Indigenous Jobs in Public Sector', *The Sydney Morning Herald*, 15 November 2021, www.smh.com.au/national/government-says-more-work-required-to-boost-indigenous-jobs-in-public-sector-20211111-p5980m.html; see also Liz Ellan, who explains that organisations that acknowledge and support community connections have an advantage over organisations that do not: Liz Ellan, 'Amplifying Indigenous Voices in the Workplace: How to Cultivate Genuine Cultural Safety for Sustainable Success'.

79 Australian Human Rights Commission, 'Human Rights and Aboriginal and Torres Strait Islander Peoples', Information Sheet (Australian Human Rights Commission), accessed 8 March 2025, humanrights.gov.au/sites/default/files/content/letstalkaboutrights/downloads/HRA_ATSI.pdf; Matthew Gray, Boyd Hunter, and Shaun Lohoar, 'Increasing Indigenous Employment Rates' (Closing the Gap Clearinghouse Issues Paper no. 3, Australian Government—Australian Institute of Health and Welfare, Australian Institute of Family Studies, March 2012), www.aihw.gov.au/getmedia/71bb346a-1b83-4038-a2f7-647e65a21445/ctg-ip03.pdf.aspx; House of Representatives Standing Committee on Indigenous Affairs, *Report on Indigenous Participation in Employment and Business* (The Parliament of the Commonwealth of Australia, August 2021), www.aph.gov.au/-/media/02_Parliamentary_Business/24_Committees/243_Reps_Committees/Indigenous/Pathways_and_Participation/Report.pdf?la=en%26hash=0FF8A974D86F9A87BB46B5F236D4FCFD110C515B.

80 Julie Lahn, 'Being Indigenous in the Bureaucracy: Narratives of Work and Exit', *The International Indigenous Policy Journal* 9, no. 1 (2018): 1–17, doi.org/10.18584/iipj.2018.9.1.3; Ellan, 'Amplifying Indigenous Voices'.

Indigenous employment in regulatory agencies, and government generally, is an essential part of reconciliation, to provide opportunities for economic empowerment, a sense of achievement and self-determination, and to ensure that First Nations people are directly interfacing with the policies and regulatory decisions affecting their communities.[81] It is recognised that recruiting First Nations people into government is challenging—the federal government experience reveals that less than a quarter of its public service agencies have First Nations employment levels of at least 3 per cent.[82] Suspicion of past government practices, socio-economic disadvantage, feelings of being undervalued, cultural preferences, racism, lack of opportunities to advance First Nations interests and lack of support for cultural obligations are some of the factors that dissuade First Nations people from entering government roles.[83]

Increasing the employment of First Nations people in regulatory agencies is important, but it must go well beyond merely setting employment targets and surface-level initiatives. Simply adding higher numbers of First Nations employees will not suffice if they are required to operate within the existing regulatory mindset and frameworks that do not fully support, understand or enable Indigenous perspectives.[84] A holistic approach is needed, one that recognises the complex nature of involving First Nations voices. This includes a commitment to making adaptive, long-term structural changes to ensure that First Nations staff are not only supported but know they are empowered to contribute their diverse worldviews—and that they will be heard and respected when they do.[85]

81 House of Representatives Standing Committee on Indigenous Affairs, *Report on Indigenous Participation*.

82 While First Nations Australians represent three per cent of Australia's population, only 21 of 90 government agencies assessed in 2021 had proportional representation, and nine had none. Gladstone and Gooley, '"More Work Required"'.

83 Leah M. Bromfield et al., *Barriers, Incentives and Strategies to Enchance [sic] Recruitment of Indigenous Carers*, (Australian Institute of Family Studies, 2007), aifs.gov.au/sites/default/files/publication-documents/paper2_0_0.pdf; Lahn, 'Being Indigenous'.

84 Lahn, 'Being Indigenous'.

85 By 'adaptive structural change', we mean that structural change should be an ongoing, evolving process that is moulded and re-envisioned by the insights, feedback and experiences of First Nations employees as they identify what works, what does not and what fails to align with their worldviews and practices. This is a shift away from assuming there is a single, easily imposed fixed way to reform structural challenges. See also Ellan, 'Amplifying Indigenous Voices'; Woodward et al., *Our Knowledge Our Way*'; 'Effective Indigenous Governance', The Australian Indigenous Governance Institute (AIGI), 2024, accessed 9 March 2025, aigi.org.au/toolkit/effective-indigenous-governance; Hunt, 'Engaging with Indigenous Australia'; Lahn, 'Being Indigenous'.

Principally, it must be recognised that First Nations people have unique expertise, lived experience and commitment to their community that can contribute in meaningful ways across governmental roles. Regulatory agencies must actively engage with the relational understandings and cultural obligations of their First Nations employees, ensuring that their cultural needs and perspectives are respected and embedded into the workplace. This requires creating an environment where First Nations cultural values and obligations are understood, supported and respected. A more nuanced approach that recognises the necessity of workplace flexibility—whether for family obligations or cultural practices such as Sorry Business[86]—will help create a genuinely inclusive, culturally responsive work environment that feels safe and nurturant for First Nations employees. When regulatory agencies embed this cultural competency into their organisational structures, First Nations' employees are more likely to feel respected, valued and empowered to contribute fully, without being reduced to a singular role or identity.[87] Additionally, research shows that embracing First Nations cultural obligations in an organisation's operations is often transformative, leading to innovation, creative problem-solving and enhanced operational resilience.[88] This approach promotes greater knowledge-sharing across the organisation and improved team collaboration and conflict resolution, while contributing to higher employee engagement and satisfaction—reflecting Indigenous practices of maintaining harmony and consensus-building.[89]

Furthermore, it is crucial to recognise that the challenges surrounding First Nations employment in government are not solely about job creation. These challenges are also about addressing deep-rooted societal and systemic issues that affect the labour market as a whole.[90] First Nations employees and businesses often bear a disproportionate burden in navigating broader historical and ongoing injustices, with disparities in health, education, incarceration and economic inequities impacting employment satisfaction and sustainability. These societal challenges require broader work and redress, NAIDOC Week being emblematic of what should be an everyday

86 'Sorry Business' refers to the cultural practices for mourning and attending funerals for family and community members, or mourning the loss of cultural connections to Country. There is no set time for Sorry Business; it is culturally contextual. Fair Work Ombudsman, 'Supporting Employees During Sorry Business', Australian Government, last modified October 2024, www.fairwork.gov.au/sites/default/files/2024-06/fd-first-nations-people-supporting-sorry-business-fact-sheet.pdf.

87 Eva et al., '"It's Self-Determination"'.

88 Ellan, 'Amplifying Indigenous Voices'.

89 Ellan, 'Amplifying Indigenous Voices'.

90 Eva et al., '"It's Self-Determination"'.

practice.[91] A commitment to long-term transformation of systemic issues would help address the historical deficit narrative while simultaneously benefiting everyone.[92] The inclusive, relational practices that First Nations cultures embody have the potential to improve the workplace experience for all employees, creating a more culturally responsive, equitable and supportive workplace.[93]

In considering a holistic approach to increasing First Nations employment in regulatory roles, a purposeful shift towards becoming a more restorative regulator may also encourage more First Nations people to be interested in taking up such roles. If First Nations people know that their worldviews, cultural needs, community obligations and Indigenous-led regulatory approaches are respected, encouraged and actively supported, the government workplace environment is likely to be more appealing, relevant and aligned with their values.

Voice with power: A pilot of Environment Protection on Country

One example of such a shift is EPA Victoria's recent pilot of Environment Protection on Country (EPOC—mentioned in Chapter 5), through which EPA Victoria sought to explore ways to 'build partnerships with Victoria's Traditional Owners and ensure our work is founded on the principles of self-determination'.[94] One expression of the EPA's commitment was the two-year pilot with six Traditional Owner corporations, starting in 2022.[95] Initially, the pilot was to be implemented with the EPA employing the EPOC positions. The idea evolved, following engagement with Traditional Owners, to involve the positioning of the EPOC roles at the corporation.

91 'NAIDOC' stands for 'National Aborigines and Islanders Day Observance Committee'. NAIDOC Week involves a week of celebrating First Nations culture, history and achievements based on a theme that changes each year. Held annually across Australia in the first week of July, it provides 'an opportunity for all Australians to learn about First Nations cultures and histories and participate in celebrations of the oldest, continuous living cultures on earth'. 'National NAIDOC Week', National NAIDOC Secretariat, accessed 8 March 2025, www.naidoc.org.au/about/naidoc-week. Both the public and private sectors across Australia provide employees with the opportunity to participate in NAIDOC week.

92 Ellan, 'Amplifying Indigenous Voices'.

93 Eva et al., '"It's Self-Determination"'.

94 Environment Protection Authority Victoria, *Strategic Plan 2022–27*, www.epa.vic.gov.au/strategic-plan.

95 In its Annual Report for 2023–24, EPA Victoria explained its approach: 'As part of developing a regulatory framework for the recognition of cultural knowledge and values, we started a 2-year Environment Protection on Country pilot program with 6 Traditional Owner corporations.' EPA Victoria, *Annual Report 2023-24*, www.epa.vic.gov.au/annual-report.

EPA Victoria agreed to fund the EPOC position (which included management overheads), along with training and capacity building to support a collaborative exploration of how the priorities for Country could be promoted within the EPA's work under the EP Act 2017.

While the pilot drew inspiration from other recent co-regulatory experimentation in the EPA,[96] the EPOC model with Traditional Owners primarily emphasised the building of relationships.[97] The EPOC roles set up as part of the pilot were not operational in the sense of exercising powers under the EP Act 2017. The roles encompassed all regulatory levels, the primary emphasis being on enabling the two-way sharing of knowledge and understanding. A work plan for each EPOC was designed to focus on the overlapping concerns for Country and the opportunities under the EP Act 2017 to prevent harm from pollution and waste. A key aspect of the program was the learning and development opportunities about the EP Act 2017 and its operational work, which helped participants to build an understanding of the EPA's operations, powers and functions. The EPOC position holders were provided with opportunities to participate in field activities, including inspections and other compliance activities, particularly where Traditional Owner corporations had concerns about pollution and waste impacts on Country.

Importantly, these roles could potentially create restorative opportunities for the healing of Country where there has been a risk of harm or where impacts have already occurred. Incorporating Traditional Owners into the regulatory process ensures the recognition of their traditional knowledge, cultural values, and environmental stewardship, informing both repair and prevention efforts and emphasising their perspectives on healing Country. This collaborative approach is inherently restorative, acknowledging the crucial role of First Nations peoples in environmental protection due to their extensive ownership and land stewardship traditions spanning millennia. Given that the pilot has concluded, it will be interesting to see whether this approach has unlocked a better understanding of cultural values, and how learnings from the pilot can inform collaborative approaches to environmental protection on the part of EPA Victoria and Traditional Owners.

96 For example, the OPLE pilot discussed in Chapter 5.

97 More details about the EPOC project are available from EPA Victoria.

Voice with power: The Aotearoa New Zealand experience

We can draw upon some additional lessons from Aotearoa New Zealand, where a new framework for a restorative health system has been developed, although it is not currently in force. This framework embraces Māori values, cultural practices and worldviews.[98] Recognising the ways in which people who are directly affected can be either empowered or excluded by government responses, the authors of this framework note the importance of supporting affected people and communities so that they can participate meaningfully in policy, program and regulatory processes. This means ensuring that the people who are directly affected have a voice in:

- who is involved
- where meetings will occur
- what questions will be asked
- what reparative or preventive actions will be required.[99]

Furthermore, the report accompanying the framework makes it clear that government agencies must learn from their failures and improve. This means they must support the affected people in the co-design, enabling them to participate meaningfully in governmental processes. Without these guarantees, 'response practices and procedures reinforce the impacts of colonisation or intergenerational trauma, or deep societal inequalities'. The authors view the restorative system in government as one inclined towards, among other things, valuing people and relationships, supporting partnerships between government agencies and iwi and Māori communities, and healing, learning and improving after harm.[100]

The inclusion of multiple knowledges

The value of unearthing and seeking to understand multiple perspectives is a fundamental Indigenous insight, deeply embedded in Indigenous wisdom and traditions and now increasingly recognised by astute contemporary scholars and policymakers who understand its significance for inclusive and

98 The National Collaborative for Restorative Initiatives in Health, *He Maungarongo Ki Ngā Iwi*.
99 The National Collaborative for Restorative Initiatives in Health, *He Maungarongo Ki Ngā Iwi*, 18.
100 The National Collaborative for Restorative Initiatives in Health, *He Maungarongo Ki Ngā Iwi*, 19.

effective governance.[101] Dr Tyson Yunkaporta refers to this as 'story-mind' in Indigenous Australian culture, 'a way of thinking that encourages dialogue about history from different perspectives, as well as the raw learning power of narrative itself'.[102]

Regrettably, however, much current empirical regulatory scholarship, as well as the most influential consultants who advise regulatory organisations, often exhibits the opposite approach.[103] Predominantly allocating their time to discussions in head offices talking to senior management, these consultants gain much of their wisdom from reading the policy documents authored by the same managers they seek to influence—a truly 'closed book' of insights that cements business as usual. Their failure to travel to the peripheries of the jurisdiction to seek out the wisdom of Indigenous peoples regarding ecological justice dooms their findings to incompleteness and reduced relevance. Even if they do talk to elders whose feet are rooted in the earth, too many consultants and regulatory advisers focus on the 'problems' perceived from their managerial or Western knowledge viewpoint, rather than on the vast and enduring Indigenous wisdom and perspectives.[104]

A restorative and regenerative focus shifts us beyond managerial preferences and calls on us to seek perspectives that transcend the C-suite and evidence-based targets grounded in conventional approaches. As scholars Marnee Shay, Grace Sarra and Jo Lampert make clear: 'What counts as evidence should privilege Indigenous voices, intellectualism, sovereignties, strengths and aspirations.'[105]

In Chapters 7 and 8, we explored how Indigenous science encompasses a holistic understanding of land, water, air, biodiversity and climate change. It is contextually informed science that relies on situated skills that often elude Western scientists trained in traditional university settings. This stands

---

101 Yunkaporta, *Sand Talk*; Eva et al., '"It's Self-Determination"'; Anthea Roberts and Nicolas Lamp, *Six Faces of Globalization: Who Wins, Who Loses, and Why It Matters*, 1st ed. (Harvard University Press, 2021), doi.org/10.4159/9780674269811.

102 Yunkaporta, *Sand Talk*, 84.

103 For example, First Nations people often report research failings that include inadequate consultation, cross-cultural insensitivities and a lack of communication, finding that 'there is little research examining what constitutes a benefit from Indigenous Australians points of view'. Roxanne Bainbridge et al., 'No One's Discussing the Elephant in the Room: Contemplating Questions of Research Impact and Benefit in Aboriginal and Torres Strait Islander Australian Health Research', *BMC Public Health* 15, no. 696 (2015): 1–10, doi.org/10.1186/s12889-015-2052-3.

104 Marnee Shay, Grace Sarra, and Jo Lampert, 'Indigenous Education Policy, Practice and Research: Unravelling the Tangled Web', *Australian Educational Researcher* 50, no. 1 (2023): 73–88, doi.org/10.1007/s13384-022-00581-w.

105 Shay et al., 'Indigenous Education Policy', 74.

in stark contrast to university-trained Indigenous citizen scientists, who uniquely offer a situated synthesis of both knowledge systems, often referred to as 'two-way science':[106]

> The salience, legitimacy and credibility of scientific knowledge is probably most apparent to scientists, whilst the salience, legitimacy and credibility of Indigenous or local knowledge is probably most apparent to Indigenous and local knowledge holders. Those who can bridge these knowledge systems have particular value in this setting.[107]

Cultural burning of Country is one example of this highly situated wisdom. Cultural burning is an Indigenous fire management practice that favours native plants over weeds, clears land for access and improves the health of Country—among other purposes.[108] Using traditional knowledge, Indigenous fire practitioners are able to determine what time of year is just right for safe burning, following strict cultural protocols.[109]

We interviewed an officer from Parks Victoria about a growing convergence between the findings of ecological science on the benefits of burning for maintaining ecological health, and traditional burns and accompanying traditional ecological knowledge.[110] The story they told us reflected an approach of keeping a light footprint of fire on Country, preparing it for adversity. The interviewee acknowledged the similarities, explaining the concept of a 'mosaic burn', which embodies the principle of 'right' fire for Country, an approach that carefully considers the unique needs of each landscape, ensuring sustainability and resilience.[111] The interviewee explained:

> Mosaic, it's about patch burning. To get patch burning, you burn in the cooler months of the year so the fire is not as intense, whereas over the spring and autumn burns … if we're trying to make the

106 Woodward et al., *Our Knowledge Our Way*.

107 Helen C. Wheeler and Meredith Root-Bernstein, 'Informing Decision-Making with Indigenous and Local Knowledge and Science', *The Journal of Applied Ecology* 57, no. 9 (2020): 1634–43, doi.org/10.1111/1365-2664.13734.

108 Michael-Shawn Fletcher et al., 'Catastrophic Bushfires, Indigenous Fire Knowledge and Reframing Science in Southeast Australia', *Fire* 4, no. 3 (2021): 61, doi.org/10.3390/fire4030061; Reynolds and Cameron, 'Yarning Up'.

109 Reynolds and Cameron, 'Yarning Up', 4.

110 Parks Victoria is a Victorian Government agency tasked with protecting and managing over 4 million hectares that include 3,000 land and marine parks and reserves. The agency works in partnership with Traditional Owners. See 'About Us', Parks Victoria, accessed 8 March 2025, www.parks.vic.gov.au/about-us.

111 Bush Heritage Australia, 'Fighting Fire in the Dry', 8 February 2023, www.bushheritage.org.au/news/fighting-fire-in-the-dry; Ricky Sproule, 'Lore of the Land: Right Fire, Right Country, Right Time', *The Citizen*, 18 October 2025, www.thecitizen.org.au/articles/lore-of-the-land-right-fire-right-country-right-time.

> forest safe and in regards to the communities, in case a big fire goes through, we'll probably burn those a bit more intense to remove as much of the fuel loads as we can.
>
> Whereas, for biodiversity values, it's about habitat management, about restoration of species. We don't want a burn that's too hot, depending on the species, of course. Some species like a really hot burn, other species prefer a cooler burn. Traditional burning is part of that. It's about probably more mosaic cool burns.[112]

Curious about the cultural context of traditional burns, we asked for more details. The officer explained further:

> [W]ith traditional burning, they burn the traditional way, so … they'll go out and they'll fire stick it, they'll go around deliberately. It's part of their culture. There's a spiritual context to the traditional burning, and they'll light up in a certain way, and they'll have members of their community, elders, getting involved. There's a real structure and approach around traditional burning. It's not just lighting up and doing mosaic burns. There's actually a spiritual connection to the land, which the Traditional Owners still carry, and it's around respect and acknowledgement, and the elders getting involved. And they'll tend to just dot fires everywhere—but strategically—to follow through on their intent as Traditional Owners.

We finished up by asking whether Indigenous people articulated healing Country through burning as also being about healing themselves, and the officer replied:

> Yes. They certainly do that talk there. Before we do our traditional burns, there will be a briefing before, to explain. The Traditional Owners will generally explain what they're trying to achieve out of these and what their aspirations are, and the message they're trying to deliver.

Rhys Swain, National Fire Program Manager with Bush Heritage Australia, an NGO that works together with Traditional Owners on fire management, further notes that: 'At the right time, and in the right conditions, fire can be a healing force.'[113] Therefore, what seems a skill of tough love of Country is actually a skill of soft mosaics that reduces the carbon entering the atmosphere and decreases the opportunity for much hotter, massive fires.

112 Interview with an officer from Parks Victoria.

113 Rhys Swain, 'Do You Know How Fire Is a Healing Force?', *Bush Heritage Australia* newsletter, 15 September 2023 (on file with authors).

In its holistic approach, traditional burning is an example of regenerative regulation that 'is reflexive to local environmental conditions and cues', respects the ecological balance through maintaining biodiversity, reduces the risk of catastrophic fire and mitigates carbon emissions.[114] It is, in effect, a practice that prevents harm to Country, helps heal it and guides the making of 'right' decisions—ensuring that the 'right fire', 'right water' and 'right plants' are used in harmony with the land, and with its human and other-than-human inhabitants.[115]

Yet, regulatory and legal attitudes that downplay Indigenous knowledge, fail to acknowledge customary laws and create confusion due to scientific uncertainties can constitute a hurdle in First Nations communities' management of landscapes.[116]

Restorative regulation can help work through such barriers by promoting dialogue and collaboration between the First Nations fire practitioners, governments and researchers, to foster a sense of shared responsibility and the co-management of resources. In supporting cultural burning, regulatory agencies are facilitating restorative values through acknowledging past mistakes, seeking to heal the land and disrupted relationships with Country, wildlife and plant kin. The recommendations from the 2020 Royal Commission into the Black Summer fires included an open called for government agencies to find ways to support Indigenous fire management.[117]

114 Fletcher et al., 'Catastrophic Bushfires', 4.

115 Fletcher et al., 'Catastrophic Bushfires', 6; Djaara, *Dhelkunyangu Gatjin Working Together to Heal Water Djaara Gatjin Strategy*, Dja Dja Wurrung Clans Aboriginal Corporation (2023), djandak.com.au/wp-content/uploads/2023/10/Dhelkunyangu-Gatjin-Working-together-to-heal-water-Gatjin-Strategy-2023.pdf; Yindjibarndi Water, 'Company Profile'; Anne Buchan et al., *Right Plant, Right Way: Report 2021: A First Nations led Review of Revegetation in Victoria*, Yindjibarndi Water, 2021, www.anpc.asn.au/wp-content/uploads/2021/10/Right-Plant-Right-Way.pdf; '"Right-Way" Science', Bush Heritage Australia, accessed 8 March 2025, www.bushheritage.org.au/what-we-do/our-priorities/science/right-way-science.

116 Fletcher et al., 'Catastrophic Bushfires', 11.

117 In the 2019–20 bushfires, over 24 million hectares were burnt, 33 people died, and around three billion non-human animals were killed or displaced, many of which were threatened species. The 2020 Royal Commission into National Natural Disaster Arrangements investigated the bushfires and recommended that 'Australian, state, territory and local governments should engage further with Traditional Owners to explore the relationship between Indigenous land and fire management and natural disaster resilience' (Recommendation 18.1). Recommendation 18.2 recommended that these governments 'explore further opportunities to leverage Indigenous land and fire management insights, in the development, planning and execution of public land management activities'. Australian Government National Emergency Management Agency, *National Report: Royal Commission into National Natural Disaster Arrangements Recommendations Implementation Status* (Australian Government, October 2020), last modified 8 September 2024, www.nema.gov.au/about-us/governance-and-reporting/reviews/royal-commission-into-natural-disaster#TheReport.

Through supporting a restorative Indigenous traditional approach to regulation and management of the environment, cultural burning can lead to the regeneration of both the environment and the communities connected to it.

Another example is the consideration of cultural flows by water regulators.[118] In the context of Victoria and First Nations people, environmental flow (or 'water for the environment') focuses on keeping waterways healthy and flowing, helping the surrounding plants and animals to thrive, while cultural flows extend this concern by aiming to improve the quality of life for First Nations people and ensuring that their traditional practices can continue.[119]

The concept of cultural flows was explained to us by a Gunditjmara man with government experience, who described it as follows:

> What's a cultural flow compared to environmental flow? Cultural flow could be something like a wetting. Big rainfall in a certain part of Victoria. Storages have fallen in that particular place, and we want to send some water down a particular stream. And then people go, 'so that's called an environmental flow.'
>
> But I think it's a lot more complex than that. We send some water down. Cultural flow in that context could be, '[Y]ou know what, through the Murray [River], long-necked turtles may be breeding in another two weeks' time, can we hold that water for another two weeks to allow that?' Why I say long-necked turtles, [they] are a totem of Yorta Yorta people. They are connected to that particular species, so something like a cultural flow of waiting two weeks for them to have fresh, cleaner water running through, for them to be able to spawn or whatever the word is. I'm not a scientist, sorry, but [for them to] be able to give birth to more long-necked turtles, for instance, during that particular time – that's classed as a cultural flow.

---

118 Cultural flows have a range of objectives, which include improving the quality of life for First Nations people, enabling them to continue their traditional practices and supporting their management to keep the waters healthy. Importantly, cultural flows involve the First Nations people 'deciding themselves where and when water should be delivered', which necessitates that they have agency in decision-making about the allocation and management of water. Siobhan Davies, Graham R. Marshall, and Malcolm Ridges, 'A Property Rights Schema for Cultural Flows in the Murray Darling Basin, Australia', *Australasian Journal of Environmental Management* 30, nos. 3–4 (2023): 393–415, 395, doi.org/10.1080/14486563.2023.2281562 (citing Weir et al.); Australian Government Murray-Darling Basin Authority, 'First Nations Cultural Flows', last modified 16 July 2024, www.mdba.gov.au/water-use/water-first-nations/first-nations-cultural-flows. Returning water, water rights and management to Traditional Owners will 'improve the spiritual, cultural, natural, environmental, social and economic conditions of their Nations.' Environmental Justice Australia, 'Cultural Flows at Margooya Lagoon', 2023, envirojustice.org.au/legal-work/first-nations-justice/cultural-flows-at-margooya-lagoon/.

119 Australian Government Murray-Darling Basin Authority, 'First Nations Cultural Flows'.

In 2023, the State Government of Victoria took a monumental step by issuing two water licences to the Gunaikurnai Land and Waters Aboriginal Corporation, the Registered Aboriginal Party representing the Gunaikurnai people, Traditional Owners of much of Gippsland in south-eastern Victoria. These allocations represent a significant move to strengthen Gunaikurnai connections to Country, supporting the Gunaikurnai people's cultural, environmental and socio-economic priorities. It follows the milestone issuance of a 2,000 megalitre water licence from the Mitchell River in 2020, marking a significant step towards restoring customary practices and protecting cultural value through the recognition of cultural flows.[120]

Such changes are essential for enabling First Nations voices to be heard, acknowledging their rights and recognising their cultural responsibilities in governance. This is not merely about granting licences or policy tweaking but involves creating a regulatory culture that actively supports the cultural responsibilities of First Nations people to care for and regenerate waters. Just as water sustains life, these reforms must provide the necessary structural framework to ensure cultural flows are recognised and upheld, and that First Nations communities are actively involved in guiding the pathways to water policymaking, planning and management decision-making.[121] This could be supported by regulatory reforms such as placing a mandatory obligation on regulators to consider cultural rights in decision-making, as well as requiring regulatory staff to engage in deeper, collaborative dialogue that honours Indigenous decision-making about what cultural water needs in order to heal and regenerate.

Another way to ensure that First Nations perspectives, knowledges and management practices are informing and guiding caring for Country is through partnerships with Traditional Owner organisations, as well as by supporting and using Indigenous rangers.[122] However, it is important to avoid repeating the issues we discussed earlier, in which problems and solutions are defined according to the regulatory partner's parameters and preferences. This can be prevented by ensuring that Indigenous worldviews

120 William Howard, 'Water Rights Returned to Gippsland Traditional Owners in Landmark Victorian Government Deal', *ABC News*, 12 October 2023, www.abc.net.au/news/2023-10-12/traditional-owners-given-more-water-in-landmark-announcement/102963860.

121 For example, see the *Baring* (pathways) to Djaara making decisions for *gatjin* (water) in Djaara, *Dhelkunyangu Gatjin*, 12–13. This covers both First Nations direct decision-making and 'provision of technical & cultural advice where others make decisions', 13.

122 Many Indigenous ranger programs are supported by relevant government agencies. This collaboration both acknowledges traditional practices and improves environmental health. See also Marcia Langton, *The Welcome to Country Handbook: A Guide to Indigenous Australia* (Hardie Grant Explore, 2023), 114; Reynolds and Cameron, 'Yarning Up'.

and needs are placed first, with the partnership recognised and respected as an Indigenous-led initiative. One good model of this can be found in the organisation Bush Heritage Australia, which is respected for its 'non-interventionist, non-managerial approach' to partnerships and ranger programs.[123] Additionally, both financial and structural support from the institutional partner(s) is crucial for the effective governance and sustainability of Traditional Owner organisations.[124]

Our short foray into the importance of embracing multiple perspectives and valuing Indigenous wisdom and traditions, both as a restorative value and as a restorative regulatory practice, has indicated that regulators must prioritise the cultivation of inclusive, regenerative spaces for dialogue and collaboration. Furthermore, it calls for a willingness to engage with worldviews that might be initially unfamiliar in the conventional regulatory context but are essential for more just and effective regulatory approaches—leading us to the First Nations tradition of yarning.

Yarning: Non-linear, culturally safe storytelling

Yarning or storytelling is an essential and engaging relational method of communication, deep listening and teaching among First Nations peoples.[125] Within Indigenous Australian culture, yarning or storytelling is a circular (non-linear), 'fluid, ongoing process, a moving dialogue interspersed with interjections, interpretations, and additions' that contains shared lived experience of family and community, keeping the storyteller intimately connected with ancestors, family, community members and outsiders.[126] Yarning is a way of immersing oneself with, and connecting to, Country relationally and spiritually, and of establishing respectful relationships.[127]

123 Martin, Bush Heritage Australia, 205.

124 Martin, Bush Heritage Australia, 204.

125 Gawaian Bodkin-Andrews et al., 'Mudjil'Dya'Djurali Dabuwa'Wurrata (How the White Waratah Became Red): D'harawal Storytelling and Welcome to Country "Controversies"', *AlterNative: An International Journal of Indigenous Peoples* 12, no. 5 (2016): 480–97, doi.org/10.20507/AlterNative.2016.12.5.4; Alasdair Vance et al., 'Culture, Health and Well-Being: Yarning with the Victorian First Nations Community', *International Journal of Indigenous Health* 19, 1 (2024): 1–17, doi.org/10.32799/ijih.v19i1.41307; Reynolds and Cameron, 'Yarning Up'.

126 Lynore K. Geia, Barbara Hayes, and Kim Usher, 'Yarning/Aboriginal Storytelling: Towards an Understanding of an Indigenous Perspective and Its Implications for Research Practice', *Contemporary Nurse* 46, 1 (2013): 13–17, doi.org/10.5172/conu.2013.46.1.13; Vance et al., 'Culture, Health and Well-Being'.

127 Reynolds and Cameron, 'Yarning Up'; Vance et al., 'Culture, Health and Well-Being'.

It includes not only the stories that can be shared but also those that cannot be told, key silences that must be adhered to and that reflect the inside/outside knowledge of women's or men's business and protocols, and the respectful, silent ways of knowing Country.[128] As a healing ritual, yarning is culturally safe and can be a way to tell a shared trauma story that helps those affected to come to terms with the emotional pain caused by what has happened to them in their past, and to make sense of their personal story in relationship to the collective, communal story.[129]

We recognise the synergies between yarning practices and restorative practices, as each opens space for meaningful dialogue—one that is safe and respectful, and opens up fresh approaches to addressing challenges, including those within regulatory contexts. Acknowledging the importance of and need for storytelling means setting aside time and creating a culturally safe place, such as a restorative or yarning circle. These spaces help ensure deep listening:

> [T]o meaningfully unlock the varying lessons and layers of meaning requires a much deeper reciprocal interaction between the story, the storyteller, the story-listener, and Country for the story itself over time.[130]

This deep listening process 'will facilitate the overcoming of non-Indigenous silences and erasures of Indigenous knowledges … It should be real listening, and hearing.'[131]

At the same time, it is important to respect and protect Indigenous cultural and intellectual property (ICIP).[132] The practices of storytelling and yarning circles should not be co-opted into regulatory frameworks or used by non-Indigenous organisations in ways that undermine, sideline or misinterpret their cultural significance. Their use in synergy with restorative regulatory approaches must remain grounded in the authentic, self-determined needs and practices of First Nations people.

---

128 Caroline Josephs, 'Silence as a Way of Knowing in Yolngu Indigenous Australian Storytelling', in *Negotiating the Sacred II: Blasphemy and Sacrilege in the Arts*, ed. Elizabeth Burns Coleman and Maria Suzette Fernandes Dias (ANU E Press, 2008), doi.org/10.22459/NS.12.2008.

129 Vance et al., 'Culture, Health and Well-Being'.

130 Bodkin-Andrews et al., 'Mudjil'Dya'Djurali Dabuwa'Wurrata', 481.

131 Bodkin-Andrews et al., 'Mudjil'Dya'Djurali Dabuwa'Wurrata, 492.

132 Shields et al., 'Creating an Authorizing Environment'. Indigenous Cultural and Intellectual Property (ICIP) is a broad term that refers what is often known as 'cultural heritage', covering 'all aspects of Aboriginal and Torres Strait Islander peoples' traditional knowledge and cultural expressions'. Arts+Law, 'Indigenous Cultural and Intellectual Property (ICIP), last modified 21 July 2024, www.artslaw.com.au/information-sheet/indigenous-cultural-intellectual-property-icip-aitb/.

Regulatory staff can deepen their understanding of First Nations people's worldviews and Indigenous regulatory approaches, and more richly appreciate their diversity, if they purposefully aim to encourage Indigenous storytelling as an integral part of restorative processes in comprehending and healing harm, and for informing everyday work practices. When yarning is seen as a way of celebrating culture, it becomes clear that 'First Nations storytelling methods are a positive and empowering process'.[133] In this way, a restorative regulator attuned to facilitating Indigenous storytelling helps to shape more inclusive and respectful regulatory approaches that centre First Nations people's lived experiences and lifeworlds.

Co-production in caring for Country: Full engagement, learning by doing

> *Engagement requires a relationship built on trust and integrity: it is a sustained relationship between groups of people working towards shared goals; on the spectrum of engagement, a high level of participation works better than lower levels (such as consultation) where problems are complex.*[134]

We complete our discussion of Indigenous-led regulatory approaches by looking at co-production as an Indigenous-led regenerative and restorative regulatory practice. Earlier in Chapter 7, we discussed a case study of a co-production for rehabilitation that involved building frog ponds as a restorative project collaboration between a local council, a local catchment authority and DJAARA, the Aboriginal Corporation of the Djaara people. Several of our interviewees, some staff from EPA Victoria and some Djaara individuals recalled this as a successful collaboration. Admittedly, one EPA staff member reflected that for the EPA, it was still early days: '[A]s an organisation … we're at a very young stage of restorative justice, and its linkage to Indigenous cultures.'[135]

This case study revealed the value of co-production as a regenerative, restorative approach that can bring regulators and other parties together into a fruitful, collaborative relationship with First Nations people. However,

133 Bodkin-Andrews et al., 'Mudjil'Dya'Djurali Dabuwa'Wurrata', 485.
134 Hunt, 'Engaging with Indigenous Australia', 1.
135 Interview with an EPA Victoria officer.

much learning remains to be done in this area, and it is essential for regulators to take a proactive stance to ensure that co-production becomes an integral part of the restorative ensemble.

There is no single, universally accepted definition of co-production or co-design.[136] However, key elements commonly recognised as integral to co-production with Indigenous peoples (and other communities) include:

- inclusion of diverse voices and perspectives
- genuine and meaningful collaboration
- recognition of Indigenous peoples and community members as 'experts in their own lives, [meaning that] policy should be designed by people with relevant lived experience'[137]
- Indigenous-led and culturally safe co-production, able to create 'ethical and creative spaces for Indigenous peoples to lead research and planning agendas to ensure multiple evidence-based, decision-making support [for] their own agendas for communities and Country'[138]
- principled self-determination, enabling 'Indigenous leadership and governance … to assist in shifting power dynamics', allowing Indigenous solutions to be brought forward[139]
- shared decision-making that legitimises different sources of knowledge 'while respecting and protecting differences in how knowledge is generated, interpreted, and applied'[140]
- shared power.[141]

136 Shay et al., 'Indigenous Education Policy, Practice and Research', 81. We use 'co-production' as the broader term, encompassing both the design and implementation of collaborative solutions. Co-design, as one phase of this process, focuses on planning and problem-solving, while co-production extends into the ongoing delivery and maintenance of outcomes and relationships. See also Chapter 8 for a discussion of co-production in relation to citizen collaboration, learning and repair.

137 Janice Rieger, *Right to Participate: Co-Designing Disability Policies in Australia*, Briefing Paper 12, QUT Centre for Justice (December 2020); Emma Blomkamp, 'The Promise of Co-Design for Public Policy' *Australian Journal of Public Administration* 77, no. 4 (2018): 729–43, doi.org/10.1111/1467-8500.12310.

138 Catherine J. Robinson et al., 'Coproduction Mechanisms to Weave Indigenous Knowledge, Artificial Intelligence, and Technical Data to Enable Indigenous-Led Adaptive Decision Making: Lessons from Australia's Joint Managed Kakadu National Park', *Ecology and Society* 27, no. 4 (2022), doi.org/10.5751/ES-13747-270436.

139 Shay, Sarra and Lampert, 'Indigenous Education Policy', 81.

140 Robinson et al., 'Coproduction Mechanisms'.

141 Emma Blomkamp, 'Navigating Power and Acknowledging Positionality' (blog), 8 February 2022, emmablomkamp.com/blog/navigating-power.

Co-production between regulators and First Nations people is 'in practice … in the spirit of reconciliation, working together interculturally'.[142] Indigenous leadership of co-production projects is essential, as is cooperation among others relevant to achieving the outcomes, including civil society, scientists and NGOs.[143] Indigenous-led co-production includes what First Nations filmmaker and author Victor Steffensen refers to as 'praction'. This term was coined by the late Kuku Thaypan Elder George Musgrave, better known as 'Poppy'. Poppy's use of the word 'praction' is a beautifully apt portmanteau of the words *practice* and *action*.[144] This notion of praction picks up on our discussion of co-production in Chapter 8, where we related the restorative concept of 'learning by doing'. As Steffensen says:

> Learning Aboriginal land management is always best done when it is practised traditionally out on country. To live the knowledge every day by going out on the land, hunting, doing bushcraft, learning about the plants and animals in between caring for every special place. You can't learn properly sitting in a classroom or talking about it. Watching the Elders doing the activities, seeing the process happen before your eyes. Following them as they take the lead in nurturing their land and culture. The best way to learn is to live the land and the knowledge as much as possible.[145]

Co-production is a relatively new experiment, and it is not without its risks, such as co-option by authorities, power imbalances, resource constraints, inertia and possible capture. But such challenges can be met restoratively with an intent to keep reorienting and supporting it, to focus on full engagement, learning by doing, and respecting the leadership and knowledge of Indigenous participants. It can be implemented from the stage of co-designing shared projects right through to their evaluation. Evaluation frameworks created by First Nations Australians already exist to draw on, and '[c]o-designing evaluations can strengthen, improve and provide a sense of ownership' for Indigenous participants.[146] Collaborative evaluation has

142 Gammage and Pascoe, *First Knowledges Country*, 6.

143 Danilo Urzedo et al., 'Indigenous Environmental Justice Through Coproduction of Mining Restoration Supply Chains in Australia', *Restoration Ecology* 30, no. S1 (2022): 1–7, doi.org/10.1111/rec.13748; Robinson et al., 'Coproduction Mechanisms'.

144 Victor Steffensen, *Fire Country: How Indigenous Fire Management Could Help Save Australia* (Hardie Grant, 2020), 145.

145 Steffenson, *Fire Country*, 143.

146 Wright et al., 'Co-Designing ', 4.

a further restorative benefit in that 'the vision is not activating evaluation as a means to an end, but rather achieving long-term sustainable benefits through deepening relationships and community inclusion'.[147]

Viewing co-production as a regenerative, Indigenous-led regulatory approach makes an important contribution to restorative regulation. Placing Indigenous voices and praction at the forefront of caring for Country initiatives undertaken with the regulator will help build trust, encourage joint consideration of the complexities involved and develop genuine, enduring partnerships. Getting to this place requires a proactive willingness on the part of regulators, along with a commitment to learn by doing and learn from mistakes. Co-production can help integrate diverse perspectives in the regeneration of Country and communities after harm, shaping a restorative regulatory framework rooted in respect for the wisdom of First Nations people and supportive of their duties to Country.

Restoring balance, healing Country and connecting wisdoms

Going back to the Creation time/the Dreaming, countless generations of First Nations people of Australia have been stewards of knowledge systems that offer profound insights into governance, environmental care and community wellbeing. Rather than seeing complex social problems as 'wicked' or insurmountable, First Nations communities are drawing upon their deeply ingrained knowledge, their stories and their relationality with Country to respond in adaptive and culturally grounded ways. The understandings generated by these sources of knowledge (including Indigenous science and traditional ecological knowledge) and interconnectedness are being brought into dialogue with contemporary scientific approaches—interpreted through Indigenous ways of knowing, being and doing—to create adaptive and enduring responses to today's challenges.[148]

147 Wright et al., 'Co-Designing', 4.

148 Rhonda Marriott and Tracy Reibel, 'Resilience, Renewal and Hope in Australian Indigenous-Led Primary Health Care Initiatives', *Primary Health Care Research & Development* 22 (2021): 1–2, doi.org/10.1017/s1463423621000712.

This culturally sensitised synthesis demonstrates how Indigenous ways of knowing, being and doing offer critical insights and solutions that are grounded in cultural practices perfected over millennia, addressing contemporary challenges while reinforcing the role of First Nations communities as leaders in governance, environmental stewardship and human and non-human community wellbeing.[149] The examples we discussed, of cultural flows and mosaic burning, which have now been incorporated into Victoria's environmental regulatory practice, amply demonstrate this.

We live in an era where corporate logic, Western views on the social and ecological determinants of wellbeing and top-down governance shape public life, political discourse and regulatory culture. Yet, the First Nations experiences and perspectives shared in this chapter demonstrate that governance imposed from above—rationalised as the dominant model—falls short of achieving environmental health and repair, and fails to recognise the holistic understandings and approaches needed for true regeneration. Sustainable, effective and holistic regeneration must be grounded in community wisdom, grassroots knowledge and diverse, deep-time perspectives.[150]

Indigenous-led regulatory approaches offer powerful insights into the restorative and regenerative practices needed to reset regulatory governance to be more attentive to 'Respect, Connect, Reflect and Direct'. These approaches emphasise fundamental principles for sustaining life, wellbeing and relationships among human and other-than-human communities: the deep interconnection of all beings and systems, our shared responsibility to protect as stewards or custodians, the importance of empowered voices and the wisdom held in multiple perspectives. These principles naturally align with restorative justice practices while contributing their own unique strengths and insights in the context of First Nations people's lived experiences and governance systems, providing an opportunity for working together and mutual learning.

---

149 Glynn-McDonald, 'First Nations Systems Thinking'.

150 Charles Taylor, Patrizia Nanz, and Madeleine Beaubien Taylor, *Reconstructing Democracy: How Citizens Are Building from the Ground Up*, 1st ed. (Harvard University Press, 2020), 2, doi.org/10.4159/9780674246652; Emmanuel Vaughan-Lee, 'Deep Time Diligence: An Interview with Tyson Yunkaporta', *Emergence Magazine*, 19 February 2024, emergencemagazine.org/conversation/deep-time-diligence/.

However, this alignment comes with an important responsibility for all regulatory practitioners and scholars: we must move beyond mere acknowledgement of Indigenous contributions. True justice requires recognising Indigenous peoples as active partners in shaping and directing how their regulatory approaches are applied and adapted, and it must involve their direct leadership in the creation and implementation of solutions grounded in their millennia knowledge and practices, integrated with contemporary science, to forge new shared pathways forward. Restorative regulation resists one-size-fits-all solutions. Instead, it creates space for diverse perspectives and practices, ensuring Indigenous communities maintain agency over their traditional knowledge and its interpretation, protection and application.[151] This collaborative approach, with Indigenous voices at its centre, points the way towards more effective and equitable regulatory systems.

We are now reaching the last stage of our research journey. In the final chapter, we gather the many seeds planted—some awaiting nourishment, others beginning to emerge and some already thriving—with the aim of cultivating a cohesive understanding of how to grow as a restorative regulator.

151 Shields et al., 'Creating an Authorizing Environment'.

10

Growing as a restorative regulator

Source: Author.

> *You could be saying one thing but your hands or your actions are doing other things. That in itself is going to … be a mark of whether there's going to be this genuine relationship that starts … Just be mindful of bringing your heart to work.*
>
> —Josephine Bourne[1]

1 Josephine Bourne, in ANZSOG, 'What is Culturally Responsive Regulation?'.

This chapter marks the final stage of our research journey. In it, we outline how to grow a restorative regulator, providing transformative recommendations for integrating restorative values across the organisation and the broader regulatory ecosystem. We advocate for a departure from rigid, mechanistic models of regulatory change, instead embracing organic, adaptive approaches grounded in relationships, trust and care. Through a three-part restorative strategy—planting opportunities, nurturing practices and cultivating internal culture—we offer a framework for embedding restorative regulation as a living, evolving practice.

In this concluding chapter, we bring together the key ideas seeded throughout the book to answer a fundamental question: How do you grow a restorative regulator?

Our central insight is that developing a restorative regulator begins with cultivating a restorative community within the organisation itself. As Ted Wachtel puts it, 'Restorative practices must be systemic, not situational.'[2] Meaningful change requires embedding restorative values across every facet of the regulatory organisation.

Moreover, regulators do not operate in isolation. As we have emphasised throughout this book, they are embedded within complex ecosystems—interacting with political systems, other regulators, regulated entities and communities. Restorative approaches must therefore be designed to operate at multiple scales: from individual interactions to community-wide processes. This broader, systemic perspective is essential.

To support this shift, we have encouraged thinking about regulatory design in organic terms, rather than relying on the more familiar metaphor of the regulatory toolbox. This shift involves two key mindset changes.

2 Ted Wachtel, 'Restorative Justice in Everyday Life: Beyond the Formal Ritual', *International Institute for Restorative Practices Graduate School*, 18 February 1999, www.iirp.edu/news/restorative-justice-in-everyday-life-beyond-the-formal-ritual.

First, a restorative approach is grounded in a relational worldview—recognising that everything is embedded within networks of relationships. In this view, regulation is not just about addressing wrongful acts, but about creating conditions that support wellbeing, accountability, relational repair and mutual flourishing.[3]

Second, regulatory change is an evolving and adaptive process. Rather than fixing problems with tools, restorative regulators work like gardeners: they observe, respond to their environment and support new growth. This adaptive management approach involves continuous learning, real-time monitoring and openness to stakeholder feedback. As interdisciplinary scholars Anthea Roberts and Taylor St John have suggested, regulators should be seen as *gardeners* or *landscape architects*—tending to the health of the whole ecosystem, not just enforcing rules.[4]

This organic framing is reinforced by recent research, such as the *Trust Flows* report.[5] A key insight of that report is that trust must flow both ways. For regulation to be legitimate and effective, governments must not only earn the trust of communities but also *demonstrate* trust in them. This reinforces the core ethos of restorative regulation: that relationships of care, accountability and mutual recognition are foundational to success.

These ideas underpin the three-part methodology for growing restorative regulation developed throughout this book. In the rest of this chapter, we illustrate how to put the three different parts into practice in the context of becoming a restorative regulatory organisation:

1. **Plant and nurture seeds of restorative practice.** Identify spaces where restorative approaches can emerge, whether through legislation (as with EPA Victoria and the EP Act 2017) or more informal innovations such as community reference groups.

3 Jenna Bednar, 'Governance for Human Social Flourishing', *Daedalus* 152, no. 1 (2023): 31–45, doi.org/10.1162/daed_a_01958; Charlotte V. O. Witvliet et al., 'Accountability: Construct Definition and Measurement of a Virtue Vital to Flourishing'.

4 Anthea Roberts and Taylor St John, 'Complex Designers and Emergent Design: Reforming the Investment Treaty System', *American Journal of International Law* 116, no. 1 (2022): 96–149, doi.org/10.1017/ajil.2021.57.

5 Mark Duckworth, Christine Horn and Michele Grossman, *Do Governments Trust Communities? The Trust Flows Project Research Report* (Centre for Resilient and Inclusive Societies, 2024), doi.org/10.56311/FZLZ2190.

2. **Embed, nurture and expand restorative practices.** Support the transition from pilot efforts to sustained and operationalised practices, recognising that restorative and conventional approaches can coexist and enrich one another.
3. **Find ways to connect restorative approaches across the entire ecosystem.** Ensure the regulator itself models restorative values by fostering a restorative culture, empowering staff, supporting innovation and creating connections across the wider ecosystem.

This is an iterative and relational process, built on learning, adaptation and feedback loops. As restorative practices take root and demonstrate value—through stronger relationships, better conflict resolution and active community engagement—they generate momentum for further growth. However, it does need to be done in a deliberate and meaningful way, with leadership and sufficient resourcing.

We now turn to each part of this approach in more detail, introducing three steps that offer practical guidance for how restorative approaches can take root, grow and thrive within the regulatory ecosystem.

Step 1: Seeding restorative justice in the regulatory terrain: Identifying opportunities

> *It's looking for those opportunities, it's trialling some things and then seeing what sticks and what doesn't stick and [asking]: What shall we try next?*[6]

Our vision sees restorative regulation growing alongside other forms of justice, such as more punitive approaches—for instance, prosecutions and licence suspensions. These adversarial methods remain necessary complements when offenders deny responsibility or continue violations, as has been comprehensively established by Braithwaite's pyramid of responsive regulation.[7] For complex regulatory issues, we need an 'and/with' mindset rather than 'either/or' choices: restorative and punitive, not restorative or punitive. Integrating restorative practices into the existing regulatory

6 Gavens, 'Incentivising Compliance'.

7 Ian Ayres and John Braithwaite, *Responsive Regulation: Transcending the Deregulation Debate* (Oxford University Press, 1992), doi.org/10.1093/oso/9780195070705.001.0001.

ecosystem expands the range of available approaches. Rather than defaulting to punitive or other standard regulatory approaches, we urge regulators to ask: *Could a restorative approach help here?*

Our opening story about the Hazelwood Mine fire showed how EPA Victoria became open to restorative justice during the early 2010s. This openness occurred parallel to an increase in the criminal prosecutions of offending corporations and a commitment to continue toughening prosecutions during the coming decade. EPA Victoria's integrative mindset indicated their realisation that not only could a restorative approach coexist alongside punitive measures—that it could actually enhance their effectiveness.

This holistic vision of restorative justice as an integral component within a regulatory ecosystem finds solid support in the comprehensive meta-analysis conducted by the University of Maryland into the effectiveness of corporate deterrence. This research found that restorative justice, while having weak deterrence effects on its own, has significantly enhanced impact when integrated into the 'regulatory mix'.[8] In other words, if seeking to change corporate behaviour, it makes sense to have many alternative arrows in your regulatory quiver, not just the arrows of deterrence. The Maryland meta-analysis included some environmental compliance studies, though most were drawn from other areas of business regulation. This hints at the possibility that our journey across the many restorative spaces in EPA Victoria's regulatory sphere has broader relevance, extending across all regulatory domains.

We would argue there is no fundamental incompatibility in strengthening both the enforcement stick and the restorative stroke. Our research into EPA Victoria has revealed that it is an astute regulator that can coax, caress *and* coerce compliance in a responsively integrated way. One senior EPA enforcement official put it well when they told us that prior to the 2017 law reforms, EPA Victoria had not yet learned the lesson that 'you don't take a knife to a gun fight'.

Incorporating a restorative element into the regulatory approach enables a regulator to avoid the frequently observed seesawing between a hands-off 'support to comply' approach at one end and coercive sanctions at the other. In other words, restorative values and practices can assist in moving up and

8 Natalie Schell-Busey et al., 'What Works? A Systematic Review of Corporate Crime Deterrence', *Criminology & Public Policy* 15, no. 2 (2016): 387–416, doi.org/10.1111/1745-9133.12195.

down the regulatory pyramid more nimbly. If both those impacted and those responsible are actively engaged in dialogue about what has happened, who has been impacted and what needs to happen to make things better, more trust and understanding can be built. This, in turn, helps to strengthen each other's ability to fulfil the compliance obligations expected from both the regulatee and the regulator. Returning to our emphasis on the value of multiple perspectives and local knowledge, bringing these to the fore can assist in ensuring that the switches between supportive and coercive approaches are more nuanced and better informed.

It is important for a regulator to leave room for experimentation when looking for opportunities to become more restorative. As author and entrepreneur Seth Godin reminds us: 'If you're not doing things that don't work, you're not trying hard enough.'[9] In Chapter 8, we spoke about the importance of learning through making mistakes. It is not about finding fault or singling out any person. It is about fixing the problem and building stronger relationships.

This approach applies equally to the broader aim of nurturing a restorative regulator. When a regulator works with opportunities as they arise, things will not always work out the way everyone hopes. Creating a safe environment for open conversations, sharing of ideas, and honest assessments of what did and did not work is vital for encouraging innovation. Godin notes that when people are aware their feedback and ideas will not be rebuked, they can devote their efforts to 'leaning into what might be possible'.[10] In this supportive context, questions that can guide the creative process of exploring restorative approaches include:

- What can we try?
- What can we learn from what we tried?
- How can we improve and continue our journey towards more restorative regulation?

This leads us to our first recommendation (Table 10.1).

9 Seth Godin, *The Song of Significance: A New Manifesto for Teams* (Penguin Random House, 2023), 100.

10 Godin, *Song of Significance*, 84.

Table 10.1. Recommendation 1

Strategies for identifying incipient restorative practice or potential spaces	
Map the restorative terrain	Proactively conduct a mapping exercise to understand fully your regulatory organisation's incipient and potential opportunities for restorative practices. Our book is an illustration of this mapping approach writ large – assessing current practices for existing and potential restorative approaches and opportunities; identifying restorative champions; being attentive to the restorative possibilities; engaging stakeholders restoratively; offering training and education; documenting and sharing the best practices; acknowledging what works and iterating on what needs improving.
Cultivate innovation	Promote creativity and open-mindedness by fostering an environment that embraces and supports diverse perspectives, values experimentation and encourages out-of-the-box thinking. Encourage team members to explore restorative approaches and challenge outdated or ineffective regulatory norms that could be improved by the inclusion of restorative practices. Provide opportunities for brainstorming, idea-sharing and cross-functional collaboration to spark innovative restorative solutions. Collaborate with other agencies where relevant; for example, by establishing a panel of trusted restorative facilitators to call upon when needed.
Encourage open conversations	Create a safe environment that helps build trust, within which staff feel comfortable to facilitate restorative conversations between each other, with senior management, with regulatees and with the wider community. Back up staff efforts with clarity of communication from senior management to make it clear that staff are supported in this endeavour, such as through performance reviews that go beyond mere evaluations to provide constructive feedback and opportunities for growth, regular check-ins to assess progress and support needs, mentoring programs and peer-led workshops that encourage restorative practices in everyday practices.

Step 2: Nurturing and expanding restorative approaches

Once the spaces for restorative approaches have been identified, the restorative regulatory landscape needs to be actively cultivated to ensure it can thrive and grow. This involves supporting the transition from the initial stage—be it developing pilots or identifying incipient restorative practices—to maintaining, routinising or operationalising them throughout the organisation.

Embedding change across a regulatory organisation is a familiar challenge for many regulators. It is essential to acknowledge the existing expertise and knowledge that many regulators already possess in these domains. Equally important is recognising that some regulatory agencies are heavily policy-oriented, others focus more on operations, yet others have their own unique mix of characteristics, requiring a multifaceted approach to growing restorative approaches. Our focus here is not to supplant existing knowledge but rather to highlight specific pathways through which restorative approaches can become an integral part of a regulatory organisation.

Empowering through leadership to embed restorative practices

> *We need, therefore, a shared vision and a strategy for building that vision. An organisation with relationships truly at the centre, and a vision owned by everyone and understood by all. The vision needs to be clearly communicated and backed up with strong leadership, leadership that exists at all levels and across all areas, driven by those who command respect for their personal attributes rather than their status.*
>
> —Mark Finnis[11]

Strong leadership from actors in key positions is essential to supporting the growth and institutionalisation of restorative approaches. Researcher and restorative justice trainer Belinda Hopkins observes:

> In school research, the evidence suggests that unless the Head teacher is 'on board' with the new approach the initiative will fail (Kane et al., 2007). This has also been my personal experience.[12]

However, Hopkins also emphasises that it is 'not enough for a senior manager or leader to be "on board"—they need to know how to drive the bus themselves'.[13] In other words, leaders must model the behaviour

11 Mark Finnis, *Independent Thinking on Restorative Practice Building Relationships, Improving Behaviour and Creating Stronger Communities* (Independent Thinking Press, 2021), 4, www.crownhouse.co.uk/assets/look-inside/9781781353387.pdf.

12 Belinda Hopkins, 'From Restorative Justice to Restorative Culture', *Revista de Asistență Socială* XIV, no. 4 (2015): 19–34, 29. The full reference for the Kane et al. citation is: Jean Kane, Gwynedd Lloyd, Gillean McCluskey, et al., *Restorative Practices in Three Scottish Councils: Final Report of the Evaluation of the First Two Years of the Pilot Projects 2004–2006*, (University of Edinburgh and University of Glasgow, 2007), restorativejustice.org.uk/sites/default/files/resources/files/Restorative%20Practices%20in%20Three%20Scottish%20Councils.pdf.

13 Hopkins, 'From Restorative Justice', 29.

they expect from others, as the proverbial saying goes—they must walk the walk as well as talk the talk. This means demonstrating the ability to listen empathetically and democratically to the team, supporting colleagues through conflict and being ready to mediate between team members.

Leaders signal to the rest of the organisation what behaviours are and are not acceptable, whether or not an organisation will admit to, and learn from, its mistakes, how innovative the culture is, whether it is status- or outcome-oriented, and the degree to which praise is valued across the organisation.[14]

It is therefore critical for leaders committed to building a restorative organisation to set a leading example. Staff members closely observe and take cues from the communications and actions of senior management: 'They notice what you say, how you react and the decisions you make.'[15] Our focus is on identifying how senior managers can empower staff across the organisation to champion, support and implement restorative practices. To that end, we present a concise list of actionable insights in Table 10.2.

Table 10.2. Actionable insights

Participate in restorative training	Provide the resources for training in restorative practices and, as much as possible, make sure that senior management engages in the training. This signals commitment to staff, inspires them to attend and ensures that senior leadership gains the restorative skillset for disseminating more widely.
Incorporate restorative practices into leadership team meetings	Run leadership meetings in a restorative way, encouraging the use of respectful dialogue, active listening and collaborative problem-solving. Experiment with the use of circles. Share key restorative approaches in senior meetings with staff.
Engage in restorative conversations	When conflict arises in the organisation – even better, *before* it arises – encourage senior staff to respond with restorative conversations rather than finger-pointing or blame. Role model deep listening to, and synthesising, multiple perspectives. Actively demonstrate and model how to address conflict in ways that promote understanding, repair, and restored relationships.

14 Melinda Muth and Bob Selden, 'Setting the Tone from the Top: How Directors Use Conversation to Shape Culture' (Australian Institute of Company Directors, 2018), 16–18, www.aicd.com.au/content/dam/aicd/pdf/tools-resources/bookstore/previews/Setting-Tone-from-top-preview.pdf.

15 Rebecca Jackson, *Where Poppies Thrive: Leadership in a Harsh World* (Ultimate World Publishing, October 2021), 129.

Demonstrate the restorative values of accountability	Encourage all senior staff to publicly acknowledge their own mistakes and outline the actions they have taken to repair them. By demonstrating accountability openly, leaders show staff that mistakes are learning opportunities. This helps develop an environment where staff feel comfortable with being accountable when they err, contributing to a culture of continuous learning and growth.[16]
Cultivate empathy	Psychologist and leadership development practitioner Rebecca Jackson says that 'empathetic leaders tend to foster greater commitment and effort'. Being an empathetic leader is a restorative practice and involves providing a safe environment in which to give feedback and innovate. It also involves coaching with care to help staff learn to problem solve, by 'asking them, "[W]hat needs to happen for you to move forward from here?"'.[17] Role modelling empathy helps all staff. It is how connection is built with colleagues, regulatees and community.[18] High stakes negotiator Scott Walker says that empathy 'creates a positive atmosphere for problem solving' and 'it doesn't matter if you don't agree with or even like them,' as empathy is 'driven by a desire to first understand before being understood'.[19] Cultivating empathy also requires attentiveness to First Nations employees' cultural needs and supporting their values in the workplace by developing cultural competencies. This supports First Nations staff and reinforces that their values are respected, as well as contributing to sustaining a harmonious and collaborative workplace for all staff (see Chapter 9).

16 As well as aligning with the concept of a learning organisation—where mistakes are viewed as 'a precious learning resource'—open accountability strengthens relational responsibility and repair while encouraging a culture of experimentation and adaptability. See Wioleta Kucharska, 'Wisdom from Experience Paradox: Organizational Learning, Mistakes, Hierarchy and Maturity Issues', *The Electronic Journal of Knowledge Management* 19, no. 2 (2021): 105–17, doi.org/10.34190/ejkm.19.2.2370. See also Witvliet et al., 'Accountability'; Wioleta Kucharska and Denise A. D. Bedford, 'Love Your Mistakes!—They Help You Adapt to Change. How Do Knowledge, Collaboration and Learning Cultures Foster Organizational Intelligence?', *Journal of Organizational Change Management* 33, no. 7 (2020): 1329–54, doi.org/10.1108/JOCM-02-2020-0052; Jackson, *Where Poppies Thrive*.

17 Jackson, *Where Poppies Thrive*, 130–32.

18 Omar Khodor and Henry Miller, 'How to Regulate with Excellence', interview with Cary Coglianese, *The Regulatory Review*, 27 August 2023, www.theregreview.org/2023/08/27/sunday-spotlight-how-to-regulate-with-excellence/.

19 Scott Walker, Order Out of Chaos: A Kidnap Negotiator's Guide to Influence and Persuasion (Harvard Business Review Press, 2023), 49.

Spend time in the field	The Royal Commission into Australia's Robodebt fiasco, in response to what it saw as senior management being too removed from on-the-ground realities, made a recommendation that senior level (SES) staff 'spend some time in a frontline service delivery role and with other community partnerships'.[20] This is a call to ensure that senior management is directly aware of the vulnerabilities, challenges and needs faced by staff, regulatees, clients and communities. This exemplifies restorative practice, as senior staff gain insights through better understanding, increased empathy and a firsthand connection to the organisation's core functions.
Encourage feedback for improvement	Make it easy for staff to provide constructive feedback or criticism about restorative practices.[21] Be committed to continuous improvement.[22] Enable stakeholders and community members to provide feedback on how the restorative organisation is performing from their perspectives as well.
Empower staff	Empower staff to identify and address specific challenges in growing a restorative environment by providing them with the encouragement, resources, autonomy and support to design and implement tailored restorative solutions. In addition, senior management should actively participate in supporting staff-led restorative initiatives. This means, among other things, regularly acknowledging and praising staff efforts, noticing positive outcomes and providing ongoing encouragement. Such visible support reinforces the organisation's commitment to restorative practices and a culture of appreciation and motivation.
Extend restorative practices beyond the organisation	Actively engage with regulatees, individuals, communities, First Nations people and their communities, and other stakeholders, in a restorative manner. Make it a habit to engage with others restoratively by listening actively, using non-judgemental and empathetic language, encouraging dialogue and creating spaces where people feel safe to express themselves freely. This relational, restorative approach demonstrates staff expertise and dedication, leading to increased respect from external stakeholders for the hard work and the knowledge they bring to their roles.

20 Catherine Holmes, 'Improving the Australian Public Service', Recommendation 23.6, in *Report: Royal Commission into the Robodebt Scheme* (Royal Commission into the Robodebt Scheme, 2023), 642.

21 Staff should have the option to provide information directly to someone or anonymously, depending on their preference.

22 Coglianese, *Listening, Learning Leading*.

In terms of leadership more broadly, it is crucial not to lose sight of the importance of appreciating and nurturing bottom-up leadership. Parallel to the development of senior management's role, it is vital to empower grassroots leadership. Jackson highlights this necessity in her discussion of the importance of fostering innovation using an empathetic approach:

> Empower people by encouraging and engaging them in proactive action. Ensure they know they are part of the solution. Involve them in projects and give them responsibilities that allow them to be productive and contribute … When you consider that a replicable finding generalised across most organisations and institutions showed that at any time only 1 in 5 people feel engaged and empowered at work, there is much opportunity for development in this space.[23]

Leaders of the incipient and evolving restorative organisation would do well to encourage and empower staff at all levels to initiate, experiment and champion restorative practices within their respective domains. Ultimately, it is by nurturing restorative leadership from the ground up that a restorative culture becomes ingrained at every level of the organisation.

Policy and resource support for restorative approaches

For restorative approaches to become routinised within an organisation, they must be embedded in the policy and regulatory frameworks that inform the regulator's daily functions and interactions. Just as building a trellis will support growth in a garden, building a frame within policy and regulatory documentation—such as compliance and enforcement policies, licensing guidance, inspection protocols and whole-of-organisation strategic plans—will support restorative approaches and help to set strong foundations. This requires dedicated resources to provide training, staff support and technological infrastructure to aid effective integration into daily operations. Once supported in this manner, the restorative principles and practices are incentivised to climb and intertwine throughout the organisation's policies and practices.

Inclusion in high-level documentation sets the expectation that restorative approaches are a valid and integral part of regulation, influencing management, staff and board members. Additionally, where policy

23 Jackson, *Where Poppies Thrive*, 131.

documentation is publicly available (as it typically would be for the examples cited), regulatees and the wider community are made aware of the organisation's commitment to restorative practices.

Legislative and judicial support for restorative approaches

As part of a broader ecosystem, a regulator's external environment greatly influences its restorative options. Regulators operate within larger political, judicial and governmental systems that profoundly shape and impact their approaches. As such, policy, judicial and legislative support are all crucial. Validation from local and national governments helps to embed restorative regulation and ensure its integration.

Including restorative justice in new or updated regulatory legislation provides important recognition, signalling that restorative approaches are valid regulatory options. This creates momentum for their practical adoption. EPA Victoria's EP Act 2017 exemplifies effective legislative implementation, as discussed in Chapter 2. Restorative approaches can also support the full application of principles in legislation that resonate with restorative regulation, such as a general duty, shared responsibility, equity, accountability and the precautionary principle.[24]

Conversely, policy environments that favour strict enforcement—marked by an unwavering commitment to 'showing the badge' in the face of defiance to laws and norms—can kill restorative initiatives. This remains a constant challenge for restorative justice and practice, given the strong populist demand for punitive approaches in many cases, despite their limited empirical support.

The judiciary also plays an important role in encouraging and authorising the use of restorative justice. A recent example is the case of *Environment Protection Authority v Forestry Corporation of NSW*, where the judge, the Honourable Justice Nicola Pain, stated the following:

24 These examples are drawn from the EP Act 2017, but many other environmental regulators, along with other regulatory domains such as occupational health and safety (OH&S), health care, financial regulation, consumer protection, education, transportation and modern slavery regulation, have such principles in their legislation.

> The Practice Note for Class 5 proceedings was amended in April 2018 to include provision for restorative justice, to the effect that where a defendant enters a plea of guilty the prosecutor and defendant are to advise the Court of any proposal for a restorative justice process in which the defendant and victims are willing to participate and of any proposed order for a restorative justice activity a defendant agrees to carry out ... So far as I am aware no prosecutor or defendant has sought to utilise that section to date. I raise that section and the Practice Note for Class 5 proceeding because it is one means by which the wider community including a local community organisation such as the BECI [Bellingen Environment Centre Incorporated] could have been engaged constructively in matters relevant to criminal sentencing for these offences. [25]

This statement shows that when a judge takes an active interest in using restorative justice, the opportunities for its application are further extended. Judicial endorsement should be paired with proactive efforts from both legal professionals and community stakeholders to embrace its potential. One strategy is to raise restorative approaches as a possibility in judicial contexts, where relevant, highlighting existing legal and regulatory successes to draw attention to the benefits of these approaches and further legitimise their application.

Development and use of shared language

One significant challenge for getting everyone on the same page is ensuring there is a common understanding of what restorative approaches involve. This is achieved through developing and using a shared language. A shared language improves communication, providing clarity, and consistency of purpose and expectations, not just for regulatory staff but also for board members, regulatees and the wider community.[26] It helps to shape the cultural shift a regulator needs in order to align with restorative values, and promotes consistency in communication and decision-making. A shared language also supports collaboration between staff, and between staff and external actors, on ideas, solutions and even cultural change.[27]

---

25 *Environment Protection Authority v Forestry Corporation of NSW* [2024], NSWLEC 84, paragraph 29.

26 Joyce Thomas and Deana McDonagh, 'Shared Language: Towards More Effective Communication', *Australasian Medical Journal* 6, no. 1 (2013): 46–54.

27 Thomas and McDonagh, 'Shared Language'.

A shared language is a key part of building both self-efficacy and collective efficacy, which are central to the values and practices of restorative justice first outlined in Chapter 1. Research by scholars Joyce Thomas and Deana McDonagh on shared language has shown that '[d]eveloping this language together helps the individual team members to self-validate their contribution, making them feel more valuable'.[28] They further note that creating a common language is an active process requiring time to establish, but that once in place, it creates understandings that may not otherwise have emerged. Additionally, a shared language can help build an 'emotional case' for change, motivating staff to move away from their entrenched ways of doing things or their strong attachment to business as usual, providing the emotional resonance needed to embrace the new journey and support new ways of working.[29] We spoke of the importance of emotional engagement in Chapter 1, and it is equally relevant to efforts to establish the restorative approach to regulating:

> This can include addressing people's concerns personally, acknowledging that it means a change to how they've been doing things, and expressing that you understand their concerns.[30]

Finally, a shared language serves to normalise the value of the opportunities offered by restorative regulation. It is through this common language that stories and narratives can be effectively shared and understood, allowing the experiences of individuals and communities impacted by harm—and affected by the corresponding regulatory actions—to be clearly communicated. As we have frequently noted, stories have a powerful emotional impact and can help convey the need for restorative approaches. However, there is another significant value in sharing these stories, which we will explore next.

Sharing the successes of restorative approaches through storytelling

> *We don't tell our own stories … restorative justice needs to be communicated.*[31]

28 Thomas and McDonagh, 'Shared Language'.

29 Kylie Denton, 'How To Embed Behaviour Change in a Complex Work Environment', Performance Advisory Group, 24 July 2020, performanceadvisorygroup.com.au/embed-behaviour-change/.

30 Denton, 'Behaviour Change'.

31 Interview with an EPA officer.

One prevalent theme we have traced throughout the book is the silence surrounding the successes of restorative approaches and how this silence prevents the sharing of valuable lessons for others to build upon. Restorative approaches often take place in the quieter, peaceful margins—with good reason. These are carefully crafted spaces designed to build trust and ensure that people feel safe and in control of their confidences. However, this means that the successful moments and results lack the big, publicised impacts of prosecutions and similar enforcement actions, with their measurable, headline-grabbing outcomes.

Yet, it is through fixing problems and forging ongoing relationships that the restorative processes pave the way for more effective regulatory action. However, like any regulatory process, restorative approaches demand resources and institutional support. Ironically, their beneficial outcomes often go unrecognised, which makes it harder to justify any regulatory agencies' investing in them.

Rather than allowing these successes to languish in obscurity, we suggest they be sought out and actively celebrated. Storytelling can be of great help. Where staff, offenders and community members are willing to share their perspectives and thoughts about their restorative experiences, the wider dissemination of their compelling narratives can increase understanding of the benefits of restorative approaches and inspire others to try them. The stories can explain what happened, how the restorative practices helped resolve the issues and how they enhanced regulatory effectiveness, shedding light on their value. When these narratives are disseminated widely—by communications and engagement teams, and street-level field officers alike—regulators can raise awareness of restorative practices, how they make a difference and, ideally, encourage their wider adoption.

This leads to our next recommendation (Table 10.3).

Table 10.3. Recommendation 2

Strategies for nurturing and expanding restorative spaces	
Build a restorative policy frame	Build a contextually tailored trellis to support restorative principles and practices in your organisation. Include restorative principles, practices and approaches in relevant high-level work documentation that reflects the regulatory policies and guidance followed by staff, such as compliance and enforcement policies, licensing guidance, inspection protocols and whole-of-organisation strategic plans, as this will help to ensure that restorative approaches are embedded in the core functions of the organisation.

<table>
<tr><th colspan="2">Strategies for nurturing and expanding restorative spaces</th></tr>
<tr><td>Provide legislative and judicial support</td><td>Where possible, recognising that legislative reform is often outside the control of regulators, engage with policymakers to advocate for the inclusion of restorative approaches in existing legislation or legislation under review. Making restorative regulation part of the suite of available approaches in compliance and enforcement, licensing, community engagement, dispute resolution and other relevant areas increases the options available to regulators for achieving restorative outcomes.

If you are in a new or transitioning regulator, seek to have restorative justice included in the regulator's foundational or new legislation, setting the tone for creating a restorative organisation from the outset.

Although beyond our research remit, we encourage the judiciary to make greater use of court rules, practice notes and relevant legislative provisions that give courts the power to apply restorative solutions to resolving disputes.</td></tr>
<tr><td>Develop a shared language</td><td>Allow space and time for your staff to develop a shared language around restorative practices. Encourage and support this usage both within the organisation and also with stakeholders, regulatees and the wider community.

Here are some ways to develop and use this shared language:

• Identify misunderstandings, inconsistencies or differing interpretations across your organisation. Develop common language and understandings.

• Hold workshops or seminars to discuss restorative approaches together. Define the key terms. Be prepared to respond to questions from staff.

• Allow exploration of the key terms. Be open to crafting meaningful definitions that reflect your organisation's focus, being sure to keep everyone on the same page.

• Create guides or aids to assist development and use of the common language around restorative approaches, such as posters, intranet pages, pamphlets, infographics and videos. Keep these on an intranet space for easy accessibility.

• Ensure that First Nations staff members are actively contributing to the development of the shared language.

• Provide a means for regular updates and revisiting progression of the shared language. Cultivating a shared language is an ongoing process. Language changes with cultural, regulatory and other shifts over time, making it essential to keep usage updated and aligned.

• Lead by example and provide recognition. Encourage senior staff to consistently use the shared language and create an environment where staff feel comfortable offering constructive feedback. Acknowledge and celebrate staff who contribute to its development and use, and who mentor and encourage peer learning on it.</td></tr>
</table>

Strategies for nurturing and expanding restorative spaces	
Make success visible	Sharing stories of success and experimentation with restorative approaches is crucial for building awareness and promoting wider adoption. Here are some ways to share the stories of success and experimentation with restorative approaches: • Share success stories internally, through staff bulletins, intranet updates and staff talks. • Incorporate the stories into training programs. • Encourage staff to make use of these stories to help regulatees and communities envision what is possible. • Share success stories with interested community leaders and First Nations leadership. Provide support for them to spread the success message in their own way, based on their firsthand experiences. • Include success stories in community newsletters, website updates, materials disseminated at community events, etc. • Share on social media platforms. • Present the stories at workshops and conferences. In pursuit of peer learning, prioritise sharing success stories with other regulators.

Step 3: Finding ways to connect restorative approaches across the entire ecosystem

Although we speak of restorative culture as the third point in this chapter, it is, in many ways, also the foundation of the first and second points. Scholars studying the use of restorative practices in institutions such as schools and care homes identify the vital role played by the surrounding environment in which the practice is happening.[32] The culture—often described as 'the way we do things around here'—acts as the soil in which restorative regulatory practices take root and grow. As Ted Wachtel observed:

> Restorative practices are not learned by sitting in lecture halls nor by reading books nor are they handed down by a company's leadership. They can only be learned by doing. An organization that truly wants to implement restorative practices must do so in a manner consistent with what those practices represent—engaging its employees in a journey of cooperative learning and change.[33]

32 See Tara Bartlett et al., '17 Programs and Practices to Promote a Safe Campus: Alternatives to School Policing and Punitive Practices', *The Urban Review* 56 (2024): 150–85, doi.org/10.1007/s11256-023-00669-2; Sean Darling-Hammond, *Fostering Belonging, Transforming Schools: The Impact of Restorative Practices*, Learning Policy Institute, 18 May 2023, learningpolicyinstitute.org/product/impact-restorative-practices-report.

33 Ted Wachtel, 'Restorative Practices in Business: Building a Community for Learning and Change Within Organizations', *International Institute for Restorative Practices Graduate School*, 18 February 1999, www.iirp.edu/news/restorative-practices-in-business-building-a-community-for-learning-and-change-within-organizations.

Belinda Hopkins, a specialist in applying restorative practices in schools, has reflected on what she and other trainers have learned about ensuring that the skills she imparts have a lasting impact on those involved. She notes: 'Our experiences have shown that the day-to-day thinking and practice within an institution is key to this.'[34]

Similarly, the *Trust Flows* report mentioned in the Introduction underscores the importance of 'tending and carefully maintaining' personal relationships as the foundation of trust. Trust, like restorative culture, cannot be engineered or imposed; it must be cultivated through consistent behaviours—openness, empathy, reliability, cultural competence and shared responsibility. These behaviours create the conditions in which both regulatory staff and community members feel safe to experiment, reflect and collaborate on shared goals.

Developing a restorative culture in practice

Many factors go towards creating a restorative culture in an organisation. The key factors are:

- support and modelling by senior leaders (as discussed above)
- alignment of restorative approaches with organisational values
- dedicated resources for supportive structures and practices, such as a restorative practices coordinator and the regular use of circles or similar restorative practices in the workplace[35]
- ongoing training and professional development to build understanding and skills.[36]

This leads us to the question: How does a restorative culture take root in an organisation?

34 Hopkins, 'From Restorative Justice', 20.

35 See, for example, the help such circles provide in the context of community mental health practitioners: Hyo Kyung Kim, Bal Hee Lee, and Kyoung A. Nam, 'Improving Interprofessional Teamwork in a Community Mental Health Team: A Team Building Circle Program Based on the Restorative Justice Paradigm', *Journal of Interprofessional Care* 38, no. 4 (2024): 642–51, doi.org/10.1080/13561820.2024.2329463. However, circles are not the only option, as outlined frequently in the book. The principle of voluntariness must be paramount—restorative practices should never be, nor be perceived as, imposed in ways that make staff feel obligated to participate or overshare. When staff do not wish to engage in circle formats, it is important to explore alternative restorative approaches that align with their comfort and preferences, while recognising that, at times, a restorative approach may not be the most appropriate option.

36 Kim et al., Improving Interprofessional Teamwork.

Damon Centola is a professor of sociology who has spent many years studying how change happens in institutions and society. He distinguishes between two types of change: superficial and deep. Superficial change—such as catchy ideas or memes—spreads rapidly through social networks, much like a virus. He likens this to a firework going off from a central node, where weak social ties are sufficient for quick dissemination through the network.

However, deeper, lasting change—especially when it involves shifts in beliefs and behaviours—is harder to achieve and requires what he calls 'complex contagion'. Unlike simple contagion, which spreads through single points of contact, complex contagion relies on strong, interconnected ties across social networks. He compares this to a fishing net, where each node is connected to many others. Strong ties create the conditions for new norms to take root, not merely by passing along information but by reinforcing its importance through multiple, trusted sources.

Centola's research suggests that meaningful change is more likely when people hear the same message from multiple sources across an organisation rather than repeatedly from top-level leaders alone. In other words, a restorative culture cannot be sustained by leadership pronouncements alone—it must be championed by individuals across different levels and sectors of an organisation.[37] Returning to Hopkins' earlier metaphor: it is not enough for just the leader to drive the bus; there must be many bus drivers within the organisation.

Academic researchers Lada Adamic and Bogdan State further support this idea:

> [I]t is easy to see why social proof obtained from multiple sources would be necessary for many individuals to show their support for a cause they believe in. Engaging in behavior that challenges the status quo carries inherent risks.[38]

These insights help to illustrate why it is critical that restorative champions within organisations have strong and diverse networks. This is borne out by the firsthand experiences of many restorative institutions—particularly schools and the growing movement of restorative cities worldwide—that focus

37 Damon Centola, *Change: How to Make Big Things Happen* (Little, Brown Spark, 2021).

38 Centola, *Change*, citing Lada Adamic and Bogdan State, 102.

on infusing a restorative culture across the urban landscape.[39] The people and institutions driving such restorative initiatives understand that a restorative ethos only takes root when a diverse range of people from across different parts of an organisation, place, city or society are dedicated to its achievement.

The restorative cities initiative

Nurturing restorative culture is an intentional, iterative and pluralist project. One compelling example of this is the restorative cities initiative, which demonstrates the transformative potential that can be unlocked by following a gradual, holistic approach towards achieving widespread societal adoption of a restorative culture.

The first restorative city began with an experiment in Kingston Upon Hull in the United Kingdom, one that continues to date. Since then, the idea of restorative cities has spread to the four corners of the world.[40] While no single definition determines what constitutes a restorative city, these initiatives share key values and practices drawing on restorative justice that inform the intentional creation of a restorative culture. In particular, restorative cities commit to being relationship-focused, inclusive and participatory.[41] Restorative cities focus on preventing harm, providing continuous learning opportunities for people of all ages and encouraging a willingness to experiment and learn from mistakes.

At its heart, the restorative city is a relational city. It puts relationships first in order to build stronger communities. It seeks to empower citizens to participate and engage in city governance, decision-making processes and restoration projects. As with all restorative approaches, for those leading the transformation, the act of asking questions is important to developing a city's restorative culture:

- What do the people and communities of this city want from a restorative city?

39 See, for example 'Restorative Justice', Oakland Unified School District, accessed 31 March 2025, www.ousd.org/restorative-justice. See also Olivia Marcucci, 'Why Restorative Justice Works in Schools: An Investigation into the Interactional Dynamics of Restorative Circles', *Learning, Culture and Social Interaction* 31, Part A, 100561 (2021), doi.org/10.1016/j.lcsi.2021.100561.

40 Examples include Como and Tempo Pausania in Italy, Brighton and Bristol in the United Kingdom, Leuven in Belgium, Whanganui in New Zealand, Canberra in Australia and Oakland in the USA.

41 Mannozzi, '"Restorative City"; Australian Capital Territory Government, Justice and Community Safety Directorate, 'Canberra as a Restorative City', accessed 27 May 2025, www.justice.act.gov.au/canberra-as-a-restorative-city.

- What do they see a restorative city as looking like?
- How will it serve their purposes and interests?

Restorative cities are gaining traction and enthusing their participants across the planet. As one activist we interviewed reflected on what makes a city restorative: 'It gets into the blood.'[42]

Cultivating a restorative culture over time

Just as a restorative city evolves over time, a restorative regulatory organisation is also a gradual work-in-progress—a journey that requires the active participation of everyone across the regulatory organisation. This participatory component also involves regulatees, stakeholders and the wider community. As the process unfolds, it is important to embrace openness to suggestions and constructive feedback, as well as continuously reflecting on key questions:

- What will *our* restorative organisation look like?
- What do our staff, regulatees, communities and stakeholders think it will look like?
- How will it serve their purposes and interests?

By sharing lessons, supporting staff in their embrace of restorative approaches and building upon restorative experiments, regulators can begin to experience the transformation to a restorative way of regulating, embedding restorative approaches into the organisation's very DNA.

Establishing communities of practice

Research makes it clear that real, systemic change happens when there are multiple champions across different areas of an organisation and its wider network.[43] One way to cultivate champions and sustain momentum is by developing communities of practice.

A community of practice brings together people who genuinely care about the same real-life problems and who interact regularly to learn from and with each other.[44] While incorporating networks where appropriate,

42 Interview with a restorative justice and environmental activist.

43 'Building a Change Champion Network Roles and Responsibilities', Change Strategists, 15 August 2024, changestrategists.com/change-champion-network-roles-and-responsibilities/.

44 Igor Pyrko, Viktor Dörfler, and Colin Eden, 'Thinking Together: What Makes Communities of Practice Work?', *Human Relations* 70, no. 4 (2016): 389–409, doi.org/10.1177/0018726716661040.

a community of practice is broader than a network because it involves a 'learning partnership', not just networking, and builds its own 'collective sense of trust and commitment'.[45] Unlike a team or taskforce that dissolves once its task is achieved, a community of practice is a sustained effort over time.[46] When well organised and resourced, it can be a powerful source of learning, knowledge-sharing and mutual support, and a place for incubating new practices collaboratively.

Learning within a community of practice is most effective when it is deeply social and relational. It helps participants deal with complex issues and build resilience by drawing on multiple perspectives.[47] Further, research has shown it can increase role efficacy and advance learning through building a shared repertoire of cases, techniques, tools, stories, concepts and perspectives,[48] many of which, such as storytelling and learning from diverse experiences, we have already discussed as key to nurturing and expanding restorative spaces.

For a restorative regulator, a supportive and collaborative space where regulatory staff can exchange ideas and experiences regarding restorative approaches—what one EPA interviewee referred to as 'an authorising environment'—is equally valuable. Developing a restorative community of practice would provide this space, whether within a single regulator or across multiple regulators working to embed a restorative culture and associated restorative approaches. Establishing such a community begins with supporting the restorative champions—those who innately embody a restorative way of being and see it as integral to their work. One way to do this is to facilitate their role in designing the community of practice and encourage them to ask and answer key questions about what they want to achieve. It is best to start small and let the community of practice evolve organically: 'The key is ensuring a core group of people are dedicated to learning together.'[49]

45 Rebecca Goodhue and Sadhana Seriamlu, *A Quick Guide to Establishing a Community of Practice* (ARACY, 2021), 6, www.aracy.org.au/wp-content/uploads/2024/09/A_quick_guide_to_Establishing_a_Community_of_Practice_ARACY_2021_-_FINAL.pdf.

46 Goodhue and Seriamlu, *A Quick Guide*, 6.

47 Adi Staempfli, *Practice Tool: Developing a Community of Practice in Your Organisation*, Practice Supervisor Development Programme (United Kingdom Department for Education, December 2020); Karine Goglio-Primard et al., 'Managing with Communities for Innovation, Agility, and Resilience', *European Management Journal* 41, no. 4 (2023): 673–75, doi.org/10.1016/j.emj.2023.07.005.

48 Goodhue and Seriamlu, *A Quick Guide*, 8.

49 Goodhue and Seriamlu, *A Quick Guide*, 13.

Senior management should communicate support for the community of practice and encourage participation, while also recognising that these communities cannot be simply created or imposed top-down. Managers can 'only create the right conditions for communities of practice to grow in and flourish'.[50] That said, senior management's influence is crucial in enabling staff to form and sustain these collaborative communities.[51]

Over time, a community of practice can help to nurture and strengthen a restorative culture across and beyond the regulatory organisation. By building up case studies and stories, and reflecting on what works and what does not, practitioners will be contributing to the restorative body of knowledge while helping to build a sense of ownership in growing a restorative regulator.

Recommendation 3 (Table 10.4) underlines the importance of connections between restorative regulatory approaches.

Table 10.4. Recommendation 3

Strategies for connecting and sustaining restorative regulatory practice	
Communicate the restorative culture	Clearly communicate the commitment to cultivating a restorative culture and organisation. Use speeches, internal websites, posters and various communications channels to convey the importance and purpose of the restorative mission.
Facilitate the growth of communities of practice	Make space for, and support the development of, a restorative community of practice. Communicate this support widely and encourage interested staff to join. Check the potential of existing networks. In cases where communities of practice already exist within or across regulators, it may be worthwhile to think of expanding their scope to include restorative practices, provided this does not dilute the overall intention to develop a restorative regulatory environment. Make use of a range of ways to connect and build the resources, from meet-ups to online platforms. Having a diversity of ways to connect will give everyone who is interested the chance to participate, making it easier to collaboratively build the repertoire of shared knowledge. Consider not only the initial incubation of restorative practices but also their transition to long-term maintenance and operationalisation. Where the regulator has the necessary scaffolding in place for restorative practices but its consistency in practice remains in development, a dedicated community of practice could provide a framework for sustaining and refining restorative approaches over time. Integrate the shared restorative insights and recommendations into the organisation's policies and practices.

50 Staempfli, *Practice Tool*, 5.

51 Staempfli, *Practice Tool*.

The restorative regulator: A long-term forecast for vibrant growth

This book has sought to reflect on what regulators can learn from decades of restorative practice, and more specifically, in this chapter, on the evolving efforts to build a restorative organisation. We have argued that for a regulator to effectively support restorative approaches beyond its own walls, it must also attend to the ways in which restorative values are lived within the organisation itself.

We know this is not easy. As one study of restorative practice in schools found, '[T]he kids do a better job of it than we [the teachers and administration] do.'[52] Yet the willingness to acknowledge difficulty—a potentially vulnerable act—is itself a restorative strength. It signals a commitment to learning, humility and improving the quality of our relationships with others, both within the workplace and beyond.

The gardening metaphor woven throughout this book has shaped our three-part approach to cultivating a restorative regulator: first, identify existing or potential spaces where restorative approaches can emerge or be seeded; second, nurture and embed these approaches to become a stable part of the ecosystem; and third, find ways to connect these approaches across the entire ecosystem, so they take deep root and flourish over time. This is not a linear process. It is an ongoing, adaptive journey, one that must respond to the conditions of the moment while holding on to long-term values of care, accountability, trust and relational responsibility.

As our research journey with EPA Victoria has progressed, we have witnessed the complexities and nuances involved in this iterative, non-linear process. We have learned that building a restorative regulator requires more than a shift in practices—it is about intentionally reshaping the very way we approach our work and our relationships. The bumps, the successes, the lessons learned and the ongoing evaluation of restorative practices within the organisation have all been invaluable in shaping our understanding. These experiences, both challenging and inspiring, have reinforced for us

52 Kristin Reimer, '"The Kids Do a Better Job of It Than We Do": A Canadian Case Study of Teachers Addressing the Hypocritical Application of Restorative Justice in Their School', *The Australian Educational Researcher* 46 (2018): 59–73, doi.org/10.1007/s13384-018-0286-7.

the importance of patience, adaptability and collective effort, whether in addressing harms, educating regulatees or engaging with local and First Nations communities.

Becoming a restorative regulator is not just about transforming our actions; it also involves transforming our interactions with others. As Josephine Bourne reminded us in this chapter's opening quote, it requires bringing our hearts to work. By aligning our internal practices with the values we espouse externally, we create the conditions—inside and out—for a more just, responsive and trustworthy regulatory system.

There will be setbacks. Some seeds will not sprout. Others will take root and grow in unexpected ways. But over time, if tended with care, the restorative regulator can become a deeply rooted presence in the regulatory landscape—one that nurtures accountability, trust and responsive relationships, helping regulators, regulatees and communities to heal ruptured relations, grow together and thrive.

The research throughout this book has revealed many possible avenues for integrating and amplifying restorative approaches across a wide range of regulatory contexts. We hope some of these examples will inspire regulators to experiment—to sow the seeds that will take root and climb the trellis, providing the structure from which a fully realised restorative regulatory organisation can bloom.

The work ahead is neither simple nor short-term. But it is necessary, and it is possible. The question now is not whether we can grow a restorative regulator—but whether we are ready to do the slow, steady work of tending one into being.

Bibliography

Abdou, Annmary S., John Brady, Amy Jane Griffiths, Alec Burrola, and Julie Vue. 'Restorative Schools: A Consultation Case Study for Moving from Theory to Practice'. *Journal of Educational and Psychological Consultation* 33, no. 4 (2023): 421–24. doi.org/10.1080/10474412.2023.2192205.

Aertsen, Ivo. 'Restorative Justice for Victims of Corporate Violence: Victims and Corporations'. In *Victims and Corporations: Legal Challenges and Empirical Findings*, edited by Gabrio Forti. Wolters Kluwer, 2018.

Al-Alosi, Hadeel, and Mark Hamilton. 'The Ingredients of Success for Effective Restorative Justice Conferencing in an Environmental Offending Context'. *University of New South Wales Law Journal* 42, no. 4 (2019): 1460–88. doi.org/10.53637/ZEAN8618.

Altman, Jon, Geoff Buchanan, and Libby Larsen. 'The Environmental Significance of the Indigenous Estate: Natural Resource Management as Economic Development in Remote Australia'. Centre for Aboriginal Economic Policy Research Discussion Paper no. 295/2007. ANU College of Arts & Social Sciences, 2007. caepr.cass.anu.edu.au/research/publications/environmental-significance-indigenous-estate-natural-resource-management.

AkzoNobel Pty Ltd. *Communications and Engagement Strategy*. March 2021. www.akzonobel.com/content/dam/akzonobel-corporate/global/en/regional-assets/australia/akzonobel-communications-and-engagement-strategy-2021.pdf.

Allan, Alfred, Justine de Mott, Isolde M. Larkins, et al. 'The Impact of Voluntariness of Apologies on Victims' Responses in Restorative Justice: Findings of a Quantitative Study'. *Psychiatry, Psychology and Law* 29, no. 4 (2022): 593–609. doi.org/10.1080/13218719.2021.1956383.

Alexander, Jon, and Ariane Conrad. *Citizens: Why the Key to Fixing Everything Is All of Us*. Canbury Press, 2022.

Allais, Lucy. 'Restorative Justice, Retributive Justice, and the South African Truth and Reconciliation Commission'. *Philosophy & Public Affairs* 39, no. 4 (2011): 331–63. doi.org/10.1111/j.1088-4963.2012.01211.x.

Amin, Dhara, Komal Bajaj, and Anita Giuntoli. 'A Need to Embrace Restorative Justice at the Heart of the Patient Safety Movement. *Journal of Medical Toxicology* 18 (2022): 183–84. doi.org/10.1007/s13181-022-00897-0.

Angel, Caroline M. 'Crime Victims Meet Their Offenders: Testing the Impact of Restorative Justice Conferences on Victims' Post-Traumatic Stress Symptoms'. PhD diss., University of Pennsylvania, 2005.

Ansell, Christopher, and Alison Gash. 'Collaborative Governance in Theory and Practice'. *Journal of Public Administration Research and Theory* 18, no. 4 (2008): 543–71. www.jstor.org/stable/25096384.

ANZSOG. 'What Is Culturally Responsive Regulation? And How Do We Work with Our Aboriginal and Torres Strait Islander Partners to Achieve It?' Panel discussion between Jacqueline McGowan-Jones, Richard Weston and Josephine Bourne, facilitated by David MacLennan. Zoom Webinar, 24 August 2022. anzsog.edu.au/learning-and-development/events-and-conferences/nrcop-culturally-responsive-regulation/.

Ardoin, Nicole M., Alison W. Bowers, and Mele Wheaton. 'Leveraging Collective Action and Environmental Literacy to Address Complex Sustainability Challenges'. *Ambio* 52 (2022): 30–44. doi.org/10.1007/s13280-022-01764-6.

Arnstein, Sherry R. 'A Ladder of Citizen Participation'. *Journal of the American Institute of Planners* 35, no. 4 (1969), doi.org/10.1080/01944366908977225.

Armytage, Penny, Jane Brockington, and Janice van Reyk. *Independent Inquiry into the Environment Protection Authority*. Environment Protection Authority Inquiry Ministerial Advisory Committee, 2016. apo.org.au/sites/default/files/resource-files/2016-03/apo-nid72340.pdf.

Arts+Law. 'Indigenous Cultural and Intellectual Property (ICIP)'. Last modified 21 July 2024. www.artslaw.com.au/information-sheet/indigenous-cultural-intellectual-property-icip-aitb/.

Australian Associated Press. 'Melbourne Public Housing Tower Residents Offered $5m Payout over Covid Lockdown'. *The Guardian* (Australian edn), 9 May 2023. www.theguardian.com/australia-news/2023/may/09/melbourne-public-housing-tower-residents-win-5m-payout-over-covid-lockdown.

Australian Capital Territory Government Justice and Community Safety Directorate. 'Canberra as a Restorative City'. Accessed 27 May 2025. www.justice.act.gov.au/canberra-as-a-restorative-city.

Australian Government. *The Australian Public Service Framework for Engagement and Participation*. Commonwealth of Australia 2020. www.industry.gov.au/sites/default/files/August%202021/document/aps-framework-for-engagement-and-participation.pdf.

Australian Government Department of Home Affairs. *Strengthening Australian Democracy: A Practical Agenda for Democratic Resilience.* Report of the Strengthening Democracy Taskforce, 2024. www.homeaffairs.gov.au/about-us-subsite/files/strengthening-australian-democracy.pdf.

Australian Government Department of Climate Change, Energy, the Environment and Water. 'Improving Community Engagement and Support For Renewable Energy Infrastructure'. Last modified 19 July 2024. www.dcceew.gov.au/energy/renewable/improving-community-engagement-support-energy-infrastructure.

Australian Government Murray-Darling Basin Authority. 'First Nations Cultural Flows'. Last modified 16 July 2024. www.mdba.gov.au/water-use/water-first-nations/first-nations-cultural-flows.

Australian Government National Emergency Management Agency. *National Report: Royal Commission into National Natural Disaster Arrangements Recommendations Implementation Status.* October 2020. Last modified 8 September 2024. www.nema.gov.au/about-us/governance-and-reporting/reviews/royal-commission-into-natural-disaster#TheReport.

Australian Human Rights Commission. 'The History of Aboriginal and Torres Strait Islander Peoples Advocating for the Right to Be Heard'. Accessed 20 February 2025. humanrights.gov.au/our-work/aboriginal-and-torres-strait-islander-social-justice/history-aboriginal-and-torres-strait.

Australian Human Rights Commission. 'Human Rights and Aboriginal and Torres Strait Islander Peoples'. Information Sheet. Accessed 8 March 2025. humanrights.gov.au/sites/default/files/content/letstalkaboutrights/downloads/HRA_ATSI.pdf.

Australian Human Rights Commission. *Wiyi Yani U Thangani (Women's Voices): Securing Our Rights, Securing Our Future Report (2020).* 9 December 2020. humanrights.gov.au/our-work/aboriginal-and-torres-strait-islander-social-justice/publications/wiyi-yani-u-thangani.

Australian Human Rights and Equal Opportunities Commission. *Bringing Them Home,* Report. Commonwealth of Australia, 1997. humanrights.gov.au/our-work/projects/bringing-them-home-report-1997.

The Australian Indigenous Governance Institute (AIGI). 'Effective Indigenous Governance', The Australian Indigenous Governance Institute. 2024. Accessed 9 March 2025. aigi.org.au/toolkit/effective-indigenous-governance.

Australian Institute of Aboriginal and Torres Strait Islander Studies (AIATSIS). 'Engaging With Traditional Owners'. 23 December 2020. aiatsis.gov.au/publication/94688.

AIATSIS. 'Map of Indigenous Australia'. Last modified 28 March 2025. aiatsis.gov.au/explore/map-indigenous-australia.

AIATSIS. 'The 1967 Referendum'. Last modified 12 July 2024. aiatsis.gov.au/explore/1967-referendum.

AIATSIS. *Overturning the Doctrine of Terra Nullius: The Mabo Case*. 27 September 2008. aiatsis.gov.au/sites/default/files/research_pub/overturning-the-doctrine-of-terra-nullius_0_3.pdf.

AIATSIS. 'Welcome to Country'. Last modified 25 May 2022. aiatsis.gov.au/explore/welcome-country.

Australian Institute of Health and Welfare (AIHW). *Aboriginal and Torres Strait Islander Health Performance Framework: Summary Report*. Australian Government, August 2024. Last updated 11 June 2025. www.indigenoushpf.gov.au/report-overview/overview/summary-report.

Australian Law Reform Commission. *Changing Policies Towards Aboriginal People*. Australian Government, 18 August 2010. www.alrc.gov.au/publication/recognition-of-aboriginal-customary-laws-alrc-report-31/3-aboriginal-societies-the-experience-of-contact/changing-policies-towards-aboriginal-people/.

Australia National Oceans Office. *Sea Country: An Indigenous Perspective: The South-east Regional Marine Plan Assessment Report*. National Oceans Office, 2002. www.dcceew.gov.au/sites/default/files/documents/indigenous.pdf.

Autesserre, Séverine. *The Frontlines of Peace: An Insider's Guide to Changing the World*. Oxford University Press, 2021. doi.org/10.1093/oso/9780197530351.001.0001.

Axtell, Paul. 'Meeting Management: Make Your Meetings a Safe Space for Honest Conversation'. *Harvard Business Review*, 11 April 2019. hbr.org/2019/04/make-your-meetings-a-safe-space-for-honest-conversation.

Ayres, Ian, and John Braithwaite. *Responsive Regulation: Transcending the Deregulation Debate*. Oxford University Press, 1992.

Baer, Miriam H. 'Designing Corporate Leniency Programs'. In *The Cambridge Handbook of Compliance*, edited by D. Daniel Sokol and Benjamin van Rooij. Cambridge University Press. doi.org/10.1017/9781108759458.025.

Bainbridge, Roxanne, Komla Tsey, Janya McCalman, et al. 'No One's Discussing the Elephant in the Room: Contemplating Questions of Research Impact and Benefit in Aboriginal and Torres Strait Islander Australian Health Research'. *BMC Public Health* 15, no. 696 (2015): 1–10. doi.org/10.1186/s12889-015-2052-3.

Baird, Julia. *Bright Shining*. HarperCollins Australia, 2023.

Balch, Oliver. 'Buen Vivir: The Social Philosophy Inspiring Movements in South America'. *Sustainable Business Blog, The Guardian*. 4 February 2013. www.theguardian.com/sustainable-business/blog/buen-vivir-philosophy-south-america-eduardo-gudynas.

Balliet, Daniel, Joshua M. Tybur, Junhui Wu, et al. 'Political Ideology, Trust, and Cooperation: In-group Favoritism Among Republicans *and* Democrats During a US National Election'. *The Journal of Conflict Resolution* 62, no. 4 (2018): 797–818. doi.org/10.1177/0022002716658694.

Banwell-Moore, Rebecca. 'Just an "Optional Extra" in the "Victim Toolkit"? The Culture, Mechanisms and Approaches of Criminal Justice Organisations Delivering Restorative Justice in England and Wales'. *International Review of Victimology* 29, no. 2 (2023): 217–35. doi.org/10.1177/02697580221079993.

Baral Abrams, Gina, Mary Jo Hebling, and Beth Smull. 'Proactive Restorative Practices: Creating the Conditions for Individuals and Communities to Flourish'. Presentation, International Institute for Restorative Practices, 25 October 2018. www.iirp.edu/images/conf_downloads/FoqHEZ_Proactive_RP_Creating_the_Conditions_for_Individuals_and_Communities_to_Flourish.pdf.

Barnes, Samantha. 'Does ESG Stand a Chance in the Trump 2.0 Era?' *International Banker*, 23 January 2025. internationalbanker.com/finance/does-esg-stand-a-chance-in-the-trump-2-0-era/.

Bartlett, Tara, Lara E. Law, Daniel Schugurensky, Marisol Juarez Díaz, and Wendy Wolfersteig. '17 Programs and Practices to Promote a Safe Campus: Alternatives to School Policing and Punitive Practices'. *The Urban Review* 56 (2024): 150–85. doi.org/10.1007/s11256-023-00669-2.

Beaty Chiste, Katherine. 'Retribution, Restoration, and White-collar Crime'. *Dalhousie Law Journal* 31, no. 1 (2008): 85–121. canlii.ca/t/t12s.

Beaufoy, Mark, and Rebecca Tompkins. 'EPA Victoria Releases Contaminated Environments Review Discussion Paper and Annual Compliance Plan 2012–13'. *Australian Environment Review* 27, no. 8 (2012). search.informit.org/doi/10.3316/agispt.20124044.

Becker, Gary, and Richard Posner. '"Capture" of Regulators by Fannie Mae and Freddie Mac'. *The Becker-Posner Blog*, 6 December 2011. becker-posner-blog.com/2011/06/capture-of-regulators-by-fannie-mae-and-freddie-mac-becker.html (site discontinued).

Bednar, Jenna. 'Governance for Human Social Flourishing'. *Daedalus* 152, no. 1 (2023): 31–45. doi.org/10.1162/daed_a_01958.

Bergstrand, Kelly, and Brian Mayer. '"The Community Helped Me:" Community Cohesion and Environmental Concerns in Personal Assessments of Post-Disaster Recovery'. *Society and Natural Resources* 33, no. 3 (2020): 386–405, doi.org/10.1080/08941920.2019.1709002.

Bhandari, Anooj. 'Restorative Practice: Developing a Community of Storytellers'. *Teaching Artist Journal* 16, no. 3–4 (2018): 100–105. doi.org/10.1080/15411796.2018.1535645.

Biggar, Susan, Louisa M. Lobigs, and Martin Fletcher. 'How Can We Make Health Regulation More Humane? A Quality Improvement Approach to Understanding Complainant and Practitioner Experiences'. *Journal of Medical Regulation* 106, no. 1 (2020): 7–15. doi.org/10.30770/2572-1852-106.1.7.

Bilmes, Linda J. 'Putting a Dollar Value on Nature Will Give Governments and Businesses More Reasons to Protect It'. *The Conversation*, 11 May 2021. theconversation.com/putting-a-dollar-value-on-nature-will-give-governments-and-businesses-more-reasons-to-protect-it-153968.

Biolinks Alliance. '$150,000 Funding Granted to Biolinks Alliance in Coliban Water vs. EPA Court Case'. 2023. biolinksalliance.org.au/coliban-water-epa-funding.

Bird Rose, Deborah. *Nourishing Terrains: Australian Aboriginal Views of Landscape and Wilderness*. Australian Heritage Commission, 1996.

Black, Julia, and Andrew Murray. 'Regulating AI and Machine Learning: Setting the Regulatory Agenda'. *European Journal of Law and Technology* 10, no. 3 (2019): 13.

Blakkarly, Jarni. 'Latrobe Valley a Litmus Test for Clean Energy Transition'. *Eureka Street* 26, no. 22, 9 November 2016. www.eurekastreet.com.au/article/latrobe-valley-a-litmus-test-for-clean-energy-transition.

Blomkamp, Emma. 'Navigating Power and Acknowledging Positionality'. *Emma Blomkamp*, 8 February 2022. emmablomkamp.com/blog/navigating-power.

Blomkamp, Emma. 'The Promise of Co-Design for Public Policy'. *Australian Journal of Public Administration* 77, no. 4 (2018): 729–43. doi.org/10.1111/1467-8500.12310.

Bodkin-Andrews, Gawaian, Aunty Frances Bodkin, Uncle Gavin Andrews, and Alison Whittaker. 'Mudjil'Dya'Djurali Dabuwa'Wurrata (How the White Waratah Became Red): D'harawal Storytelling and Welcome to Country "Controversies"'. *AlterNative: An International Journal of Indigenous Peoples* 12, no. 5 (2016): 480–97. doi.org/10.20507/AlterNative.2016.12.5.4.

Bonfanti, Rubinia Celeste, Benedetta Oberti, Elisa Ravazzoli, Anna Rinaldi, Stefano Ruggieri, and Adriano Schimmenti. 'The Role of Trust in Disaster Risk Reduction: A Critical Review'. *International Journal of Environmental Research and Public Health* 21, no. 1 (2023): 1–21. doi.org/10.3390/ijerph21010029.

Bonney, Rick, Caren B. Cooper, Janis Dickinson, et al. 'Citizen Science: A Developing Tool for Expanding Science Knowledge and Scientific Literacy'. *BioScience* 59, no. 11 (2009): 977–84. doi.org/10.1525/bio.2009.59.11.9.

Bouffard, Jeff, Maisha Cooper, and Kathleen Bergseth. 'The Effectiveness of Various Restorative Justice Interventions on Recidivism Outcomes Among Juvenile Offenders'. *Youth Violence and Juvenile Justice* 15, no. 4 (2017): 465–80. doi.org/10.1177/1541204016647428.

Bourne, Josephine. 'Indigenous Organisation Leaders: Balancing Tensions Between Achieving Political Goals and Regulatory Requirements'. *Australia and New Zealand School of Government (ANZSOG)*. 16 August 2022. anzsog.edu.au/news/indigenous-organisation-leaders-balancing-tensions-between-achieving-political-goals-and-regulatory-requirements/.

Bradshaw, William, David Roseborough, and Mark S. Umbreit. 'The Effect of Victim Offender Mediation on Juvenile Offender Recidivism: A Meta-Analysis'. *Conflict Resolution Quarterly* 24, no. 1 (2006): 87–98. doi.org/10.1002/crq.159.

Brady Spalding, Andrew. 'Restorative Justice for Multinational Corporations'. *Ohio State Law* 76, no. 2 (2015): 357–408. doi.org/10.31228/osf.io/2ez96.

Braithwaite, John. 'Accountability and Responsibility Through Restorative Justice'. In *Public Accountability: Designs, Dilemmas and Experiences,* edited by Michael Dowdle. Cambridge University Press, 2006.

Braithwaite, John. *Crime, Shame and Reintegration*. Cambridge University Press, 1989. doi.org/10.1017/CBO9780511804618.

Braithwaite, John. 'Minimally Sufficient Deterrence'. *Crime and Justice* 47, no. 1 (2018): 69–118. doi.org/10.1086/696043.

Braithwaite, John. 'Motivational Interviewing and Restorative Justice Praxis'. In *The Praxis of Justice: Liber Amicorum Ivo Aertsen,* edited by Brunilda Pali, Katrien Lauwaert and Stefaan Pleysier. Eleven, 2019.

Braithwaite, John. 'Regulating Nursing Homes: The Challenge of Regulating Care for Older People in Australia. *British Medical Journal* 323, no. 7310 (2001). doi.org/10.1136/bmj.323.7310.443.

Braithwaite, John. 'Responsive Excellence'. Working Paper, University of Pennsylvania, 2015.

Braithwaite, John. 'Restorative Justice and De-Professionalization', *The Good Society* 13, no. 1 (2004): 28–31. Project Muse. muse.jhu.edu/article/175203.

Braithwaite, John. *Restorative Justice and Corporate Regulation*. Routledge, 2003.

Braithwaite, John. *Restorative Justice and Responsive Regulation*. Oxford University Press, 2002. doi.org/10.1093/oso/9780195136395.001.0001.

Braithwaite, John. *Restorative Justice and Responsive Regulation: The Question of Evidence*. RegNet Research Paper no. 2016/51, 14 September 2016. doi.org/10.2139/ssrn.2839086.

Braithwaite, John. 'Types of Responsiveness'. In *Regulatory Theory: Foundations and Applications*, edited by Peter Drahos. ANU Press, 2017. doi.org/10.22459/RT.02.2017.

Braithwaite, John. 'Motivational Interviewing and Restorative Justice Praxis'. In *The Praxis of Justice*, edited by Brunilda Pali, Katrien Lauwaert and Stefaan Pleysier. Eleven International, 2019.

Braithwaite, John. 'Regulatory Mix, Collective Efficacy, and Crimes of the Powerful'. *Journal of White Collar and Corporate Crime* 1, no. 1 (2020): 62–71. doi.org/10.1177/2631309x19872430.

Braithwaite, John. 'Street-Level Meta-Strategies: Evidence on Restorative Justice and Responsive Regulation'. *Annual Review of Law and Social Science* 17 (2021): 205–25. doi.org/10.1146/annurev-lawsocsci-111720-013149.

Braithwaite, John. 'Scaling Up Crime Prevention and Justice'. *Crime and Justice* 50, no. 1 (2021): 247–99. doi.org/10.1086/716093.

Braithwaite, John. 'Restorative Justice'. *John Braithwaite: War, Crime, Regulation*. (blog). Accessed 20 February 2025. johnbraithwaite.com/restorative-justice.

Braithwaite, John, and Declan Roche. 'Responsibility and Restorative Justice'. In *Restorative Community Justice, Repairing Harm and Transforming Communities*, edited by Gordon Bazemore and Mara Schiff. Rockefeller University Press, 2001.

Braithwaite, John, Toni Makkai, and Valerie Braithwaite. *Regulating Aged Care: Ritualism and the New Pyramid*. Edward Elgar, 2007. doi.org/10.4337/9781847206855.

Braithwaite, John, Valerie Braithwaite and Gale Burford. 'Broadening the Applications of Responsive Regulation'. In *Restorative and Responsive Human Services*, edited by Gale Burford, John Braithwaite, and Valerie Braithwaite. Routledge, 2019. doi.org/10.4324/9780429398704-2.

Braithwaite, Valerie. 'Collective Hope'. *The Annals of the American Academy of Political and Social Science* 592, no. 1 (2004). doi.org/10.1177/0002716203262049.

Braithwaite, Valerie. 'The Hope Process and Social Inclusion'. *The Annals of the American Academy of Political and Social Science* 592, no. 1 (2004). doi.org/10.1177/0002716203262049.

Braithwaite, Valerie. *Defiance in Taxation and Governance: Resisting and Dismissing Authority in a Democracy*. Edward Elgar, 2009. doi.org/10.4337/9781848449077.

Braithwaite, Valerie. 'Tax Evasion'. In *The Oxford Handbook of Crime and Public Policy*, edited by Michael Tonry. Oxford University Press, 2012. doi.org/10.1093/oxfordhb/9780199844654.013.0016.

Braithwaite, Valerie. 'Beyond the Bubble that is Robodebt: How Governments That Lose Integrity Threaten Democracy'. *The Australian Journal of Social Issues* 55, no. 3 (2020): 242–59. doi.org/10.1002/ajs4.122.

Braithwaite, Valerie. 'Understanding and Managing Trust Norms'. *International Journal for Court Administration* 12, no. 3 (2021): 1–13. doi.org/10.36745/ijca.425.

Braithwaite, Valerie, Gerben Bruinsma, and David Weisburd. 'Defiance and Motivational Postures'. In *Encyclopedia of Criminology and Criminal Justice*, edited by Gerben Bruinsma and David Weisburd. Springer, 2014.

Braithwaite, Valerie, Kristina Murphy, and Monika Reinhart, 'Taxation Threat, Motivational Postures and Responsive Regulation'. *Law and Policy* 29, no. 1 (2007): 137–58. doi.org/10.1111/j.1467-9930.2007.00250.x.

Bromfield, Leah M., Jenny R. Higgins, Daryl J. Higgins, and Nick Richardson. *Barriers, Incentives and Strategies to Enchance [sic] Recruitment of Indigenous Carers*. Australian Government: Australian Institute of Family Studies, 2007. aifs.gov.au/sites/default/files/publication-documents/paper2_0_0.pdf.

Buchan, Anne, Amos Atkinson, Angela Muscatello, et al. *Right Plant, Right Way: Report 2021: A First Nations led Review of Revegetation in Victoria*. Dja Dja Wurrung Enterprises Pty Ltd (DJANDAK), 2021. www.anpc.asn.au/wp-content/uploads/2021/10/Right-Plant-Right-Way.pdf.

Burford, Gale, John Braithwaite, and Valerie Braithwaite. *Restorative and Responsive Human Services*. Routledge, 2022. doi.org/10.4324/9780429398704.

Burns, Danny. 'Systemic Action Research: Changing System Dynamics to Support Sustainable Change'. *Action Research* 12, no. 1 (2014): 3–18. doi.org/10.1177/1476750313513910.

Burnes, David, Marie-Therese Connolly, Erin Salvo, Patricia F. Kimball, Geoff Rogers, and Stuart Lewis. 'RISE: A Conceptual Model of Integrated and Restorative Elder Abuse Intervention', *The Gerontologist* 63, no. 6 (2022): 966–73. doi.org/10.1093/geront/gnac083.

Bush Heritage Australia. 'Fighting Fire in the Dry'. 8 February 2023. www.bushheritage.org.au/news/fighting-fire-in-the-dry.

Bush Heritage Australia. '"Right-Way" Science'. Accessed 8 March 2025. www.bushheritage.org.au/what-we-do/our-priorities/science/right-way-science.

Calo, Ryan, and Danielle Keats Citron. 'The Automated Administrative State: A Crisis of Legitimacy'. *Emory Law Journal* 70, no. 4 (2021): 797–845.

Cameron, Jenny, and Katherine Gibson. 'Alternative Pathways to Community and Economic Development: The Latrobe Valley Community Partnering Project'. *Geographical Research* 43, no. 3 (2005): 274–85. doi.org/10.1111/j.1745-5871.2005.00327.x.

Cameron, Sarah, Ian McAllister, Simon Jackman, et al. *The 2022 Australian Federal Election: Results from the Australian Election Study*. Australian Election Study, 5 December 2022. apo.org.au/node/321025.

Campbell, Jenny. 'Why Perspective Matters: Understanding the Importance of Different Viewpoints'. *Resilience Dynamic*. Accessed 23 January 2025. resiliencedynamic.com/resilient-thinking/why-perspective-matters/.

Cary, Joanna, Henry Jackson, and Wayne Gumley. 'Statutory Tools for Environmental Protection in Victoria – The Next Generation. *National Environmental Law Review*, no. 2 (2004): 38. www5.austlii.edu.au/au/journals/NatEnvLawRw/2004/34.pdf, accessed 13 February 2025.

Centola, Damon. *Change: How to Make Big Things Happen*. Little, Brown Spark, 2021.

Change Strategists. 'Building a Change Champion Network Roles and Responsibilities'. 15 August 2024. changestrategists.com/change-champion-network-roles-and-responsibilities/.

Chartrand, Larry, and Kanatase Horn. *A Report on the Relationship Between Restorative Justice and Indigenous Legal Traditions in Canada*. Department of Justice Canada, October 2016. www.justice.gc.ca/eng/rp-pr/jr/rjilt-jrtja/rjilt-jrtja.pdf.

Choi, Yongjin, and Ashley M. Fox. 'Mistrust in Public Health Institutions is a Stronger Predictor of Vaccine Hesitancy and Uptake Than Trust in Trump'. *Social Science & Medicine* 314 (2022): 1–10. doi.org/10.1016/j.socscimed.2022.115440.

Chouinard, Yvon. 'Earth is Now Our Only Shareholder'. Patagonia.com, 14 September 2022. www.patagonia.com/ownership/.

Christ, Carol. 'The Chancellor of Berkeley Weighs In'. Interview by Molly Fischer. *The New Yorker*, 17 December 2023. www.newyorker.com/news/the-new-yorker-interview/the-chancellor-of-berkeley-weighs-in.

Christensen, Helen. 'Legislating Community Engagement at the Australian Local Government Level'. *Commonwealth Journal of Local Governance*, no. 21 (2019): 1–30. doi.org/10.5130/cjlg.v0i21.6515.

Christie, Nils. 'Conflicts as Property'. *The British Journal of Criminology* 17, no. 1 (1977): 1–15. doi.org/10.1093/oxfordjournals.bjc.a046783.

Clark, Janine Natalya. 'Storytelling, Resilience and Transitional Justice: Reversing Narrative Social Bulimia'. *Theoretical Criminology* 26, no. 3 (2022): 456–74. doi.org/10.1177/1362480620933230.

Clott, Alec. 'Restorative Justice as a Form of Collaborative Governance: A Theoretical Analysis of Mediation and Collaboration'. *SPECTRA* 5, no. 1 (2016). spectra journal.org/articles/73.

Coaldrake, Peter. *Let the Sunshine In: Review of Culture and Accountability in the Queensland Public Sector: Final Report*. Government of Queensland, 28 June 2022. apo.org.au/node/318405.

Coffee, John C., Jr. *Corporate Crime and Punishment: The Crisis of Underenforcement*. Berrett-Koehler, 2020.

Coglianese, Cary. *Listening, Learning Leading: A Framework for Regulatory Excellence*. The Penn Program on Regulation, 2015.

Coglianese, Cary. 'Empathy in an Automated State'. *The Regulatory Review.* The Penn Program on Regulation, 10 January 2022. www.theregreview.org/2022/01/10/coglianese-empathy-automated-state/.

Coleman, Peter, T. *The Way Out: How to Overcome Toxic Polarization*. Columbia University Press, 2021. doi.org/10.7312/cole19740.

Coliban Water. 'Business Case to Examine Efficiency of Key Murray Water System'. 25 August 2023. coliban.com.au/business-case-examine-efficiency-key-murray-water-system.

Coliban Water. 'Innovate Reconcilation Action Plan: July 2023–July 2025'. August 2023. coliban.com.au/about-us/reconciliation-action-plan.

Contact. 'Restoration of Environmental and Cultural Impacts of the 2019 Karapiti Incident'. 3 December 2023. contact.co.nz/aboutus/media-centre/2021/05/13/karapiti-incident-report.

Contact Energy. *2024 Integrated Report*. Contact Energy, 2024. contact.co.nz/investor-centre/reports-and-results/integrated-report.

Crepaldiet, Maura, Giulia Fusi, Alice Cancer, Paola Iannello, and Maria Luisa Rusconi. 'The Bidirectional Relationship Between Risk and Creativity: A Systematic Review'. *TPM – Testing, Psychometrics, Methodology in Applied Psychology* 31, no. 1 (2024): 41–57, doi.org/10.4473/TPM31.1.3.

Cross, Andi. 'How Businesses Can Give Back to the Environment and Their Communities'. *Forbes*, 3 April 2024. www.forbes.com/councils/forbesbusinesscouncil/2024/04/03/how-businesses-can-give-back-to-the-environment-and-their-communities/.

Cross, Donna S., Kevin C. Runions, Ken A. Resnicow, Eileen F. Britt, and Caitlin Gray. 'Motivational Interviewing as a Positive Response to High-School Bullying'. *Psychology in the Schools* 55, no. 5 (2018): 464–75. doi.org/10.1002/pits.22120.

Cunneen, Chris, and Juan Tiari. 'Indigenous Criminology'. In *The Routledge Companion to Criminological Theory and Concepts*, edited by Avi Brisman, Eamonn Carrabine, and Nigel South. Routledge, 2017. doi.org/10.4324/9781315744902.

Czabán, Samu. 'A Lawyer's View of Irrelevant Influences in the Courtroom'. *Psyche*, 23 January 2025. psyche.co/ideas/a-lawyers-view-of-irrelevant-influences-in-the-courtroom.

Dadich, Ann, Cris Townley, Rebekah Grace, and Lynn Kemp. 'Building Resilient Australian Communities'. *JMI Policy Insights* (2025), James Martin Institute for Public Policy. researchers.westernsydney.edu.au/en/publications/building-resilient-australian-communities-policy-insights-paper.

Dandurand, Yvon, and Annette Vogt. *Handbook on Restorative Justice Programmes*. 2nd edition. Criminal Justice Handbook Series. United Nations Office on Drugs and Crime, 2020. www.unodc.org/documents/justice-and-prison-reform/20-01146_Handbook_on_Restorative_Justice_Programmes.pdf.

Danson, Natasha. 'The Case for Empathy by Regulators'. *Grey Areas: A Commentary on Legal Issues Affecting Professional Regulation*, no. 248 (2020). Steinecke Maciura LeBlanc Barristers & Solicitors. www.sml-law.com/wp-content/uploads/2020/07/Greyar248.pdf.

Darling-Hammond, Sean, *Fostering Belonging, Transforming Schools: The Impact of Restorative Practices*. Learning Policy Institute, 18 May 2023. learningpolicyinstitute.org/product/impact-restorative-practices-report.

Davies, Siobhan, Graham R. Marshall, and Malcolm Ridges. 'A Property Rights Schema for Cultural Flows in the Murray Darling Basin, Australia'. *Australasian Journal of Environmental Management* 30, nos. 3–4 (2023): 393–415. doi.org/10.1080/14486563.2023.2281562.

Dawson, Neil M., Brendan Coolsaet, Eleanor J. Sterling, et al. 'The Role of Indigenous Peoples and Local Communities in Effective and Equitable Conservation'. *Ecology and Society* 26, no. 3 (2021). doi.org/10.5751/ES-12625-260319.

Deci, Edward L., and Richard M. Ryan. 'The "What" and "Why" of Goal Pursuits: Human Needs and the Self-Determination of Behavior'. *Psychological Inquiry* 11, no. 4 (2000): 227–68. doi.org/10.1207/S15327965PLI1104_01.

Dekker, Sidney, Amanda Oates, and Joseph Rafferty, eds. *Restorative Just Culture in Practice: Implementation and Evaluation*. Productivity Press, 2022. doi.org/10.4324/9781003162582.

Delta Group. 'Inner West Dust and Air Quality Has a Better Plan'. (n.d.). www.deltagroup.com.au/inner-west-dust-and-air-quality-has-a-better-plan/.

Denton, Kylie. 'How To Embed Behaviour Change in a Complex Work Environment'. Performance Advisory Group, 24 July 2020. performanceadvisorygroup.com.au/embed-behaviour-change/.

DeStigter, Todd. 'Public Displays of Affection: Political Community Through Critical Empathy'. *Research in the Teaching of English*, 33, no. 3 (1999): 235–44. doi.org/10.58680/rte19991669.

di Salvia, Daniela. 'Pachamama'. In *Encyclopedia of Latin American Religions*, edited by Henri Gooren. Springer International Publishing, 2019. doi.org/10.1007/978-3-319-27078-4_65.

Djaara. *Dhelkunya Dja: Dja Dja Wurrung Country Plan 2014–2034*. Dja Dja Wurrung Clans Aboriginal Corporation, 2014. djadjawurrung.com.au/wp-content/uploads/2021/04/Dhelkunya-Dja-Country-Plan-2014-2034.pdf.

Djaara. *Dhelkunyangu Gatjin: Working Together to Heal Water. Djaara Gatjin Strategy*. Dja Dja Wurrung Clans Aboriginal Corporation, 2023. djandak.com.au/wp-content/uploads/2023/10/Dhelkunyangu-Gatjin-Working-together-to-heal-water-Gatjin-Strategy-2023.pdf.

Downie, Jocelyn, and Jennifer L. Llewellyn. *Being Relational: Reflections on Relational Theory and Health Law*. University of British Columbia Press, 2011. doi.org/10.59962/9780774821902.

Douglas, Susan. 'Neutrality in Mediation: A Study of Mediator Perceptions'. *QUT Law Review* 8, no. 1 (2008): 139–57. doi.org/10.5204/qutlr.v8i1.88.

Duckworth, Mark, Christine Horn, and Michele Grossman. *Do Governments Trust Communities? The Trust Flows Project Research Report.* Centre for Resilient and Inclusive Societies, 2024, doi.org/10.56311/FZLZ2190.

Dudgeon, Pat, Shol Blustein, Abigail Bray, Tom Calma, Rob McPhee, and Ian Ring. *Connection Between Family, Kinship and Social and Emotional Wellbeing.* Australian Institute of Health and Welfare (AIHW), 2021. www.indigenousmhspc.gov.au/getattachment/e129c621-58a4-4966-8730-dcf6e3a533a8/dudgeon-et-al-2021-family-kinship-20210802.pdf.

Dudley, Susan E., and Zhoudan Xie. 'Designing a Choice Architecture for Regulators'. *Public Administration Review* 80, no. 1 (2020): 151–56. doi.org/10.1111/puar.13112.

Duffy, Michelle, Sue Yell, Larissa Walker, et al. 'The Social Justice Issues of Smoke Im/Mobilities'. *Australian Geographer* 54, no. 4 (2023): 573–87. doi.org/10.1080/00049182.2023.2256595.

Dynes, Russell R. 'Social Capital: Dealing with Community Emergencies'. *Homeland Security Affairs* 2, no. 2 (2006): 1–26.

Eburn, Michael. 'Looking to Courts of Law for Disaster Justice'. In *Natural Hazards and Disaster Justice: Challenges for Australia and Its Neighbours*, edited by Anna Lukasiewicz and Claudia Baldwin. Springer, 2020. doi.org/10.1007/978-981-15-0466-2_7.

Edelman. *Trust Barometer 2022 Australia.* Edelman, 16 February 2022. www.edelman.com.au/trust-barometer-2022-australia.

Edwards, Anne. 'Relational Agency: Learning to Be a Resourceful Practitioner'. *International Journal of Educational Research* 43, no. 3 (2005): 174. doi.org/10.1016/j.ijer.2006.06.010.

Edwards, Joel, Eric Windholz, Nicholas Faulkner, Lara Werbeloff. 'Implementing General Environmental Duties: Challenges and Opportunities', *Australian Journal of Public Administration* 80, no. 3 (2021): 474–492. doi.org/10.1111/1467-8500.12456.

Eldridge, Kevin. 'Is It Enquiry or Inquiry? Australian Spelling'. 2024–25. www.australian-dictionary.com.au/dictionary/is-it-enquiry-or-inquiry.php.

Ellan, Liz. 'Amplifying Indigenous Voices in the Workplace: How to Cultivate Genuine Cultural Safety for Sustainable Success'. Liz Ellan. Accessed 9 March 2025.

Emergency Management Victoria. *Community Based Emergency Management: Better Connected, and Working Together—Before, During and After: Overview 2023.* Emergency Management Victoria, 2023. www.emv.vic.gov.au/how-we-help/community/community-based-emergency-management/community-based-emergency-management-overview.

Emergency Management Victoria. 'Victoria's Emergency Management Planning Framework'. Accessed 17 February 2025. www.emv.vic.gov.au/responsibilities/emergency-management-planning/emergency-management-planning-resource-library-0/victorias-emergency-management-planning-framework.

Engage Victoria. 'EPA Development Licence Applications'. State Government of Victoria. Accessed 15 February 2025. engage.vic.gov.au/epa-development-licence-applications.

Environmental Defender's Office (EDO). *Implementing Effective Independent Environmental Protection Agencies in Australia: Best Practice Environmental Governance for Environmental Justice.* EDO, January 2022. www.edo.org.au/wp-content/uploads/2022/01/Implementing-effective-independent-EPAs-in-Australia-Report.pdf.

Environmental Justice Australia. 'Cultural Flows at Margooya Lagoon'. 2023. envirojustice.org.au/legal-work/first-nations-justice/cultural-flows-at-margooya-lagoon/.

Environment Protection Authority Inquiry Ministerial Advisory Committee. *Independent Inquiry into the Environment Protection Authority/ Environment.* State Government of Victoria, August 2015.

Environment Protection Authority (EPA) Victoria. *Air Emissions from Non-Hazardous Waste Landfills – Update of 2013 Literature Review.* State Government of Victoria, December 2016. cleanaway2stor.blob.core.windows.net/cleanaway2-blob-container/2019/11/Air-Emissions-from-Non-Hazardous-Waste-EPA2016.pdf.

EPA Victoria. *Annual Report of Operations 2023–24.* www.epa.vic.gov.au/annual-report.

EPA Victoria. 'The Build Aware Campaign'. Archived 19 October 2022, at the Wayback Machine, web.archive.org/web/20250426203551/https://www.epa.vic.gov.au/about-epa/laws/laws-and-your-business/build-aware.

EPA Victoria. *Charter of Consultation.* Publication 1928. 15 June 2021. www.epa.vic.gov.au/about-epa/publications/1928.

EPA Victoria. 'Coliban Region Water Corporation ABN: 96 549 082 360'. Last modified 3 October 2023. www.epa.vic.gov.au/public-registers?q=Coliban.

EPA Victoria. *Compliance and Enforcement Policy.* 29 January 2025. www.epa.vic.gov.au/about-epa/publications/1798-2.

EPA Victoria. 'Continual Improvement and Review'. Archived 27 March 2022, at the Wayback Machine, web.archive.org/web/20250428025229/https://www.epa.vic.gov.au/for-business/find-a-topic/environment-protection-laws-and-regulations/implementing-the-general-environmental-duty---a-guide-for-licence-holders/continual-improvement-and-review.

EPA Victoria. *1814: Sanction Powers Policy.* Last modified 31 August 2023.

EPA Victoria. 'Environment Reference Standard'. Environment Protection Act 2017 no. S245 Gazette 26 May 2021. www.epa.vic.gov.au/environment-reference-standard.

EPA Victoria. *EPA Environmental Citizenship Strategy*. EPA Victoria, February 2013. Archived 26 March 2020, at the Wayback Machine. web.archive.org/web/20250420193958/https://www.epa.vic.gov.au/about-epa/publications/1519.

EPA Victoria. 'EPA's Focus on Protection and Prevention'. Last modified 4 July 2022. www.epa.vic.gov.au/about-epa/what-we-do/epa-is-changing.

EPA Victoria. 'Hallam Road Landfill'. Last modified 20 June 2025. www.epa.vic.gov.au/hallam-road-landfill.

EPA Victoria. 'Implementing the General Enviromental Duty for Licence Holders.' Last modified 2 May 2025. www.epa.vic.gov.au/implementing-general-environmental-duty-licence-holders.

EPA Victoria. *EPA Victoria Compliance and Enforcement Policy*. Publication 1798.3.29. January 2025. www.epa.vic.gov.au/compliance-and-enforcement-policy.

EPA Victoria. *EPA Victoria Compliance and Enforcement Policy*. Publication 1388. June 2011. hazelwoodinquiry.archive.vic.gov.au/wp-content/uploads/2014/08/EPA.0001.004.0049.pdf.

EPA Victoria. 'EPA Victoria Upgrades Its Compliance and Enforcement Action'. *Australian Environment Review* 26, no. 7 (2011): 201–04.

EPA Victoria. 'Inspiring Environmental Solutions'. Archived 22 September 2020, at the Wayback Machine. web.archive.org/web/20250521144033/https://www.epa.vic.gov.au/about-epa/our-programs-and-projects/inspiring-environmental-solutions.

EPA Victoria. *Inspiring Environmental Solutions: EPA's Community Funding Program.* Program Guidelines. 2011. Archived 12 April 2020, at the Wayback Machine. web.archive.org/web/20250414050624/https://www.epa.vic.gov.au/-/media/epa/files/publications/1419.pdf.

EPA Victoria. 'Officers for the Protection of the Local Environment'. Last modified 17 December 2024. www.epa.vic.gov.au/officers-protection-local-environment.

EPA Victoria. 'Our Regulatory Approach'. Environment Protection Authority Victoria. Last modified 25 May 2025. www.epa.vic.gov.au/our-regulatory-approach.

EPA Victoria. 'Permissions Scheme Policy'. Publication 1799.3. Last modified 29 January 2025. www.epa.vic.gov.au/17993-permissions-scheme-policy.

EPA Victoria. 'Recognition of the Traditional Owners and Victoria's First Peoples'. Last modified 9 December 2022. Archived 21 May 2025, at the Wayback Machine. web.archive.org/web/20250521052331/https://www.epa.vic.gov.au/about-epa/recognition-and-inclusion-of-victorian-aboriginal-people-and-traditional-owners.

EPA Victoria. 'Register of Advisory Panels'. Last modified 18 March 2025. www.epa.vic.gov.au/public-registers?register=advisory-panels.

EPA Victoria. *Strategic Plan 2022–27.* www.epa.vic.gov.au/strategic-plan.

EPA Victoria. 'The Tottenham Industrial Fire'. Last modified 12 May 2025. www.epa.vic.gov.au/tottenham-industrial-fire.

EPA Victoria. 'Using SEPPs and WMPs in the New Environment Protection Framework Guide'. 1994, last modified 30 June 2021. www.epa.vic.gov.au/1994-using-sepps-and-wmps-new-environment-protection-framework-guide.

Environment Southland Regional Council. 'Environment Southland Diversion Scheme'. In Environmental Southland Regional Council, *Diversion Policies.* October 2017. www.es.govt.nz/repository/libraries/id:26gi9ayo517q9stt81sd/hierarchy/about-us/plans-and-strategies/policies/compliance-policies/documents/ES%20Compliance%20Policies.pdf.

Epstein, Ronald M., and Mary Catherine Beach. '"I Don't Need Your Pills, I Need Your Attention:" Steps Toward Deep Listening in Medical Encounters'. *Current Opinion on Psychology* 53 (2023): 1–6. doi.org/10.1016/j.copsyc.2023.101685.

Eva, Christian, Jessica Harris, Kerry Bodle, Dennis Foley, Boyd Hunter, and Nina Nichols. '"It's Self-Determination. Blackfullas Making Right Decisions for Blackfullas": Why Indigenous-Owned Businesses Create Better Indigenous Employment Outcomes'. *Australian Journal of Social Issues* 59, no. 1 (2024): 29–56. doi.org/10.1002/ajs4.292.

Evans, Katherine, and Dorothy Vaandering. *The Little Book of Restorative Justice in Education: Fostering Responsibility, Healing, and Hope in Schools*. Good Books, 2016.

Evolve Communities. 'Connection to Country—Why is Country Important to Aboriginal and Torres Strait Islander People?' *Sites at Scale* (blog). Accessed 7 March 2025, www.evolves.com.au/connection-to-country/.

Executive Office of the President, Office of Management and Budget. 'Broadening Public Participation and Community Engagement in the Regulatory Process'. Memorandum for the Heads of Executive Departments and Agencies, Executive Office of the President, 19 July 2023. www.reginfo.gov/public/jsp/EO/fedReg Review/Broadening-Public-Participation-and-Community-Engagement-in-the-Regulatory-Process.pdf.

Fair Work Ombudsman. 'Supporting Employees During Sorry Business'. Australian Government. Last modified October 2024. www.fairwork.gov.au/sites/default/files/2024-06/fd-first-nations-people-supporting-sorry-business-fact-sheet.pdf.

Federal Bureau of Investigation. 'Al Capone'. Accessed 1 March 2025. vault.fbi.gov/Al%20Capone.

Feller, Kirk. 'Giving Back Is a Business's Moral Responsibility'. *Rolling Stone*, 1 August 2023. www.rollingstone.com/culture-council/articles/giving-back-is-good-business-1234797862/.

Field, Rachel. 'The Theory and Practice of Neutrality in Mediation'. *The Arbitrator and Mediator* 22 no. 1 (2003): 79–89. eprints.qut.edu.au/6290/.

Finnis, Mark. *Independent* Thinking on Restorative Practice: Building Relationships, Improving Behaviour and Creating Stronger Communities. Independent Thinking Press, 2021. www.crownhouse.co.uk/assets/look-inside/978178135 3387.pdf.

Fisse, Brent. 'Reconstructing Corporate Criminal Law: Deterrence, Retribution, Fault and Sanctions'. *Southern California Law Review* 56 (1982): 1141–246.

Fisse, Brent, and John Braithwaite. *Corporations, Crime and Accountability*. Cambridge University Press, 1994. doi.org/10.1017/CBO9780511659133.

Fletcher, Michael-Shawn, Anthony Romano, Simon Connor, Michela Mariani, and Shira Yoshi Maezumi. 'Catastrophic Bushfires, Indigenous Fire Knowledge and Reframing Science in Southeast Australia'. *Fire* 4, no. 3 (2021): 61. doi.org/10.3390/fire4030061.

Florini, Ann, Gordon LaForge, and Anne-Marie Slaughter. 'Democratic Governance for the Long Emergency'. In *Democracy in a Hotter Time: Climate Change and Democratic Transformation,* edited by David W. Orr. MIT Press, 2023. doi.org/10.7551/mitpress/15122.003.0016.

Forsberg, Lars, Hans Wickström, and Håkan Källmén. 'Motivational Interviewing May Facilitate Professional Interactions with Inspectees During Environmental Inspections and Enforcement Conversations'. *PeerJ* 2, no. e508 (2014): 14, doi.org/10.7717/peerj.508.

Forsyth, Miranda. 'Turning Up the Restorative Dial in Environmental Regulation with an Adaptive Learning Loop'. In *The Palgrave Handbook of Environmental Restorative Justice*, edited by Brunilda Pali, Miranda Forsyth, and Felicity Tepper. Palgrave Macmillan, 2022. doi.org/10.1007/978-3-031-04223-2_7.

Forsyth, Miranda, Deborah Cleland, Felicity Tepper, et al. 'A Future Agenda for Environmental Restorative Justice?' *The International Journal of Restorative Justice* 4, no. 1 (2021): 17–40. doi.org/10.5553/tijrj.000063.

Forsyth, Miranda, and Felicity Tepper. 'Environmental Enforceable Undertakings: An Innovative Tool to Repair and Prevent Environmental Harm'. *Journal of Environmental Law* 36 (2024): 385–411. doi.org/10.1093/jel/eqae021.

Fox Koob, Simone, Melissa Cunningham, Sarah Emery, Benjamin Preiss, and Noel Towell. 'Scores of Dead Fish, Eels Wash Up After Melbourne Factory Fire'. *The Age*, 31 August 2018. www.theage.com.au/national/victoria/scores-of-dead-fish-eels-wash-up-after-melbourne-factory-fire-20180831-p500z5.html.

Fredericks, Anthony D. 'Why Taking Risks is Critical for Creativity'. *Psychology Today* (blog), 21 January 2022. www.psychologytoday.com/au/blog/creative-insights/202201/why-taking-risks-is-critical-creativity.

Freeman, David. 'In Conversation: Terry Pratchett and Gerald Seymour'. *The Guardian*, 9 November 2001. www.theguardian.com/books/2001/nov/08/fiction.terrypratchett.

Freedman, Jeri. *The Establishment of the Environmental Protection Agency.* Cavendish Square, 2018.

Frewer, Lynn, and Brian Salter. 'Public Attitudes, Scientific Advice and the Politics of Regulatory Policy: The Case of BSE'. *Science and Public Policy* 29, no. 2 (2002): 137–45. doi.org/10.3152/147154302781781092.

Fulham, Lindsay, Julie Blais, Elizabeth A. Schultheis, et al. 'The Effectiveness of Restorative Justice Programs: A Meta-Analysis of Recidivism and Other Relevant Outcomes'. *Criminology & Criminal Justice* 25, no. 5 (2023): 1–27. doi.org/10.1177/17488958231215228.

Gabbay, Zvi D. 'Exploring the Limits of the Restorative Justice Paradigm: Restorative Justice and White Collar Crime'. *Cardozo Journal of Conflict Resolution* 8, no. 421 (2006–2007): 421–86.

Gammage, Bill, and Bruce Pascoe. *First Knowledges Country: Future Fire, Future Farming*. First Knowledges series, edited by Margo Neale. Thames & Hudson, 2021.

Garner, Jake. 'Restorative Practices in ResLife: The Role of Fair Process in Curriculum Development'. *Roompact* (blog). August 2022. blog.roompact.com/2022/08/restorative-practices-in-reslife-the-role-of-fair-process-in-curricular-development/.

Gavens, Kate. 'Incentivising Compliance: Using Behavioural Insights to Encourage and Persuade' (panel discussion with Liam Smith and John Merritt, Australia and New Zealand School of Government [ANSZOG] and the National Regulators Community of Practice, Melbourne Business School and online, 2 June 2023). anzsog.edu.au/learning-and-development/events-and-conferences/incentivising-compliance-using-behavioural-insights-to-encourage-and-persuade/.

Gavrielides, Theo. 'Domestic Violence and Power Abuse Within the Family: The Restorative Justice Approach'. In *Violence in Families: Integrating Research into Practice*, edited by Peter Sturmey. Springer International Publishing, 2023. doi.org/10.1007/978-3-031-31549-7_18.

Gavrielides, Theo. 'Restorative Justice—the Perplexing Concept: Conceptual Fault-lines and Power Battles Within the Restorative Justice Movement'. *Criminology & Criminal Justice* 8, no. 2 (2008): 165–83. doi.org/10.1177/1748895808088993.

Geia, Lynore, K., Barbara Hayes, and Kim Usher. 'Yarning/Aboriginal Storytelling: Towards an Understanding of an Indigenous Perspective and Its Implications for Research Practice'. *Contemporary Nurse* 46, 1 (2013): 13–17. doi.org/10.5172/conu.2013.46.1.13.

Giles, Cynthia. *Next Generation Compliance: Environmental Regulation for the Modern Era*. Oxford University Press, 2022. doi.org/10.1093/oso/9780197656747.001.0001.

Gladstone, Nigel, and Cameron Gooley. 'Government Says "More Work Required" to Boost Indigenous Jobs in Public Sector'. *The Sydney Morning Herald*. 15 November 2021. www.smh.com.au/national/government-says-more-work-required-to-boost-indigenous-jobs-in-public-sector-20211111-p5980m.html.

Glynn-McDonald, Rona. 'First Nations Systems Thinking'. *Common Ground.* 14 July 2021. Last modified 20 October 2022. www.commonground.org.au/article/first-nations-systems-thinking.

Godin, Seth. *The Song of Significance: A New Manifesto for Teams.* Penguin Random House, 2023.

Goglio, Karine, Florence Crespin-Mazet, Laurent Simon, Patrick Cohendet, and Etienne Wenger-Trayner. 'Managing with Communities for Innovation, Agility, and Resilience'. *European Management Journal* 41, no. 4 (2023): 673–75. doi.org/10.1016/j.emj.2023.07.005.

Goodhue, Rebecca, and Sadhana Seriamlu. *A Quick Guide to Establishing a Community of Practice.* ARACY, 2021. www.aracy.org.au/wp-content/uploads/2024/09/A_quick_guide_to_Establishing_a_Community_of_Practice_ARACY_2021_-_FINAL.pdf.

Goolmeer, Teagan, Oliver Costello, Culturally Signiticant Entities workshop participants, Anja Skroblin, Libby Rumpf, and Brendan A. Whittle. 'Indigenous-Led Designation and Management of Culturally Significant Species'. *Nature Ecology & Evolution* 8 (2024): 1623–31. doi.org/10.1038/s41559-024-02466-w.

Gottman, John, and Nan Silver. *The Seven Principles for Making Marriage Work: A Practical Guide from the Country's Foremost Relationship Expert.* Second ed. Harmony Books, 2015.

Grabowski, Daniel. 'Considering Multiple Perspectives In Critical Thinking'. *Oxford Open Learning,* 23 March 2023. www.ool.co.uk/blog/considering-multiple-perspectives-in-critical-thinking/.

Graham, Mary. 'Some Thoughts About the Philosophical Underpinnings of Aboriginal Worldviews'. *Australian Humanities Review.* Accessed 7 March 2025. australianhumanitiesreview.org/2008/11/01/some-thoughts-about-the-philosophical-underpinnings-of-aboriginal-worldviews/.

Graham, Mary. 'Some Thoughts About the Philosophical Underpinnings of Aboriginal Worldviews'. *Worldviews: Global Religions, Culture, and Ecology* 3, no. 2 (1999): 105–18. doi.org/10.1163/156853599X00090.

Gray, Matthew, Boyd Hunter, and Shaun Lohoar. 'Increasing Indigenous Employment Rates'. Australian Government—Australian Institute of Health and Welfare, Australian Institute of Family Studies, March 2012. www.aihw.gov.au/getmedia/71bb346a-1b83-4038-a2f7-647e65a21445/ctg-ip03.pdf.aspx.

Grieve-Williams, Victoria. 'Makarrata: The Aboriginal Healing Process We Should All Know About'. *SBS Voices*. 4 July 2019. Last modified 09 July 2019. www.sbs.com.au/voices/article/makarrata-the-aboriginal-healing-process-we-should-all-know-about/8nd8avji8.

Guirguis, Ayman, James Gray, Tess Kane, and Jenna S. Yim. 'Australia Greenwashing: Half-Yearly Review of ASIC and ACCC Prosecutions—and ACCC Position on Environmental Collaborations'. *K&L Gates Hub*, 21 October 2024. www.klgates.com/Australia-Greenwashing-Half-Yearly-Review-of-ASIC-and-ACCC-Prosecutions-and-ACCC-Position-on-Environmental-Collaborations-10-21-2024.

Gunningham, Neil, Peter N. Grabosky, and Darren Sinclair. *Smart Regulation: Designing Environmental Policy*. Clarendon Press, 1998. doi.org/10.1093/oso/9780198268574.001.0001.

Gunningham, Neil, Cameron Holley, and Clifford Shearing. 'Neighbourhood Environment Improvement Plans: Community Empowerment, Voluntary Collaboration and Legislative Design'. *Environmental and Planning Law Journal* 24, no. 2 (2007): 126.

Gunningham, Neil, and Darren Sinclair. 'Regulation and the Role of Trust: Reflections from the Mining Industry'. *Journal of Law and Society* 36, no. 2 (2009): 167–94. doi.org/10.1111/j.1467-6478.2009.00462.x.

Gunningham, Neil, and Darren Sinclair. 'Smart Regulation' in *Regulatory Theory Foundations and Applications*, edited by Peter Drahos. ANU Press, 2017. doi.org/10.22459/rt.02.2017.08.

Hall, Jane. 'Review of the Victorian EPA—What May Change?' *Australian Environment Review* (2016): 138–44.

Hall, Tom, and Robin James Smith. 'Care and Repair and the Politics of Urban Kindness'. *Sociology* 49, no. 1 (2015): 3–18. doi.org/10.1177/0038038514546662.

Haller, Linda. 'Restorative Lawyer Discipline in Australia'. *Nevada Law Journal* 12, no. 2 (2012): 316–32.

Hamilton, Mark. *Environmental Crime and Restorative Justice: Justice as Meaningful Involvement*. Palgrave Macmillan, 2021. doi.org/10.1007/978-3-030-69052-6.

Hamilton, Mark. 'Restorative Justice Conferencing in an Environmental Offending Context: The Role of Legislation'. *Asia Pacific Journal of Environmental Law* 25 (2022): 51–76. doi.org/10.4337/apjel.2022.01.03.

Hamilton, Mark. 'Restorative Justice Conferencing in Australia and New Zealand: Application and Potential in an Environmental and Aboriginal Cultural Heritage Protection Context'. *International Journal of Restorative Justice* 4, no. 1 (2021): 81–97. doi.org/10.5553/tijrj.000064.

Hamilton, Mark, and Ellie Stanton. 'Characteristics of Restorative Justice Conferencing in a New Zealand Environmental Offending Context'. *New Zealand Law Review* 32, no. 4 (2024): 585–616.

Handsaker, Renee. 'Narrative Approaches to Restorative Justice Settings: Considerations of Power, Struggle and Social Transformation'. In *Intersecting Stories: Narrative Therapy Reflections on Gender, Culture and Justice,* edited by Dulwich Centre. Dulwich Centre Publications, 2020.

Haraway, Donna. 'Situated Knowledges: The Science Question in Feminism and the Privilege of Partial Perspective'. *Feminist Studies* 14, no. 3 (1988). doi.org/10.2307/3178066.

Harris, Nathan, Lode Walgrave, and John Braithwaite. 'Emotional Dynamics in Restorative Conferences'. *Theoretical Criminology* 8, no. 2 (2004): 191–210. www.ojp.gov/ncjrs/virtual-library/abstracts/emotional-dynamics-restorative-conferences.

Hazelwood Mine Fire Inquiry. 'Mine Rehabilitation Community Consultations – 4 & 5 August 2015: Summary of Discussion'. State Government of Victoria, 2015. hazelwoodinquiry.archive.vic.gov.au/wp-content/uploads/2015/08/Summary-of-Mine-Rehabilitation-community-consultations-PDF-383KB.pdf.

Hettema, Jennifer, Julie Steele, and William R. Miller. 'Motivational Interviewing'. *Annual Review of Clinical Psychology* 1, no. 1 (2005): 91–111. doi.org/10.1146/annurev.clinpsy.1.102803.143833.

Hill, Brittany. 'Restoring Justice for Animal Victims'. *Animal & Natural Resource Law Review* (2021): 217–46.

Hill, Meg. 'Health Fears for Tunnel Project'. *Dockland News*, 4 September 2019. www.docklandsnews.com.au/health-fears-for-tunnel-project_15623.

Hobson, Jonathan. Anamika Twyman-Ghoshal, Rebecca Banwell-Moore, et al., 'Restorative Justice, Youth Violence, and Policing: A Review of the Evidence'. *Laws* 11, no. 4 (2022): 62. doi.org/10.3390/laws11040062.

Holley, Cameron, and Darren Sinclair. 'Deliberative Participation, Environmental Law and Collaborative Governance: Insights from Surface and Groundwater Studies'. *Environmental and Planning Law Journal* 30, no. 1 (2013): 32–55.

Holmes, Catherine. 'Improving the Australian Public Service'. Recommendation 23.6. In *Report: Royal Commission into the Robodebt Scheme*. Royal Commission into the Robodebt Scheme, 2023.

Hopkins, Belinda. 'From Restorative Justice to Restorative Culture. *Revista de Asistența Sociala* 14, no. 4 (2015): 19–34.

Howard, William. 'Water Rights Returned to Gippsland Traditional Owners in Landmark Victorian Government Deal'. *ABC News*, 12 October 2023. www.abc.net.au/news/2023-10-12/traditional-owners-given-more-water-in-landmark-announcement/102963860.

Houghton, James. 'Communicating About COVID-19: Health Literacy and Language Services During the Pandemic'. *Issue Brief*, Ethnic Communities' Council of Victoria, October 2020: 7. eccv.org.au/communicating-about-covid-19-health-literacy-and-language-services-during-pandemic/.

House of Representatives Standing Committee on Indigenous Affairs. *Report on Indigenous Participation in Employment and Business*. The Parliament of the Commonwealth of Australia. Canberra, August 2021. www.aph.gov.au/-/media/02_Parliamentary_Business/24_Committees/243_Reps_Committees/Indigenous/Pathways_and_Participation/Report.pdf?la=en%26hash=0FF8A974D86F9A87BB46B5F236D4FCFD110C515B.

Hyder, Kieran, Serena Wright, Mark Kirby, and Jan Brant, 'The Role of Citizen Science in Monitoring Small-Scale Pollution Events'. *Marine Pollution Bulletin* 120, no. 1 (2017): 51–57. doi.org/10.1016/j.marpolbul.2017.04.038.

Hunt, Janet. 'Engaging with Indigenous Australia—Exploring the Conditions for Effective Relationships with Aboriginal and Torres Strait Islander Communities'. Australian Government—Australian Institute of Health and Welfare, Australian Institute of Family Studies, October 2013. www.aihw.gov.au/getmedia/7d54eac8-4c95-4de1-91bb-0d6b1cf348e2/ctgc-ip05.pdf?v=20230605181119&inline=true.

Inspector-General for Emergency Management Victoria. *Hazelwood Mine Fire Inquiry Progress Report 2021*. State Government Victoria. February 2022. Last modified 19 August 2024. www.igem.vic.gov.au/publications/publications/hazelwood-mine-fire-inquiry-progress-report-2021.

Inspector-General for Emergency Management Victoria. *Hazelwood Mine Fire Inquiry: Implementation of Recommendations and Affirmations. Progress Report 2021*. State Government of Victoria, 2021. issuu.com/igemvic/docs/hazelwood_mine_fire_inquiry_-_progress_report_2021.

Inspector-General for Emergency Management. *Hazelwood Mine Fire Inquiry: Implementation of Recommendations and Affirmations Progress Report 2022. Victorian Government, 2023.* www.igem.vic.gov.au/publications/publications/hazelwood-mine-fire-inquiry-progress-report-2022.

International Association for Public Participation. 'IAP2 Spectrum of Public Participation'. International Association for Public Participation. 2007. hdl.handle.net/10214/3123.

International Institute for Restorative Practices Graduate School. 'Facilitating Listening Circles: Advanced Training and Essential Skills for Facilitators'. Accessed 20 February 2025. www.iirp.edu/professional-development/facilitating-listening-circles.

Intihani, Siti Nur. *Regulation of Deviations Local Government Grant Funds to the Private Sector Through Restorative Justice*. Proceedings of the 2nd International Conference on Law, Economy, Social and Sharia, vol 2 (2024): 545–67.

Jackson, Rebecca. *Where Poppies Thrive: Leadership in a Harsh World.* Ultimate World Publishing, October 2021.

Jacobs, Emily, and Richard J. Keegan. 'Sustaining Optimal Performance When the Stakes Could Not Be Higher: Emotional Awareness and Resilience in Emergency Service Personnel (With Learnings for Elite Sport)'. *Frontiers in Psychology* 13 (2022): 1–15. doi.org/10.3389/fpsyg.2022.891585.

Janke, Terri, Zena Cumpston, Rosemary Hill, et al. 'Indigenous: National and international Frameworks That Support Caring for Country'. In *Australia State of the Environment 2021* (Australian Government Department of Agriculture, Water and the Environment, 2021). soe.dcceew.gov.au/indigenous/management/national-and-international-frameworks-support-caring-country.

Jenkins, Bryan. 'Environmental Restorative Justice: Canterbury Cases'. Presentation at the 38th Annual Conference of the International Association for Impact Assessment, Durban, South Africa, May 2018. www.researchgate.net/publication/338955180_Environmental_Restorative_Justice_Canterbury_Cases.

Jenkins, Simon. 'Want Justice for the Victims of Grenfell? It's Now Clearer Than Ever That Public Inquiries Are Not the Answer'. *The Guardian,* 6 September 2024. www.theguardian.com/commentisfree/article/2024/sep/05/justice-victims-grenfell-public-inquiries-not-answer.

Jessup, Brad. 'Environmental Justice as Spatial and Scalar Justice: A Regional Waster Facility or a Local Rubbish Dump Out of Place?' *McGill International Journal of Sustainable Development Law and Policy* 9, no. 2 (2013): 69–107. www.jstor.org/stable/24352643.

Johnson, Sian. 'What Desire Paths Can Tell Us About Safer, Better Public Spaces'. *ABC News*, 23 April 2023. www.abc.net.au/news/2023-04-23/desire-paths-offer-insight-into-use-of-public-spaces/102191044.

Johnson, Tom, Tanya Allport, and Amohia Boulton. 'Te Ruru: Co-creating an Indigenous Systems Change Framework'. *Journal of Awareness-Based Systems Change* 4, no. 1 (2024): 49–75. doi.org/10.47061/jasc.v4i1.7006.

Johnston, Kim A. 'Community Engagement: Exploring a Relational Approach to Consultation and Collaborative Practice in Australia'. *Journal of Promotion Management* 16, no. 1–2 (2010): 217–34. doi.org/10.1080/1049649090357 8550.

Johnstone, Gerry, and Daniel W. Van Ness. *Handbook of Restorative Justice*. Willan Publishing, 2007.

Johnstone, Gerry and Daniel W. Van Ness. 'The Idea of Restorative Justice'. In *Handbook of Restorative Justice,* edited by Gerry Johnstone and Daniel Van Ness. Willan Publishing, 2007.

Jones, Ashanti. The Heart of Facilitation in Restorative Justice'. *Learning for Justice* 6 (2024). www.learningforjustice.org/magazine/fall-2024/the-heart-of-facilitation-in-restorative-justice.

Josephs, Caroline. 'Silence as a Way of Knowing in Yolngu Indigenous Australian Storytelling'. In *Negotiating the Sacred II: Blasphemy and Sacrilege in the Arts,* edited by Elizabeth Burns Coleman and Maria Suzette Fernandes Dias. ANU E Press, 2008. doi.org/10.22459/NS.12.2008.

Joudo Larsen, Jacqueline. *Restorative Justice in the Australian Criminal Justice System.* AIC Reports Research and Public Policy Series 127. Australian Institute of Criminology, 2014. www.aic.gov.au/publications/rpp/rpp127.

Jülich, Shirley, and Noel S. B. Cox. 'Good Workplaces: Alternative Dispute Resolution and Restorative Justice'. In *The Big Issues in Employment: HR Management and Employment Relations in NZ,* edited by Jane Parker. CCH New Zealand, 2013.

Kahn, Shahid, and Mia Lucas. 'The Effectiveness of Restorative Justice Programs in Reducing Recidivism'. Department of Public Health, Yale University.

Karp, David, and Megan Schachter. 'Restorative Justice in Universities: Case Studies of What Works with Restorative Responses to Student Misconduct'. In *Routledge International Handbook of Restorative Justice*, edited by Theo Gavrielides. Routledge, 2018.

Kasriel, Emily. 'Deep Listening'. *Stanford Social Innovation Review* 20, no. 1 (2021): 32–37. doi.org/10.48558/K52F-1711.

Kass, Edward. 'The Power of Nice: Active Listening, Procedural and Interpersonal Fairness Perceptions and Prosocial and Antisocial Negotiation Behaviors'. (2010). repository.usfca.edu/olc/6.

Kelln, Brad R. C., and John H. Ellard. 'An Equity Theory Analysis of the Impact of Forgiveness and Retribution on Transgressor Compliance', *Personality and Social Psychology Bulletin* 25, no. 7 (1999): 864–72. doi.org/10.1177/0146167299025007008.

Kerr, Jack, and Dan Oates. 'Chemical Stockpiles Found at Melbourne Warehouses Linked to West Footscray Inferno'. *ABC News*, 2 January 2019. www.abc.net.au/news/2019-01-02/illegal-chemicals-stored-in-melbourne-warehouses-epa-claims/10678258.

Kershen, Lawrence. 'Can Environmental Mediation Save the Planet?' *Passlenet*, 28 January 2023. passle-net.s3.amazonaws.com/Passle/5b3f2cb9780ebf0410d034b3/MediaLibrary/Document/2023-01-26-17-20-50-655-CanEnvironmentalMediationsavethePlanet.pdf.

Kettaneh, Celeste A., William T. Chung, and Kevin C. Chung. 'First Impressions: Setting the Stage for Better Relationships'. *Plastic and Reconstructive Surgery* 152, no. 4 (2023): 693–98. doi.org/10.1097/PRS.0000000000010661.

Khodor, Omar, and Henry Miller. 'How to Regulate with Excellence'. Interview with Cary Coglianese. *The Regulatory Review*, 27 August 2023. www.theregreview.org/2023/08/27/sunday-spotlight-how-to-regulate-with-excellence/.

Kilmer, Derek. *Final Report: Select Committee on the Modernization of Congress*. Select Committee on the Modernization of Congress, 15 December 2022. www.congress.gov/117/crpt/CRPT-117hrpt646/GPO-CRPT-117hrpt646.pdf?itid=lk_inline_enhanced-template.

Kirkwood, Steve. 'A Practice Framework for Restorative Justice'. *Aggression and Violent Behavior* 63 (2022): 1–10. doi.org/10.1016/j.avb.2021.101688.

Klein, Gary, Helen Altman Klein, Brian Lande, Joseph Borders, and James C. Whitacre. 'Police and Military as Good Strangers'. *Journal of Occupational and Organizational Psychology* 88, no. 2 (2015): 231–50. doi.org/10.1111/joop.12110.

Koch, Jochen, Martin Eisend, and Arne Petermann. 'Path Dependence in Decision-Making Processes: Exploring the Impact of Complexity Under Increasing Returns'. *BuR—Business Research* 2, no. 1 (2009): 67–84. doi.org/10.1007/bf03343529.

Koorey, Dean. 'Q&A: Inquire vs Enquire'. *Australian Writers' Centre*. 18 February 2015. www.writerscentre.com.au/blog/qa-inquire-vs-enquire/.

Krasny, Marianne E., and Keith G. Tidball. *Civic Ecology: Adaptation and Transformation from the Ground Up*. The MIT Press, 2015. doi.org/10.7551/mitpress/9780262028653.001.0001.

Krpan, Stan. *Compliance and Enforcement Review: A Review of EPA Victoria's Approach*. Publication 1368. EPA Victoria, February 2011. www.vgls.vic.gov.au/client/en_AU/vgls/search/detailnonmodal/ent:$002f$002fSD_ILS$002f0$002fSD_ILS:268802/one.

Kyung Kim, Hyo, Bal Hee Lee, and Kyoung A. Nam. 'Improving Interprofessional Teamwork in a Community Mental Health Team: A Team Building Circle Program Based on the Restorative Justice Paradigm'. *Journal of Interprofessional Care* 38, no. 4 (2024): 642–51. doi.org/10.1080/13561820.2024.2329463.

Kucharska, Wioleta. 'Wisdom from Experience Paradox: Organizational Learning, Mistakes, Hierarchy and Maturity Issues'. *The Electronic Journal of Knowledge Management* 19, no. 2 (2021): 105–17. doi.org/10.34190/ejkm.19.2.2370.

Kucharska, Wioleta, and Denise A. D. Bedford. 'Love Your Mistakes!—They Help You Adapt to Change. How Do Knowledge, Collaboration and Learning Cultures Foster Organizational Intelligence?' *Journal of Organizational Change Management* 33, no. 7 (2020): 1329–54. doi.org/10.1108/JOCM-02-2020-0052.

Lahn, Julie. 'Being Indigenous in the Bureaucracy: Narratives of Work and Exit'. *The International Indigenous Policy Journal* 9, no. 1 (2018): 1–17. doi.org/10.18584/iipj.2018.9.1.3.

Langton, Marcia, and Aaron Corn. *The Way of the Ancestors*. Thames & Hudson Australia, 2023.

Lansing, Amy E., Natalie J. Romero, Elizabeth Siantz, et al. 'Building Trust: Leadership Reflections on Community Empowerment and Engagement in a Large Urban Initiative'. *BMC Public Health* 23 (2023): 1–25. doi.org/10.1186/s12889-023-15860-z.

Latimer, Jeff. 'A Meta-Analytic Examination of Youth Delinquency, Family Treatment, and Recidivism'. *Canadian Journal of Criminology and Criminal Justice* 43, no. 2 (2001): 237–53. doi.org/10.3138/cjcrim.43.2.237.

Latimer, Jeff, Craig Dowden, and Danielle Muise. 'The Effectiveness of Restorative Justice Practices: A Meta-Analysis'. *The Prison Journal* 85, no. 2 (2005): 127–44. doi.org/10.1177/0032885505276969.

Lawrence, Darlene. 'The Pursuit of Social Justice by the Care-leavers from the Nova Scotia Home for Coloured Children and the Production of Knowledge'. M.A. diss., Mount Saint Vincent University, 2019). ec.msvu.ca/server/api/core/bitstreams/34c03b71-b4a6-4252-a01e-dd99440aa26c/content.

Leeper Piquero, N. S. K. Rice, and A. R. Piquero. 'Power, Profit and Pluralism: New Avenues for Research on Restorative Justice and White Collar Crime'. In *Restorative Justice from Theory to Practice*, edited by H. Ventura Miller. Emerald Group Publishing Limited, 2008. doi.org/10.1016/S1521-6136(08)00409-0.

Levi-Faur, David. 'Regulation and Regulatory Governance'. In *Handbook on the Politics of Regulation,* edited by David Levi-Faur. Edward Elgar, 2011.

Levitats, Zehavit, and Eran Vigoda-Gadot. 'Yours Emotionally: How Emotional Intelligence Infuses Public Service Motivation and Affects the Job Outcomes of Public Personnel'. *Public Administration* 95, no. 3 (2017): 770. doi.org/10.1111/padm.12342.

Li, Shike, Ivana Radivojevic, Kriti Jain, and Carlina Conrad. 'When Apologizing Hurts: Felt Transgression and Restoration Efforts'. *Journal of Organizational Behavior* 44, no. 1 (2023): 42–63. doi.org/10.1002/job.2672.

Lilburn, Jen. (BCRG convenor). *BCRG Brooklyn Community Representative Group: Background and Achievements*. January 2014. www.brooklynip.com.au/wp-content/uploads/2014/02/BCRG-BackgroundAndAchievements-Report-A4-170114-web.pdf.

Liotta, Morgan, 'Tower Lockdown "Confusion and Distress" Could Have Been Prevented: GP'. *NewsGP*, 6 August 2020. www1.racgp.org.au/newsgp/clinical/tower-lockdown-confusion-and-distress-could-have-b.

Lipsey, Mark W. 'The Primary Factors that Characterize Effective Interventions with Juvenile Offenders: A Meta-Analytic Overview', *Victims & Offenders* 4, no. 2 (2009): 141–42, doi.org/10.1080/15564880802612573.

Little, Adrian. 'The Politics of Makarrata: Understanding Indigenous-Settler Relations in Australia'. *Political Theory* 48, no. 1 (2020): 30–56. doi.org/10.1177/0090591719849023.

Llewellyn, Jennifer J. 'Responding Restoratively to Student Misconduct and Professional Regulation: The Case of Dalhousie Dentistry'. In *Restorative and Responsive Human Services*, edited by Valerie Braithwaite, Gale Burford, and John Braithwaite. Routledge, 2019. doi.org/10.4324/9780429398704-9.

Llewellyn, Jennifer J. 'Restorative Justice: Thinking Relationally About Justice'. In *Being Relational: Reflections on Relational Theory and Health Law*, edited by Jocelyn Downie and Jennifer L. Llewellyn. UBC Press, 2012. doi.org/10.59962/9780774821902.

Llewellyn, Jennifer J. 'Transforming Restorative Justice'. *The International Journal of Restorative Justice* 4, no. 3 (2021): 374–96. doi.org/10.5553/TIJRJ.000096.

Llewellyn, Jennifer, Jean Flynn, Chief Judge Pam Williams, et al. *Nova Scotia Home for Colored Children Restorative Inquiry: Council of Parties Third Public Report.* Dalhousie University, 2018. digitalcommons.schulichlaw.dal.ca/reports/64/.

Lodi, Ernesto, Lucrezia Perrella, Gian Luigi Lepri, Maria Luisa Scarpa, and Patrizia Patrizi. 'Use of Restorative Justice and Restorative Practices at School: A Systematic Literature Review'. *International Journal of Environmental Research and Public Health* 19, no. 1 (2022): 1–34. doi.org/10.3390/ijerph19010096.

Loeffler, Elke, and Tony Bovaird, eds. *The Palgrave Handbook of Co-Production of Public Services and Outcomes*. Palgrave Macmillan, 2021. doi.org/10.1007/978-3-030-53705-0.

Long, Ruby, Emily C. Cleveland Manchanda, Annette M. Dekker, et al. 'Community Engagement Via Restorative Justice to Build Equity-oriented Crisis Standards of Care'. *Journal of the National Medical Association* 114, no. 4 (2022): 377–89. doi.org/10.1016/j.jnma.2022.02.010.

Lount Jr., Robert B., and Nathan C. Pettit. 'The Social Context of Trust: The Role of Status'. *Organizational Behavior and Human Decision Processes* 117, no. 1 (2012): 15–23. doi.org/10.1016/j.obhdp.2011.07.005.

Lundahl, Brad W., Chelsea Kunz, Cynthia Brownell, Derrik Tollefson, and Brian L. Burke. 'A Meta-Analysis of Motivational Interviewing: Twenty-Five Years of Empirical Studies'. *Research on Social Work Practice* 20, no. 2 (2010): 137–60. doi.org/10.1177/1049731509347850.

Mackenzie, Polly. *The Social State: From Transactional to Relational Public Services.* Demos, 8 July 2021. demos.co.uk/research/the-social-state-from-transactional-to-relational-public-services/.

Macpherson, Elizabeth Jane. *Indigenous Water Rights in Law and Regulation: Lessons from Comparative Experience*. Cambridge University Press, 2019. doi.org/10.1017/9781108611091.

Macrory, Richard. *Regulatory Justice: Making Sanctions: Final report.* Better Regulation Executive, November 2006. www.regulation.org.uk/library/2006_macrory_report.pdf.

Makkai, Toni, and John Braithwaite. 'Praise, Pride and Corporate Compliance'. *International Journal of the Sociology of Law* 21, no. 1 (1993): 73–91.

Manaaki Whenua Landcare Research. 'Key Māori Principles, 1996–2025'.

Mannozzi, Grazia. 'The Emergence of the Idea of a "Restorative City" and Its Link to Restorative Justice'. *International Journal of Restorative Justice* 2 (2019): 288–92. doi.org/10.5553/IJRJ/258908912019002002006.

Marawili, Djambawa, and Annette Kogolo, with Christina Balcombe Davidson. 'The Land and the Sea Can't Talk: We Have to Talk for Them'. *Artlink* 36, no. 2 (2016): 26–33.

Marcucci, Olivia. 'Why Restorative Justice Works in Schools: An Investigation into the Interactional Dynamics of Restorative Circles'. *Learning, Culture and Social Interaction* 31, Part A, 100561 (2021). doi.org/10.1016/j.lcsi.2021.100561.

Marriott, Rhonda, and Tracy Reibel. 'Resilience, Renewal and Hope in Australian Indigenous-Led Primary Health Care Initiatives'. *Primary Health Care Research & Development* 22, no. e65 (2021): 1–2. doi.org/10.1017/s1463423621000712.

Marshall, Christopher D. *All Things Reconciled: Essays on Restorative Justice, Religious Violence, and the Interpretation of Scripture*. Cascade Books, 2018.

Marshall, Christopher D. 'Justice as Care'. *The International Journal of Restorative Justice* 2, no. 2 (2019): 175–85. doi.org/10.5553/IJRJ/258908912019002002001.

Martin, Sarah. *Bush Heritage Australia: Restoring Nature Step by Step*. 1st ed. NewSouth, UNSW Press, 2016.

Matthews, Veronica, Kristina Vine, Amba-Rose Atkinson, et al. 'Justice, Culture, and Relationships: Australian Indigenous Prescription for Planetary Health'. *Science* 381 (2023): 636–41. doi.org/10.1126/science.adh9949.

McCormack, Phillipa. 'Assessing an Assertive EPA Victoria'. *Waste Management and Environment (WME) Magazine*, November 2010: 16–17.

McElrea, Fred W. M. 'The Role of Restorative Justice in RMA Prosecutions'. *Resource Management Journal* 3, no. 7 (2004): 1. www.napierlibrary.co.nz/assets/Judge-McElrea/RJ-and-the-Resource-Management-Act-RM-Law-Assoc-200407.pdf.

McKay, Daniel. 'Uluru Statement: A Quick Guide'. *Parliamentary Library Research Paper Series* 2016–17. 19 June 2017. parlinfo.aph.gov.au/parlInfo/download/library/prspub/5345708/upload_binary/5345708.pdf.

McKinnon, Katharine, Katherine Gibson, and Linda Malam. 'Introduction: Critical and Hopeful Area Studies—Emerging Work in Asia and the Pacific'. *Asia Pacific Viewpoint* 49, no. 3 (2008). doi.org/10.1111/j.1467-8373.2008.00376.x.

Meadows, Donella. *Leverage Points: Places to Intervene in a System*. The Sustainability Institute, 1999.

Meidinger, Errol. 'Regulatory Culture: A Theoretical Outline'. *Law & Policy* 9, no. 4 (1987): 355–86. doi.org/10.1111/j.1467-9930.1987.tb00416.x.

Melbourne Water Corporation. *Stony Creek Rehabilitation Plan 2019–2029*. Melbourne Water Corporation, 8 September 2019. www.melbournewater.com.au/about/what-we-do/publications/stony-creek-rehabilitation-plan.

Menkel-Meadow, Carrie. 'Restorative Justice: What Is It and Does it Work?' *Annual Review of Law and Social Science* 3 (2007): 161–87. doi.org/10.1146/annurev.lawsocsci.2.081805.110005.

Merritt, John. 'Incentivising Compliance: Using Behavioural Insights to Encourage and Persuade'. Panel discussion with Liam Smith and Kate Gavens, ANSZOG and the National Regulators Community of Practice, Melbourne Business School and online: ANZSOG, 2 June 2023. anzsog.edu.au/learning-and-development/events-and-conferences/incentivising-compliance-using-behavioural-insights-to-encourage-and-persuade/.

Metz, Thaddeus. 'Ubuntu: The Good Life'. In *Encyclopedia of Quality of Life and Well-Being Research*, edited by Filomena Maggino. Springer International Publishing, 2024. doi.org/10.1007/978-3-031-17299-1_4029.

Millar, Benjamin. 'Community Highlights Toxic Tottenham Fire Impact'. *Star Weekly*, 14 August 2019. maribyrnonghobsonsbay.starweekly.com.au/news/community-highlights-toxic-tottenham-fire-impact/.

Miller, Susan L. 'The Importance of Storytelling for Restorative Justice'. In *After the Crime: The Power of Restorative Justice Dialogues between Victims and Violent Offenders*. New York University Press, 2011. doi.org/10.18574/nyu/9780814770382.001.0001.

Mills, Donald Lee. 'The Crashing Tide: Blending Restorative Practices and Trauma-Informed Care'. IIRP Graduate School, 2013.

Ministry of Justice. 'Policy Name: Restorative Practice (Incorporating Restorative Justice Services) Policy Framework'. Ministry of Justice and HM Prison & Probation Service (UK). 6 February 2023. assets.publishing.service.gov.uk/media/63e12cb3e90e076264193957/restorative-practice-incorporating-restorative-justice-services-policy-framework.pdf.

Minority Rights Group. '"Just-Us for All": Indigenous Wisdom for Human and Planetary Well-being'. Minority and Indigenous Trends 2023—Focus on Water. *Digital Reports*. 20 June 2023. minorityrights.org/resources/trends2023-just-us-for-all-indigenous-wisdom-for-human-and-planetary-well-being.

Moola, Faisal, Helina Jolly, Joli Borah, and Robin Roth. 'The Potential for Indigenous-Led Conservation in Urbanized Landscapes in Canada'. *Frontiers in Human Dynamics* 6 (2024): 1–18. doi.org/10.3389/fhumd.2024.1340379.

Moore, David B., and Alikki Vernon. *Setting Relations Right in Restorative Practice: Broadening Mindsets and Skill Sets*. Routledge, 2024.

Mouffe, Chantal. *Agonistics: Thinking the World Politically*. Verso, 2013.

Mouffe, Chantal. *For a Left Populism*. Verso, 2018.

Mouffe, Chantal. *On the Political*. Routledge, 2005.

Mulhan, Kathryn. 'Managing the Costs of Emotional Labor in Emergency Ambulance Call-Taking'. *The Journal of Emergency Dispatch*, 22 July 2020. www.iaedjournal.org/managing-the-costs-of-emotional-labor-in-emergency-ambulance-call-taking.

Muller, Jerry Z. *The Tyranny of Metrics*. Princeton University Press, 2018. doi.org/10.2307/j.ctvc77h85.

Muller, Samantha, Steve Hemming, and Daryle Rigney. 'Indigenous Sovereignties: Relational Ontologies and Environmental Management'. *Geographical Research* 57, no. 4 (2019): 399–410. doi.org/10.1111/1745-5871.12362.

Murray-Atfield, Yara. 'Melbourne Public Housing Tower Resident Says Community Is Being "Treated Like Criminals" Amid Coronavirus Lockdown'. *ABC News*, 7 July 2020. www.abc.net.au/news/2020-07-05/coronavirus-lockdown-melbourne-public-housing-residents-speak/12423170.

Muth, Melinda, and Bob Selden. 'Setting the Tone from the Top: How Directors Use Conversation to Shape Culture'. Australian Institute of Company Directors, 2018. www.aicd.com.au/content/dam/aicd/pdf/tools-resources/book store/previews/Setting-Tone-from-top-preview.pdf.

Mycock, Andrew. 'The Anglosphere or Anglospheres? The English-Speaking World in Flux'. *Analysis* (blog). Centre for International Policy Studies, 14 October. 2020 www.cips-cepi.ca/2020/10/14/the-anglosphere-or-anglospheres-the-english-speaking-world-in-flux-2/.

NAIDOC. '2021 Theme: Heal Country'. 2021. www.naidoc.org.au/get-involved/2021-theme.

Nascimento, Ana M., Joana Andrade, Andreia de Castro Rodrigues, et al. 'The Psychological Impact of Restorative Justice Practices on Victims of Crimes—a Systematic Review'. *Trauma Violence Abuse* 24, no. 3 (2023). doi.org/10.1177/15248380221082085.

National Advisory Council for Environmental Policy and Technology (NACEPT). *Information to Action: Strengthening EPA Citizen Science Partnerships for Environmental Protection.* National Advisory Council for Environmental Policy and Technology, April 2018. www.epa.gov/sites/default/files/2018-04/documents/nacept_2018_citizen_science_publication_eng_final_v2_508_0.pdf.

National Emergency Management Agency. '2019–2020 Royal Commissions and Inquiries'. A webpage listing State and federal inquiries into the 2019–2020 bushfires. Accessed 2 March 2025. knowledge.aidr.org.au/resources/2019-20-royal-commission-and-inquiries/.

National Museum Australia. 'Indigenous Australians' Right to Vote'. Last modified 16 May 2023, www.nma.gov.au/defining-moments/resources/indigenous-australians-right-to-vote.

National NAIDOC Secretariat. 'National NAIDOC Week'. Accessed 8 March 2025. www.naidoc.org.au/about/naidoc-week.

Neale, Nathan Robert, Kenneth D. Butterfield, Jerry Goodstein, and Thomas M. Tripp. 'Managers' Restorative Versus Punitive Responses to Employee Wrongdoing: A Qualitative Investigation'. *Journal of Business Ethics* 161 (2020): 603–25. doi.org/10.1007/s10551-018-3935-x.

Nehme, Marina, Jessica Anderson, Olivia Dixon, and Dimity Kingsford-Smith. *The General Deterrence Effects of Enforceable Undertakings on Financial Services and Credit Providers.* Centre for Law, Markets and Regulation UNSW,, 2018. download.asic.gov.au/media/4916053/18-325mr-deterrence-effects-of-enforceable-undertakings-on-financial-services-and-credit-providers.pdf.

New South Wales Government. Health Sydney Local Health District. 'Heal Country, Heal Our Nation'. NAIDOC Week 2021, Heal Country! 4–11 July 2021. www.slhd.nsw.gov.au/pdfs/NAIDOC-Week-2021.pdf.

New South Wales Environment Protection Authority. 'Guidelines for Seeking Environmental Court Orders'. Last modified 26 March 2025. www.epa.nsw.gov.au/licensing-and-regulation/regulation/policies-and-guidelines/guidelines-for-seeking-environmental-court-orders.

News from Brown. 'U.S. Is Polarizing Faster Than Other Democracies, Study Finds'. *Brown,* 21 January 2020. www.brown.edu/news/2020-01-21/polarization.

Nixon, Monty. 'Here's What "Deep Listening" Can Tell Us About the Natural World and Our Place in It'. *The Conversation,* 28 January 2025. theconversation.com/heres-what-deep-listening-can-tell-us-about-the-natural-world-and-our-place-in-it-235868.

Nygren, Anja. 'Contested Lands and Incompatible Images: The Political Ecology of Struggles Over Resources in Nicaragua's Indio-Maíz Reserve'. *Society & Natural Resources* 17, no. 3 (2004): 189–205. doi.org/10.1080/08941920490270221.

O'Brien, Justin. 'Creating Space: Comanagement Considerations in Kakadu National Park'. In *Reclaiming Indigenous Governance: Reflections and Insights from Australia, Canada, New Zealand, and the United States*, edited by William Nikolakis et al. University of Arizona Press, 2019. doi.org/10.2307/j.ctvqc6jwv.15.

O'Flynn, Janine, and Gary L. Sturgess. *2030 and Beyond: Getting the Work of Government Done: An ANZSOG Research Paper for the Australian Public Service Review Panel.* Australia and New Zealand School of Government, 1 March 2019. anzsog.edu.au/research-insights-and-resources/research/2030-and-beyond-getting-the-work-of-government-done/.

OECDgov. 'Building Trust to Reinforce Democracy' (video). 5 August 2022. www.youtube.com/watch?v=xNc45gpZJao.

Oakland Unified School District. 'Restorative Justice'. Accessed 31 March 2025. www.ousd.org/restorative-justice.

Ojeda, Jaime, Anne K. Salomon, James K. Rowe, and Natalie C. Ban. 'Reciprocal Contributions Between People and Nature: A Conceptual Intervention', *BioScience* 72, no. 10 (2022), doi.org/10.1093/biosci/biac053.

'OPLE to Shine in Gippsland'. *Mirage News*, 28 August 2019. www.miragenews.com/ople-to-shine-in-gippsland/.

Organization for Economic Co-operation and Development (OECD). 'Eight Ways to Institutionalise Deliberative Democracy'. *OECD Public Governance Policy Paper*. OECD, 2021. www.oecd.org/content/dam/oecd/en/publications/reports/2021/12/eight-ways-to-institutionalise-deliberative-democracy_e1f898a0/4fcf1da5-en.pdf.

OECD. 'Ensuring Environmental Compliance'. Accessed 23 February 2025. www.oecd.org/en/topics/ensuring-environmental-compliance.html.

Orrnert, Anna. *Youth Initiatives: Supporting Citizen Engagement with Government and Civic Life*. GSDRC Helpdesk Research Report 1418. GSDRC, University of Birmingham, 2018. gsdrc.org/wp-content/uploads/2018/03/Youth_initiatives_citizen_engagement.pdf.

Orsina, Amalia. *La Responsabilità da Reato Dell'ente Tra Colpa di Organizzazione e Colpa de Reazione* [*Corporate Criminal Liability Between Organizational Fault and Reactive Fault*]. Giappichelli Editore, 2024.

Ostrom, Elinor. 'Crossing the Great Divide: Coproduction, Synergy, and Development'. *World Development* 24, no. 6 (1996): 1073–87. doi.org/10.1016/0305-750x(96)00023-x.

Pabon, John. *The Great Greenwashing: How Brands, Governments and Influencers Are Lying to You*. Melbourne Books, 2023.

Pain, Nicola. 'Encouraging Restorative Justice in Environmental Crime'. *The Newcastle Law Review* 13 (2018): 29.

Pain, Nicola, Rachel Pepper, and Millicent McCreath. 'Restorative Justice for Environmental Crime: An Antipodean Experience'. *Australian Environment Review* 31, no. 8 (2016): 290. search.informit.org/doi/abs/10.3316/agispt.20171125.

Painter, Anthony. 'A Crisis of Legitimacy?' *RSA Journal* 165, no. 3 (2019): 10–15. www.jstor.org/stable/26907473.

Pali, Brunilda, Miranda Forsyth, and Felicity Tepper, eds. *The Palgrave Handbook of Environmental Restorative Justice*. Palgrave Macmillan, 2022.

Pandeli, Jenna, Neil Sutherland, and Hugo Gaggiotti. 'Outlining a Practical, Emotional and Reflexive Approach to Organizational Ethnography'. In *Organizational Ethnography: An Experiential and Practical Guide*, edited by Jenna Pandeli, Neil Sutherland, and Hugo Gaggiotti. Routledge, 2022. doi.org/10.4324/9781003021582-1.

Parker, Christina, and Kathy Bickmore. 'Complexity in Restorative Justice Education Circles: Power and Privilege in Voicing Perspectives About Sexual Health, Identities, and Relationships'. *Journal of Moral Education* 50, no. 4 (2021): 471–93. doi.org/10.1080/03057240.2020.1832451.

Parker, Christine. 'Restorative Justice in Business Regulation? The Australian Competition and Consumer Commission's Use of Enforceable Undertakings'. *Modern Law Review* 67, no. 2 (2004): 209–46. doi.org/10.1111/j.1468-2230.2004.00484.x.

Parker, Christine, and John Braithwaite. 'Regulation'. In *The Oxford Handbook of Legal Studies,* edited by Peter Cane and Mark Tushnet. Oxford University Press, 2003.

Parkinson, Lesley. *Restorative Practices at Work*. Crown House Publishing, 2023.

Parks Victoria. 'About Us'. Accessed 8 March 2025. www.parks.vic.gov.au/about-us.

Parliament of Victoria Legislative Council Environment and Planning Committee. *Inquiry into Recycling and Waste Management: Interim Report*. Victorian Government Printer, August 2019. new.parliament.vic.gov.au/4a4bf9/content assets/631c8359ad7f4dc487aef9d986fae1e7/interim-report-inquiry-into-recycling-and-waste.pdf.

Participedia. 'Scotland's Climate Assembly: Recommendations for Action'. *Participedia*, last modified 10 June 2023. participedia.net/case/12537.

Pascoe, Bruce. *Dark Emu, Black Seeds: Agriculture or Accident?* Magabala Books, 2014.

Pascoe, Katherine Margaret. 'Subverting, Challenging and Working Within Bureaucratic and Managerialist Systems: Strategies for Upholding Relationship-Based Social Work Practice'. *Journal of Social Work Practice* 39, no. 2 (2025). doi.org/10.1080/02650533.2024.2411044.

Paul , Gregory D., and Ian M. Borton. *Creating Restorative Justice: A Communication Perspective of Justice, Restoration, and Community*. Lexington Books, 2021.

Payne, Anne Maree, and Heidi Norman. *Findings from the Literature Review*. Indigenous Land and Justice Research Group, School of Humanities and Languages, University of NSW, 2024. www.reconciliation.org.au/wp-content/uploads/2024/03/Coming-to-terms-with-the-past-Literature-review.pdf.

Payne, Anne Maree, and Heidi Norman. *Coming to Terms with the Past? Identifying Barriers and Enablers of Truth-Telling and Strategies to Promote Historical Acceptance*. Research report of Indigenous Land and Justice Research Group, School of Humanities & Languages, University of NSW. UNSW and Reconciliation Australia, 2024. www.reconciliation.org.au/wp-content/uploads/2024/04/Barriers-and-enablers-to-truth-telling-report.pdf.

Pazzanese, Christina. 'Democrats and Republicans Do Live in Different Worlds'. *The Harvard Gazette*, 16 March 2021, National & World Affairs. news.harvard.edu/gazette/story/2021/03/democrats-and-republicans-live-in-partisan-bubbles-study-finds/.

Pearson, Luke. 'What is a Makarrata? It's More Than a Synonym for Treaty'. *ABC News*. 10 August 2017. RN. www.abc.net.au/news/2017-08-10/makarrata-explainer-yolngu-word-more-than-synonym-for-treaty/8790452.

Perel, Esther, and Mary Alice Miller. 'Letters from Esther #50: Could it Really Be That Easy to Resolve Conflict?'. *Letters from Esther* (blog), 2023. www.estherperel.com/blog/letters-from-esther-50-could-it-really-be-that-easy-to-resolve-conflict.

Pew Research Center. *Americans' Views of Government: Decades of Distrust, Enduring Support for Its Role*. 6 June 2022. www.pewresearch.org/politics/2022/06/06/americans-views-of-government-decades-of-distrust-enduring-support-for-its-role/.

Phillips, Jake, Jaime Waters, Chalen Westaby, and Andrew Fowler. *Emotional Labour in Criminal Justice and Criminology*, 1st edn. Routledge, 2020. doi.org/10.4324/9780429055669.

Philipp-Muller, Aviva, Spike W. S. Lee, and Richard E. Petty. 'Why Are People Antiscience, and What Can We Do About It?' *Proceedings of the National Academy of Sciences* 119, no. 30 (2022): 1–10. doi.org/10.1073/pnas.2120755119.

Poelina, Anna, Donna Bagnall, Mary Graham, et al. *Declaration of Peace for Indigenous Australians and Nature: A Legal Pluralist Approach to First Laws and Earth Laws*. Springer, 2024. doi.org/10.1007/978-981-99-9327-7.

Pointer, Lindsey. 'Learning to Work "with" (the Social Discipline Window)'. *Lindsay Pointer, PhD* (blog). 18 February 2018. lindseypointer.com/2018/02/18/learning-to-work-with-the-social-discipline-window/.

Poulson, Barton. 'A Third Voice: A Review of Empirical Research on the Psychological Outcomes of Restorative Justice'. *Utah Law Review* 1 (2003): 167–204.

Pranis, Kay. 'Individual and Collective Accountability in a Restorative Framework'. Online presentation. 12 November 2018.

Premier of Victoria. 'New App to Put People First During Emergencies'. State Government of Victoria, 16 November 2016. www.premier.vic.gov.au/new-app-put-people-first-during-emergencies.

Premier of Victoria. *Statement on Victorian Ombudsman Housing Report*. State Government of Victoria, 17 December 2020. www.premier.vic.gov.au/statement-victorian-ombudsman-housing-report.

Premier of Victoria. 'Strengthening Air Monitoring in the Latrobe Valley'. State Government of Victoria, 7 December 2017. www.premier.vic.gov.au/site-4/strengthening-air-monitoring-latrobe-valley.

Preston, Brian J. 'The Use of Restorative Justice for Environmental Crime'. *Criminal Law Journal* 35, no. 3 (2011): 136. papers.ssrn.com/sol3/Delivery.cfm/SSRN_ID1831822_code1005507.pdf?abstractid=1831822&mirid=.

Putnam, Robert D. *Bowling Alone: The Collapse and Revival of American Community*. Simon & Schuster, 2000.

Pyrko, Igor, Viktor Dörfler, and Colin Eden. 'Thinking Together: What Makes Communities of Practice Work?' *Human Relations* 70, no. 4 (2016): 389–409. doi.org/10.1177/0018726716661040.

Rane, Nitin Liladhar, Saurabh P. Choudhary, and Jayesh Rane. 'Artificial Intelligence for Enhancing Resilience'. *Journal of Applied Artificial Intelligence* 5, no. 2 (2024): 1–33. doi.org/10.48185/jaai.v5i2.1053.

Rapa, Luke J., Candice W. Bolding, and Cari Allyn Brooks. 'Integrating Critical Consciousness and Social Empathy: A New Framework to Enhance Conscientization'. In *Critical Consciousness: Expanding Theory and Measurement*, edited by Luke J. Rapa and Erin B. Godfrey. Cambridge University Press, 2023. doi.org/10.1017/9781009153751.004.

Rawsthorne, Margot, Amanda Howard, Pam Joseph, and Dara Sampson. 'Understanding Community-Led Disaster Preparedness'. *Australian Journal of Emergency Management,* April 2023: 49–54. doi.org/10.47389/38.2.49.

Reconciliation Australia. 'We Need to Celebrate Success'. News release. 25 February 2013. www.reconciliation.org.au/we-need-to-celebrate-success.

Reconciliation Australia. 'Reconciliation Australia Board: New Co-Chairs', *News*, Reconciliation Australia. 16 December 2024. www.reconciliation.org.au/changes-to-reconciliation-australia-board/.

Recovered Energy Australia. 'What We Do'. 2018. Accessed 13 February 2025. www.recoveredenergy.com.au/what-we-do.

Rehm, Peter H., and Denise R. Beatty. 'Legal Consequences of Apologizing', *Journal of Dispute Resolution* 1996, no. 1 (1996): 116–30. scholarship.law.missouri.edu/jdr/vol1996/iss1/7.

Reimer, Kristin. '"The Kids Do a Better Job of It Than We Do": A Canadian Case Study of Teachers Addressing the Hypocritical Application of Restorative Justice in Their School'. *The Australian Educational Researcher* 46 (2018): 59–73. doi.org/10.1007/s13384-018-0286-7.

Resilience Dynamic. 'Why Perspective Matters: Understanding the Importance of Different Viewpoints'. Updated 27 April, 2023. resiliencedynamic.com/resilient-thinking/why-perspective-matters/.

Restorative Inquiry Council of Parties. *A Journey to Light: A Different Way Forward.* Final Report of the NSHCC Restorative Inquiry. Province of Nova Scotia, 2019. restorativeinquiry.ca/report/Restorative-Justice-Inquiry-Final-Report.pdf.

Restorative Justice 101. 'Restorative Cities: 8 Examples Changing the World'.

Retamal, Monique, Elsa Dominish, Le Xuan Thinh, Nguyen, Anh Tuan, and Samantha Sharpe. 'Here's What Happens to Our Plastic Recycling When It Goes Offshore', *The Conversation*, 30 January 2019, theconversation.com/heres-what-happens-to-our-plastic-recycling-when-it-goes-offshore-110356.

Reynolds, Doc, and Liz Cameron. 'Yarning Up with Doc Reynolds: An Interview About Country from an Indigenous Perspective'. *Wildlife Research* 52, (2025): 1–7. doi.org/10.1071/WR24104.

Ricklefs, Natalie. 'Why Your In-Person Town Halls Aren't Reaching People'. *Citizen Lab,* 19 July 2022. Wayback Machine, archived 19 August 2022. web.archive.org/web/20231026135212/https://www.citizenlab.co/blog/civic-engagement/why-your-in-person-town-halls-arent-reaching-people/.

Rieger, Janice. *Right to Participate: Co-Designing Disability Policies in Australia.* Briefing Paper 12. QUT Centre for Justice, December 2020.

Ripley, Amanda. 'These Radically Simple Changes Helped Lawmakers Actually Get Things Done'. *The Washington Post,* 9 February 2023. www.washingtonpost.com/opinions/2023/02/09/house-modernization-committee-bipartisan-collaboration-lessons/.

RMIT Centre for Restorative Justice. 'What Is Restorative Justice?' Open Circle. 24 May2024. cij.org.au/opencircle/what-is-restorative-justice.

Roberts, Anthea. 'Risk, Reward, and Resilience Framework: Integrative Policy Making in a Complex World'. *Journal of International Economic Law* 26, no. 2 (2023): 233–265. doi.org/10.1093/jiel/jgad009.

Roberts, Anthea, and Nicolas Lamp. *Six Faces of Globalization: Who Wins, Who Loses, and Why It Matters.* 1st ed. Harvard University Press, 2021.

Roberts, Anthea, and Taylor St John. 'Complex Designers and Emergent Design: Reforming the Investment Treaty System'. *American Journal of International Law* 116, no. 1 (2022): 96–149. doi.org/10.1017/ajil.2021.57.

Robinson, Catherine J., Jennifer Mairi Macdonald, Justin Perry, , et al. 'Coproduction Mechanisms to Weave Indigenous Knowledge, Artificial Intelligence, and Technical Data to Enable Indigenous-Led Adaptive Decision Making: Lessons from Australia's Joint Managed Kakadu National Park'. *Ecology and Society* 27, no. 4 (2022). doi.org/10.5751/ES-13747-270436.

Roffey, Sue, and Florence McCarthy. 'Circle Solutions, A Philosophy and Pedagogy for Learning Positive Relationships: What Promotes and Inhibits Sustainable Outcomes?' *The International Journal of Emotional Education* 5, no. 1 (2013): 36–55. files.eric.ed.gov/fulltext/EJ1085741.pdf.

Rossignoli, Paula. 'Matt Beech | Polarized Peoples—Examining the Culture Wars and How They Can be Transcended'. *Institute of European Studies*, 20 June 2024. ies.berkeley.edu/news/matt-beech-polarized-peoples-examining-culture-wars-and-how-they-can-be-transcended.

Rossner, Meredith. 'Emotions and Interaction Ritual: A Micro Analysis of Restorative Justice'. *The British Journal of Criminology* 51, no. 1 (2011): 95–119. doi.org/10.1093/bjc/azq075.

Rossner, Meredith. *Just Emotions: Rituals of Restorative Justice*. Oxford University Press, 2013. doi.org/10.1093/acprof:oso/9780199655045.001.0001.

Rossner, Meredith. 'Restorative Justice in the 21st Century: Making Emotions Mainstream'. In *The Oxford Handbook of Criminology*, edited by Alison Liebling, Shadd Maruna and Lesley McAra. Oxford University Press, 2017. eprints.lse.ac.uk/76789.

Rossner, Meredith, and Helen Taylor. 'The Transformative Potential of Restorative Justice: What the Mainstream Can Learn from the Margins'. *Annual Review of Criminology* 7 (2024): 357–81. www. doi.org/10.1146/annurev-criminol-030421-040921.

Rutledge, David. 'Stability, Security and Survival: A Conversation with Mary Graham'. An episode of the ABC Radio National program *The Philosopher's Zone*, broadcast 8 December 2023. www.abc.net.au/listen/programs/philosopherszone/the-philosophers-zone/102961342.

Sahani, Mateus Kambale, Harro Maat, Dina Balabanova, et al. 'Engaging Communities as Partners in Health Crisis Response: A Realist-Informed Scoping Review for Research and Policy'. *Health Research Policy and Systems* 22, no. 1 (2024): 1–15. doi.org/10.1186/s12961-024-01139-1.

Sampson, Robert J., Stephen W. Raudenbush, and Felton Earls. 'Neighborhoods and Violent Crime: A Multilevel Study of Collective Efficacy'. *Science* 277, no. 5328 (1997): 918–24. doi.org//10.1126/science.277.5328.918.

Sanders, Elizabeth B.-N., and Pieter Jan Stappers. 'Co-Creation and the New Landscapes of Design'. *CoDesign* 4, vol. 1 (2008): 5–18. doi.org/10.1080/15710880701875068.

Sandu, Antonio, and Simona Damian. 'Applying Appreciative Inquiry Principles in the Restorative Justice Field'. Postmodern Openings 3, no. 2 (2012): 37–52. postmodernopenings.com/wp-content/uploads/2012/06/3-Applying-Appreciative-Inquiry-Principles.pdf.

Sant'Ambrogio, Michael, and Glen Staszewski. 'Public Engagement with Agency Rulemaking: Final Report'. Paper presented at the Administrative Conference of the United States, 19 November 2018.

Sarkissian, Wendy, PhD (blog). Accessed 13 February 2025. sarkissian.com.au/publications/inspired-books/speakout-the-ultimate-workshop-guide/what-exactly-is-a-speakout/.

Sarkissian, Wendy, and Andrea Cook. *Speaking Out in Community Engagement: A Review of Fifteen Years of the* SpeakOut *Model*. Social Planning and Research Council of B.C. (2000). www.sparc.bc.ca/wp-content/uploads/2020/11/speaking-out-in-community-engagement.pdf.

SBI Group. 'Community Consultative Committee'. 2023. www.sbiinertlandfill.com/community-investment/.

Schiff, Mara. 'Taking Responsibility: A Conversation on Restorative Justice and Youth'. Interview by Sarah Schweig, 23 October 2012. Center for Justice Innovation. www.innovatingjustice.org/publications/taking-responsibility-conversation-restorative-justice-and-youth.

Scholl, Mark B., and Christopher B. Townsend. 'Restorative Justice: A Humanistic Paradigm for Addressing the Needs of Victims, Offenders, and Communities'. *The Journal of Humanistic Counseling* 63, no. 3 (2023): 184–200. doi.org/10.1002/johc.12204.

Semuels, Alana. 'Is This the End of Recycling?' *The Atlantic*, 5 March 2019. www.theatlantic.com/technology/archive/2019/03/china-has-stopped-accepting-our-trash/584131.

Severs, Eline, and Alexander Mattelaer. 'A Crisis of Democratic Legitimacy? It's about Legitimation, Stupid!'. *European Policy Brief* 21 (March 2014). Egmont Royal Institute for International Relations. aei.pitt.edu/63549/.

Shapland, Joanna, Gwen Robinson, and Angela Sorsby. *Restorative Justice in Practice: Evaluating What Works for Victims and Offenders*. Routledge, 2011. doi.org/10.4324/9780203806104.

Shay, Marnee, and Grace Sarra. '"Co-Design" Is the Latest Buzzword in Indigenous Education Policy. Does It Live Up to the Hype?' *The Conversation*. 4 September 2023. theconversation.com/co-design-is-the-latest-buzzword-in-indigenous-education-policy-does-it-live-up-to-the-hype-212194.

Shay, Marnee, Grace Sarra, and Jo Lampert. 'Indigenous Education Policy, Practice and Research: Unravelling the Tangled Web'. *Australian Educational Researcher* 50, no. 1 (2023): 73–88. doi.org/10.1007/s13384-022-00581-w.

Schell-Busey, Natalie, Sally S. Simpson, Melissa Rorie, and Mariel Alper. 'What Works? A Systematic Review of Corporate Crime Deterrence'. *Criminology & Public Policy* 15, no. 2 (2016): 387–416. doi.org/10.1111/1745-9133.12195.

Sherman, Lawrence W., Peter Neyroud, and Ken Pease. *Offender-Desistance Policing and the Sword of Damocles*. Civitas, 2012.

Sherman, Lawrence W., Heather Strang, Evan Mayo-Wilson, Daniel J. Woods, and Barak Ariel. 'Are Restorative Justice Conferences Effective in Reducing Repeat Offending? Findings from a Campbell Systematic Review'. *Journal of Quantitative Criminology* 31, no. 1 (2014): 1–24. doi.org/10.1007/s10940-014-9222-9.

Sherman, Lawrence, W., Heather Strang, Caroline Angel, et al. 'Effects of Face-to-face Restorative Justice on Victims of Crime in Four Randomized, Controlled Trials'. *Journal of Experimental Criminology* 1, no. 3 (2005): 367–95. doi.org/10.1007/s11292-005-8126-y.

Shields, Tegan, Leah Talbot, Jack Pascoe, et al. 'Creating an Authorizing Environment to Care for Country'. *Conservation Letters* 8 (2025): 1–6. doi.org/10.1111/conl.13075.

Shiva, Vandana. *Staying Alive*. Indraprastha Press, 1988.

Short, Rose, Gill Case, and Karen McKenzie. 'The Long-Term Impact of a Whole School Approach of Restorative Practice: The Views of Secondary School Teachers'. *Pastoral Care in Education* 36, no. 4 (2018): 313–24. doi.org/10.1080/02643944.2018.1528625.

Silbernagel, Jaclyn. 'Systemic Change—Indigenous People and the Legal System'. Podcast. Episode 12 in series Let's Talk Poverty. *enough for all*, 1 June 2022. enoughforall.ca/podcasts/systemic-change-indigenous-people-and-the-legal-system.

Sims Metal. 'About Us: A Leading Metal Recycling Company'. Accessed 13 February 2025. www.simsmm.com/about-us/.

Simu, Octavian, Paul McGorrery, and Melanie Hull. *Sentencing Occupational Health and Safety Offences in Victoria: Report and Recommendations*. Sentencing Advisory Council, 2025. www.sentencingcouncil.vic.gov.au/sites/default/files/2025-02/sentencing_ohs_offences_report_and_recommendations.pdf.

Skarlatidou, Artemis, Muki Haklay, Simon Hoyte, Michiel van Oudheusden, and Isabel J. Bishop. 'How Can Bottom-up Citizen Science Restore Public Trust in Environmental Governance and Sciences? Recommendations from Three Case Studies'. *Environmental Science and Policy* 160 (2024): 1–10. doi.org/10.1016/j.envsci.2024.103854.

Smith, Christopher. 'Reparative Readings'. *Anatomies of Power* (blog). 20 December 2021. anatomiesofpower.wordpress.com/2021/12/20/reparative-readings/.

Smith, Liam. 'Incentivising Compliance: Using Behavioural Insights to Encourage and Persuade' (panel discussion with Kate Gaven and John Merritt, Australia and New Zealand School of Government [ANSZOG] and the National Regulators Community of Practice. Melbourne Business School and online, 2 June 2023). anzsog.edu.au/learning-and-development/events-and-conferences/incentivising-compliance-using-behavioural-insights-to-encourage-and-persuade/.

Smith, Liam, Peter Bragge, Jim Curtis, and Paul Kellner (eds). *Inspiring Change: How to Influence Behaviour for a Better World.* Monash University Publishing, 2024.

Sparrow, Malcolm K. *The Character of Harms: Operational Challenges in Control.* Cambridge University Press, 2008. doi.org/10.1017/CBO9780511753862.

Sparrow, Malcolm K. *Fundamentals of Regulatory Design*. Published by author, 2020.

Sparrow, Malcolm K. *The Regulatory Craft: Controlling Risks, Solving Problems, and Managing Compliance*. Brookings Institution Press, 2011.

Sproule, Ricky. 'Lore of the Land: Right Fire, Right Country, Right Time'. *The Citizen*, 18 October 2025. www.thecitizen.org.au/articles/lore-of-the-land-right-fire-right-country-right-time.

Staempfli, Adi. *Practice Tool: Developing a Community of Practice in Your Organisation.* Practice Supervisor Development Programme. United Kingdom Department for Education, December 2020.

Stapleton, Amy B., Jeffrey Lating, Matthew Kirkhart, and George S. Everly Jr. 'Effects of Medical Crisis Intervention on Anxiety, and Posttraumatic Stress Symptoms: A Meta-Analysis'. *Psychiatric Quarterly* 77, no. 3 (2006): 231–38. doi.org/10.1007/s11126-006-9010-2.

State Government of Victoria. *Hazelwood Mine Fire Inquiry Report 2014.* Victorian Government Printer, 2014. www.latrobe.vic.gov.au/sites/default/files/2024-06/Hazelwood%20Mine%20Fire%20Inquiry%20Report%20%282009%29.pdf.

State Government of Victoria. *Hazelwood Mine Fire Inquiry: Victorian Government Implementation Plan.* Department of Premier and Cabinet, June 2016. www.healthassembly.org.au/wp-content/uploads/2024/08/Hazelwood-Mine-Fire-Inquiry-Implementation-Plan.pdf.

Steffensen, Victor. Fire Country: How Indigenous Fire Management Could Help Save Australia. Hardie Grant Travel, 2020.

Stevens, Francis, and Katherine Taber. 'The Neuroscience of Empathy and Compassion in Pro-Social Behaviour'. *Neuropsychologia* 159 (2021). doi.org/10.1016/j.neuropsychologia.2021.107925.

Strang, Heather, Lawrence W Sherman, Evan Mayo-Wilson, et al. 'Restorative Justice Conferencing (RJC) Using Face-to-Face Meetings of Offenders and Victims: Effects on Offender Recidivism and Victim Satisfaction. A Systematic Review'. *Campbell Systematic Reviews* 9, no. 1 (2013): 1–59. doi.org/10.4073/csr.2013.12.

Stroh, David Peter. *Systems Thinking for Social Change*. Chelsea Green Publishing, 2015.

Stromberg, Per M., and Ranjula Bali Swain. 'Citizen Monitoring in Environmental Disclosure: An Economics Perspective'. *Journal of Environmental Management* 356 (2024): 18. doi.org/10.1016/j.jenvman.2024.120567.

Suff, Rachel. *Report: Managing Conflict in the Modern Workplace*. Chartered Institute of Personnel and Development, 2020. www.cipd.org/globalassets/media/knowledge/knowledge-hub/reports/managing-conflict-in-the-workplace-2_tcm18-70655.pdf.

Surdek, Steffan. 'Why Understanding Other Perspectives Is A Key Leadership Skill'. *Forbes.com*. 17 November 2016. www.forbes.com/sites/forbescoachescouncil/2016/11/17/why-understanding-other-perspectives-is-a-key-leadership-skill/.

Suzuki, Masahiro, and Xiaoyu Yuan. 'How Does Restorative Justice Work? A Qualitative Metasynthesis'. *Criminal Justice and Behavior* 48, no. 10 (2021): 1347–65. doi.org/10.1177/0093854821994622.

Suzuki, Masahiro. 'Possibility of Sincere Apology in Restorative Justice: When and How?', International Journal of Offender Therapy and Comparative Criminology 68, no. 13–14 (2022): 1342–1356. doi.org/10.1177/0306624x221132238.

Suzuki, Masahiro, and Tamera Jenkins. 'Apology–Forgiveness Cycle in Restorative Justice, But How?' *International Review of Victimology* 29, no. 2 (2023): 259–76. doi.org/10.1177/02697580221079994.

Swain, Rhys. 'Do You Know How Fire Is a Healing Force?' *Bush Heritage Australia* newsletter, 15 September 2023.

Szydlowski, Gabriela, Noortje de Boer, and Lars Tummers. 'Compassion, Bureaucrat Bashing, and Public Administration'. *Public Administration Review* 82, no. 4 (2022): 619–33. doi.org/10.1111/puar.13485.

Taylor, Charles, Patrizia Nanz, and Madeleine Beaubien Taylor. *Reconstructing Democracy: How Citizens Are Building from the Ground Up*. 1st ed. Harvard University Press, 2020. doi.org/10.4159/9780674246652.

Te Ara. 'Kaitiakitanga—Guardianship and Conservation'. *Te Ara: The Encyclopedia of New Zealand*, 2007. teara.govt.nz/en/kaitiakitanga-guardianship-and-conservation.

tebrakunna country, Emma Lee, and Robyn Eversole. 'Rethinking the Regions: Indigenous Peoples and Regional Development'. *Regional Studies* 53, no. 11 (2019): 1510–19. doi.org/10.1080/00343404.2019.1587159.

Tepper, Felicity. 'Amplifying Edge-Awareness: Socio-Ecological Restorative Approaches to Human-Wildlife Coexistence' in *Criminología verde: alternativas a la impunidad y al punitivismo ante los daños bio-socio-ecológicos* [*Green Criminology: Alternatives to Impunity and Punitivism Facing Bio-Socio-Ecological Harms*], edited by Gema Varona. Dykinson, 2025.

Tepper, Felicity. 'The Animal Question in Ecosystem Restoration: Foregrounding Animal Kin Through Environmental Restorative Justice (ERJ)'. *Revista de Victimologia | Journal of Victimology* 15 (2023): 99–146.

Tepper, Felicity. 'Koala Perspective of a Restorative Circle Facilitation'. In *Justicia Restaurativa Medioambiental y Animal*, edited by Gema Varona. Dykinson, 2024.

Tepper, Felicity. 'Restorative Justice for Animal Harm'. *Power to Persuade* (blog). 5 July 2023. www.powertopersuade.org.au/blog/restorative-justice-for-animals.

Thomas, Joyce, and Deana McDonagh. 'Shared Language: Towards More Effective Communication'. *Australasian Medical Journal* 6, no. 1 (2013): 46–54.

Torina Coulthard, Claire. 'The Land is Sacred: Bunji'. *The Oxford Blue Student Newspaper CIC*. 13 November 2022. theoxfordblue.co.uk/the-land-is-sacred-bunji/.

Tormey, Simon. 'The Contemporary Crisis of Representative Democracy'. *Democratic Theory* 1, no. 2 (2014). doi.org/10.3167/dt.2014.010211.

Torre, Giovanni. 'Dja Dja Wurrung Clans Call for Water Rights and Greater Say in Water Management'. *National Indigenous Times*, 28 June 2023. nit.com.au/28-06-2023/6550/dja-dja-wurrung-clans-call-for-water-rights-and-greater-say-in-water-management.

Tyler, Tom R. (ed.). *Why People Obey the Law*. Princeton University Press, 2006. doi.org/10.1515/9781400828609.

Tronto, Joan C. *Caring Democracy: Markets, Equality, and Justice*. 1st ed. NYU Press, 2013.

Tronto, Joan. 'Creating Caring Institutions: Politics, Plurality, and Purpose'. *Ethics and Social Welfare* 4, no. 2 (2010): 158–71. doi.org/10.1080/17496535.2010.484259.

Twopeny, Richard Ernest Nowell. *Town Life in Australia*. Elliot Stock, 1883. Cited in Helen Doyle. *Thematic History – A History of the City of Melbourne's Urban Environment: Planning for Future Growth*, 92. Context Pty Ltd, 2011. mvga-prod-files.s3.ap-southeast-4.amazonaws.com/public/2024-05/history-city-of-melbourne-urban-environment.pdf.

Tūwharetoa Māori Trust Board. *Tūwharetoa Māori Trust Board: Position Description*. Tūwharetoa Māori Trust Board, June 2021. www.tuwharetoa.co.nz/app/uploads/2021/07/Kaiawhina-Karapiti-JD.pdf.

Tūwharetoa Māori Trust Board Waikato River Committee. *Karapiti Incident: Waipuwerawera/Waikato River Cultural Impact Assessment*. Tūwharetoa Māori Trust Board, September 2020.

Tuurnas, Sanna. 'Skilling and Motivating Staff for Co-production'. In *The Palgrave Handbook of Co-Production of Public Services and Outcomes*, edited by Elke Loeffler and Tony Bovaird. Palgrave Macmillan, 2021. doi.org/10.1007/978-3-030-53705-0_25.

Umbreit, Mark S., Betty Vos, and Robert B. Coates. 'Restorative Justice Dialogue: Evidence-Based Practice'. Center for Restorative Justice & Peacemaking, 1 January 2006. www.antoniocasella.eu/restorative/Umbreit_2006.pdf.

Umbreit, Mark, and Marilyn Peterson Armour. *Restorative Justice Dialogue: An Essential Guide for Research and Practice*. Springer Publishing Company, 2010. doi.org/10.1891/9780826122599.

Unglik, Ari. *Between a Rock and a Hard Place: The Story of the Development of the EPA*. Environment Protection Authority, 1996.

Ungunmerr-Baumann, Miriam-Rose, Rachel A. Groom, Emma L. Schuberg, et al. 'Dadirri: An Indigenous Place-Based Research Methodology'. *AlterNative: An International Journal of Indigenous Peoples* 18, no. 1 (2022): 94. doi.org/10.1177/11771801221085353.

United Nations Environment Programme (UNEP). 'Indigenous People and Nature: A Tradition of Conservation'. *News, Stories & Speeches*, 26 April 2017. www.unep.org/news-and-stories/story/indigenous-people-and-nature-tradition-conservation.

United Nations Environment Programme (UNEP). 'Indigenous Peoples and the Nature They Protect'. *News, Stories & Speeches*, 8 June 2020. www.unep.org/news-and-stories/story/indigenous-peoples-and-nature-they-protect.

United Nations Office on Drugs and Crime. 'Topic 2—Justifying Punishment in the Community. First published March 2019. www.unodc.org/e4j/en/crime-prevention-criminal-justice/module-7/key-issues/2--justifying-punishment-in-the-community.html.

United States Government, 'Framework for Public Participation and Community Engagement (PPCE)'. Accessed 24 February 2025. www.opengovpartnership.org/the-open-gov-challenge/united-states-framework-for-public-participation-and-community-engagement/.

Urzedo, Danilo, Simone Pedrini, Clancy Hearps, Kingsley Dixon, and Stephen van Leeuwen. 'Indigenous Environmental Justice Through Coproduction of Mining Restoration Supply Chains in Australia'. *Restoration Ecology* 30, no. S1 (2022): 1–7. doi.org/10.1111/rec.13748.

Vance, Alasdair, Janet McGaw, Di O'Rorke, Selena White, and Sandra Eades. 'Culture, Health and Well-Being: Yarning with the Victorian First Nations Community'. *International Journal of Indigenous Health* 19, 1 (2024): 1–17. doi.org/10.32799/ijih.v19i1.41307.

Vallier, Kevin. *Trust in a Polarized Age.* Oxford University Press, 2020.

Vance, Alasdair, Janet McGaw, Di O'Rorke, Selena White, and Sandra Eades. 'Culture, Health and Well-Being: Yarning with the Victorian First Nations Community'. *International Journal of Indigenous Health* 19, no. 1 (2024): 1–17.

Vaughan-Lee, Emmanuel. 'Deep Time Diligence: An Interview with Tyson Yunkaporta'. *Emergence Magazine,* 19 February 2024. emergencemagazine.org/conversation/deep-time-diligence/.

Veolia. 'Hallam Road Landfill'. Accessed 20 February 2025. www.anz.veolia.com/our-facilities/landfills/hallam-road-landfill.

Veolia. 'Hampton Park Outlook Transfer Station'. Accessed 20 February 2025. www.anz.veolia.com/our-facilities/transfer-stations/hampton-park-outlook-transfer-station.

Victorian Aboriginal Heritage Council. 'Land Is Our Future: Caring for Country'. In '"Taking Care of Culture": State of Victoria's Aboriginal Cultural Heritage Report'. Discussion Paper, Victorian Aboriginal Heritage Council, November 2020. www.aboriginalheritagecouncil.vic.gov.au/sites/default/files/2021-01/Taking%20Care%20of%20Culture%20Discussion%20Paper_04012021_2.pdf.

Victorian Government Inspector-General for Emergency Management. *Report into the West Footscray Industrial Fire (August 2018).* State of Victoria, 2020. www.igem.vic.gov.au/publications/report-into-the-west-footscray-industrial-fire-august-2018.

Victorian Local Governance Association. 'Citizen Juries—An Overview'. Accessed 13 February 2025. www.vlga.org.au/citizen-juries-overview.

Victorian Public Sector Commission and State Government of Victoria. 'Aboriginal and Torres Strait Islander Culture and History'.

Victorian Ombudsman. 'Good Practice Guide: Managing Complex Complainant Behaviour'. 2 February 2022. www.ombudsman.vic.gov.au/learn-from-us/practice-guides/managing-complex-complainant-behaviour/.

Victorian Ombudsman, *Investigation into the Detention and Treatment of Public Housing Residents Arising from a COVID-19 'hard lockdown' in July 2020.* 17 December 2020. State Government of Victoria, December 2020. www.ombudsman.vic.gov.au/our-impact/investigation-reports/investigation-into-the-detention-and-treatment-of-public-housing-residents-arising-from-a-covid-19-hard-lockdown-in-july-2020/.

Villegas, Sam. 'For Better Engagement, Torch the Town Hall (Meeting)'. Raftelis. Accessed 13 February 2025. www.raftelis.com/insight/for-better-engagement-torch-the-town-hall-meeting.

Vines, Prue. 'Apologising to Avoid Liability: Cynical Civility or Practical Morality?' *Sydney Law Review*, 23 (2005): 483–505.

Vines, Prue. 'The Power of Apology: Mercy, Forgiveness or Corrective Justice in the Civil Liability Arena?' *University of New South Wales Law Review* 30 (2007). doi.org//10.5130/psjlsj.v1i1.535.

Vines, Prue. 'The Value of Apologising Within a Moral Community: Making Apologies Work. *Oñati Socio-Legal Series* 7, no. 3 (2017): 370–89.

Wachtel, Ted. 'Defining Restorative'. *International Institute for Restorative Practices Graduate School* (2016): 1–12. www.iirp.edu/images/pdf/Defining-Restorative_Nov-2016.pdf.

Wachtel, Ted. 'Restorative Justice in Everyday Life: Beyond the Formal Ritual'. *International Institute for Restorative Practices Graduate School*, 18 February 1999. www.iirp.edu/news/restorative-justice-in-everyday-life-beyond-the-formal-ritual.

Wachtel, Ted. 'Restorative Practices in Business: Building a Community for Learning and Change Within Organizations'. *International Institute for Restorative Practices Graduate School*, 18 February 1999. www.iirp.edu/news/restorative-practices-in-business-building-a-community-for-learning-and-change-within-organizations.

Wachtel, Ted, and Paul McCold. 'From Restorative Justice to Restorative Practices: Expanding the Paradigm'. *IIRP News*. International Institute for Restorative Practices, 5 August 2004. www.iirp.edu/news/from-restorative-justice-to-restorative-practices-expanding-the-paradigm.

Wailling, Jo, Allison Kooijman, Joanne Hughes, and Jane K. O'Hara. 'Humanizing Harm: Using a Restorative Approach to Heal and Learn From Adverse Events'. *Health Expectations: An International Journal of Public Participation in Health Care and Health Policy* 25, no. 4 (2022): 1193–99. doi.org/10.1111/hex.13478.

Walgrave, Lode. 'Restorative Justice, Punishment, and the Law'. In *The Palgrave Handbook on the Philosophy of Punishment,* edited by Matthew C. Altman. Palgrave Macmillan, 2023.

Walker, Scott. *Order Out of Chaos: A Kidnap Negotiator's Guide to Influence and Persuasion*. Harvard Business Review Press, 2023.

Wall Kimmerer, Robin. *Braiding Sweetgrass: Indigenous Wisdom, Scientific Knowledge and the Teachings of Plants*. Penguin Press, 2020.

Wallace, Harry M., Julia Juola Exline, and Roy F. Baumeister. 'Interpersonal Consequences of Forgiveness: Does Forgiveness Deter or Encourage Repeat Offenses?' *Journal of Experimental Social Psychology* 43, no. 7, (2008): 1446–58. doi.org/10.1016/j.jesp.2007.02.012.

Weisberg, Robert. 'Restorative Justice and the Dangers of Community'. Research Paper No. 50. Stanford Law School, February 2003. papers.ssrn.com/sol3/papers.cfm?abstract_id=373483.

Weller, Sally A. 'Just Transition? Strategic Framing and the Challenges Facing Coal Dependent Communities'. *Environment and Planning C: Politics and Space* 37, no. 2 (2019): 298–316. doi.org/10.1177/2399654418784304.

West Coast Regional Council. *Compliance and Enforcement Policy*. March 2018. www.wcrc.govt.nz/repository/libraries/id:2459ikxj617q9ser65rr/hierarchy/Documents/Services/Consents%20and%20Compliance/Forms/Compliance%20Forms/Compliance%20and%20Enforcement%20Policy%20March%202018%20Final.pdf.

West Coast Regional Council. 'Alternative Justice Outcome Reached for Westland District Council'. Media release, 20 May 2019. www.wcrc.govt.nz/repository/libraries/id:2459ikxj617q9ser65rr/hierarchy/Documents/Council/News%20and%20Announcements/News%20%28media%20releases%29/2019/Media%20Release%20-%20WDC%20-%20Alternative%20Justice%20Outcome.pdf.

West Gate Tunnel Project. 'What We're Building: About'. 18 February 2022. bigbuild.vic.gov.au/projects/west-gate-tunnel-project/about.

Weir, Jessica K., Claire Stacey, and Kara Youngetob. *The Benefits Associated with Caring for Country, Literature Review*. Caring for Our Country, Australian Institute of Aboriginal and Torres Strait Islander Studies (AIATSIS, June 2011). aiatsis.gov.au/sites/default/files/research_pub/benefits-cfc_0_2.pdf.

Wexler, Lesley, and Jennifer K. Robbennolt. '#METOO AND RESTORATIVE JUSTICE'. *GP Solo*, July/August, 2020. files.webservices.illinois.edu/9316/me-too-restorative-justice.pdf.

Wheeler, Helen C., and Meredith Root-Bernstein. 'Informing Decision-Making with Indigenous and Local Knowledge and Science'. *The Journal of Applied Ecology* 57, no. 9 (2020): 1634–43. doi.org/10.1111/1365-2664.13734.

Wijdekop, Femke. 'Reconnecting with the Living Earth Through Restorative Justice'. *KOSMOS*, 10 April 2019. web.archive.org/web/20231123071740/https://www.kosmosjournal.org/news/reconnecting-with-the-living-earth-through-restorative-justice/.

Wijdekop, Femke. *Restorative Justice Responses to Environmental Harm*. IUCN, 2019. files.harmonywithnatureun.org/uploads/upload864.pdf.

Wijntjens, Lianne. 'The (Non-Existent) Legal Risks of Apologising: Courts Do Not See Apologies as a Way to Accept Civil Liability'. *Journal of European Tort Law* 13, no. 3 (2022): 271–301. doi.org/10.1515/jetl-2022-0014.

Williamson, Bhiamie. '"Although We Didn't Produce These Problems, We Suffer Them": 3 Ways You Can Help in NAIDOC's Call to Heal Country'. *The Conversation*, 5 July 2021. theconversation.com/although-we-didnt-produce-these-problems-we-suffer-them-3-ways-you-can-help-in-naidocs-call-to-heal-country-163362.

Wilson, David B., Ajima Olaghere, and Catherine S. Kimbrell. *Effectiveness of Restorative Justice Principles in Juvenile Justice: A Meta-Analysis*. U.S. Department of Justice Office of Justice Programs, June 2017. www.ojp.gov/pdffiles1/ojjdp/grants/250872.pdf.

Wilson, Eleanor. 'Landfill Causing a Stink for Locals'. *StarNews*, 2 July 2022. Berwick. berwicknews.starcommunity.com.au/news/2022-07-02/landfill-causing-a-stink-for-locals/.

Wilson, Rob, Max French, Hannah Hesselgreaves, Toby Lowe, and Mark Smith. 'New Development: Relational Public Services—Reform and Research Agenda'. *Public Money & Management* 44, no. 6 (2024): 553–58. doi.org/10.1080/09540962.2024.2344902.

Wilson, Samuel, Melissa A. Wheeler, and Vlad Demsar. '5 Charts Show How Trust in Australia's Leaders and Institutions Has Collapsed'. *The Conversation*, 20 May 2022. theconversation.com/5-charts-show-how-trust-in-australias-leaders-and-institutions-has-collapsed-183441.

Winter, Kawika B., Mehana Blaich Vaughan, Natalie Kurashima, et al. 'Indigenous Stewardship Through Novel Approaches to Collaborative Management in Hawai'i'. *Ecology and Society* 28, no. 1 (2023). doi.org/10.5751/ES-13662-280126.

Witvliet, Charlotte V. O., Sung Joon Jang, Byron R. Johnson, et al'Accountability: Construct Definition and Measurement of a Virtue Vital to Flourishing'. *The Journal of Positive Psychology* 18, no. 5 (2022): 660–73. doi.org/10.1080/17439760.2022.2109203.

Wong, Jennifer S., Jessica Bouchard, Jason Gravel, Martin Bouchard, and Carlo Morselli. 'Can At-Risk Youth Be Diverted From Crime? A Meta-Analysis of Restorative Diversion Programs'. *Criminal Justice and Behavior* 43, no. 10 (2016): 1310–29. doi.org/10.1177/0093854816640835.

Wood, William R., and Masahiro Suzuki. 'Getting to Accountability in Restorative Justice'. *Victims & Offenders* 19, no. 7 (2024): 1400–23. doi.org/10.1080/15564886.2024.2333304.

Woodward, Emma, Rosemary Hill, Pia Harkness, and Ricky Archer. *Our Knowledge Our Way in Caring for Country: Indigenous-Led Approaches to Strengthening and Sharing Our Knowledge for Land and Sea Management.* Australian Government National Environmental Science Programme.North Australian Indigenous Land and Sea Management Alliance (NAILSMA) and CSIRO, 30 July 2020. apo.org.au/sites/default/files/resource-files/2020-07/apo-nid307687.pdf.

World Bank Group. 'Citizen Engagement and the CIVIC Facility'. Accessed 6 June 2025. www.worldbank.org/en/topic/citizen-engagement#.

Wright, Michael, Aunty Doris Getta, Aunty Oriel Green, et al. 'Co-Designing Health Service Evaluation Tools That Foreground First Nation Worldviews for Better Mental Health and Wellbeing Outcomes'. *International Journal of Environmental Research and Public Health* 18, no. 16, 8555 (2021): 1–14. doi.org/10.3390/ijerph18168555.

Wucker, Michele. 'The Surprising Link Between Creativity and Risk'. *Strategy + Business*. 29 July 2021. www.strategy-business.com/blog/The-surprising-link-between-creativity-and-risk.

Yell, Susan, and Michelle Duffy. 'Community Empowerment and Trust: Social Media Use During the Hazelwood Mine Fire'. *Australian Journal of Emergency Management* 33, no. 2 (2018): 66–69.

Yindjibarndi Water. 'Company Profile'. Accessed 8 March 2025. yindjibarndi.com.au/wp-content/uploads/2023/10/Yindjibarndi-Water.pdf.

Yoorook Justice Commission. 'About Yoorook'. Accessed 2 March 2025. yoorrook justicecommission.org.au/about/.

Yunkaporta, Tyson. *Sand Talk: How Indigenous Thinking Can Save the World*. 1st ed. Text Publishing Company, 2020.

Young, Iris Marion. *Inclusion and Democracy*. Oxford University Press, 2002.

Zehr, Howard. *The Little Book of Restorative Justice*. Good Books, 2002.

Zehr, Howard. *Changing Lenses: Restorative Justice for Our Times*. Herald Press Harrisonburg, 2015.

Zuckerman, Ethan. *Mistrust: Why Losing Faith in Institutions Provides the Tools to Transform Them*. W. W. Norton & Company, 2021.

Zuckerman, Michael. 'Mirage of Democracy: The Town Meeting in America'. *Journal of Deliberative Democracy* 15, no. 2 (2019). doi.org/10.16997/jdd.331.

Author biographies

Miranda Forsyth is a Professor in the School of Regulation and Global Governance (RegNet) in the College of Law, Governance and Policy at The Australian National University (ANU), and co-Director of the ANU Centre for Restorative Justice. With over two decades of experience in restorative justice, she is a leading voice in restorative regulation and socio-legal approaches to peacebuilding and violence prevention. As the lead investigator of the ARC Linkage project informing this book, she brings extensive knowledge and expertise to advancing restorative approaches to regulation. Her research and advisory work—conducted for governments, international bodies and NGOs—focuses on reconceptualising justice to move beyond adversarial enforcement and offer practical solutions to conflict resolution.

Felicity Tepper is a Senior Researcher at RegNet, ANU, with postgraduate qualifications in environmental law and policy, disaster resilience and recovery, and the humanities. Her professional experience spans the government, private, NGO, and academic sectors, with expertise in environment, health, gender and democratic governance. With an extensive background in regulatory reform, policy development and advocacy, Felicity understands the complexities and multiple dimensions of environmental and public health challenges. Her community facilitation experience continues to shape her research, which centres on the needs of both human and more-than-human communities affected by environmental harm.

Deborah Hollingworth holds a Master of Laws from the University of Melbourne and has practised as a legal professional across government and the not-for-profit sector. For the past decade, she has worked at the Environment Protection Authority Victoria (EPA), where she pioneered restorative and environmental justice policy and practice. In 2015, she was awarded the EPA's Mark Payton Scholarship to develop a framework for regulatory environmental justice. She has been a champion for change, particularly in the recognition of the role of First Nations in environmental protection. Her work includes contributing to the 2017 Environment Protection Act, which incorporates the principles of environmental restorative justice.

Alistair Nairn completed postgraduate study in conflict resolution and environmental management, and has worked for EPA Victoria since 2007, involved in a wide variety of issues and projects. His work in environmental regulation has focused on stakeholder engagement and public participation, with a key interest in environmental and restorative justice.

www.ingramcontent.com/pod-product-compliance
Lightning Source LLC
LaVergne TN
LVHW011817200926
848484LV00005B/1223